THE
HUMANITY
ARCHIVE

JERMAINE FOWLER

THE HUMANITY ARCHIVE

Recovering the Soul of Black History from a Whitewashed American Myth

For Amora and Jacari.

And anyone who has lost themselves in stories
to find out who they are.

Row House Publishing recognizes that the power of justice-centered storytelling isn't a phenomenon; it is essential for progress. We believe in equity and activism, and that books—and the culture around them—have the potential to transform the universal conversation around what it means to be human.

Part of honoring that conversation is protecting the intellectual property of authors. Reproducing any portion of this book (except for the use of short quotations for review purposes) without the expressed written permission of the copyright owner(s) is strictly prohibited. Submit all requests for usage to rights@rowhousepublishing.com.

Thank you for being an important part of the conversation and holding sacred the critical work of our authors.

Library of Congress Cataloging-in-Publication Data Available Upon Request
ISBN 978-1-955905-14-5 (HC)
ISBN 978-1-955905-15-2 (eBook)
Printed in the United States
Distributed by Simon & Schuster

Book design by Aubrey Khan, Neuwirth & Associates, Inc.

First edition
10 9 8 7 6 5 4 3 2 1

CONTENTS

"There are the stories that made America, and the stories that America made up . . ."

PROLOGUE

EVERY FEBRUARY, I THINK BACK on my "Black History Month" education, when time-strapped teachers hurried to add Black stories to the curriculum, usually settling on Martin Luther King Jr., Harriet Tubman, Frederick Douglass, and George Washington Carver as the honorable representatives of all things great, Black, and historical. I have to imagine, if you sat in a public-school classroom, you learned about Rosa Parks, who ignored the demand to surrender her seat to a white passenger on a crowded bus, because the forty-two-year-old seamstress was tired. As the story goes, an incredulous driver stopped the bus and swiftly called the police, who promptly arrested Parks for violating the racial segregation law. That evening, she spent a couple of uncomfortable hours in a bleak little jail cell, before local civil rights leaders posted her bail. Which was taught to us as though this singular event shifted the moral universe and catalyzed the Civil Rights Movement.

To this and similarly narrow stories, I attached my concept of Black history in America. There it was. An unassuming, bespectacled woman named Rosa Parks stumbled onto a city bus after a long day at her department store job and into the towering arc of American history. A red, white, and blue curve eternally bending toward moral progress. Sensing more to the story, I went to the most logical place—the library. Keep in mind I grew up in the nineties, so my generation was the last group of kids without Wikipedia and Google searches at our fingertips. Library catalogs weren't even online yet. To find a book, we sifted through thousands of oatmeal-colored cards lined up in file draws, each alphabetically separated by author, title, and subject. I loved it. The library was like an intellectual smorgasbord. And, yes! I sampled it all. I paced between shelves, ran my fingertips across book spines, peered into forgotten lives, and forged camaraderie with authors dearly departed. Rules are made to be broken; I even folded page corners for bookmarks. The library was clean, warm, and friendly; a welcomed escape from the confrontational, poverty-ridden streets on which I was raised. Oh, yeah,

I almost forgot, the genre was biography, the author—*N, O, P, Parks*. There it is. I grabbed the card out of the drawer and went searching for the book, *Rosa Parks: My Story*.

Well before her legendary bus face-off, Rosa Louise McCauley Parks was a curious child growing up in in Tuskegee, Alabama, which was brimming in Black history, including that of the Tuskegee Institute (now Tuskegee University). The town was, at the time, the wicked underbelly of sweet-tea-sipping Southern racism. At six years old, Parks watched her grandfather, loaded shotgun in hand, vowing to contest death itself as Klansmen terrorized the Black community. "I wanted to see him kill a Ku-Kluxer," she recalled. Far from her reputation as a modest bus passenger, Parks grew up in a deep tradition of self-defense, progressive racial politics, and activism. Her family was connected to the Black nationalist struggle of Marcus Garvey, and she considered Malcolm X a personal hero, marrying a like-minded activist.

"I talked and talked of everything I know about the white man's inhuman treatment of the negro," she once said. By 1943, she worked as branch secretary for the Montgomery chapter of the NAACP (National Association for the Advancement of Colored People). Despite her radical leaning politics, she always seemed so centered. Maybe that's why later in life she enjoyed the restorative power of yoga. From there, she spent more than a decade registering voters, counseling youth, fighting fire-breathing segregationists, and investigating racial violence. Some stories haunt, like her interviews with lynching witnesses and sexual assault victims. Recy Taylor and Gertrude Perkins were two of them, both young women abducted and raped by white men. Despite threats of violence if they did not remain silent, they courageously told the story of their traumas. The sworn officers of the judicial system refused to believe them. Side note, or rather a question: Is speaking about these heinous acts too nerve-shattering and too terrible for an adolescent brain? I think not. Isn't it strange that most American children are exposed to violence in their daily lives, yet we seldom give voice to its victims? What's more, this renders violence meaningless, silence acting like a moral sanction for its continuance.

Parks went to the scene of the crimes. She consoled the victims. She sought out elusive justice. Back in 1963, she descended on Washington with a human tidal wave of more than two hundred thousand civil rights soldiers of all creeds, religions, and colors, who, together, stood under the colossal shadow of the Lincoln Memorial to demand that the nation expand its ideal of "the people." Parks almost didn't make it to the National Mall that day. The male-dominated Southern Christian Leadership Conference was progressive on civil rights, but deeply conservative in its treatment of women. The leaders planned to march them in a separate, segregated procession and disallow them to speak to the masses at the podium. Parks would have none of it. She protested, only joining the march when the leadership reversed its decision.

Far from a singular moment, Parks's life embodied a journey made for a great cause. To oversimplify that life estranges her from a civil rights movement beginning in the mid-1700s. It severs her ties to a prolonged Black history of dissent. It cuts her off from a continuum of confrontation and cleaves her from a legacy of heroes who fought the juggernaut of legalized segregation. She was but one in a steady line of Black people to use civil disobedience on public transportation as an act of freedom. Freedom! Elizabeth Jennings Graham. Ida B. Wells-Barnett. Freedom! Barbara E. Pope. Ellen Harris. Sarah Louise Keys. Claudette Colvin. Aurelia S. Browder. Freedom! Their names read like poetry. A rhythmic meter against injustice. They rebelled on streetcars, objected on trains, and opposed on buses. They broke criminal laws, abiding instead by moral ones. For Black people, the lives of our grandfathers and great-great-grandmothers and those before them were shaded by segregated experiences. We'll never know exactly how most of them fought for equality, but when they did, they became part of an extraordinary tradition. "I wasn't tired," Parks once recalled. "No, the only tired I was, was tired of giving in."

In a perfect world, Black history would be told with textured nuance. Instead, it is reduced to a panorama of caricatures and marketing slogans aimed at a consumer niche hungry for Black culture. Black History Month sits in the bargain bin of education, the place a thing goes after losing its value—its essence, its very soul. We should not be surprised, then, that it's been unable to move us beyond a pseudo-celebration. But did you know it was never supposed to last this long?

When Carter G. Woodson founded Negro History Week in 1926, the precursor of Black History Month, he dreamed of a day when the observance would no longer be necessary. There is a photo of him, taken in 1915, where he's gazing stoically outward, clean shaven, and dapper in a well-cut suit with a polka-dot tie that belies his upbringing. Despite being a brilliant historian, it's a miracle he earned the title. He grew up desperately poor, only one generation removed from chattel slavery. He almost lost his education to the hard labor of dusky Virginian coal mines. He worked breathlessly to supplement his parents' meager income, but somehow mustered the time to teach himself reading and math, finally graduating high school at twenty, then earning a bachelor of literature. Like a plant refusing to surrender to concrete, he grew through his rigid circumstances. His ambition landed him at the prestigious Harvard University, and he walked out as one of the first Black minds to earn a PhD. He was a man determined, it seemed, to turn the traditional telling of American history on its head. That is because the word *American* was synonymous with *Anglo-Saxon, Caucasian*, and *white*.

Woodson rewrote Black history, combating the lies in thousands of Eurocentric textbooks. Imagine the heroic effort to upend the towering myth of Black inferiority, liberating Black history from a prison of racist fantasies constructed to alienate Black existence as an inconvenient fact. Woodson must have gone into those lonely archives like a grizzled old detective intent on solving a mystery with inadequate evidence. Undeterred, he threw himself into the investigation. His every thought, every journal, every book written acting in service to uplift Black contributions to America. But here is the shocker: The venerated father of Black history said we should not study Black history. Rather, he said we should study Black people in history. Therein lies a subtle distinction, one that America has failed to grasp, because it requires a simple but, at the same time, radical revisioning of a shared past.

In this future, we would study our collective humanity year-round. Not solely based on race, we would not have to, because our national narrative would be free from the venomous drip of nationalism and bigotry. Woodson cast his history in the best ideals of democracy, where every voice might be heard in our history books. Carter G. Woodson was one of the first Black historians I ever read. The first time I picked up his book *The Mis-Education of the Negro* (1933), I painted it yellow with a highlighter. In that little book, I learned one of life's greatest lessons: Education is to freedom what the sun is to life. To learn is to survive, and without a knowledge of history, a part of you is effectively dead. A good thing to know.

And so, on we go. In this book, I've recovered a few of the millions of stories from Black history to frame the contours of our humanity. But first, let me tell you my own story. Conventionally speaking, I'm no one's historian. I've defended no dissertations, have no PhD to proudly display, no real academic bona fides. I poked around the university for a while as a nomad drifting from architecture courses to mechanical engineering courses, then to marketing courses before jumping ship with an undergraduate degree. The only thing better than hindsight is foresight, much better to anticipate future problems than agonize over how you could've avoided them. Back then I had neither. I can now say with certainty my passions lie in scholarship and teaching. However, staring down the double barrel of student loans and monthly rent, a PhD in history looked very much like financial suicide. Then, the Great Recession of 2007 gutted anything left of my higher education dreams, yet my love of learning remained undiminished.

Curiosity is, and has been, my highest credential. I'm an intellectual adventurer, always trying to experience the high of discovering a dose of wisdom, a measure of history, a capsule of humanity. The library is my alma mater. Books are my professors. For what it's worth, my nickname as a kid was *the professor*, because I was always reading and sharing stuff I learned. An adolescent history buff, I remember picking up an old, dusty hardcover copy of a book in the library by Joel Augustus Rogers, written in 1934, called, *100 Amazing Facts About the Negro: With Complete Proof: A Short Cut to the World History of the Negro.* I read about how he traveled the globe to find the undocumented lives of African-descended people. From that point on, I wanted to read as much as I could about the Black people who impacted the globe. If I psychoanalyze my younger self, some of my study was an act of vindication, because somewhere along the line, I'd swallowed that bitter pill of self-loathing, and debunking America's pathological lie of Black inferiority through history books was a curative. I needed to prove I existed, that we deserved to exist, as much as anyone else. I know, a shaky substitute for cognitive behavioral therapy, but in those moments, history books were all I had.

I'll never forget the time a librarian led me back into the shelves and showed me every Black history book in the library's collection. It's funny how the smallest gestures can have the biggest impact on your life. I spent whole summers reading my way out of that library. I helped enslaved carpenters cut and frame America's colonies and statehouses from timber—artisans constructing porticoes, balustrades, and ornate columns—then, joiners detailing windows, mantles, sashes, and doors. In another book, I created the tools of humanity with Black inventors. Then, I learned business with unsung Black entrepreneurs like Sara Spencer Washington, who founded the start-up Apex, an international empire of beauty schools and products.

I felt a kindred spirit with Arthur Alfonso Schomburg—his life was a manifesto of research and dedication to forgotten history. Without an advanced degree in the subject, he became one of the most meticulous curators and scholars who ever lived, so much so that his home resembled a packed elevator, stuffed with thousands of books and miscellaneous collections. He often joked that his wife gave an ultimatum: The stuff goes, or I go. Eventually his prolific collection laid the foundation for what is now The Schomburg Center for Research in Black Culture, currently incorporated into the New York Public Library.

I appreciated the poets, able to structure life's truths in verse. To this day I remember sitting on the carpet in between the four-tiered wooden shelves flipping through Gwendolyn Brooks and Amiri Baraka. I then helped Josiah Henson shuttle fugitives along the Underground Railroad and joined Elizabeth Freeman in the courtroom to sue for freedom before rebelling against slavery with Nat Turner. I remember learning about Paul R. Williams, the Black architect who shaped the environment of Southern California, where more than 2,500 buildings stand as a testament to his impeccable design skill. His story inspired me to study the discipline of architecture and how the built environment leaves its signature on human behavior. I read about the Black men who fought in the 24th Infantry Regiment during the Korean War, which ravaged the peninsula with artillery fire and death, leaving hundreds of thousands dead. I learned about Rebecca Lee Crumpler, the first Black woman to become a doctor in 1864, who immediately put those skills to use helping poor, underprivileged children and the formerly enslaved. I was determined to find the marginalized and underemphasized. I planned the Civil Rights Movement with Ella Baker and Bayard Rustin. Rustin, along with Audre Lorde, inspired me to take a stance against heterosexism. Every book had been like a conversation between me and the writer. Some confirmed my opinion, and others taunted me to change my mind.

Meanwhile, I was frustrated by the dramatic contradictions. I can only assume my school thought its history lessons were colorblind, but the more I learned, the clearer it became that Black history was just a cursory scribble. Europe stood as the sole measure of human achievement. Even Black heroes were presented in whiteface: Toussaint Louverture, the astounding general who expelled the French forces from Haiti, was called "the Black Napoleon"; famed scientist George Washington Carver, "the Black Leonardo"; Granville Woods was "the Black Edison"; Alain Locke, "the Black Plato"; and the classic beauty of Dorothy Dandridge got her dubbed "the Black Marilyn Monroe." In everything from civilization to culture, white history was the yardstick of progression. I realized then what I'd internalized after swallowing anti-Black stereotypes. They went down like unaged corn whiskey—cheap, raw, and unpalatable. I couldn't believe I'd unwittingly bought into the idea that white was the only color of possibility, and that Europe was inherently better than the rest of the world. So, I began my own journey out of the gloomy, dank cave of ignorance.

In my indignation, I dove headfirst into Afrocentrism. I took a narrow view of Western civilization, mocking racist Europeans, who, in a bid for geopolitical domination, set up a pernicious racial hierarchy that continued to exploit Black people. Back then, I thought, *To hell with those Enlightenment thinkers like Voltaire, David Hume, and Immanuel Kant.* Who were they to sit there in their goofy wigs theorizing that the white race is the greatest perfection of humanity? Afrocentrism was my sword, shield, and body armor.

I fought to clear my mind of the lies degrading all things African. The lies that debased the intelligence, beauty, possibility, and capability of African-descended people. The lies that said Europeans founded everything. In response, my whole worldview became Black, and that made me gullible to all sorts of conspiracies, half-truths, and questionable facts. Ancient Egyptians, all Black Africans. Human civilization, yep, that sprang exclusively from Black Africa. Black Africans not only had a presence in ancient America, they founded its civilizations. Jesus was Black. Ludwig van Beethoven was Black. I discarded any evidence that didn't support my beliefs. If anyone disagreed or challenged me, I conveniently told them that European scholars hid the evidence.

I even trolled my intellectual adversaries with insignificant truths. Yes, polar bears look white, but underneath their plush transparent undercoat—the skin, black. Everything black, not just a little, no, like Vantablack, the scientific, lab-created coating that absorbs 99.965 percent of visible light.

I even stopped celebrating Christmas because it was a European holiday. I thought, if white Europeans think Black Africa is not worthy of consideration and only condemnation, then white Europe is not worthy of consideration and only condemnation. All of this was rooted in pain. It rested on pessimism. An eye for an eye makes the world blind.

An African-centered worldview provided me with counterclaims against the myth of Black inferiority. It opened a window for me to see how people of African descent made unique contributions to human civilization, pursuing their own values and ways of life. It deepened my understanding of the psychological, social, spiritual, and cultural destruction of African civilization. But I began to realize my deference to a set of assumptions that I never questioned. In a sense, with an all-Black worldview, I'd baptized myself in ink. And yet, I found no salvation.

In fact, the worst of Afrocentrism was xenophobic, inward looking, and uncritical of its own limitations, not unlike Eurocentrism. Afrocentrism reduced another race to its worst qualities—white supremacist pathology, colonialism, and imperialism. There was a certain madness in it, too, watching people indict Europe using the critical theories and psychoanalysis crafted by her native-born philosophers, psychologists, and social scientists—the Marxes, the Freuds, the Gramscis, and de Beauvoirs of the West.

So, I moved beyond the sanctified myths of history to see the interlocking truths that connect all seven billion of us dwelling on Earth. I loved Africa no less. Only then, when I followed the river of Black history, I could detour down the tributaries, inlets, creeks, and channels of all races. On my new journey, no matter what cultural stream I drifted on, they all fed back into the great ocean of humanity.

Compared with a typical American-authored history book, which tends to sway toward uncritical celebration or museum of atrocity, this book is a little different. We will not shy from our ever-present power struggles, the spectrum of inequality, nor the deeply flawed history from which they stem, but my aim is to underscore our inextricably linked humanness. No easy thing. Not when media, government, academia, and algorithms exploit our divisions in service to their respective power bases. The dangerous undercurrents of history always pull at us—one million differences divide us, and misunderstandings separate us, but we need a sort of double vision, so that we still see in common. The fact that any of us were born is a miracle we all share, then we live strange and unique lives until meeting our expiration date.

Yet, we'd be foolish not to acknowledge that American history has sacrificed Black humanity to its whitewashing and elisions. The stories are either triumphs or cautionary tales, but Black history is too complex for simple binaries and Manichaean interpretations. So, just like the history of Rosa Parks, we connect on the surface, but seldom in the deep. Black history becomes like a bus tour of Mt. Rushmore with big Black faces. A few figures like Frederick Douglass, Harriet Tubman, and Martin Luther King Jr. loom so large it's difficult to see them as human beings. Without self-study or at-home education, most of us would leave school remembering nothing more than the promise of King's dream, and how Harriet Tubman traveled the Underground Railroad after tying off her headwrap. Beyond these central historical figures, millions of other dark human bodies are defined by a simplistic tale of slavery in a strange land somewhere south. They were nameless masses in the pages of the past, lacking depth—breath—action—emotion.

I don't think it's unfair to say that history books are still made of ink, wood pulp, and ignorance. In 2021, a Portland, Oregon, mother found her fifth grader reading dehumanizing passages from her school textbook, *A History of US: War, Terrible War: 1855–1865* by author Joy Hakim, which teaches children the following stories about Harriet Tubman: "She could lift great weights, withstand cold and heat, chop down big trees, and go without food when necessary. She had been trained, in childhood, to take abuse. That was part of what it meant to be a slave."

Far from isolated incidents, these news stories act as flag posts across the landscape of racial prejudice. One of the worst examples I remember is from 2017, when teachers at a high school near Los Angeles decided to reenact the "experience" of slavery by taping students' wrists together and making them lie in the dark before watching a clip from the movie *Roots*. At universities across the nation, Black intellectuals who theorize about race are prime targets of far-right conservatives. State legislators pass sweeping education bills limiting the teaching of Black pain to protect white students who might feel upset about it. These concerns operate from an assumption that racial tensions come from discussion, rather than the conditions these discussions arise in response to. Instead of telling the truth about the foundations of racial power and how it exists in the present, young minds are taught a comforting narrative of national innocence.

In bookstores, I always find myself in the US history section. Then, somewhere else. Trying to locate anyone who isn't white, male, a president, a sports icon, a descendant of royalty, or a model minority who "made it." Often, African American history is segregated into another section. Situated next to all the other hyphenated Americans: Chicano-American, Asian-American, Native-American, women, and otherwise. Black history is an elective in high school, deemed optional if offered at all. It is a separate Africana studies department on college campuses. It is set aside 337 days out of the year. These gestures may seem insignificant, but they stand as claims that Black history is not part of the American story. The stubborn insistence on the separation of Black people, their history, and experiences, or anyone else's—is a denial of their humanity.

When I think of all this, it reminds me why I started *The Humanity Archive* in the first place. After all of my life's twists and detours, I remembered myself as a kid in the library. The one frustrated by the omissions in my school lessons. The kid who could talk about how, in fourteen hundred and ninety-two, Columbus sailed the ocean blue, quote Shakespeare, tell you about Homer's *Odyssey*, the innermost thoughts of Emily Dickinson, the exceptionalism of the Constitution, and the apocryphal kite flown by Benjamin Franklin in a thunderstorm, but who knew little to nothing about Black history. We tamed the wilderness with an adventurous Daniel Boone, and even learned to empathize with the internal struggle of the founding fathers as they held the wolf of slavery by the ears, as Jefferson said, unable to safely hold it or let it go. We even felt the pain of rural white farmers, their poverty and hopelessness frozen forever in the harrowing photos of the Great Depression.

When painting the delicate brushstrokes of humanity, white was the primary color. I don't know if you've ever felt compelled to do something, like a deep, inaudible voice is beckoning you to some purpose. I did, and it was calling on me to share my curiosity, as well as my love of knowledge and history, with the world. So, I bought a cheap microphone and started narrating the stories on my podcast. In one episode, I told the story of Benjamin Banneker, a free Black man in the 1700s who wrote to Thomas Jefferson, asking him to end slavery. I told the story of Katsushika Hokusai, a Japanese ukiyo-e artist who once dipped the feet of a chicken in red paint, then chased it to produce fall leaves for an art competition. He won. Then another on Pocahontas, but from the perspective of her people. Socrates, Fred Hampton, Queen Nzinga (more on her in chapter nine), Juneteenth, and one on "The History of Police in America." I just kept telling the stories of humanity. The stories of the historically unheard. It all led me here, to writing this book. When you turn the final page, I hope you understand three things:

1. How Black history has been whitewashed.
2. How to make connections between past, present, and future.
3. The important role Black people have played in human history.

This is not a textbook. And it is not a book with any groundbreaking original research. This is not a Herculean attempt to cover all Black history in a few hundred pages, nor is it a neat, little, linear timeline of history. This is a book that follows the pendulum of history as it swings back and forth. This is a book where we'll jump into the mess of history and sort our way out of it. I offer few prescriptions, and I have more questions than answers. What I am offering is an outline of Black humanity stitched from images stretching into a far-reaching past. Think of this as a reconnaissance mission. We'll scout the routes of knowledge, map the obstacles of whitewashing, and survey the Black historical landscape. We'll probe, seek, and sometimes stumble into the stuff that makes us human.

I've broken this book into four parts to guide us. First, we will explore how the truth has been hidden from us. And how our history shapes not only our identity, but our concepts of truth.

Second, we will build the foundation. Looking back, way back, millions of years into time to show how Black people have been essential to the development of our entire species and to the world, to America, to the flowering of our humanity. Only then will we see that Western culture is not the sole proprietor of freedom, wisdom, and virtue. Nor is it the sole source of exploitation, greed, and tribal indifference.

Then, we take a closer look at the walk from slavery to freedom. Or what we might call anti-Black history, but also we will show its resistance. Stories of oppression are highly visible in this book, because they feature heavily in the Black American experience. This history still ripples through our institutions, and I'm far from the first to point out how it is still evident in our justice, health, education, housing, and environmental inequalities. Individual racism as a pathology refuses to die and, like most deep-seated prejudices, it'll likely never be fully eradicated, springing up like a weed year after year through fear-based myths and stereotypes. We choose to rewrite that history in our own hearts and minds, or not, to our personal liberation or peril.

Finally, we will chart possibilities. And look at how modes of thinking, belief, and action have helped people transcend mere circumstance to live lives of meaning and transform the world. You'll likely notice that I don't have a chapter on the 1954–1968 Civil Rights Movement. I tell a lot of stories from that era throughout the book, but those years get enough attention. Likely, because they fit neatly into the national narrative of American progress.

Together we will reimagine history. We will question. Who are we? And what has America become by denying Black experiences? We will see that the soul of Black folk is infused into American music, food, art, language, literature, science, thought, politics, values, and encoded into the double helix of our collective being. We will confront the atrocities of American history, because there are still Black descendants of Thomas figuring out what it means to be in the lineage of Jefferson. And because the past still lingers into the present with its consequences.

Then, most importantly, we will move beyond dark truths and briny tears. I wrote this not only as a confrontation with the past, but out of love for it. When I look back, I also see endless human possibility. I see life, laughter, and the eternal sunrise in the faces of those who've come before us. History is the autobiography of the universe. It holds our shared memories, transporting our lived experiences across space and time. We need our history. Charles C. Seifert said a people without a history is like a tree without roots. We are the branches, forever reaching upward. But it is human nature to long for our origins. It's no wonder genealogy and ancestry tests are so popular, because without our identity, we are rendered inhuman. Black people were rendered inhuman. We still are in many ways, which is why this book is dedicated to rendering Black humanity as a visible part of the whole. My favorite quote, and the ethos of this book, comes from a second-century African-Roman playwright named Terence, and in Latin it goes: "*Homo sum, humani nihil a me alienum puto,*" which can be translated as, or, "I am human, and I think nothing human is alien to me."

As I write this, there are 331 million people living in America. We have centuries-old divisions that have yet to be mended and scars that have yet to heal, but the only way this American experiment continues is by finding some uniting principle. Something that can resonate beyond race, religion, politics, ethnic background, gender, sexual orientation, or culture. That thing will be and always has been our humanity. That's all I was searching for as I wandered through those libraries, Black humanity. And I hope, whoever you are, as you flip through these pages, as you read these stories, you see yourself and find your own.

PART 1

Buried Truth

Herein lie buried many things. . . .
—W. E. B. Du Bois, *The Souls of Black Folk*

Whitewashing American History

whitewash /ˈwaɪtwɒʃ/ Verb:
deliberately attempt to conceal unpleasant or incriminating facts
about (someone or something) to make it seem better than it is.
—*Oxford English Dictionary*

CHARLESTON, South Carolina—Squinting against the rays of a lumbering sun, I walked down a cobblestone path to the memorial for Robert Smalls. There, partially covered by bushes, sat a simple bronzed plaque barely raised from the ground and littered with bits of trash and cigarette butts. *What a small pittance for an extraordinary life*, I thought. Especially in a city of outsized beauty. The coastal town streets were lined with palmetto trees, waterfront restaurants, and stately Georgian architecture. The city hugs you with serene Southern charm, but Smalls's life stood in stark contradiction. He lived through the darkest decades of American history. An estimated 40 percent of enslaved people were funneled through Charleston Harbor. Human horrors echo through the hallways of homes now magnetizing global tourists with their antebellum elegance.

Born in 1839 on Beaufort, a South Carolina island, into the fierce protectiveness of his mother, Lydia Polite, the young Robert lived a life apart from the worst brutalities of chattel slavery. No slavery was idyllic, but not all was deliberately cruel, so to prepare him for the racial injustice he'd surely face, Lydia took her son to the auction block to witness the trafficking of human flesh. The skin-tearing beatings. The muted tears. The wasted pleas. It was a harsh and real-world-oriented kind of love.

In her book about Smalls's life, author Dorothy Sterling teases out a conversation young Robert may have had with his mother: "When I'm a man, I'm going to be just like Master. Going to have a house like his and a boat like his and a plantation like his."

Lydia responded, "You ain't never going to be a man. You're a boy now, and it'll be boy till you're sixty. When you're stooped and limping along with a cane, you'll grow up to be uncle."

Perhaps her tough-love approach was to prepare Robert for the degrading social realities he'd surely face. Later, Smalls found himself at Charleston Harbor as hired labor on the bustling docks of that Southern town. He found hope on the water's edge. And love.

Smalls was allowed to marry his sweetheart, an enslaved hotel maid named Hannah Jones, who likewise was given permission to marry. Deemed property, consent was required to seal the bonds of love in holy matrimony. Likely, you'd have had no ceremony, save the ritual of jumping over a broomstick. There was no white muslin wedding gown. No bride's ring. No officiant. No reception. Yet, love is a power unmatched and, despite everything, many said they felt no less married.

Robert and Hannah etched out a life together and a growing family. They welcomed two daughters, Elizabeth and Sarah, into the world. They suffered through the devastating grief of losing a third child, Robert Jr., to the ravages of smallpox. But while supporting his family on those long days as a lamplighter, stevedore foreman, sailmaker, rigger, and finally, a sailor, Smalls longed for liberty. Miraculously, in 1862, after the start of the Civil War, the water provided him the opening to make one of the most daring escapes in all history. Entrusted to steer the CSS *Planter*, a lightly armored Confederate Navy vessel, Smalls began laying his escape plan. He'd steal the ship and navigate to freedom. To fail was to die. One evening, the white officers disembarked from the ship to spend the night ashore, creating just the right opportunity for Smalls and seven other enslaved crew members to execute a lively escape. It was time to take the ship. If caught, they'd shoot its guns to the last round of ammunition in a death-defying fight for freedom. If that didn't work, suicide. They'd sink the ship and go down with it.

I've often wondered who those other seven men were, and though Smalls was exceptional, his extraordinary actions lay rooted in the courage of Black community, a community that, even within the struggles of the world as it was, spared no effort in getting free. Most of us desire self-determination or at least some control over our own destiny. We want to believe that our actions will close the distance to our dreams. So, Smalls and the others would row, quite literally, toward freedom.

Buttoning his white naval jacket and donning a straw hat, in the darkness Smalls resembled the ship's captain just enough to pass by five Confederate harbor ports. And it didn't hurt that he'd mentally mapped the waterways and memorized the proper hand signals to make it past those checkpoints. At the risk of his life, and that of seven other crew members, his wife and children, and eight others who boarded along the way, he deftly maneuvered a heavily guarded harbor. They prayed. They trembled. They cried. They despaired. Nonetheless, Smalls was steadfast. After passing the Confederate fortifications, he barreled toward the US Navy's South Atlantic Blockading Squadron, lowering the South Carolina and Confederate flags, hoisting a white bedsheet signifying surrender. "I am delivering this war material including these cannons and I think Uncle Abraham Lincoln can put them to good use," he said to the Union officers, who were surely shocked. He'd crossed the line of freedom, but his story doesn't end there.

Having enough courage and naval intelligence to help shape the Civil War, Smalls then served with the Union Navy and Army. He spied for the Union, recruited some five thousand Black soldiers, and took part in seventeen military engagements as one of the first Black Navy pilots in the northern effort. After the war, he purchased his former enslaver's house in Beaufort with money paid to him by the US government for half the appraised value of the CSS *Planter*, a ship originally used by those whose interest was to keep him enslaved.

During the Reconstruction period, he served in the South Carolina state assembly, went to Washington as a congressman, and served five terms in the US House of Representatives. Robert Smalls's statesmanship saw restrictive Black codes abolished, public schools constructed, salaries for teachers and laborers increased, and the Charleston harbor improved.

Sidelining resentment, he even pushed a relief bill for former Confederate farmers.

His was one of the most inspiring stories in American history. Smalls died in 1915, but it took a century for the city of Charleston to resuscitate his legacy.

In recent years, the city has erected a statue of Denmark Vesey, a marker to the slave-led Stono Rebellion, and the International African American Museum. But as internal conflicts became public in 2021, the museum's reputation was put in jeopardy. A well-respected museum director of operations quit, accusing the museum board of allowing it to become a "racist and misogynistic organization," and a local retired history professor said the museum should have been committed to a racial truth and reconciliation process. That makes me wonder, are we naïve to expect any museum whose primary funding comes from state and corporate dollars to infuse the reconciliation between past and present into its core values? The city of Charleston, like the rest of America, is stuck between those who want to reckon with its dark history and those who do not. Our nation stands at the uneasy intersection between whitewashing and recovery, while Black history and the legacies of those like Robert Smalls hang in the balance.

A Ritual of Forgetting

As I stood on the short, bright-green grass of the waterfront, I couldn't help but think about how Black history is crushed under the weight of reductions and simplifications. Only minutes away stood a statue honoring "The Confederate Defenders of Charleston," a towering monument commissioned by the United Daughters of the Confederacy. The UDC is a group of Southern socialites who, with their textbook committees, influenced school boards to ban books deemed disparaging of the South. The group has had historic affiliations with white supremacist groups, feeding the public a strict diet of Anglo-Saxonism and mobilizing against desegregation under the guise of honoring their ancestors. In their theory of race, Black inferiority was the natural hierarchy of human existence. The UDC still exists, and while no one is naïve enough to think it still exerts control over school curriculum, its ideas wield stubbornly persistent staying power.

"It was not that the textbooks had to preach black inferiority and white supremacy," said historian Elizabeth Gillespie McRae. "They just had to erase African Americans from American history in all but the most decorative moments, and in those moments, they became inferior historical subjects not worthy of individual attention. Jim Crow politics relied on the stories it told and the symbols it created, which were replicated decade after decade in public schools."

These ideas were etched in stone as thousands of Confederate monuments were scattered across America. In fact, the one in Charleston stands almost twenty-five feet tall. So, as my six-foot-two-inch frame hovered over the Robert Smalls plaque, I thought about how history is the biography of power. Those who hold it shape history like sculptor's wax, molding public opinion in their favor. Think of all the atrocities formed into denial, even in the face of indisputable evidence. Until relatively recently, the Turkish government denied the Armenian genocide of 1915. Japan long refused to acknowledge its colossal war crimes, including the Nanjing Massacre in which hundreds of thousands of Chinese were killed. The United States has been slow to call the slaughter of indigenous people genocide, and has censored the voices of the enslaved. Denialism pollutes history, minimalizes acts of inhumanity, and stalls acts of reconciliation. Denialism weaves itself into US history, censoring the voices of the enslaved.

Modern historians use the concept of *damnatio memoriae*—a Latin phrase meaning "condemnation of memory"—to describe society's efforts to erase official histories. Ancient Romans used memory sanctions to expunge public figures considered tyrants, traitors, and enemies of the state from the public record. Faces on statues were chiseled to bits, written records deleted, books burned, inscriptions effaced, visual depictions scratched from currency, and paintings buffered beyond recognition. It was a ban on remembrance, a fate considered worse than death. This orchestrated forgetting was, as it is now, a deliberate act. A choice. The Romans knew that public history feeds our cultural identity, nourishes power, and sustains political authority.

The omissions of Black history have been used in service of white power. They said slavery was humane. They blamed the victims. They justified the unjustifiable. This helped keep a legalized caste system in place in America some one hundred years after the Emancipation Proclamation. It doesn't stop there. The whole world has witnessed how they set fire to our memories; what was lost will never be fully recovered.

But we do the work. We move through the dust and soot trying to restore our treasured heirlooms. We reexamine the legacies. We seek—and we find—exemplary figures like Robert Smalls, and we accent their brilliance. In this way, we keep in contact with the best of our American past. And we can apply his vision, self-determination, and courage to our own struggles. But we cannot stop there. We are obliged to remember that his heroism came at a cost. The melancholy reality of life, especially political life, is that it is a constant battle. So, it seems to me that we dishonor the legacy of those like Smalls by overlooking the biggest battle he fought, the war against white supremacy. While awaiting repairs on the *Planter* in 1864, a year when Philadelphia enforced explicitly racist segregation laws, Smalls was ejected from an all-white streetcar. He presents an early example of celebrity activism: As a famed Civil War hero, he led a mass boycott of segregated public transportation. The constitutional right to boycott remains a powerful countermeasure to remedy injustice.

Even the most qualified Black people have their credentials, qualifications, and birth certificates placed under the microscope. Smalls himself was jailed on baseless accusations of bribery as an elected official. All during a time when white politicians organized the intimidation and murder of Black voters. He, too, faced death threats from white supremacists and was effectively removed from office through the terror tactics of organized racists. And while the extremes may be different, Black politicians still face more scrutiny. Like Smalls, how many Black people have followed the advice of their parents to work twice as hard and be twice as smart, talented, and dependable? When we only examine the upper stratum of history, we miss the deep layers that allow us to define the structure of the present.

Some important questions simply aren't asked enough. Whose monuments ascend toward the heavens? Whose stories are told with dignity? Whose lives are appreciated? Whose dead deserve our tears? On a trip to Washington, DC, I cast a skeptical eye on another monument. When looking at the Emancipation Memorial, the goal to juxtapose slavery and freedom is clear, but it is bereft of truth. President Abraham Lincoln's tall frame towers over a half-naked Black freedman kneeling at his feet. Lincoln clutches the Emancipation Proclamation in one hand. The other is waving over the man's head, as if to say, *abracadabra, you're free*. I get the temptation to mythologize heroes, and it would be absurd to think that a whole history could be captured in a single monument. But one cast in truth would have, at least, had them standing side by side.

We've grown accustomed to the idea that Lincoln "freed the slaves." To be fair, the mild and moderate approach Lincoln took to end the institution of chattel slavery was likely the only way to obliterate the institution. At its best, Lincoln's story is that of a unifier, a man who underwent a long evolution. However, such narrow generalizations of history render the 186,000 Black people who buttoned up their Union Army blues and grabbed muskets to fight for Black liberty obsolete. And they wipe out the almost three hundred years Black people had already spent trying to get free. Even more, these generalizations aim to conceal Lincoln's blemishes.

Contrary to his hatred of slavery, for much of his political career, Lincoln was ambivalent about emancipation. Most of us are familiar with the lines of his 1862 letter, in which he wrote: "If I could save the union without freeing any slaves I would do it; and if I could save it by freeing all the slaves I would do it; and if I could save it by freeing some and leaving others alone, I would also do that." But less highlighted is how, in 1861, he supported the Corwin Amendment, which, if passed, would have maintained US slavery indefinitely. It is well known that he didn't like slavery, which makes it more glaring that he was, for a moment, willing to sacrifice millions of Black lives to hold the Union together.

We hear much about his evolution, but I have thought a lot about the Black people in his orbit. In *Life and Times of Frederick Douglass*, the famed abolitionist gives us a glimpse into his complicated relationship with the president. And historians say that Lincoln's barber, his associate for more than two decades, the free Black entrepreneur William Florville, advised him on racial matters while lining up that Amish-style beard. But in US history, Black people have been a footnote under Lincoln's heel. And speaking of that, the name of the man kneeling in the Emancipation Memorial? It was Archer Alexander. He was the model for the freedman kneeling under Lincoln. Alexander became a fugitive in 1863, and courageously alerted

Union authorities about a plan by his enslaver to demolish a bridge used by the Union Army. A dashing man with a friendly smile, his great-great-great-grandson would grow up to become the quick-jabbing, fast-talking civil rights activist and heavyweight champion of the world, Muhammad Ali. I'm always amazed to see dots connecting like this.

It was formerly enslaved Black people like Alexander who donated every penny to fund the Emancipation Memorial, yet white people had control over its design and commission. A formerly enslaved woman named Charlotte Scott gave the first donation—five dollars—to the construction of the statue. In all, $20,000 was raised by Black people for its construction. But the monument was immediately seen for what it was. "The negro here, though rising," wrote Frederick Douglass a few days after at the dedication ceremony, "is still on his knees and nude. What I want to see before I die is a monument representing the negro, not couchant on his knees like a four-footed animal, but erect on his feet like a man."

These aren't details people just overlooked. Those who erected these statues knew full well they were degrading Black people, as do those who continue to whitewash history.

Written Out

One of America's first historians was Chief Justice John Marshall. Legend has it, when he died in 1835, the Liberty Bell cracked at his funeral, never to be heard again. He is lionized as America's great chief justice, a mover, shaker, and shaper of constitutional law. So much so that legal decisions from the Marshall Court are routinely used as precedent, like *Marbury v. Madison,* which set the Supreme Court as the final interpreter of the Constitution and legalized its ability to overrule the president, Congress, and state governments. Marshall also bought and sold humans with amoral intensity, keeping more than 250 people in perpetual bondage during his lifetime.

Modern biographers rarely mention it. One said that he was the "owner of a modest number of slaves." Who were they? Edey, Harry. Kate. Moses. Ben. Dick. "A negro woman." "Woman," that is how he recorded them as property. We give more thought to naming cats and dogs. In cases like these, the enslaved are like cutouts from an American portrait—the gaping hole and outline reminds us they were there, but we'll never see the details. When Marshall wrote one of the first books on the American story, a massive work on George Washington and America's founding, he said little of those he considered "pests" and "criminals."

Early writers and historians viewed history as a way of explaining statecraft and politics, whose main characters were elite white males, thereby ignoring everyone else. In this same era, George Bancroft, known as "the father of American history," oriented his massive, ten-volume, *History of the United States of America: From the Discovery of the Continent* (1848) around the same principles of exceptionalism and unimpeded progress that animate many American histories today. His romantic historical drama centered on a story of Anglo-Saxon zeal and heroism. Black people were written as a soulless labor force extracting bounties of rice, cotton, and tobacco. I searched hundreds of pages of his books, trying to find Black humanity, and came up empty. There was a similar denial of indigenous genocide. They were but "a few scattered tribes of feeble barbarians, destitute of commerce and of political connection." Millions of people accepted this as truth. Deep down, millions still do. That is because the building blocks of American memory—citizenship, liberty, patriotism, and elite white American power—have always depended on it.

Deep into the twentieth century, professional historians, poets and intellectuals, politicians, teachers, military personnel, lawyers, journalists, and others wrote glaringly racist histories without raising many eyebrows. They were unafraid to say—on the record, out loud, into microphones, in books and other publications—that Black people were inferior. Johns Hopkins University–educated Thomas F. Dixon Jr., a Baptist minister and politician who thought that Black people did nothing to affect the world, reflected the dominant ideas of his era:

> Since the dawn of history, the negro has owned the continent of Africa—rich beyond the dream of poet's fancy, crunching acres of diamonds beneath his bare black feet. Yet he never picked one up from the dust until a white man showed to him its glittering light. His land swarmed with powerful and docile animals, yet he never dreamed a harness, cart, or sled. A hunter by necessity, he never made an axe, spear, or arrowhead worth preserving

beyond the moment of its use. He lived as an ox, content to graze for an hour. In a land of stone and timber he never sawed a foot of lumber, carved a block, or built a house save of broken sticks and mud.

Racism is more guarded these days, but I'm stating the obvious to say it still exists. Cultural illiteracy feeds it, and there yet remains a shortage of in-depth and nuanced reporting about the African continent from outside of it. Often, it is presented as a no-man's-land, or a giant game preserve, or chimpanzee sanctuary, or hotbed of terrorists, or massive, disease-infested continent with a few isolated cities and beachfront hotels. As I'm writing this book, in 2022, Vladimir Putin has ordered an invasion into Ukraine, there is war, the death toll widens, the threat of nuclear catastrophe has the world on edge. I flip through a news story about how civilians outside Kyiv are being executed— hands bound, necrotized bodies lying curled next to trash littering the streets. The world weeps. At the same time, in the Tigray Region of Ethiopia, famine is being used as a weapon of war, up to half a million dead. Northern Tigrayan civilians are sandwiched into mass executions by the Ethiopian government and Eritrean militias, atrocities on all sides. I flip through the news to see a young child with a horrifyingly distended belly. He is starving to death. I compared the outpouring of cash and empathy for the Ukrainian civilians, whose death toll is no less important, but pales in comparison.

I have never seen anything like this for a Black or Brown nation. In comparison to Ukraine's hourly and daily coverage, Tigray barely registers. Journalists around the world dropped their oath to be unbiased, because, as one Ukrainian official said, there were "European people with blue eyes and blonde hair being killed." Only the buzzards count the dead in Africa. An overstatement, of course, but let your attention rest on the fact that the dehumanizing ideas of a whitewashed history still exist. After centuries, they have hardened into dangerous assumptions, laws, social norms, and government policies against Black people all over the globe. These are the attitudes that, if left unchecked, are used to justify orgies of atrocity—mass graves, the blocking of humanitarian aid, torture, and genocide. The past connects to the present.

Uncovering history can be like walking up to a log in the woods that looks usable on the surface until you kick it over and find the underside rotten. We can trace much of today's ideological decay to a seemingly benign US history that was in fact used to deny reparative justice and justify the segregation of Black people. Remember earlier I mentioned the United Daughters of the Confederacy? Well, their influence extended much further than a single statue. In 1915, Mildred Rutherford, a Southern educator with an axe to grind, boldly said that "patriotic men and women of the north as well as the south, are demanding a new history." As the national historian of the group, she promoted the Confederacy as the true spirit of America. If you want to know the origins of the whitewashed slavery lessons in public schools, you don't have to look much further than Rutherford. Looking back, this is probably why we read *The Adventures of Huckleberry Finn* (1855) instead of *The Confessions of Nat Turner* (1967). Rutherford was a foremother of the book ban. Groups like hers denied schoolchildren access to accurate knowledge of the past.

In the early twentieth century, a wave of Southern historians graduated from Columbia University under the ideas of renowned historian William A. Dunning. In the so-called Dunning School, Reconstruction was a failure. As historian Eric Foner writes in his book *The Second Founding: How the Civil War and Reconstruction Remade the Constitution* (2019), those early historians believed that "blacks lacked the capacity to participate intelligently in political democracy." In addition, Dunning believed that Black and white were so distinct in characteristics that coexistence was impossible without a system that accounted for the so-called fact of Black inferiority. Thus, the failure of Reconstruction, which gave and protected the voting rights of Black people, was considered a necessary evil.

These historians were no stand-in for all white historical scholarship, but their ideas lived on in public memory. You have to remember the pro-Confederate book of love, loss, and propaganda, *Gone with the Wind* (1936), was the cultural zeitgeist of its era. That author described newly freed Black people "like monkeys or small children turned loose among treasured objects whose value is beyond their comprehension." This was a book that has made lists alongside the Holy Bible for top worldwide sellers. I haven't been to church in years, but sometimes nothing captures an idea like a bit of biblical prose. "There is no remembrance of former things, Nor will there be any remembrance of things that are to come by those who will come after," says a passage from the book of Ecclesiastes 1:11. Just think, less than a hundred years after our deaths, our descendants will no longer drop tears on our headstones. But when it comes to US history, Black people have been forgotten much quicker. On purpose. And that is how the past has been whitewashed.

To Tell Our Own Stories

In October 1833, a young Black abolitionist named William C. Nell stood to speak in front of the Juvenile Garrison Independent Society at the African Meeting House in Boston. As a boy, he'd peeked into the window to see an antislavery meeting being held by abolitionist William Lloyd Garrison. Sometimes gentle influences are the most powerful, as soon after, Nell became Garrison's antislavery apprentice. His parents were equally committed to the antislavery cause, so it's no surprise to find him, at only sixteen years old, intensely focused on uniting Black people to fight slavery and anti-Black prejudice. But aside from his storied life as an abolitionist and desegregationist, it is worth remembering that Nell was part of a largely overlooked canon of Black historians and scholars. This group took on the burden of reframing Black history, correcting errors, and reshaping the Black image. The white publishing establishment seldom took their work seriously, but they self-published, covering facts and depictions of Black life, ever on a mission to set the record straight.

In 1841 James W. C. Pennington wrote *A Textbook of the Origin and History of the Colored People*, which sought to "unembarrass" the origin of Black people in history. In his 1855 book, *The Colored Patriots of the American Revolution*, William C. Nell gives a brisk accounting of Black existence during the British North American war. William Wells Brown published his book in 1863, telling about *The Black Man: His Antecedents, His Genius, and His Achievements* with a knife-edge sharpness. To sketch the biographies of Black people as slaves, soldiers, and citizens, George Washington Williams published the two-volume *History of the Negro Race in America from 1619 to 1880,* in 1887. Anna J. Cooper, "the mother of Black feminism," earned a PhD in history in 1925, and stands as a towering figure in Black American scholarship.

Evading prejudicial degree programs, nonacademic scholars breathed life into history. Those like Leila Amos Pendleton, Elizabeth Lindsay Davis, and Laura Eliza Wilkes are all worthy of the title *historian*, even with only a high school diploma. Of almost two thousand history doctorates awarded by 1935, only six were given to Black people. But as they trickled into the profession, not a second was wasted debunking the lies. Compiling thousands of papers, books, and articles, they began the difficult work of clearing out the racist historical sewage. In the cold isolation of segregated libraries, and within the walls of historically Black colleges, they infused the peculiarities of the Black experience into the American one. Each generation built on the other to create an interconnected Black historical universe. Sometimes they wrote to replace psychological anguish with self-respect, sometimes for redemption. Some wrote from biblical inspiration and others from political awakening. Black voices became louder.

In sheer intellectual output, W. E. B. Du Bois was unparalleled in the scholarly universe. *The Suppression of the African Slave-Trade: Trade to the United States of America, 1638–1870* (1892), *The Negro Church* (1903), and *Black Reconstruction in America: Toward a History of the Part Which Black Folk Played in the Attempt to Reconstruct Democracy in America, 1860–1880* (1935) are but a few fantastic titles he cranked out over his decades-long career. Dorothy Porter Wesley revolutionized how we learn about Black history in America. In her long and prolific career (1930–1995), she transformed the library from her desk at Howard University. When Black history was organized into only two categories, slavery and colonization, the enterprising librarian highlighted Black people in every subject: literature, health and medicine, music, philosophy, mathematics, history, biology, religion, and other specific subject areas. With a shoestring budget and student staff, she amassed a collection of eighteen thousand items; when she began, there were only three thousand. A genius curator with an eye for the important, she saved irreplaceable history from the trash bin.

It was the 1962 book *Before the Mayflower: A History of Black America,* by Lerone Bennett Jr., that mainstreamed 1619 as the most important date in Black American history. Bennett graduated from Morehouse the same year as Martin Luther King Jr., and died in 2018. It makes me wonder, *What if King had lived that long?* In 1966, John Hope Franklin put forth his meticulously researched and massive book, *From Slavery to Freedom*, which appealed to Black and white audiences alike.

And like Du Bois incarnate, a bookshelf would groan under the weight of Henry Louis Gates Jr. texts. His body of work includes hundreds of books written and coauthored, documentaries, articles, and TV series. I referenced his work *The Annotated African American Folktales* (2017) in the writing of this book.

Others drifted far off the radar, like John Henrik Clarke, John Wesley Blassingame, Helen Grey Edmonds, Rosalyn Terborg-Penn, Rayford W. Logan, Charles H. Wesley. The list goes on. Not to leave anyone out, but I could take up twenty more pages listing all the scholars who laid the foundations for my work and all the other contemporary, Black-authored history books you see on the shelf. More and more Black historians came forward who refused to sugarcoat their narratives. Hundreds of book clubs and writers groups have supported them. But I still wrestle with some of the same issues as my predecessors. Race, class, gender, freedom, redemption, identity, and the absurdity of American life. Black scholars producing history today continue to scrub the whitewash, helping to shape a collective memory.

Whose History Now

America is a young nation, too immature to deal with the trauma of our national childhood. In every decade the question is argued—how do we teach American history? In the 1990s the architects of multiculturalism, a political theory of tolerance and diversity, found themselves embroiled in a culture war—a straw man target of the political right, which saw it as political correctness and excessive tolerance. They railed against multicultural content in textbooks and saw the framework as a threat to social cohesion, an invitation for unrestricted mass immigration, and an attack on Western liberalism.

If this sounds a bit familiar, it may be because it shares some similarities with the debates surrounding critical race theory. There is nothing new under the sun, but in the war over history, people are still dug into the same trenches. As a multinational movement, the American flavor of multiculturalism sought to fill the void of tolerance with a multiethnic chorus of voices in American literature and history. The sociological metaphor of a salad bowl became common and diametrically opposed to the long-used idea of the melting pot. It was the idea that the historically un-meltable—Black people, Hispanics, women, Asians, indigenous, disabled folk and beyond—could retain their unique identities, integrating with, but not disappearing into, the whole.

A Black professor, C. James Trotman, stated in his 2002 book, *Multiculturalism: Roots and Realities*, that it "uses several disciplines to highlight neglected aspects of our social history, particularly the histories of women and minorities [and] promotes respect for the dignity of the lives and voices of the forgotten." Well intentioned as that definition stands, its critics accused it of disguising uniculturalism, where people can disparage any culture but their own, especially if it is "white" and "oppressive." There is some validity to this. When we adhere uncritically to any ideology, it can become like looking through a keyhole, but when I read books like Ronald Takaki's *Different Mirror: A History of Multicultural America* (2012), a collage history in which he sketches a multiethnic history ranging from Native Americans, Black, Irish, Mexicans, Chinese, Japanese, Korean, Afghan, and Jewish, I see it as a worthy effort. But the soul of Black history is lost in such sweeping narratives, which fail to adequately delve into the history of anti-Blackness. I'm totally for discovering everyone's history; I just don't think we can do it from one textbook. We need the tools to dig for historical truth on our own, along with a critique on our flawed approaches to teaching history.

In 2020, when the brutal killings of Black Americans at the hands of police became a horrific staple on cell phones and television screens, a mélange of citizens and corporations opened up to the forbidden truths of American history that many Black people already knew. Culturally, history has occupied a formidable space in Black homes. US Black history was always a part of who we were. It was the intersection of history and the televised denial of Black humanity that caused the wider interest in Black stories, and in some cases the acknowledgment of whitewashing.

In 2021, the American Historical Association, the oldest professional association of historians, formally acknowledged its role in "generating, disseminating, legitimating, and promoting histories that have helped contribute to the evolution and institutionalization of racist ideas, racial discrimination, and racist violence in the United States." Coming to the realization that, throughout American history, this pattern of anti-Blackness has been a major determinant not only of Black social, economic, and political life, but in the writing of it. There was an outpouring of effort to learn marginal histories for about six months, but that amount of high-octane interest was bound to run low on fuel. Change happens in fits, starts, outrages, and atrocities. So much changed, and so much stayed the same.

When I first began this book, I stumbled upon Ralph Ellison's 1953 classic, *Invisible Man*. In his surreal masterpiece, Ellison introduces us to an unidentified Black narrator high-wiring across the abyss of our racial divide. Later, we find him working at a paint manufacturing company called Liberty Paints. The building was unmistakable because of the brightly lit advertising sign that read, "Keep America Pure with Liberty Paints." Liberty is a cut above the competition because of a very special pigment, a proprietary blend that produces a brilliant white marketed as "Optic White." Then the mystery is revealed. Only after ten drops of a black chemical are squirted into the mixture does it reach perfection. Undetectable in the finished product, the contribution of the black chemical makes the dazzling white paint possible. Unlike that paint, it is easy to detect Ellison's symbolism. The author sought to show the desire to keep America white.

The tragedy is that generations have grown up knowing little about their own history. In classic vampire lore, the undead blood sipper is unable to see his or her own reflection, because mirrors don't reflect soulless creatures. When Black history is whitewashed, American history becomes soulless, unable to see itself, its moral depths, and its true identity. Black brilliance has been the unseen ingredient in the history of the United States.

And yet, from the beginning, Black people have been told that they have created nothing of consequence. As a result, our dreams have been kept secret from us. Many were never told that they were capable of great things, so they never tried. Progress has been made to update our narratives, but our history remains segregated. An afterthought. Like the story of Robert Smalls, a national hero, covered by the foliage of exclusion. But more people are reexamining the past with all its complexities and contradictions. They know, as I do, it is up to each generation to rewrite the past with new vision. Because if we don't, if the attempts to whitewash Black stories succeed, our history will be as someone once said, a set of lies agreed upon.

2

Who Are You?

In America, the traditional routes to
Black identity have hardly been normal.
—June Jordan, *Civil War*

As a human being, I cannot allow myself to be fragmented into Negro
at one time, woman at another or worker at another, I must find a
unifying principle in all these movements to which I can adhere.
—Pauli Murray, 1967

He was a thin, jet-black man with sharp features. His silver goatee complemented his hair, which was receding into baldness as he proceeded in age. He looked weary. Deep-set wrinkles protruded from his forehead, but his eyes still gazed out with the same bright, piercing focus we might imagine they had when he was nineteen years old and soon to be married. But raiders from the West African kingdom of Dahomey (present-day Benin) had other plans. Embroiled in intertribal warfare, he found himself on the losing side. In 1860, Oluale Kossola was kidnapped. Wrenched from home and stripped of clothing, Kossola was shoved into a barracoon (a temporary prison enclosure) to await a new fate.

The kingdom of Dahomey had grown rich through such raids, and Kossola was now captive to a major supplier of the US slave addiction. The United States banned the importation of enslaved people in 1808, with New Jersey becoming the last Northern state to abolish the practice altogether only four years earlier. The seedy flow of human cargo continued south of the Mason-Dixon. Kossola, along with 110 others, were packed into a schooner named the *Clotilda,* destined for Mobile, Alabama. All was done on a bet by plantation owner Timothy Meaher, who told friends he could pull it off. It was the last known ship to bring enslaved Africans to the United States.

By the time Oluale Kossola met Zora Neale Hurston, who captures his story in the book *Barracoon*, completed in 1931, he was called Cudjo Lewis. Nearing a century in age, he looked out from deep-set eyes, gripping his smoking pipe with knotty fingers, and told his story. Staying true to his linguistic humanity, Hurston captured his words in dialect, just as he spoke them. Lewis recounted in detail the detestable cruelty of his ordeal, but it was these words that really moved me: "When I think 'bout dat time I try not to cry no mo," he said, presumably in pain. "My eyes dey stop cryin' but de tears runnee down inside me all de time. I no see none my family."

Lewis helps us fulfill our relentless need to recover what was lost on the unimaginable journey from Africa to America. It is impossible to survey the annihilation—of family, of gods, and cultural practices—completely, but his story helps us understand the identities lost to all Black Americans who are descendants of the enslaved. Freed in 1865, after the conclusion of the Civil War, Lewis stood at the crossroads of Africa and America, longing for what he called "de Affica soil."

Sensing he would never return, his group resolved to appeal for compensation. Lewis approached his former enslaver, Timothy Meaher, who was sitting on a felled tree. "Cap'n Tim, you brought us from our country where we had lan'," Lewis asserted. "Why doan you give us piece dis land so we kin buildee ourself a home?"

His words had the effect of fire to the log Meaher was sitting on. "Cap'n jump on his feet," Lewis recalled, embittered and angry. "Fool do you think I goin' give you property on top of property? I tookee good keer my slaves and derefo' I doan owe dem nothin.'"

This might have smothered the dreams of the most hopeful, but the budding community reckoned with reality took nothing and made something. They ate bread and molasses, saved pennies, pooled resources, and acted as a unit. They were bound, not by blood kinship, but traumatic experience. Through mutual aid, they founded Africatown, a community that still exists in Alabama, albeit under industrial and economic threat. But the collective effort of the original enslaved people allowed them to buy the land refused to them as payment for their purloined labor. There was Jinnie/

Jenny and Cuffy/Cuffee (a variation of the Akan name Kofi), also husband and wife, and most likely *Clotilda* survivors. And there was Matilda Mc-Crear a woman said to wear her hair in inventive Yoruban hairstyles until the day she died. Another one of the original African born was named Redoshi, who lived there with her husband, "William" or "Billy" whom she was forced to marry at twelve years old, until becoming a widow in the 1920s. It is all too bad Hurston did not capture her story. Firsthand accounts of women who survived the Middle Passage are scant.

Most of their stories lie buried under the seabed. Even what we know about an Africatown resident named Redoshi comes from a white journalist projecting exotic fantasies. His description of her belies virtue and accuracy. In his eyes, she was a "dark, supple princess . . . imbued with the love of life in the jungles." Contrary to the dismal accounts of other *Clotilda* survivors, the interviewer attested to a jovial interview in which Redoshi said she was treated and fed well. But this reinforced pre–Civil War histories of benevolent slavery, and we might also wonder, with white oversight, how many stories of true injustice were withheld.

But those in Africatown went on. They self-governed under and retained what African traditions they could. In her yard, Redoshi kept flowers "painted in circles surrounded by half-buried bottles in geometrical formation," a common practice among Black people in the nineteenth and early twentieth centuries, as it was thought to ward off evil spirits. They blended their languages and customs with aspects of their new home in America. *Clotilda* survivors are the only descendants of slavery in the United States who can trace their African ancestry to an exact location. And it is stories like theirs that offer the only verifiable beginning of who we are. Psychologists have identified what is called a cognitive need for closure. Or the desire for an absolute answer to a question, trying to fill that hole, that longing, for a time before—the time when we knew, without a shadow of a doubt, our exact lineage and heritage, the place from which we came.

Lost Origin

If you are Black, a descendant of the enslaved, and turn your eye to the past, you will likely never know your true origin. You might descend from the

Yoruba, Fula, Akan, Mande, Woloof, Angola, Whydah, Igbo, or any other one of three thousand ethnic groups on the continent. Not just bodies, but identities were stolen. Our ethnicities were fragmented. But out of the memory shards of a forgone motherland, a Black identity was constructed, acting as a global home for those who trace their roots to Africa.

Colonists didn't just export slavery across the globe, they exported Africa, creating a culture that lives on forever, despite the many millions who perished. In America, they remembered Africa. The tongue spoke its language. The body moved to its rhythms. The mind recounted its wisdom. The soul reanimated its religions. But the American doctrine of Anglo-conformity forced silence on all things African.

Think about the seemingly innocent task of giving someone a name. Then think of it as an act of destruction. When Ben, Homer, Venus, and Matilde were shuttled from Augusta, Georgia, to Charleston, South Carolina, in 1833, their names held little meaning. Most likely, they were picked at random from a King James Bible or a classical piece of Western literature to register on a slave manifest. "What's in a name?" Shakespeare has Juliet ask in his most enduring play. "That which we call a rose by any other name would smell as sweet" (*Romeo and Juliet*, Act II, Scene II).

But names have meaning, especially when yours is taken from you. To lose a name is to lose a form of self-expression. It is to sever ties with a social group, your peers, community, and even spirituality. So, the tragedy of re-naming enslaved people was not that they ceased to be themselves, it was that they still were. For this reason, the first generations of enslaved people clung to the complex naming traditions of their homeland. Some had the names of beloved relatives; other names bore significance in society. Some names had deep religious meaning. Others used day-names, indicating the day of the week an individual was born. For many, slave names were simply masks, put on when called by enslavers, but in private, they used their original names. They clung to meaningful identifiers rather than tags of property rights. It was also a tactic of psychological survival. We can clearly see the unraveling of identity by reading a fugitive slave ad:

$10 REWARD - Ran away on the 6th inst. the black boy JOHN or JOHN BULL, aged about 30 years, five feet four inches in height, very stout built, round face, badly marked by smallpox, and a scar produced from an attempt to cut his throat. The said boy was bought some nine months since from— Miller, and is supposed to be loitering about the Old Basin or Lake end of the Railroad. The above reward will be paid to any one who will produce him to me or lodge him in any jail so that I may get him.

A thirty-year-old man spoken of as a toddler or child. Imagine going by Quash, Cuffee, Sukey, or Mustapha to be called Boy, Girl, Uncle, Old Man, or Auntie. These names, whether said condescendingly or affectionately, re-inforced a subordinate relationship between those using names as control and those forced to answer to them. Accounts vary, but best estimates sug-gest that thousands, maybe tens of thousands of first-generation Africans in North America were Muslim, forced to renounce their Islamic faith and take on Christianity. In 1774, the name Fatimer was included on an accounting document at Mount Vernon, a person listed by George Washington as part of his tax responsibilities. Fatima, a name meaning "Shining One" in Arabic, offers possibilities of a Muslim connection. If we imagine all those who came over with birthright names imbued with human essence, we can see why they continued to use them in private, disassociating from their dehumaniz-ing English ones. Their names faded away with each passing generation.

Their ethnic backgrounds and nationalities faded, too. Over a long his-tory, and a bit of etymology acrobatics, Americans now considered Black or (b)lack depending on whom you ask, have been called simply African, slave, mulatto, quadroon, octoroon, colored, the n-word, *nigger*, negro, Afro-American, African American. Let me catch my breath . . . okay. Some of those labels were chosen and others imposed. Some imbued pride, oth-ers denigration. Once upon a time, in a world not long ago, like Europeans, Asians, Mesoamericans, or people anywhere else, African societies didn't use these racial terms to identify themselves. But that would all change.

As Europe achieved global dominance, its philosophers and scientists began categorizing humans based on geography, skin color, and cranial di-mensions. And as slavery progressed in America, Black and white skin clas-sifications quickly followed. Not so simple, though, as people mixed consensually or not, migrated forcefully or not, and America became more colored. At first, white was built on an Anglo-Saxon myth, meaning native to Britain. The national popularity of this idea is well evidenced, but it is interesting to note that the 1889 book *Anglo-Saxon Superiority* by Edmond Demolins was a cherished possession of US president Theodore Roosevelt. To maintain power in a more colorful America, the rules of whiteness changed. Formerly marginalized groups—like the Irish—who, at one point, forged class solidarity with poor Black people, abandoned their revolutionary roots and collaborated in anti-Black oppression.

In our modern era, the definition of white has shifted again on the US census to include white-identifying Hispanics. By all available evidence, the measuring stick for white becomes more inclusive when it needs to swell numbers and to maintain power. And though non-white groups were also colored and marginalized (Yellow, Red, Brown), they retained the option of anchoring their identity in their ethnicity: Filipino, Chippewa, Chinese, Puerto Rican, Hawaiian, or any other number of groups. And the enduring legacy of race and slavery is that Black is what all other colors are defined by. But it is the formerly enslaved, perhaps more than any other group in America, who will never know their origins beyond the docking of those ships full of human cargo.

Identity and Power

Orlando Patterson was correct to say that few other groups "have contributed more to the culture of the group that dominated and excluded them, than black Americans—in music, dance, theatre, literature, sports and more generally in the style and vibrancy of its dominant culture, America is indelibly blackish." Few would argue against this, but Black Americans have often found themselves exiles in their new home.

Some, like Marcus Garvey, embraced this fully. A Jamaican, Garvey's Black nationalist influence extended throughout the Caribbean, North America, and Africa. Pessimistic about US racial progress, he believed that if Black people stayed in the United States, it would lead to their demise. Speaking in the 1920s, he asserted, "Those who . . . believe that the race problem will be solved in America through higher education, they will walk between now and eternity and never see the problem solved. That day will never happen until Africa is redeemed."

A deft speaker who would walk around in a Napoleonic hat decorated with brilliant plumage, a brass-buttoned suit laced with golden braids, and a ceremonial sword, Garvey cast an imposing figure. And yet, his message was simple. Black people need to rebuild Black identity through racial pride and unity among Africa's global descendants. Perhaps Garvey's most significant message was that Black people should cast off their European overlords, board steamships bound for Africa, and rebuild in the motherland.

For those feeling alienated and pessimistic about America's commitment to racial justice, Garvey's message still resonates. Some have called for leaving altogether, and it is here we can see the interplay between identity and power.

As part of a "Back to Africa" movement in 1834, the American Colonization Society, a white-run organization seeking to purge the nation of its "unfortunate and degraded" free Black population, established a colony on the west coast of Africa called the Republic of Maryland, an independent African country that merged into what is now Liberia. By 1867, the group had resettled some thirteen thousand free and formerly enslaved Black people.

American history is full of contradictions. The United States was at once smuggling in enslaved Africans, while at the same time sending them back to Africa. So, when Black people returned to Africa they were called Americo-Liberians and the indigenous Liberians were called Congoes. As a small percentage of the population, the Americo-Liberians became an elite class and oppressed the natives. Though they did stamp out ongoing tribal slavery and bring economic stability, they denied citizenship and then voting rights to indigenous Liberians into the twentieth century, and set up a one-party oligarchic rule for 133 years. I'm certain this is not what Garvey had in mind. What does this tell us about the relationship between identity and power? In this case, a rapid thrust from powerless to powerful obliterated the notion of a collective Black identity.

I suspect that, with the corrupting nature of power, people who are subordinated often reproduce the same asymmetrical relationships they vowed to never repeat. Understandably, we pay a great deal of attention to how the politics of white power represses the Black identity. And yet, we forget how identity filters through power in other ways. Imbalances related to class (middle-/underclass Black people), color (dark/light), and countless other identifiers that cause social conflicts not only between groups but within them. Often, to distance ourselves from powerlessness, we replicate, duplicate, and mimic the same oppressive dynamics exercised against us. We have been made to believe that power can only be constructed as A over B, but power can also work as A through B. Then reciprocal as B through A. The Black colonizers might have chosen to work with the native population instead of over it. It is a painful admission, but when the history of Liberia is overlooked, we miss a valuable discussion on how easy it is to imitate and project the same abuse onto others as has been done to us.

Outlined in Black

We all choose different shores on which to anchor our identity. Many have gone back to the coasts of Africa, not on a ship, but through genealogy, to answer that existential question that comes to us all: Who am I? But genealogical research as a Black American can be painful. As you march along the bridge to the past, there is a hole known as the 1870 Brick Wall. Before that year, no surnames were recorded of African descendants. It is not impossible to find your ancestors beyond it, but you'll have to rummage through US customs records showing the ships that transported your ancestors, tax records itemizing them as property; wills showing them zigzagging between different family owners, and the bills accounting their sale; all of these things invalidating their existence as humans. All reminders that they were enslaved. Sometimes records will show you where they were sold. So, your search might pulsate with pain as you follow their paths.

Genetic testing has provided new bridges to the past, across which millions of people are walking, hoping to find their African homelands. In her 2016 book, *The Social Life of DNA: Race, Reparations, and Reconciliation After the Genome*, Professor Alondra Nelson talks about the overwhelming power of tracing our roots. One group who found out their ancestors were from Sierra Leone met for a ceremony of remembrance at a ferry landing known for slave auctions. According to Nelson, it's "not just about identity in a narcissistic way, but about people trying to reconcile the history of slavery, and scaling up from their ancestry test to what it means for the history of the US." Yet others see things differently, choosing not to find their identity in

DNA. Suspicious of labs that send vials for you to package your genetic makeup, likely to sell it into a study or database. Even more, there are those who don't associate their identity with Africa at all, giving up on the kente cloth ideas, and dashiki dreams. Instead finding personhood in what we have built here. Perhaps they are skeptical of a monolithic vision of Africa's past. One that loses the infinite nuances of the earth's second largest continent.

As people navigated a new culture, the Black identity has not easily blended with an American one. Not for lack of effort. The soul of Black people is tied up in America, though the nation has been slow to recognize it. Black people have been removed from the country, segregated into ghettos, discriminated out of suburbs, thrust into impoverished enclaves, and segmented into housing projects. All leaving us to wonder, can Black people ever transcend race in America? In 1869, while advocating the unpopular position of accepting Chinese immigration, Frederick Douglass said, "We are a country of all extremes—, ends and opposites; the most conspicuous example of composite nationality in the world."

But courts thought otherwise, forwarding the idea that non-white people could never be integrated into American society. In the 1854 case *People v. Hall*, the California Supreme Court ruled that Black, mulatto, Chinese, and Native American people were not white, and therefore could not testify against a white man in court. Calling back to this history, Toni Morrison wrote, "American means white, and Africanist people struggle to make the term applicable to themselves with ethnicity and hyphen after hyphen after hyphen." So, if American means white, and identity is, at least in part, socially negotiated, non-white people are left with few bargaining chips. The one-drop rule, which applies to no other group, effectively bars anyone with a microscopic trace of African ancestry from identifying as white. Dark skin, thick lips, tight curls, and a broad nose have been the identification cards of Blackness. One drop of Blackness has been seen as an indelible stain of inferiority. In a history where sex and race collide, this was enforced to ensure white purity. But genetics continue to prove that most of us are racially ambiguous. We might wonder how many white people have hidden their Black identities in secrecy and shame. We are left to wonder how many fathers abandoned their sons, or how many mothers aborted their daughters, all to uphold the construct of a pure race. It is all absurd, but the idea of racial purity is built on centuries of lies. When the one-drop rule was proposed to become law in 1895, South Carolina politician George D. Tillman railed against it. A reporter from the *News and Courier* captured his words this way:

> It is a scientific fact that there is not one full-blooded Caucasian on the floor of this convention. Every member has in him a certain mixture of . . . colored blood. . . . It would be a cruel injustice and the source of endless litigation, of scandal, horror, feud, and bloodshed to undertake to annul or forbid marriage for a remote, perhaps obsolete trace of Negro blood. The doors would be open to scandal, malice, and greed.

But in Virginia, it was made law, passed as the Racial Integrity Act of 1924. White people defined race in America. And they did so to their own whim. For instance, when elite Virginians who claimed descent from Pocahontas and John Rolfe demanded an exception to the law to keep their categorization as white, a Pocahontas exemption was added. They could maintain their white status in the racial order despite their non-white ancestry. But the Black identity adapted, accommodating all phenotypes, just like the continent of Africa itself. From light-skinned people with aquiline noses, to dark people with kinky hair, ever expanding to represent a mosaic of colors. But the effects of racism took a toll on Black personhood. Colorism and "shadeism" share similarly hideous features as racism when we assign value and intelligence to people based on the relative lightness or darkness of their Blackness. One story that has long circulated in the Black community is that, through the twentieth century, dark-skinned people were excluded from churches, sororities, fraternities, and social clubs if they could not pass the infamous "brown paper bag test." If you were darker than the bag, you were out. Biracial people, light enough, also "passed" as white. Exploiting the loophole and staking a claim in the land of white identity, they attempted to reap the privilege, social, and economic benefits denied darker hues of Black Americans.

But everyone dealt with their identity differently. Actress Fredericka "Fredi" Washington, a fair-skinned, green-eyed Black woman with a smoldering screen presence, was pale enough to "pass," but refused. Obsessed more with her race than talent, no one could believe her choice: "I can't for the life of me, find any valid reason why anyone should lie about their origin or anything else for that matter. Frankly, I do not ascribe to the stupid theory of white supremacy and to try to hide the fact that I am a Negro for economic or any other reasons . . . people can't believe that I'm proud to be a Negro and not white. To prove I don't buy white superiority I chose to be a Negro."

But according to a friend she did pass for white, "when she was traveling in the South with Duke Ellington and his band." They could not go into ice-cream parlors, he said, so she would go in and buy the ice cream, then go outside and give it to Ellington and the band. Whites screamed at her, "Nigger lover!" Washington was able to live on her own terms, evoking her identity with integrity, acting out her agency through her own self-conception.

Self or Socially Constructed

There is great power in defining yourself. But as social animals, our culture has a profound influence on who we are. How the world perceives us directly influences how we see ourselves and how our brains develop. It impacts how we negotiate and understand our relationships. And when it comes to race, America has fed Black people a diet of lies about their identity. Lie long enough and the lie can become indistinguishable from truth. Black people have been sambo, Aunt Jemima, brutish, lazy, lawn jockey, niggerized, exotic, hackneyed, clichéd, and stereotyped. In 1976, Ronald Reagan mainstreamed the idea of a "welfare queen," by accusing single Black mothers like Linda Taylor of living large on taxpayers' hard-earned dollars, collecting government checks while covered in jewels. So, too, did descriptions of welfare recipients using food stamps to buy T-bone steaks, living in New York housing projects with eleven-foot ceilings and swimming pools feature in his rhetoric.

In the 1940s, a husband and wife team of psychologists named Dr. Kenneth and Dr. Mamie Clark designed "doll tests" to gauge the effects of racial segregation on children. They asked Black children their preferences for Black or white dolls. Mostly, they chose white dolls. What could account for this at such a young age? Here you had children as young as three and four years old, who not only recognized racial differences, but who ascribed less value to darker skin. Unwittingly, the children must have thought they were making a simple choice. But underneath, there was a pained reality about internalized inferiority. Black children valued themselves less than whites.

People are not immune to negative messages about their group. From a young age, Black children see the pervasive discrimination of others who look like them. These negative perceptions of Black people—in books, on screens, and from speakers—then shape how they see themselves. Psychologically, how many white dolls have been chosen before and how many have been chosen since?

One of the earliest Black psychoanalysts to explore race and identity was Afro-Caribbean psychiatrist Frantz Fanon, who, while completing his residency in France in 1952, wrote and published his first book, *Black Skin, White Masks*. At only twenty-seven years old, he was heavily influenced by the brutal colonization of Africa and carried those melancholic visions of terror and violence into his book. He explores the violence of colonization inflicted on the Black body and the endless depths of agony in the sea of the subconscious mind. Fanon then switches perspective to the reciprocal violence of the colonized trying to recover their history, dignity, and sense of self. The book is fascinating for its insights into the psychic hurt that comes along with the social penalties of Black skin. One of my biggest takeaways was how oppression results in a sort of mutually assured spiritual destruction between one who is dominating and the other who is dominated. He warned against the false self-image Black people have adopted from whites. He encouraged Black people to retain a Black identity because, so long as they tried to be a carbon copy of white, they would sink into the quicksand of despair. But he ended his book to the tune of a common humanity saying, "The Negro is not. Any more than the white man. Both must turn their backs on the inhuman voices which were those of their respective ancestors in order that authentic communication be possible. Before it can adopt a positive voice, freedom requires an effort at disalienation."

For those of us who have struggled to figure out who we are, psychology provides four helpful concepts when thinking about identity: realignment, reflection, retreat, and reconciliation. Realignment is where one identity is chosen over another. This might mean to embrace a Black nationalistic identity in the spirit of Martin Delany, abolitionist, writer, editor, and doctor. He fought his whole life for Black freedom and civil rights, and was a contemporary of and cofounder of *The North Star* with Frederick Douglass, though he is much less known. Douglass was an assimilationist, a point with which Delany came to disagree as he would become known as the "Father of Black American Nationalism." Delany fundamentally rejected America as it is. He made two trips to Africa and traveled along the Niger River looking for land to settle, "We are a nation within a nation, we must go from our oppressors," he once said. He was antagonistic toward a country that so often scoffed at Blackness, relegating it to the status of inferior, excluding it from its schools, rejecting it from its social circles, denying it from its neighborhoods, enslaving it, lynching it, telling it to straighten its hair and disproportionately locking it up in its prisons. In 1857 in the seminal *Dred Scott v. Sandford* decision, Chief Justice Roger Taney said Blacks were not "acknowledged as part of the people" who had declared independence from Britain and ratified the Constitution, and as such were ineligible citizens of the United States. In the twenty-first century, when Black people have been in America almost five hundred years, people still say, go back to Africa. Yes, this has driven so many into realignment. Unconvinced, and sometimes unwilling, to act toward social integration.

But what of those who chose reflection, which is to "fit" or assimilate in America? In a fit of World War I xenophobia, Theodore Roosevelt said when speaking on immigration in 1907: "It is an outrage to discriminate against any such man because of creed, or birthplace, or origin. But this is predicated upon the person's becoming in every facet an American, and nothing but an American. . . . There can be no divided allegiance here. Any man who says he is an American, but something else also, isn't an American at all." Black people have tried this. Leaning into the refrain, *God, Family, Country*. Subordinating their ethnicity and their Blackness. They watched as white immigrants like the Irish, Italians, and Jews were, minus some enduring stereotypes, tepidly accepted into American society. Black people have been the most Christian, most patriotic, most hardworking, and most embracing of America. And still rejected. But assimilation comes at a cost: the acceptance of a dominant group, who also control the criteria. Anyone who doesn't assimilate is seen as a failure in not doing so. They are socially distanced. We are not wrong to wonder why assimilation has been seen as the only path to ethnic and racial harmony. Is it the best option, or for the most excluded? Is it really an option at all? Some have retreated, what psychologists define as rejecting both identities. Born of a Black American mother and white British father, Guns N' Roses guitarist Slash had this to say when questioned on race: "When I started doing my own thing, especially playing guitar, it wasn't so much of a thing. I never really cared to have to identify one way or another." I can't speak much to Slash's motives for erasing his Black identity, but let's follow him down that path.

The orthodox, scientific opinion has moved beyond *The Bell Curve: Intelligence and Class Structure in American Life,* a 1994 book staking out claims about the biological roots of racial IQ gaps, only to be pushed aside by more current evidence that suggests more genetic variations within groups than outside of them. Several plausible scientific theories explain the variations in human skin tone, one being that melanin developed as a protective adaptation to higher UV radiation in certain geographies. The point is, no modernly respected theory of racial difference is based in Black inferiority. So, why should we craft our identity from a cancerous concept that metastasized in sixteenth-century Europe? Race was born from the worst of philosophy, pseudoscience, and religion. It is a social construct.

Not even science, however, which confirmed that any two human beings are 99.9 percent identical, has been enough to tear down these racial structures that seem indestructible. But it may be possible to deconstruct it if we find out why it was created in the first place.

Last in the psychological toolkit is reconciliation, where we integrate our identities. This seems to be the most promising. The more we reconcile, the more whole we can be. Every day we reconcile the different parts of ourselves. But when you must parse out parts of yourself, it is exhausting. Negotiating and renegotiating who you are in varying social situations. A woman around men. An atheist around Christians. A youth around elders. Reconciliation is much easier person to person. Much harder for a whole society. This is especially true for Black people. No matter how hard they try to reconcile their Blackness to America, there is an awareness of difference, often reinforced by social cues. A never-ending balancing act, of staying true to a cultural identity while trying to synchronize with the dominant one, negotiating the difference between who you are and who you are perceived to be.

To Be Human

The Autobiography of Malcom X (1965) had a deep and personal impact on me. The public image of the man once known as "Detroit Red" is usually that of a militant Black extremist who eviscerated "white devils" with acidic eloquence. But in his brief life Malcolm underwent stunning transformations. Malcolm had the courage to speak the truth of his conviction, then, considering new evidence, use that same courage to admit that the conviction he once held as true was false. In this way he began as a ruthlessly opportunistic drug-dealing pimp surviving the harshness of the inner city. Then, during a stint in prison, he became a devout Muslim, rising through the ranks to become the national spokesperson for the Nation of Islam. That's the short version. *The Autobiography of Malcolm X* (1965) and *The Dead Are Arising: The Life of Malcolm X* (2020) by Les and Tamara Payne move beyond the legend to capture his flawed, internal struggles. People take from his philosophy what they wish, but what moves me most was his transition from a claustrophobic nationalism into a radical humanism.

Like a snake shedding its skin, after a life-changing trip to Mecca, where he saw all races coming together in the name of God, he abandoned his anti-white rhetoric. He laid a new foundation on the idea of the oneness of humanity: "I'm for truth, no matter who tells it . . . I'm a human being, first and foremost, and as such I'm for whoever and whatever benefits humanity as a whole." Malcolm X did not abandon his struggle for racial justice, Black solidarity, or global liberation for the darker race, but he found a unifying principle in humanity. This I learned from him and the danger of "*isms*." Whether it's liberalism, Nazism, capitalism, conservatism, communism, or nationalism—and even skepticism about all these can become its own dogma. In their demands of ideological purity, all chart their own descent into rigidity. Inflexible ideologies demand loyalty to strict principles but the world requires flexibility, and more of it. So, while they can provide important frameworks for thinking and being in the world, they should not compose our sole worldview. No one holds a monopoly on truth. Knowing this is the first step toward freedom. For once you have made that realization, you are forever free of the ideological prison in which so many spend their lives.

It is here that I think I resolved my own inner crisis of the Black intellectual. Able to, as the astute scholar Harold Cruse said, "deal intimately with the white power structure and cultural apparatus, and the inner realities of the black world at one and the same time," I fell in love with, developed a passion for, and found truth in the human experience. I put my ear to the ground and, in the sands of history, I heard ancestral voices on all seven continents and the islands. I flashed back to the library as the meeting place of all citizens in search of knowledge. I saw myself, not only in Africa, but in Asia, Europe, Australia, and in South America, all while staying rooted in the uniqueness of my own experience as a Black man in America.

What, then, is the solution? Perhaps we need a fifth psychological mechanism: revolutionary acceptance. An embrace of our infinitely changeable identities. Yes, we must understand that our identities rest on pudding. They are malleable, changeable, fluid—like water changing its form in different contexts. No matter how much you embrace or reject any part of yourself is up to you; it is wholly personal. You will be rejected by some, but who is fully embraced? You will be hated by others, but who is universally loved? This is where freedom lies.

As I rested my worldview on a stable affection, commitment, and understanding of people, I saw with new eyes. Like a doctor I could examine the disease, decay, and sickness of humans in history while seeing their endless possibilities for health and life. So, I continued in that library. Plato taught me about the republic, and Alexis de Tocqueville introduced me to democracy. The Egyptians and Aztecs showed me their innovative civilizations.

Then, I sat at the feet of Confucius, Kierkegaard, Aquinas, and Heidegger to learn philosophy. I solved mysteries with Sherlock Holmes, ran through Middle-earth with Hobbits, and looked into the bluest eye with Toni Morrison. I studied Buddhism, flipped the pages of the Koran, and had a Bible so thick it could double as a doorstop. I learned about Cleopatra VII Philopator of Egypt, Elizabeth I of England and Ireland, and Amanikasheto of Kush. I borrowed books in political science, economics, anthropology, archaeology, and geography. If it was a subject, I studied it. I found humanity in the free public library, the most democratic institution in the world.

One thing is clear: We have the tendency to stick with one sole identity at the betrayal of all others. But we are Black, men, women, American, young, elderly, middle age, Christian, Buddhist, Muslim—we have one body that carries multitudes. So, how might we come together with such varying identities? Some say that in the human race, everyone loses. But I think the principle of humanity is our best chance of winning. If the goal is democracy, to be ourselves together, we need to connect not around identity, which in the end is too fickle, but our underlying values and shared interests. In this way, we avoid the homogenization of diverse cultures while also achieving a sense of solidarity. The strongest people have principles, and the strongest nations remember they are indivisible. Some gulfs are unbridgeable but, divisions aside, I see a shared humanity as the moral rallying point for those of us trying to hold it all together. Principled humanity unifies against anti-Black oppression and not only Blackness. Life, liberty, and the pursuit of happiness and not blind patriotism. It forms groups around antipoverty rather than a class war. Not to monopolize power but ensure it stays with the people. One way is exclusive, the other inclusive. Collective American identity will come when we redefine American values, with its foundation resting on the firm bedrock of humanity, recognition, and dignity. Only time might tell if this is practical. But in a nation with such extreme differences in identity, the bedrock of principle is the only way to negotiate inclusion and belonging. To be human first, for the benefit of all humanity.

3

Miseducated

Education is the most powerful weapon
which you can use to change the world.
—**Nelson Mandela**

May those whose holy task it is,
To guide impulsive youth,
Fail not to cherish in their souls
A reverence for truth
—**Charlotte Forten Grimké**

Before cofounding the Mississippi Freedom Democratic Party with Ella Baker and Fannie Lou Hamer, which forced the integration of the mainstream Democratic Party, before being beaten relentlessly by police after paying a ticket, before organizing registration drives for poor, illiterate voters, before his military service, before being shot at, before being awarded a MacArthur Genius Grant (formally, the MacArthur Fellows Program), Bob Moses began his career teaching quadratic equations at a private school in the Bronx. In 1960, he left it all to join the sit-in movement. But as the Civil Rights Movement receded like seawater after a storm, leaders' wives became widows, activists became politicians, organizers became professors, and young clench-fisted Black Panthers retired into civilian life, only stepping out for an occasional interview. Few, if any, I'd venture to say, shifted into teaching algebra as a new outlet for their activism.

The quiet leadership style of Bob Moses hasn't landed him on many bookshelves despite his outsized role in the Civil Rights Movement. But his work after the movement is just as inspiring. Moses saw the financial shambles of poor communities of color and determined the new fight for Black people was economic access. And he had the foresight to see that this would be directly tied to literacy in math and science, an area for which Black people were woefully behind. In his book *Radical Equations: Civil Rights from Mississippi to the Algebra Project*, he made a radical statement: We should educate kids to change the world.

> In the sixties everyone said sharecroppers were apathetic until we got them demanding to vote. That finally got attention. Here, where kids are falling wholesale through the cracks—or chasms—dropping out of sight, becoming fodder for jails, people say they do not want to learn. The only ones who can dispel that notion are the kids themselves.

I had a lot of joys when I was a kid, but math wasn't one of them. Teaching is no easy business, so imagine the virtue required to dedicate your life to solving one of the Black community's most overlooked issues—math proficiency. Working through his nonprofit, the Algebra Project, Moses taught thousands of underserved children, never giving up on them. His teaching methods were transformative. With calm confidence, he connected algebra to real-world problems, teaching ratios with African drumming and the number line through field trips.

The stories of those like Moses are often told as polemical tales of civil rights heroes drummed up for political purpose, but at the root was an extraordinary individual whose real work was in the day-in, day-out task of making breakthroughs with frustrated groups of sharecroppers and bored students. Moses used his grassroots organizing ability to unite students, teachers, and parents to build a culture of success through child-centered education. Learning calculus alone won't solve inequality, but it's the Moses philosophy that stuck with me. He understood that we have been miseducated, and he knew that education needed to address the main concern our kids will face as they emerge from high school—how to survive and thrive in the world.

I had a teacher or two like Bob Moses, but they were exceptions. My only Black teacher in K–12 public school was Mr. Brown. I remember on the first day of class we had to sign our names on an attendance sheet for a morning roll call. The resident jokester wrote "Seymour Butts," and Mr. Brown read it aloud, thinking it was a student's name. The class burst into juvenile laughter. Mr. Brown cut through it like a katana, leaving only a shredded silence. "If anyone disrupts my classroom again, we're gonna see more butts seated in detention."

Statistics have long shown that having teachers of color is beneficial to all students, including the 2017 study by the Institute of Labor Economics, which found that low-income, Black, male, elementary school students taught by a Black teacher in the third, fourth, or fifth grade were 39 percent less likely to drop out of high school. I didn't drop out, but many I know did. And I wonder what an impact a couple of Mr. or Ms. Browns might have made. I had my parents guiding me, but having a Black educator to connect with for the first time made a tremendous impact.

I am not a teacher, so I cannot speak much on pedagogy or how to solve the many issues teachers and students face, but I am an observer of past and present. I imagine most teachers get chewed up and spit out not long after they go into the field. I know how it is to go into an institution and think you alone can change the system, only to leave with gray hair and defeat. I did a speaking event at a middle school as I was writing this book where the teachers looked as young as the students. Maybe I'm just getting old, but judging by the fresh-out-of-college faces, there weren't very many even close to retirement age. Then I put myself in the shoes of a modern student, and it is easy to see how the education system miseducates them. Kids in class today, faces aglow from the light of computer screens, probably feel given up on. They are the subject of centuries-old national hostilities waged as a forever war over what and how they will be taught, or even who will teach them as educators disappear from the field. Who knows? In the future, algorithms and automated learning may fill in teacher shortage gaps, while school lunches are seamlessly delivered by drone.

Whatever our future looks like, we were all kids once and grew up to become more bitter and less tolerant. Education reforms are touted year in and out while our kids are stressed out and depressed, staring into wars, extreme inequality, and a rapidly warming planet. Parents fear that school won't prepare their children for the real world, but they are already living in it. If they see the glass as half empty, I wouldn't blame them. If they see the glass as half full, I wouldn't blame them either. But I think it's helpful to see it both ways.

In this chapter, I want to do just that—I want to explore the difference between miseducation and education, showing how, instead of sparking a desire for self-learning and an ability to understand, think, and question, public education has been used as a tool of indoctrination. Teaching us to memorize. Cramming all manner of intelligence into a Stanford-Binet test. Then showing us how to swallow, then regurgitate, a prescribed diet of conformity. And this doctrine of compliance with what the world is, instead of what it could be, has been unequally applied to the darker races of America. To be educated is to be inspired. To question. To think. To doubt. To understand. Education gives us the freedom to make mistakes and learn from them. A democratic education would teach us to move beyond the skin to understand why others believe the way they believe. And to hope that, as our youth grow up, they can refill the glass.

Education or Indoctrination

Everything has its origins, and in 1647, the Puritans of Massachusetts passed the first colonial mandate requiring community schooling. Rather than focus on free thought, the laws were passed so that children would be literate enough to read and obey the laws of God and man. In years to come, education became a public responsibility. Colonial funds were allocated to hire headmasters, one-room schools were constructed, and children shuffled along to learn in them. Finding themselves either conditionally free, enslaved, or in servitude, this educational expansion was not welcoming of many Black children. But there is a story of one who was able to learn.

Born in Baltimore County, Maryland, in 1731, Benjamin Banneker grew up among slavery but free, conditionally. The Black codes, with restrictive curfews and travel permits, arbitrary taxes to ensure "good behavior," the ban on gun or dog ownership, the silencing of testimony against a white person in court, and regulation of large gatherings, governing Black existence were far from freedom. The thing about the Black codes was that nowhere in America could a Black person participate equally in society with a white one. Racism and restrictions aside, Banneker did have some privilege. Most Black people were trapped in an infinite loop of endless labor, busy harvesting tobacco, so important to the colonies that it was used as currency. They caulked the hulls of ships with cotton soaked in pine tar to make them watertight. With curved, bladed sickles, they reaped harvests of wheat, which were bundled and transported to Europe on those same boats. In 1979, skeletons were found scattered around the site of the Catoctin Furnace, an iron forge in Frederick County, Maryland. Little is told of the enslaved labor on the iron plantations central to colonial economic development, smelting, smithing, and mining ore. Unfree and semi-free labor built America. So, with their sole existence directed toward processing natural resources, most received no education, aside from what helped them perform their daily drudgery. When there isn't much to do but work, the light of humanity becomes a flicker. Alienated from the wisdom of Africa and the West, the vast majority of Black people learned from experience. They shared theories among themselves, observed life, and reflected.

But Banneker was an exception. The woman believed to be his maternal grandmother, Molly Welsh, is thought to be one of the indentured servants who made up almost half of English migrants before 1775, and his grandfather was said to be a progeny of West African royalty. In the colonies, most poor children began their education in the home, but as grammar and secondary schools grew, Maryland counties were not required to provide public schools for Black students until 1872. It was through his proximity to his white grandmother, who taught him how to read the Bible, and the Quakers, one of the earliest groups to pivot from slave owners to abolitionists, that Banneker beat the odds favoring his illiteracy. A family friend, Andrew Ellicott, taught him astronomy and arithmetic. This may be more myth than fact, but one historian theorized that Banneker was also the recipient of knowledge from his father, a member of the Dogon tribe of West Africa, a people thought to have advanced knowledge of grand cosmic events. Free to learn, young Banneker befriended the stars. He devised astronomical calculations. He thought about the infinite dimensions of the universe. He predicted lunar and solar eclipses with exacting accuracy. He observed the positions of celestial bodies. And then published his findings in a widely circulating almanac.

In his lonely diversions, he loved to tinker. Once, he reverse-engineered a pocket watch, uncovering the mysteries of the time-telling machine with its chronometer and balance spring regulating the progress of the hands. A naturalist, he even documented cicada swarms. And later, he worked as an assistant surveyor, helping plot the federal district and location of the capital of the United States. It is difficult to imagine him doing any of this without openness and curiosity. It is something that Banneker faced the extreme challenge of learning as a free Black man in America with little opportunity, but he was also one of the first in a long tradition to use his education to help the miseducated. At fifty-nine years old, from his farm in Oella, Baltimore County, at the edge of its streams and woodlands, he sent a pressing letter to then secretary of state Thomas Jefferson along with one of his almanacs:

> Sir how pitiable is it to reflect, that although you were so fully convinced of the benevolence of the father of mankind, and of his equal and impartial distribution of those rights and privileges which he had conferred upon them, that you should at the same time counteract his mercies, in detaining by fraud and violence so numerous a part of my brethren under groaning captivity and cruel oppression, that you should at the same time be found guilty of that most criminal act, which you professedly detested in others, with respect to yourselves.

Banneker stood on the doorstep of humanity and was refused entry. As a vain consolation, Jefferson responded, saying that he wished nothing more than for Black chattel to prove their intelligence, but until a system is devised to raise the condition of Black people to what it "ought to be," chattel slavery would remain. And thus, Jefferson set the terms. Knowledge was and is the only way to be truly free in America. The story of Banneker reminds me that a miseducation is an incomplete one. Here was someone brimming with talent, who crafted genius from educational scraps, but lived in a nation where he would never reach his full potential, because the opportunity would always be denied.

A second early example of Black education comes through the life of Phillis Wheatley Peters, who was forcibly kidnapped from Senegambia at no more than seven years old. After surviving the Middle Passage, she was sold to John and Susanna Wheatley, a wealthy and well-connected Boston family, "for a trifle," because she was so frail the ship's captain thought she would soon die. Living in the Wheatley household as a servant, she would've seen the comings and goings of the vastly powerful. Prominent philanthropists, Presbyterian, Anglican, and Methodist ministers dined in their home; a tailor, John Wheatley had clientele including the likes of John Hancock.

One day, Phillis was found writing on the wall with chalk. Instead of punishment, she was taught to read and write by the children of her enslavers. She learned Greek and Latin. She read Ovid, Terence, and Homer. She was baptized as a devout Protestant Congregationalist. The silences in her story scream. Where exactly was her homeland? What was her original name? What are the details of her experience on the Middle Passage? After finding a publisher while on a trip in London, the young prodigy released the first book of classical poetry ever created by a Black person in the United States, *Poems on Various Subjects, Religious and Moral*. History has given way to show us her poetic rhyme, logic, allusion, and Christian ideals.

So strong was the racist belief in Black inferiority that, in 1772, Phillis found herself in the thick of the scrutiny by an elite circle. Eighteen Massachusetts men, including the colony governors, lawyers, and clergymen, most Harvard graduates, wanted to know if she really could master the written word. The teenager was on trial, not for theft, assault, or any other offense— rather, it was for displaying her intelligence. There are still people who downplay their brightness for fear of being outcast. After proving the poems were indeed hers, Phillis was paraded into the soirées and evening parties of privileged white women like a rarified exception to the rule of Black stupidity. With Phillis objectified as an ornament, her mistress, Susanna Wheatley, made her recite her poems for the colonial aristocracy at tea parties. In the shadow of whites, and not permitted to associate with the other enslaved people, Phillis Wheatley Peters was trapped in a palace of power. She had to fight for survival in a world that only valued her if she remained a submissive, docile, and ardently Christian, Black girl.

After the publication of her book, Phillis was freed. Much of her life after is obscure, but we know she married John Peters, a shopkeeper who earned quite a reputation. He shows up in the record earlier as a peculiarity because he was a Black in an unofficial business partnership with a white man named Josias Byles, trading sugar, tea, and nails in front of bars and inns.

People wondered what they were doing together and at one point ordered John detained and searched for papers. He went to jail for debt in 1784, and despite Phillis's status as a prodigy and minor celebrity, she was relegated to the job of scullery maid at a boardinghouse. She died in obscurity, her body laid to rest in an unmarked grave.

TRACING THE LATIN ROOTS of the word *education*, we come away with two meanings. *Educare* means "to mold." In this view a student is like a vessel into which you pour information. *Educere* means "to lead out." Think of this like throwing a student a long and loose string. The student is guided along the way, but can still explore his or her own directions. It has been common, I think, that our most important civic institution, the public school, has been much better at the latter than the former. Schools have come a long way, educational attainment is higher than ever before, but kids are molded and taught what to think, not how to think. For most parents, no amount of scrimping and saving will be enough to get their kids into the highest quality schools that not only double as prep for the best universities, but also instill intangible skills like intrinsic motivation. Education is lost to standardized testing, teachers made invisible by exam scores and an over-emphasis on memorization.

Somehow, we've failed to infuse public schools with a democratic humanity, which only comes from empathy, debate, consideration, reading, persuading, and searching for solutions together, no matter our differences. It requires the virtue of humility. The ability to face one of life's greatest challenges, which is, and I truly believe this, to have the courage to speak the truth of your convictions, then, considering valid new evidence, turn around and admit the conviction you once held true was false. We are taught within the same prejudices of our predecessors, and then when we grow old enough, we replicate the cycle. This type of education is not about change. You are taught to fit the needs of your society. The authoritarian culture of our schools does not teach children to live in a democracy, instead institutionalizing them in thought and action, reinforcing the school-to-prison pipeline for those without the resources to find a higher path.

And as with Banneker's life, that path is usually self-taught. Most history makers are the ones who challenged the system. Those who not only discovered their talents, but used them to effect change in the world. True freedom in education comes when you not only make your way in society as it is, but when you can change it.

The restrictions on Black education continued. Prior to the 1830s, restrictions on Black literacy were harsh but not universally enforced. But this was before the revolt of Nat Turner. On August 21, 1831, Turner led around seventy enslaved and free Black people into the valley and shadow of death. Turner was a stout thirty-one-year-old with a scar on his temple from a mule kick, believed to have given him sublime visions. Not of the concussive but the prophetic type. The voice of God spoke to him, so he said. He had visions of Black and white spirits mingling in blood. He harbored the vengeance of Isaiah, whom the Bible quotes: "Ah! I will vent my wrath on my foes and avenge myself on my enemies."

Turner was a nightmare turned real for slave owners. In Southampton County, Virginia, Turner and the revolters went house to house freeing enslaved people. They murdered indiscriminately—men, women, children. The end goal was liberation. State militia and armed civilians crushed the rebellion in less than a day. Vigilantes killed some two hundred Black people, most of whom had nothing to do with the rebellion. Turner hid in the depths of the woods for months, but was captured, hanged, and skinned. Some say he was turned into a lampshade. But the retribution was not only physical; restrictions on Black education would also be more crushingly enforced. The man who documented his confession said that Turner's "natural intelligence and quickness of apprehension is surpassed by few men I have ever seen."

Education was seen as a threat—if you can read and write, you can read and write about your liberation. The response was clear as evidenced by a write-up in the *Richmond Inquirer*: "No black man ought to be permitted to turn a preacher in the country. The law must be enforced or the tragedy of Southampton appeals to us in vain." The mood was dark.

"The brightest and best men were killed in Nat's time. Such ones are always suspected. Black people were afraid to pray out loud at the time of the old prophet Nat," said Charity Bowery, an enslaved woman likely in her fifties at the time. "Whites threatened to punish 'em dreadfully."

After Turner's revolt, the literary oppression of the era became so severe, it prompted *Harper's Weekly* to declare that "the alphabet is an abolitionist. If you would keep a people enslaved refuse to teach them to read."

Of the 3,428 responses collected from formerly enslaved people interviewed for the Federal Writers Project—the ambitious New Deal program gathering oral history from thousands of Americans—a little more than 5 percent learned to read and write during slavery. Within the tens of thousands of pages compiled for what is the largest archive of its kind are some horrifying experiences of indoctrination. Those who were enslaved as children in Mississippi, Texas, Georgia, and South Carolina recounted the same threat—learn to read and be grievously injured. "The first time you was taught trying to read or write, you was whipped with a cow-hide, the next time with a cat-o-nine-tails, and the next time they cut first jint offen your forefinger," said Doc Daniel Dowdy, an ex-enslaved man in Madison County, Georgia. Most of us could scarcely imagine the punishing fear of having fingers torn off for using them to turn the pages of a book. They had little choice but to conform to the dictates of an oppressive slavocracy.

Another ex-slave from Georgia, recollecting the terror, said: "If they caught you trying to write they would cut your finger off, and if they caught you again they would cut your head off." Georgia Baker, who grew up on a Georgia plantation before the Civil War, said that Black people were more afraid of newspapers than they were of snakes. None of the ex-slaves interviewed had experienced these punishments themselves but claimed personal knowledge that it happened.

Regardless, the psychological terror, coupled with an intense paranoia, surely acted as a reading repellent for most. But the enslaved moved to the rhythm of resilience and, even in places with brutally enforced rules, they found a way. In the depth of the woods, they dug pits, covering them with branches and sticks to hide Bibles and scraps of discarded paper. Then they snuck back to their secret schools under the blanket of nighttime to decipher written language under the glimmer of the moon. They "borrowed" spelling books from their enslavers, appealed to sympathetic whites, used storytelling, and learned to write using sticks in the sand. They hid books under their beds and exchanged fleeting periods of leisure for fleeting periods of learning. In turn they taught others. In the 1830s, Washington lawyer Elias B. Caldwell expressed a common sentiment of the era:

> The more you improve the condition of these people [Blacks], the more you cultivate their minds, the more miserable you make them, in their present state. You give them a higher relish for those privileges which they can never attain and turn what we intend for a blessing into a curse. No, if they must remain in their present situation, keep them in the lowest state of degradation and ignorance. The nearer you bring them to the condition of brutes, the better chance do you give them of possessing their apathy.

This sentiment extended not only to the enslaved, but the conditionally free. Black intelligence was imprisoned to control Black people. The South is often pointed to as the seedbed of inequality, but the first literacy tests for voters were introduced in Connecticut in the mid-1800s. In fact, Jim Crow was born in Boston. In 1848, five-year-old Sarah Roberts was enrolled in an all-Black public elementary school in Massachusetts. Her parents, one of whom was Benjamin Roberts, one of the nation's first Black printers, had practical reasons to challenge the decision. The segregated school was too far from their home, and they passed five white schools before reaching one for Black children. Robert Morris, one of the first Black lawyers in the United States, mounted a spirited legal response on behalf of the family, and his work influenced waves of legal challenges to segregation. He argued that under Commonwealth statutes, "[a]ny child unlawfully excluded from public school instruction, in this Commonwealth, shall recover damages against the city or town by which such public school instruction is supported." It is telling that one of the first Black people to practice law used his powers in service to equity in public education.

But in 1850, Chief Justice Memuel Shaw held that racial segregation was legal under the Massachusetts constitution, a decision that would be felt across the nation for the next hundred years. During the trial, Morris's co-counsel, Charles Sumner, argued, "[Education] in . . . two schools may be precisely the same, but a school devoted to one class must differ essentially in spirit and character from [one] where all classes meet together in equality. . . . Prejudice is the child of ignorance . . . sure to prevail where people do not know each other." But the schools were not precisely the same—far less support and funding went into Black schools compared to white ones. With every denial of education, Black Americans were denied the heritage of the nation. The founding ideal that the survival of a republic depends on a broad electorate of educated voters. The founders knew that ignorant populations were more susceptible to the domination of tyrants and monarchs. Black Americans knew that with no education they could never enjoy the promise of democracy.

Radical Self-Reliance

Only months after the Civil War, in the fall of 1865, Northern missionaries went to the war-torn South expecting to find dehumanized Black victims needing refinement in the ways of civilized society after the brutality of slavery. When they arrived, they were shocked. In a significant number of towns, the formerly enslaved had established educational collectives, staffed schools with Black teachers, and were preparing their children for the world they'd inherit. They were reluctant to give up control of their own education to white Northerners. General Superintendent of Education for the Bureau of Refugees, Freedmen, and Abandoned Lands (Freedmen's Bureau) John W. Alvord was compelled to understand the complexities of Black education and traveled through nearly all the former Confederate states to document it. By January 1866, he'd written his first report. In no uncertain terms, he said: "Throughout the entire south an effort is being made by the colored people to educate themselves." Alvord estimated that by 1866, there were some five hundred community-built Black schools. In Goldsboro, North Carolina, he found: "Two colored young men, who but a little time before commenced to learn themselves, had gathered, 150 pupils, all quite orderly and hard at study." They found schools like the one in Savannah, Georgia, that had been opened years earlier by Catherine Deveaux and her daughter Jane, when teaching the enslaved was punishable by a $500 fine and up to thirty-two lashes in the public square. Careful to avoid detection and finding ingenious ways to dodge the surveillance of the slave state, the children lingered around the playground, then one by one walked off to a predetermined location. Appearing to be on an errand, they carried buckets, wrapped their books in newspaper, and picked up wood chips as if collecting them for fires.

The chasm between what Blacks were doing for their own education and the perception of them was a wide one. The sheer amount of self-determination necessary after generations of enslavement is evidence that education was not only valued but directly tied to the idea of freedom. In 1866, a convention of freedmen gathered in Charleston, South Carolina, and could have led with any of a thousand grievances surely felt by those just out of enslavement. But their foremost concern was education. At an 1865 convention of freedmen in South Carolina, they made it clear: "Whereas, 'Knowledge is power,' and an educated and intelligent people can neither be held in, nor reduced to slavery; Therefore [be it] Resolved, that we will insist upon the establishment of good schools for the thorough education of our children." As Alvord went on to say: "In the absence of other teaching, they are determined to be self-taught; and everywhere some elementary text-book, or the fragment of one, may be seen in the hands of negroes."

It was nothing less than an educational revolution.

One of the first official Black schools in the post-slavery South was near Fortress Monroe in Virginia. It was there that a Black woman with wavy hair, hopeful eyes, and a gentle smile named Mary Smith Kelsey Peake ex-emplified the spirit of a determined teacher. As part of the Black elite in Hampton, Virginia, she was born into the era of "race uplift," where it was expected that middle-class Blacks would use their education and financial privilege for the economic, political, and social improvement of the whole race. It was seen as a sacred duty.

Described as "charitable with a benevolent heart," Peake secretly educated enslaved Blacks prior to the Civil War. During the war, much of Hampton was razed to the ground by rebel troops, including Mary's home. Undeterred, after the war she taught a class of fifty children in the day and twenty adults at night. Sick with tuberculosis, she taught children at her bedside. Not everyone who teaches is a teacher; the defining characteristic is passion. That is the only thing that could carry a person through full-body chills and bloody coughs to educate others.

As the Freedmen's Bureau gained control over the Southern Black schools, it ushered in an era of white control over Black education. Was this good? If education is the greatest tool to lead people out of poverty and into the knowledge necessary to enter society as well-informed citizens, then not at all. Even among the most good-natured white Americans, it was a radical idea to conceive of a truly multiracial democracy where Black people could rise to the heights of human possibility in America.

The mudsill theory, proposed in 1858 by South Carolina senator James Hammond, echoed an idea resounding through much of human history, that higher learning is an elite privilege available only to the wealthy. He argued that "there must be a class to do the menial duties, to perform the drudgery of life." In his view, educated people shouldn't perform manual labor. They only ate the bread labor harvested, at the table labor constructed, in the home labor built. The toil of production fell to the uneducated, an underclass purposefully kept ignorant and eternally divided by race while the educated sat atop an embarrassment of riches.

Without education, we are unaware of the ways we're being manipulated. In 1910, about 90 percent of Black Americans still lived in Southern states. By nature of class and skin, they were the most likely to be stuck in the soul-crushing cycle of labor exploitation and wealth creation, not for themselves but for others. They dug, planted, chopped, weeded, and pruned crops in Arkansas. They donated aching backs to heavy loads, picking and cleaning and carrying up to two hundred pounds of raw white cotton across Mississippi delta farmland daily. They gave calloused hands to tilling the soil along the sluggish Louisiana bayou. They hunched over in sun-bleached bib overalls, working on the sprawling pastoral farms of Alabama. They were exploited by the foxlike cunning of politicians, the coercion of farm owners, and the unequally applied force of the law. As many children began working as young as ten, there was little time for education beyond primary school, if they even received that much.

Many Black people did indeed go off in search of better opportunities, abandoning one farm after finishing a lease to work at one with marginally better opportunities, but this moving disrupted any educational stability the children might have had. Work drove life, and education took a back seat. Work was survival, education a luxury. Yet Southern Black people kept on pushing. Many Southern whites were ambivalent to Black education, but as throngs of white Northerners traveled South to help, it became intolerable. Interracial schools were burned to the ground, and the white teachers were threatened with violence. It's estimated that arsonists burned down

631 schools between 1864 and 1876. Imagine hammering the last nail into a school building it took months to build, only to come back the next day to smoldering ashes. A female teacher in Northern Virginia fled her job after being shunned by the white community there. Another instructor in Alabama was told to "prepare for travail," should they not leave immediately. Captain James McCleery, superintendent of education of the Freedmen's Bureau in Texas and northwestern Louisiana, only escaped a band of attackers in Louisiana by hiding in a swamp all night.

After *Plessy v. Ferguson* cemented segregation into law in 1896, the great question of Black education was incorporated into a larger fight between Northerners and Southerners, who debated universal education for all children. Reluctant, because the coercive agriculture of the South required an ignorant populace, Southerners kept Black education poor and terrible. But the universal demand for education, spearheaded by the agitation of Black people, served as a major factor in bringing public schools to the South. Unable to stop it and eager to push away Northern intervention, Southern whites shifted their strategy to controlling and restricting the expansion of public schooling rather than stopping it.

All the while, with meager support, Black families were working with teachers to maintain their school buildings and foot the bill for athletic teams and cultural events, paying what many have called the "Black Tax," which was a double tax, because they had to pay local taxes while putting up money for their own underfunded schools. Molded after Northern liberal arts academies, the Black-run schools not only taught practical skills but reflected the duties and obligations inherent in their rightful place in a democratic citizenship. They focused heavily on developing Black leadership, politicians, managers, ministers, and businesspeople.

But the conservative Southerners in power would never go along with a school system teaching Blacks to challenge their racial order, only to work within it. It was inconceivable to give Black people the gift of an education that would empower them to craft their own destiny. In the first decade of the twentieth century, the Southern Education Board, an organization made up mostly of Northern philanthropists and Southern college presidents, met to mold the future of public education in the war-ravaged South. Heavy on the agenda was the so-called Negro crisis. The Northerners acquiesced to the ideas of social Darwinism, which greatly influenced the era, pronouncing a racial hierarchy of nature and universe. In this theory, those best fitted for survival compete with and subordinate those who are not. Stay out of politics, be patient, work hard, be morally upright, leave expert jobs to whites, and in generations those Black people fit to succeed would.

Southerners like Charles W. Dabney were specific: "We must use common sense in the education of the negro. We must recognize in all its relations that momentous fact that the negro is a child race, at least two-thousand years behind the Anglo-Saxon in its development." He went on to insist they must work in the industrial arts and that it was ridiculous for them to waste time with Greek, Latin, or anything to do with the liberal arts.

Fork in the Road

In the cold of November 14, 1915, Booker T. Washington, renowned educator and leader, died in his home near the Tuskegee Institute in Alabama, which he helped to found. The years between 1895 and 1915 have been called the age of Washington, because the controversial leader became the ranking spokesman of Black America during this era. After a life of dogged advocacy for Black education, he died of malignant hypertension at fifty-nine. Near death on a trip to New York, he demanded to visit home one last time, saying: "I was born in the South, have lived all my life in the South, and expect to die and be buried in the South." Born in a one-room log hut in Virginia in 1856 (or 1858 or 1859, he never knew for sure), he rose from the wreckage of slavery. Driven as though by fire to learn, at sixteen, he walked five hundred miles and enrolled in the Hampton Normal Agricultural Institute in Virginia. It is almost incomprehensible to me that someone had to walk so far to find a school, but it was one of the few institutions of higher education for Black students in the South. It wasn't long before he was a favorite student of Hampton's white founder, General Samuel Chapman Armstrong, under whom Washington would forge his ideas in education, framed by Armstrong's program of hard work and respectability. There was no political knowledge. No preparation to challenge Southern social power and wealth. Even more,

Washington's mentor dissuaded Black voting and aspirations for political office.

A Northerner, Armstrong amplified the common bond between North and South—white supremacy. Hampton schools were known to overwork Black students, making them rise at 4:00 a.m. to work "ten hours of drudgery," according to the Hampton doctrine, this would shape them for "the struggle of life." Suffering was something to be accepted with pride. This program, which tied Black people to the soil, won over even the most conservative Southern whites. Philanthropy was acceptable if it reinforced the very caste system other Black people worked to disrupt.

Steeped in the ideals of the Hampton Institute, Washington charted a meteoric rise. He became the head of a school in Tuskegee, where a new generation of Black teachers, farmers, and skilled workers would be trained. When Tuskegee Institute swung open its doors on July 4, 1881, it only had one teacher and thirty students. It had no land or buildings, and $2,000 a year granted by the Alabama legislature. By the time the institute reached its twentieth year, it had expanded to two thousand acres, nearly one hundred large and small buildings, fifteen hundred students, and two hundred faculty members teaching at least forty trades.

Ever the pragmatist, Washington cited the need for Black communities to become financially independent above all else, stay out of the way, and eventually their rights would come. "No race can prosper till it learns that there is as much dignity in tilling a field as in writing a poem," Washington once said. On its own, this idea was practical and found wide support. Focus education on making a living, work, save, and buy land. Washington had many detractors, angry about his conservative call for gradual progress, and his seeming willingness to accept the subservience of Black people. Publicly he said, we give up. Keep your right to vote. Just leave us alone to till our farms and make our living.

"In all things that are purely social we can be as separate as the fingers," said Washington, "yet one as the hand in all things essential to mutual progress." Then, after telling followers to concede to social segregation, Washington accepted an invitation from Theodore Roosevelt to dine at the White House. It was the first time a Black person had ever eaten a meal there. They had been invited to offices, but dining there was unheard of, as it was a mark of social equality. Some responded positively, but there was severe backlash. Senator Benjamin Tillman of South Carolina said, "The action of President Roosevelt entertaining that nigger will necessitate our killing a thousand niggers in the South before they will learn their place again."

There may be no other six-letter word in the English lexicon that carries so much poison. Makes your stomach turn, doesn't it? If not, I wonder why not. That one word opens a Pandora's box of all the ominous dimensions of American racism. Underneath the rancor of that word, though, was Washington's near silence on the racial hierarchy it helped uphold. This set several Black leaders against Washington, who saw him as a Black ventriloquist for the voice of white power. For this reason, he was about to enter one of the biggest Black rivalries until Ali fought Frazier. What some have called Bookerism, or Black acquiescence to a racially unjust status quo, made him enemies with Black militants and progressives. Especially those like William Edward Burghardt Du Bois, born in Great Barrington, Massachusetts. The same year he debated Washington, Du Bois had become the first Black man to earn a PhD from Harvard. When asked about the accomplishment, he reportedly said, "The honor, I assure you, was Harvard's." This penetrating wit and poetic defiance mark Du Bois's life work, which unlike Washington, was vocal in its call for Black civil rights and racial justice.

It was Du Bois who said that the basic human rights of Black people could not wait. Then, in *The Souls of Black Folk*, a book that immediately sold out of stock three times over and launched Du Bois into national prominence, he went nuclear. In a chapter titled "Of Mr. Washington and Others," he lampooned Washington's ideas about segregation. In his view, Washington was a conformist aligning his behavior with the white power structure. Even the brightest moon has a dark side. No matter his conservative politics, Washington could be ruthless toward his more radical Black enemies, even hiring spies and provocateurs to counteract them. Du Bois was not without flaw either, as he promoted the elitist strategy encouraged by Northern white liberals including Reverend Henry Lyman Morehouse called the Talented Tenth, an undemocratic idea that a select group of educated Black men should lead Black America. Du Bois changed later, but it stands as a stain on his legacy. Yet on the matter of education, Du Bois was unwavering. In 1906, he said, "Unless we develop our full capabilities, we cannot survive. If we are to be trained grudgingly and suspiciously, trained not with reference to what we can be, but with sole reference to what somebody wants us to be, we simply are trying to follow the line of least resistance." Washington's words from 1895 exist as a response:

> The wisest among my race understand that the agitation of questions of social equality is the extremest folly, and that progress in the enjoyment of all the privileges that will come to us must be the result of severe and constant struggle rather than of artificial forcing. No race that has anything to contribute to the markets of the world is long in any degree ostracized. It is important and right that all privileges of the law be ours, but it is vastly more important that we be prepared for the exercises of these privileges.

These two men do not represent the entirety of Black thought—Marcus Garvey would have something to say about that—but they both saw education as a path to empowerment. They changed the nature of Black political debate. Washington's uneasy truce with white supremacists is not without premise; he was in the belly of the beast. We know that America has only recently moved closer to the definition of multiracial democracy, but Washington lived in an anti-Black, authoritarian enclave. The few civil liberties Black Americans had existed under constant threat. Once while traveling to a speaking engagement by train, Washington rode past a lynched Black body hanging close to the tracks, seemingly to say, this is what happens to you if you step out of line. I'm not one to entrench myself in an opinion about what I would have done in a century in which I didn't live. I find it more useful to walk in the shoes of those who did, look at the footsteps, and see how they led us to where we now stand.

From his seat in Tuskegee, in the gut of the Southern regime, we must ask if Washington was simply a pragmatist, teaching Black Southerners not to be idealistic, but to survive and compete within the system. Du Bois, on the other hand, with his highly educated Northern background, came from a different place. His primary position was that of a writer, not an organizer. With the pen, he challenged lynching, Jim Crow laws, and discrimination. He was a challenger, one trying to force change on the system or to change the system entirely. He built a towering intellectual legacy, becoming a pioneer in the field of sociology, uplifting Black history to challenge its racist interpretations, and founded *The Crisis* magazine, which published articles about Black life and concerns in a way white publishers never would. But even though the two disagreed, they listened to each other. There is much to be learned from Black history at its most radical extremes, but too little is made of the antagonistic coexistence between the edges. Despite their much-highlighted public debate, they coauthored a book in 1907, *The Negro in the South*. Washington secretly financed legal challenges to racial discrimination.

Marcus Garvey had a deep respect for Washington, likely because of his economic self-sufficiency program. I'm paraphrasing here but I once read that years after Washington's death, a young man began to disparage him in the presence of Du Bois, who promptly cut him short. He told the indignant youth that, unlike him, the man he was criticizing bore the mark of Cain on his back. Washington was the last of the slavery generation of civil rights leaders, and the younger Du Bois ushered in a second. It is interesting that we are still operating within the same debates. Should we focus on vocational schools or PhDs? Should we empower ourselves through economics or broad-based knowledge? How do we meet the needs of our communities? All of these are valid questions, and the ultimate irony is that, if we are miseducated, we will never think to ask them.

Reclaiming Youth

In 1950, the president of Morehouse College, Benjamin E. Mays, made a piercing observation:

> The Jim Crow system with its inevitable consequences of inequality has warped the minds and spirits of thousands of Negro youths. They either grow to manhood accepting the system, in which case they aspire to limited, racial standards; or they grow up with bitterness in their minds. It is the rare Negro child who comes through perfectly normal and poised under the segregated system.

Mays concluded that "the greatest thing that anyone can do to improve the morale of Negro children and youth is to continue to fight to destroy legalized segregation." Not everyone agreed, but after failing over and over to get equal funding for Black schools, desegregation became the major strategy of the NAACP. Four years later, in 1954, *Brown v. Board of Education of Topeka* legally struck down the doctrine of separate but equal—and the decision was unanimous. It was a major blow to Jim Crow, a system of apartheid so insidious that they even segregated the use of Black students' textbooks. This ruling was perhaps the biggest milestone in the educational history of the United States of America. It was a fundamental fulfillment of democracy that no one could discriminate against you entering a school because of your skin. But there is a difference between keeping people out of schools and forcing people into them. Especially when you are not wanted.

As Black students were bused to white schools in compliance with court orders, a tidal wave of white resistance came crashing down. I still see the innocence on six-year-old Ruby Bridges's face as she was hustled into William Frantz Elementary School in New Orleans, Louisiana, as the first Black student to desegregate the school in 1960. Protesting white mothers, fathers, and their children directed their fanatical anger toward Bridges, a small child, who had to be taught alone by a single teacher in a classroom for an entire year.

I think about the looks on those white faces and am reminded that hate transfers from generation to generation. The same ideas of white superiority crowded the minds of the nationalists who marched in the deadly Unite the Right rally in Charlottesville (August 11–12, 2017) in which far-right groups opposed the removal of a Robert E. Lee statue. The rally ended with the death of one counter-protester, Heather Heyer, who was struck by a car purposely driven into the crowd. Another counter-protester, DeAndre Harris, received eight staples in his head after being beaten with pipes and boards. Following the rally, President Donald Trump said, "There were fine people on both sides," drawing equivalents rather than outright condemning the white supremacist groups. Between 1960 and 2017, the faces may have been different, but the hatred was the same. And that hatred didn't leave the school system as states fought desegregation until the 1970s. Many others dodged the process altogether, and now we are witnessing an income-based segregation all over again.

The 1983 report *A Nation at Risk: The Imperative for Educational Reform* provides a cautionary tale predicting our current approach to schools. It fomented the idea that failure was inherent in our public school system and the idea stuck. It was followed by recommendations for more homework, longer school hours, more high stakes tests, and other ineffective changes that remain as popular solutions. Failure and reform are still the battle cry. I truly believe we should rethink our whole public school system to better meet the needs of the poor, which includes roughly half of Black and Brown kids. "You got to start with little things that are not in the book," said Ruby Middleton Forsythe, a Black educator who taught for more than six decades in South Carolina schools and went on to say that we should plant "the best seed into whatever soil we come into contact with, watching the growth, and the reproduction of the product sent forth."

Current conversations focus so much on Black student failure that the historic successes are forgotten. But the truth usually lives beyond the binary. The history of Black American education is an illustration of those who have responded to political, economic, and environmental barriers in fascinating ways to realize their humanity by way of education. And though I am not a teacher, allow me to muse for a moment as a concerned citizen. I think most of us can agree that strong schools filled with educators who motivate, demand, and expect high levels of achievement often get high levels of achievement. This is difficult for many white teachers teaching Black students, because data shows expectations for Black students are lower than everyone else, which naturally correlates to lower achievement. This is a problem that white people have to figure out for themselves. But in my opinion, we need those teachers to have the same commitment and care as Barbara Henry, then a young white woman from Boston, and the only one in the entire school willing to teach Ruby Bridges in the lion's den she walked into. I believe integration was a worthy goal, but the destruction of the Black school was an unintended consequence. Many of those schools were based on a general "we don't stand unless you stand" communal philosophy. Defined by togetherness and teachers committed to caring for and educating the whole child. And as I reflect on the photos of Black children being escorted into schools by armed national guardsmen, we might wonder if sending Black children into schools to learn with the lions was a good idea.

Now Black students disproportionately find themselves labeled as special education, are punished more, and given a lower quality of education. They aren't told that they can. They are denied an honest history. Though well studied, anti-Black racial bias remains largely unresolved because colorblind approaches sidestep the issue. Black teachers who are better able to relate to Black students are overwhelmed when called on to handle issues in white teachers' classrooms. They keep going because they know they are making an impact but many leave from exhaustion. "You don't even see what I can bring to the table. . . . All you do see is that I don't belong at your table," said a teacher from Houston, Texas, in 2016.

Many teachers put forth a heroic effort to supplement curriculum, but often they are ground into the machine. I'm no expert, but I'm a product of public schools. I experienced the lack of community that makes learning more than a challenge. Underemployed single mothers, incarcerated fathers, fistfights, teenage pregnancy, and drug deals in the bathroom. When I was twelve, one of my childhood friends took a shotgun from his father's closet and fired it point-blank into the chest of another. I used to play on the same Nintendo they were playing on; it easily could've been me. There was no real community-engagement effort, no lessons in cooperation, self-awareness, or emotional regulation.

We were expected to fail. We were not taught skills to help us exist in the real world. There were absentee parents, too overworked to be more than a little involved. Schools were not a part of the community; almost all of the Black kids were bused in from the other side of town. We cannot outrun our history. It is now as it was then: Unless education can find space to address the political and economic problems facing Black people and prepare all students to be participants in the democratic process, then the problems will remain. Socially just schools will seldom spring from socially unjust neighborhoods. Just imagine all the ready, sharp, and daring intelligence it took for Black people to survive in America, then think of the possibilities had it been able to thrive.

The Search
for Truth

Truth is a letter from courage.
—**Zora Neale Hurston**

In the mid-1960s and early 1970s, a new social movement emerged on the heels of the Civil Rights Movement. Desegregation and the Voting Rights Act of 1965 could not quell nearly four hundred years of frustration for the Black underclass. But unlike the nonviolent visage of their elders, the new face of Black liberation contorted into a militant grimace. They called it Black Power. The gradualism of civil rights politics crumbled under the heavy despair of poor, inner-city Black youth, whose pent-up rage exploded onto quiet Ivy League and state university campuses. Far from the hazy, hippie nostalgia often defining 1960s youth, students were organized and angry. Various forms of national outrage created a hurricane of restless student movements on college campuses. Students scathingly dissected the status quo. A furious anti-war movement chided President Lyndon B. Johnson and the years-long campaign in Vietnam with chants of, "Hey, hey, LBJ, how many kids did you kill today?" Black Power antagonized Western culture. A second wave of feminism confronted patriarchy and gender inequality. The gay liberation movement released centuries of sexual repression from the closet. Others subordinated their Blackness, whiteness, and gender to a Marxist class struggle trying to penetrate the dense economic realities of capitalism. Mario Savio, best known as the leader of the Free Speech Movement in Berkeley, summed up the mood:

There's a time when the operation of the machine becomes so odious, makes you so sick at heart, that you can't take part, you can't even passively take part, and you've got to put your bodies upon the gears and upon the wheels, upon the levers, upon all the apparatus, and you've got to make it stop! And you've got to indicate to the people who run it, to the people who own it, that unless you're free, the machine will be prevented from working at all!

After a federal push, or maybe it was a shove, threatened to withhold grant funding and accreditation, universities opened enrollment to Black students. Black enrollment shot up, but by 1965, Black students still only represented 4.8 percent of college admissions. Now remember these institutions purported the highest values with their mottos that rang of universal truths. *Veritas,* said Harvard, which, in Latin, translates "to the spirit of truth." "The wind of freedom blows," said Stanford. "Let there be light," said UCLA. "Light and Truth" is emblazoned on the Yale coat of arms. Those are beautiful words and all, but universities are a microcosm of society. America's higher learning institutions had long been a playground for an intellectual aristocracy. They chart an extended history of excluding white women, non-whites, Catholics, Jews, and non-Protestant Christians.

As the fight for civil rights and equal opportunity progressed, increased Black enrollment on college campuses jolted the status quo and aroused the ever-restless spirit of the racist mob. Protests were organized, crosses were burned, and in one instance white students organized a gala to mock Black students. "The university fancied itself free of bigotry, imbued with the belief that it is the man, not the color, that counts," said historian Allen Ballard. "But self-perception is often fatally in conflict with the perception of others. The white American university, as viewed by Blacks, was white and racist."

A chainsaw could've barely cut the tension. Black students demanded that administrators become more attentive to their needs. "What universities have failed to realize in almost every case," said campus observers sizing up the situation, "is that the American educational experience has been a white experience, an experience based on white history, white tradition, white culture, white customs, and white thinking, an education designed primarily to produce a culturally sophisticated, middle class, white American."

Protests were pervasive. Some say as many as one million students joined in on campuses across the country. At San Francisco State College, a student-led protest that started on November 6, 1968, lasted 134 days. The peaceful 142-acre campus collapsed into mayhem. A multiracial coalition of students, disruptive and militant, shook the rigid structures of academia with cries of "On strike! Shut it down!"

Joseph White, who was dean of undergraduate studies, said: "We were invisible on the faculty, in the curriculum and on the staff. And we were almost invisible in the student body." Inspired by the Civil Rights Movement at home and the revolutions in Latin America, Africa, and Asia, existing student organizations came at the calling of the Black Student Union to form a multiracial coalition of students demanding the campus shut down until their demands were met. Many called for an end to racial discrimination on campuses. At SFSC, those demands included the creation of a Third World college, which would represent all ethnicities, and a Black studies program. Faculty, trustees, and California governor Ronald Reagan refused to buckle. They kept the university open. As it is, unmet demands almost always end in a clash. Strikers banged on classroom doors, threatened students and teachers, overflowed toilets and bathroom sinks into hallways, and severed phone cords. Met with brutal force, officers lined up in riot gear with batons, then beat the students mercilessly. Blood stained the pavement. Officers had no sympathy for the protests, one officer later saying, "Did their . . . demands justify the bombings? Hell no," he said. "They placed a bomb in the administrative offices while school was in session. They were setting fires in the library. They were putting people's lives in danger."

A Pulitzer Prize–winning photo on the cover of *Newsweek*'s May 15, 1969, edition captured the national sentiment, titled "Universities Under the Gun." Yet, this was not always the case, as many universities were already prepared to incorporate Black studies into the curriculum. What happened when the smoke cleared? After the students were released from jail and the faculty uneasily settled back into campus life, universities did what one contemporary called "buying confrontation insurance," quickly putting together Black studies departments and urban affairs centers. Others said this was a concession to Black militancy. But the protest worked. Black studies departments sprang up everywhere. So, too, did women's studies, Native American studies, Chicano studies, and departments dedicated to the past, present, and future of other historically marginalized groups.

When I was in my last year of high school, the necessity of college hung over my head. With hard work, my parents thought, it would open doors that would otherwise stay closed. I left with an undergraduate degree and $50,000 in student loans, but I also left with the first genuine experience in Black history I've ever had in an educational institution. For the first time, I felt that my instructors tried to correct the misrepresentation of Black history, and place those who were omitted back in the record. For this reason, Black studies departments are necessary. It has been the scholars in those departments, often with scant research budgets, who reinvigorated Black history in only a few decades. But we cannot expect ethnic studies departments to fill in for eighteen years of culturally illiterate histories. One course cannot make up for what our public primary and secondary schools have failed to teach.

Watching the protests on campuses in the 1960s, historian C. L. R. James attempted to persuade American universities that Black studies was not a concession but an opening into the intellectual life and understanding of Black students: "There is an opportunity to extend the field of intellectual inquiry, which they have neglected up to now, a chance to penetrate more into the fundamentals of Western civilization, which cannot be understood unless black studies is involved." Yes, Western civilization cannot be understand outside the context of African civilization. And American history cannot be understood outside of Black history. But even further, we cannot understand any history without first understanding the truth of humanity. And for that I think we need an introductory course that provides all these frameworks, in a spirit that might inspire people to dig deeper on their own.

A Mind for History

Thinking about *Reading Rainbow*, a show that ran on PBS from 1983 to 2006, sends my mind wandering down the back road of sentimentalized 1990s nostalgia. Each show featured a book, narrated by celebrities, reviewed by children, and then host LeVar Burton would go to a location connected to the book. One episode featured a book about a ranch, and he went to an old western town to imagine life in the 1800s. It's ironic that a TV show bolstered my love of reading, but in the last segment of each episode, before giving us some reading recommendations, he'd say, "But you don't have to take *my* word for it." Those words always stuck with me. It's all too easy to allow your views to be molded by a dominant opinion. What Burton understood was the importance of investigating information for yourself. To think for oneself. So, before we move into part two of this book, I want to give you my toolkit for studying history. Think of this as a brief manual on how to find your own truth by looking backward, or at least, a framework for how I've spent the last decade cutting through the whitewashed—yet popular—retellings of American history to extract the human essence of it all:

1. Never stop learning. Learning doesn't stop after the cap and gown comes off a first, second, or even third time. Be a curiosity-driven lifelong learner. Explore the experiences of humanity to enrich your life and transform the world.

2. Get a library card. Read your way through history. Read this book and that book. New and old. I prefer the crisp yellowing pages of old books. I wander through antique book shops and sniff them like a wine sommelier searching for hints of walnut and vanilla. No, seriously, read many accounts of the same event. Read a diversity of opinions and viewpoints. If you know that one view is overrepresented, read the one that is underrepresented. It will confirm your opinion or change your mind, but either way, it will bring you closer to the truth. Read a diversity of historians and authors. Read the mainstream and the controversial. Read biography, social history, military history, journalistic history, then history across race, gender, and class.

   If history is a set of stories scattered with facts, then you need to hear from more than one storyteller. Read about saints and read about tyrants. Read the book that venerates someone as a saint, then the one that calls that saint a tyrant. If you do this, you will be able to identify the motives of authors much easier. Read your way around the globe, West, East, North, and South. Read radical history and patriotic, diplomatic, conservative, and liberal. This will be hard. Most people only read that which confirms their current worldview, but if only we would receive information from an opposing perspective, we would be closer to finding something in common. Some books you'll taste test; others you'll devour. But then you'll have a sampling of ideas and be able to decide from which you wish to compile your own. This is what historians do; it's called historiography. When we read everyone's history, no one's history will be lost.

3. Understand the uses and abuses of history. Philosopher Friedrich Nietzsche left a compelling mental framework for us to use on our journey for historical truth. And he was very interested in the study of history not for its own sake, but to help people live more meaningful lives. The only way to do this, he thought, was to avoid getting lost in the quicksand of history, rather using it to serve us in the present.

In his essay "On the Use and Abuse of History for Life" (1874) he gives us three modes of using past knowledge for the present: antiquarian, monumental, and critical. Antiquarian history is museum history. It preserves the artifacts of humanity. It is the love of history. It is the person who wants to know what Napoleon was wearing when he died. I dabble in this sort of history. I have a small collection of old magazines. One is a 1973 *Sports Illustrated* issue, in which Muhammad Ali gave an interview through clenched teeth. His jaw was wired shut from a break caused by the flying fists of Ken Norton in a shocking upset victory. Colonial Williamsburg is a whole town built as a relic for no other purpose than to reenact life in mid-eighteenth-century America. This history helps keep us rooted and carries on tradition. But when you apply this to something like a battle flag from the Confederate Army, long used as a hate symbol, you can begin to see where the problem lies. Some say it is simply tradition, but just because something is old does not make it good. At some point, we have to be bold enough to take a hatchet to the hardened stone of traditions if breaking them creates positive change.

Monumental history is the history that inspires us. They are the people who've shown us what is possible. They are the ones we look back to for guidance. We live vicariously through them and try to channel their thoughts, work, and accomplishments into our own lives. It is the writer who aspires to construct a surgically clean sentence like Ernest Hemingway. Or the pianist who studies Beethoven. I like to think of these as historic mentors. Close your eyes and imagine bringing back from history any four people of your choice to mentor you. They visit you every evening for thirty minutes, and you can keep or choose different mentors nightly according to your needs. Every night you have their ear, honesty, constructive feedback, expertise, and guidance. Mine might go something like this:

ME: I've sought solutions to my problems and come up empty.

ZORA NEALE HURSTON: There are years that ask questions and years that answer.

ME: Sometimes I wonder if I'm making the right decisions.

NELSON MANDELA: May your choices reflect your hopes, not your fears.

ME: People are obsessed with smartness; so many claim to know everything.

SOCRATES: The only true wisdom is in knowing that you know nothing.

ME: I've struggled to ease the tension between my desire for self-reliance and community.

MARCUS GARVEY: The ends you serve that are selfish will take you no further than yourself, but the ends you serve that are for all, in common, will take you into eternity.

Each person, group, and nation is inclined to uplift heroes according to their purpose and principles. For someone it is the dauntless pioneers who braved hardships to bring America West. For someone else, it is the fearless Native American warriors who fought against those colonizers. If you're an aspiring boxer, you're likely studying the uncanny speed and adaptive technique of Sugar Ray Robinson. A feminist's bookshelf likely holds space for bell hooks. There is a hero for every cause and saints for every doctrine. But gone too far, a monumental history quickly becomes a whitewashed one. We evangelize people and move their lives beyond debate. When we project our ideas, visions, and fantasies onto historical figures, we risk making them not what they were but what we want them to be. We are only to remember that Winston Churchill defended Europe against Nazis in World War II, but not that he was also a white supremacist, sure that those of "Aryan stock" would triumph over the barbarous minorities. Stuck in monumental nostalgia, there are those who refuse to puncture the façade of Bill Cosby as "America's Dad," even after he admitted under oath to drugging and assaulting women. People get most upset when their heroes are challenged. It is painful to find out the person you lifted to the status of demigod is merely a Homo sapien.

Finally, there is critical history, which requires us to confront the horrors of the past. To take on a critical framework is to question, judge, and condemn our histories. It hunts through the thicket of facts to prey on injustices. A critical historian condemns the past and sentences it to death. History is full of cancer, and yet, when we are too critical, it can become like chemotherapy, a treatment that can't differentiate between malignant and healthy cells. From a strict, critical perspective, you get students who want to eliminate Walt Whitman from the curriculum because he called Black people "baboons" and "brutes." But he also wrote with tenderness about the enslaved, and his writings produced beautiful visions of democracy. I'm not sure how stringent Whitman's prejudice was, but I am in favor of a history that holds a magnifying glass to the bearded bard's racist words while also appreciating the universal truths he offered like:

Do I contradict myself?
Very well then I contradict myself,
(I am large, I contain multitudes.)

As a Black American, this can be hard to reconcile. The architects of Western culture built an oppressive racial hierarchy into their new world. Cruel racial prejudice dwelled deep in the consciousness of America's

founders. American nightmares still harbor civilizational terror, state violence, and smiling faces in white spaces that betray the truth of our unbelonging. And then we read from the pages of an American literary canon
whose greatest writers typed racist drivel from the goose-down comfort of
a society blanketed in bigotry. How do we reconcile this? I think we can
confront the vile ideas of Whitman and the systemic intolerance of the society that made him, and then still revel in the prophetic and the brilliant.
Destroy only the malignant.

James Baldwin is here to help us as he offers his words in *Notes of a Native
Son*: "I know, in any case, that the most crucial time in my own development came when I was forced to recognize that I was a kind of bastard of
the West . . . I would have to appropriate these white centuries. I would have
to make them mine—I would have to accept my special attitude, my special
place in this scheme—otherwise I would have no place in any scheme."

Mr. Baldwin understood that, even when dealing with problematic figures, we still should take what can be made useful to us in the present. So,
if used in harmony, the antiquarian, the monumental, and the critical act as
a sort of checks and balances. Then all at once we can appreciate the past,
we can celebrate the beauty of humanity, and also confront its horrors.

The Heart of History

Sally Hemings left no records behind. But what historians hid for centuries,
science has revealed. The nation was not ready to accept that an enslaved
Hemings birthed six children all paternally linked to their founding father,
Thomas Jefferson. Or that those light-skinned, enslaved children working
on the Monticello plantation who looked like him were indeed his. Only
after DNA evidence was revealed in 1998 did the Thomas Jefferson Foundation form a committee to weigh the facts—and concluded the likelihood
of what many long believed was true. To fit the master narrative, the public
created a myth that they were in love. Jefferson defenders have no shortage of
defenses and sympathy for him. They say this was common for the time and
describe Hemings as his mistress. And, if cultural consumption offers any
evidence, last I checked the movie *Sally Hemings: An American Love Story*
(2000) charted 4.6 stars out of nearly seven hundred reviews on Amazon.

The historical record suggests Hemings was fourteen years old, and a play-mate of his daughter at the time. Jefferson faced scrutiny for this in his own time, but generations of authors and historians have come to his defense, heavily outweighing the injustice done to Hemings. She was at the mercy of Jefferson, dependent on his every whim. Who sympathizes with her abuse, manipulation, or coercion? What of her descendants, who whispered of their relationship to Jefferson for generations? They suffer in silence. Because America has not been ready to deal with the pain of its history.

The reason I weaved the stories of enslavement so thoroughly into the beginning of this book is because, if we want to understand our scars, we must look back to our injuries. In the 1780s, a young abolitionist named John Riland befriended an old African man named Caesar, who had deep scars from the iron fetters he wore on the slave ship during the Middle Passage. It was impactful enough for Riland to note that the skin on his ankles was "seamed and rugged." On that shuttle of sadism, Caesar had his limbs strapped with iron manacles. Chained, he sat inches from a man whose language he did not know as they sailed some four thousand miles across the Atlantic. When the ship strained, groaned, and rocked within the violent swells of ocean chaos, the men could not coordinate their movements. At times the man next to Caesar grew sick and convulsed violently. The fetters lacerated both men's flesh. They cut deeper with each frenzied movement. Like Lazarus, Caesar arose from the clutches of death. But he would later say it was as if "the iron entered onto our souls."

History is painful. The multigenerational legacy of chattel slavery, Jim Crow, racial terror, and residual racism has, as Caesar said, "entered onto our souls." What would it take for us all to truly feel this history? There is a tendency to look at these stories coldly and objectively, like the medical dissection of a cadaver. Empathy is unequally distributed to the powerful at the expense of the marginal. The will to understand these experiences has come slowly in America, and there seems to be a calcification of the body's most powerful muscle.

"The need to let suffering speak is a condition of all truth," said philosopher Theodor Adorno. History is not just a cold set of facts and figures; it is personal. It crawls under our skin and imposes itself on our memories. We are only just understanding the transference of past trauma. We all can imagine the pain accompanying a broken ankle, a deep cut, a severe burn, or an injured back, but society has been slower to understand those unseen inner wounds that go unspoken. Yet research is coming to light to support what psychiatrists have termed as intergenerational trauma. Studies, like the ones involving Holocaust survivors, are acknowledging that exposure to extremely adverse events also impacts one's offspring, who find themselves wrestling with their parents' and grandparents' post-traumatic stress. In effect, trauma is passed from one generation to the next. Proactive theories even suggest that an epigenetic transfer of trauma can affect DNA function.

Furthermore, researchers found that this trauma was expressed in three different ways, which might be helpful to understand the Black experience as it relates to nearly four hundred years of racial terror and discrimination in America. The researchers, when studying the Holocaust survivors and their children, identified three variations of intergenerational response: the victim, the numb, and the fighter. The victim is stuck in the trauma, overprotective and emotionally volatile. The numb slips into emotional isolation, showing an intolerance of weakness, and pushes a conspiracy of silence in the family. The fighter possesses a strong sense of justice and a desire to maintain group identity. All of these, it seems to me, are predictive of the responses of Black people as they come to realize their history in America.

For many Black people, eager to explore their history, it has now come time for us to explore the nuances of being Black in America, beyond our shared injustices and victimization. Beyond the slave ship, the Klan, and the lynching. Understandably, people want to divorce themselves from the suffering and focus on joy, to explore and celebrate love, art, wealth, and even ordinary lives. This is desperately needed. Black history isn't a continuously running horror show. But we should also remember these words from Maya Angelou: "History, despite its wrenching pain, cannot be un-lived; but if faced with courage, need not be lived again." Yes, history is tragic. It is interwoven with pain, grief, sorrow, and heartache. We all bear the scars, bruises, and wounds of our collective pasts. If we rummage through the wreckage of that past, we can find bright stars glowing in the blackened void.

This very idea is what I see in the brilliant photography work of Gordon Parks, who found universal dignity in the high-poverty misery of America's slums. He saw it from behind the lens of his first camera, a Voigtländer Brilliant he bought at a Seattle pawnshop for $12.50 in 1937. In more than half a century of work, from the 1940s to the 2000s, he captured the beauty of a composite America because he didn't give in to the trauma. Not even after what he experienced growing up in Fort Scott, Kansas, in the midnight of American racism. Not even after the death of his mother when he was fourteen. Not even after his homelessness. He didn't go numb. And he didn't turn inward; instead, he looked out, capturing the commonalities that lie within us all.

"I have for a long time, worked under the premise that everyone is worth something," Parks once said, "that every life is valuable to our own existence. Consequently, I've felt it was my camera's responsibility to shed light on any condition that hinders growth or warps the spirit." He stood behind the camera and captured the essence of America with visceral urgency. He traveled everywhere, from small towns to big cities. From Shady Grove, Alabama, to San Francisco, New York, and Los Angeles. I flipped through one of his photo books. In one picture, Parks fills the frame with a Black couple in their mid-fifties, dressed for church. The man has on a straw boater hat, lips wrapped tightly around a cigar, his right hand clutching a tattered Bible. The woman wears a black fascinator hat, which reminds me of a crown. Her right arm wrapped around the man. They both wear stern smiles. They look dignified and unified. Polished. A picture of spiritual character. It was 1950, and they are staring directly into the face of injustice.

I came across another photo. Fort Scott, Kansas, 1950. A father crouches down, surrounded by his wife, son, and two daughters. He's changing what appears to be a flat tire. He has laid a cloth on the ground to keep his pants from getting dirty. Parks translated humanism through the language of the camera. Known for his celebrity photos, he humanized humanity.

And not just the Black poor but also the stark poverty of white families, capturing all, even those in Latin America, with the same care. He photographed Black Muslims in prayer rituals when many others distanced themselves from the group. Another photo essay presented by

Life magazine, "Segregation in the South," confirms the Black experience through a lens of segregation. One photo captures a sign that says, "FOR SALE LOTS FOR COLORED." Another shows a group of Black children standing in front of a segregated playground, separated not by some childhood intolerance, but by a metal fence keeping them out. Another image then contradicts stereotypes, but lends to images of violent masculinity, captured in Alabama, two Black boys and a white one playing with guns. This is revealing. Segregation was the law, but people still mixed, in work and in friendship. Gordon Parks was willing to look at the pain, and what did he find? The heart of history, the interconnectedness of us all.

The Spirit of History

What is the spirit of history? Now, I don't want to get all supernatural on you here, and this is not theology—so, let me frame this in a way that I think might be more relatable. Spirit is like music, which has a quality that is indiscernible, something felt so deeply that it goes beyond the five senses. It goes beyond theory, and method, and analysis, for these have their limits. The brain can be cold and unfeeling. And it goes beyond even empathy, which is not unlimited. We can only take on so many problems before we're exhausted. I believe that what drives us beyond these limitations is the spirit. The higher virtue and the channeling of something divine. It is Augusta Savage with the clay, it's Michael Jordan with the basketball, it is Jimi Hendrix riffing on the guitar. For me, the spirit of history lies in the Akan philosophy of Sankofa, a word captured in the phrase "*Se wo were fi na wo Sankofa a yenkyi,*" translated as "It is not wrong to go back for that which you have left behind." The word is represented by a bird reaching for an egg on its back. The definition seems simple but communicates the symbiotic relationship between the three dimensions of time—past, present, and future.

Sociologist Alfred Kofi Quarcoo says this about Sankofa: "Learn from or build on the past. Pick up the gems of the past. [It is a] constant reminder that the past is not all shameful and the future may profitably be built on aspects of the past. Indeed, there must be a movement with the times but as the forward march proceeds, the gems must be picked up from behind and carried forward on the march."

Sankofa means we go back to recover the best of the past and acknowledge the debt we owe our ancestors. It is an attempt, I believe, to be fluid, to step outside of our current framework into something different. Through Sankofa we can mine the unlimited resources in the fields of ancestral wisdom. To apply Sankofa to American enslavement is to believe that the will to survive lives on through us. It is to say that their subjugation does not have to be the last word. It transcends what I can write here, because it is something spiritual, casting itself beyond words. The history is felt. It allows us to tap into the everlasting resonance of our most harmonic evolutions: love, hope, integrity, community, fortitude, and equality. It is a cosmic carrying forth of the sacred flame given to us by our predecessors, and then using it to illuminate our path into an unknown future.

THE VERY USE OF and carrying forward of Sankofa in the Black American community represents the meaning of this philosophy. It is a deep desire to go back and find a fragment of the beautiful. American Sankofa is the signature sweet barbecue of Henry Perry, who after moving from Memphis, Tennessee, to Kansas City, perfected the recipe. An amalgamation that traveled from the Chickasaw tribe, who cooked meat over indirect flame, combining the basting techniques of the Chickasaw with those from the British colonists, and throwing in a hearty dash of the sweet-spicy mustard brought by French and German immigrants, traveling state to state until Perry put his hands on it and became the "Father of Kansas City Barbecue." And bringing that forward generation to generation.

And for me, this Sankofa of American history is to bring all of this together with an all-embracing moral vision. Or what I might call the humanity ethic. A recognition that any two human beings are 99.9 percent similar based on DNA. So, to express everything that we are, at some point we have to stop exaggerating our differences, because we know that nothing human is alien. Sankofa is a transmission of the spirit, showing up in other ways, sometimes unknowingly, often in our art, our music, our style, and other elements of our culture. Sankofa dares us to find the faintest light in the pitch black of inhumanity. It goads us to find beauty, like the words of poet Lucille Clifton: "someone inside me remembers . . . the voice of the universe at peace . . . at the beginning of creation." Forgetfulness does not exist. The best is behind us. The worst is behind us. Our power lies in how we bring it forward."

PART 2

Foundational
Presence

The future is built on the foundation of the past.
—**Unknown**

5

Into Africa

Africa is a dark continent not merely because its people
are dark skinned or by reason of its extreme impenetrability,
but because its history is lost.
—**Paul Robeson**

In 1961, Louis Armstrong, along with his wife, Lucille Wilson, found themselves an ocean away from America on a tour of Egypt. It was a purposeful excursion. The US government sent the famed horn player, affectionately known as Satchmo, as a goodwill world ambassador to thaw some ice in the Cold War. What better than jazz—a form unburdened by rigid structure, the improvisational style where one can shine individually, with the goal to always elevate the entire group—to represent the best ideals of American democracy? Armstrong's band played shows from Sierra Leone to Khartoum, Sudan. In Cairo, not long after his vocalist had a paralyzing stroke from tour exhaustion, he serenaded his wife with his brass trumpet, gazed on by the Great Sphinx of Giza. This moment was photographed, and every time I see it, I see the intersection of Black America and Africa. One of history's greatest artists carrying the hybrid eloquence of jazz back to the motherland. It is as though he went there to remind Africa of the beauty she helped to spread across the world. But why do we so rarely look back to her?

To be clear, humans have always had the capacity for prejudice. But the walls of Eurocentrism have formed an intellectual and emotional fortress around the African continent. For centuries, those who lived there have been seen as less. Less worthy, less beautiful, less pious, less human. No one knows exactly when these walls began their construction. According to the historian Nell Irvin Painter: "Americans still struggle to understand that race is an ideology, not a biological fact, more like witchcraft than empirical science. Just as difficult to grasp, it seems, is the idea that our idea of one big white race, which you're either in or out of, is less than a century old."

But the seeds were planted much earlier, which explains why the tree will be difficult to uproot. As early as 1449, city leaders in Toledo, Spain, used legalized racism to define those of Jewish or Moorish ancestry as having impure blood. Then, in the eighteenth century, Europeans started ranking humans as superior and inferior based on skin, ranking intelligence by skull size, and ranking beauty by proximity to the Caucasus Mountains. Africa was called the dark continent as a backdrop to the European enlightenment, which insinuated it was backward.

European scholars performed all sorts of intellectual acrobatics to obscure the truth about African advancement. "Some even suggested that African accomplishments were the result of visitors from outer space. Any wild idea was more acceptable than to admit that Africans had the intellect and ingenuity to develop and control well-ordered empires. The purpose of all these erroneous theories was simply to justify slavery and attitudes of racial superiority," explained Patricia McKissack, the prolific author who penned scores of Black history inspired books for children and teens, and who once stated her mission was to "build bridges with books."

White supremacists built their bridges as well, constructed of lies to fill the gap between real African sophistication and false African inferiority. Because of this, a devastatingly unknowable amount of history is lost forever. Pair that with half-hearted archaeology, and the Western tendency to ignore the oral histories of indigenous Africans, and you see how difficult it is to be recovered. And history was more than lost, it was banished. As the sun set on the British Empire in the mid-twentieth century, officials destroyed, removed, and renamed records of imperialist crimes all over the world. "What's burnt won't be missed!" cried a British officer as he frantically sifted piles of papers, in what was called Operation Legacy, a systematic effort to shape the legacy of the Empire post-colonization.

Lured by the siren song of the unknown, some have spent their lives seeking the lost African history that racism destroyed. And because of their efforts, it is now commonly accepted that Europe, Asia, and Egypt were not the only civilizations in history with advanced technology. I was astonished to read the account of a European traveler who spent time in the great Benin City in West Africa (present-day Nigeria) around the seventeenth century:

> The town seems to be very great. When you enter into it, you go into a great broad street, not paved, which seems to be seven or eight times broader than the Warmoes street in Amsterdam. . . . The king's palace is a collection of buildings which occupy as much space as the town of Harlem, and which is enclosed with walls. There are numerous apartments for the Prince's ministers and fine galleries, most of which are as big as those on the Exchange at Amsterdam. They are supported by wooden pillars encased with copper, where their victories are depicted, and which are carefully kept very clean. The town is composed of thirty main streets, very straight and 120 feet wide, apart from an infinity of small intersecting streets. The houses are close to one another, arranged in good order. These people are in no way inferior to the Dutch as regards cleanliness; they wash and scrub their houses so well that they are polished and shining like a looking glass.

The pillage of Benin City was meticulous and the destruction swift. In 1897, British forces captured and exiled the *oba* (king), stole some ten thousand sculptures, plaques, and ceremonial artifacts, then burned the city to the ground. Plaques of warriors in bronze, figures of horn blowers, and altars thought to facilitate communication with ancestors found their way behind reflection-controlled museum glass at places like the Metropolitan Museum of Art and the British Museum. Occasionally, institutions repatriate a few artifacts, inviting news journalists to make a show of it. But there is something deeply paternalistic in the assumption that, unethically looted or not, these relics are better off displaced in museums outside of Africa rather than the natural home from which they were stolen.

At an African higher education summit in 2014, scholars from Tanzania, South Africa, Uganda, Nigeria, and Ethiopia delivered a sweeping report titled *Recommendations for Reinvigorating the Humanities in Africa* that called for a reappraisal of the world-enhancing contributions of African history and culture. A 2019 update on the project quoted the original report: "It is clear that the marginalization of the humanities must be remedied, because no knowledge-led development strategy can succeed without a solid core of humanistic understanding and humane values. To envision the future, we must understand the lessons of the past. To act in the present, we must be sensitive to current cultural complexities."

To those with the willingness to listen, Africa will fill their ear with its wisdom and beauty. Approximately 10 percent of an iceberg's mass is visible above water; Africa is its own iceberg. If ancient Egyptian history is visible, the rest is submerged. Ancient Egypt is at once magisterial, intimidating, and gorgeous to behold, yet, if you're willing to dive deep, there is a massive amount of history to discover on the continent of Africa beyond its pyramids and pharaohs.

When the Present Visits the Past

Before we explore the history of Africa, we have to deal with the problem of presentism. Always, we project our current views onto the past to make it meaningful for us in the present. Yet, when we do this uncritically, we risk falling into rabbit holes we can never make our way out of. As the main progenitor of human civilization, Egypt has been the most contested racial battleground. Afrocentrists clash with Eurocentrists over the skin pigmentation of ancient Egyptians. Depending on whom you ask, you will hear that Egypt was exclusively Black, white, or that they have always looked as they do now. Each worldview tainted by the desire to claim its perceived glory. It is a tragedy of modern history that the construction of race imposes itself onto a past where it did not exist. There is more genetic diversity within Africa than anywhere in the world. There are infinite numbers of hair types, nose shapes, eye colors, and color swatches across the vast continent. Geneticists have recognized four language families: Afro-Asiatic, Nilo-Saharan, Khoisan, and Niger, all of which migrated within the continent. And, of course, people migrated, traded, and made incursions from outside each. Africa has always been part of the international and intercultural transmission of humanity, trading in ideas, culture, customs, and beliefs. Africa was constantly developing.

And yet, we force race into a past where it is an unwelcome intruder. These same arguments rarely exist over, say, how Asian Europe is, though recent genome research argues that northern Europeans share about 12 percent of their ancestry with the Mongol empire from the days of Genghis Khan, or how European innovations were heavily influenced by Asia. We still apply these sweeping assumptions of noninfluence with terms like "Western thought," when we know those thinkers embraced Chinese, Persian, and indigenous ideas. Enlightenment thinker Gottfried Wilhelm Leibniz was rare in his admittance that European governments borrowed ideas from Chinese statecraft. This denial stems from colonial assumptions of European superiority in all things—knowledge, civilization, and development. To retain their identity, Black people have looked to reconnect with their historical contributions, ones that have been largely ignored in the Western accounts of history and that require greatness as the price of recognition. Many Black people have claimed Egypt for their own, not out of malice, even though they overstate their sources of what was Black then, but as an attempt to be recognized in a human history that often excludes them. I am not here to join these arguments, but I will speak on what is certain.

Egypt is part of Africa. Early archaeologists and Egyptologists didn't lock their racism in a case while they excavated and interpreted African sites of civilization, identifying Egypt as white. Nubia is part of Africa, and it, too, was a foundational civilization. There was no impenetrable barrier; not even the vastness of the Sahara Desert separated the so-called sub-Saharan Nubia from its northern neighbors. They influenced one another as powerful neighbors for some 1,400 years. Nubia should be taught right alongside Egypt and Rome. It is not. Scholars whitewashed Nubians because they were indisputably Black in the modern sense. How can you say people are inferior when you find their cities, pyramids, writings, infrastructure, and evidence of a sophisticated civilization in an indisputably Black nation? You can't, so they ignored it. And it is still ignored.

That said, here is a rare opportunity to explore the complexity and subtlety of humanity and to find fundamental truths without the burden of race. It is an opportunity to acknowledge that every culture we explore is based on fragments of another. Each precedent has an antecedent. Africa had a multitude of cultures. So, here we will categorize people by tribe, kingdom, ethnicity, clan, locale, religion, or any other number of features while understanding a fundamental truth that, no matter the shade, they were African. This is the Africa we will tour. A place described beautifully by the late historian Basil Davidson. He spoke of the dominant proportions of the continent, its wild variations in climate, temperature, and landscape, diversity of animals, its crawling bugs, its overwhelming magnificence:

> If you tramp through the African bush, you will soon wonder how anyone could ever impose human settlement on this land, much less keep footing here and steadily enlarge it. All this wild profusion stands there vast and looming, like a conscious presence waiting to move in again the moment your back is turned. Give this giant the merest chance, you will feel, and the whole surrounding scenery will again invade these narrow fields and possess the land once more, possess it utterly, as though humanity had never been. Every African culture bears profound witness to this dominating "spirit of the land."

The Glory Days

Ancient Egypt fascinated me as a kid. My love of that great African culture emerged in endless documentaries and rotating book stacks. I vividly remember reading about mummification. How the brains were removed through the nose, the flesh embalmed, and bodies reunified with souls in the afterlife. One wonders what those wealthy Egyptians and royalty would think, after being buried with their riches so they could take them into the afterlife, now stolen and resting in museums as reminders of colonial pillage. I thought I knew a lot about that civilization from reading about Tutankhamun and first inventions like the modern calendar, surgery, and breath mints. But that would be like saying I knew a lot about a car by kicking its tire. There was so much more to learn.

Later, I went through an adolescent phase where I sped through books on arcane religions. I'd scour the library for texts on the mythological and supernatural. I tried to decode Egypt's mysteries in astrology, theology, and philosophy. I thought about the priesthoods, deities, and rituals hoping to reveal the divine origin of the cosmos. I read the classics of ancient Egyptian literature. The narratives, hymns, tales, and guides, like *The Instruction of*

Ptahhotep, in which a high-ranking official offered a transition plan to his son on the eve of retirement. It is interesting to think that, over four thousand years ago, someone thought in the same ways we do, speaking timeless truths that would relate to life today. As if rebuking us in our own time for the pathology of elitism, where people are ranked by who is the smartest, Ptahhotep writes, "Be not proud because thou art learned; but discourse with the ignorant man, as with the sage." I thought about how much of Egypt was remixed and reformed into Greco-Roman culture, and how their civilizational achievements are rarely traced back to Africa.

Egypt's neighbors were just as fascinating. To continue right under the surface of the iceberg, we find the Kushites, later called Nubians, who were an old people, with roots stretching back as deep as 8,000 BCE. From its tribal infancy, it grew into one of Africa's first global powers. The Kush Kingdom was a dominant presence in Nubia for over three thousand years. Yearly, millions arrive in Egypt to tour its sprawling pyramids, but it was the Meroites (later one of the Kush empires in modern Sudan) who boasted the most triangular monuments. Go there and you can see over two hundred of them chiseled in sandstone and granite standing in defiance of time. These with its elephant gods and lion temples, ornate tombs, and royal burial chambers. Kush kings invaded and ruled over Egypt, and Egyptian kings invaded and ruled over Kush.

The largest fortresses the Egyptians ever constructed were on the border of Kush, which speaks to the military prowess of the Kushites. The Egyptians, with their air of superiority, called them "wretched kush," but they also held low opinions about Asiatics and Libyans. Deep into history, we can feel the gusts of xenophobia, nationalism, and intolerance. And we see the elements of ethnicity sharpened by war with one group defining its superiority against the other. But these attitudes were fluid. Kush was rich with resources and served as an international trading center. From its metropolises in Kerma, Napata, and Meroe, they facilitated the business of the state. Its merchants traveled as far as Persia to trade in gold, animal skins, ebony, incense, and other exotic goods from their prestige economy. Kush was culturally rich. Priests consulted oracles for untold prophecies. They wrote scripts in hieroglyphs and cursive language, still indecipherable. They were mainly farmers raising wheat watered by the Nile. To overcome challenges presented by lack of rain, they used a shadoof, a highly efficient irrigation tool for raising buckets of water. In addition, state-sponsored infrastructure included massive water tanks, deep wells, and production facilities for iron and pottery.

Women walked the streets in colorful clothing and hair beaded with ornaments, fanning themselves with ostrich feathers. The wealthy draped themselves in gold, silver, quartz, and other precious jewelry. Nubia (Kush) was known as "the land of the bow," for its archers were adept in its use. Greek historians Homer and Herodotus described people they called the *Aithiopians* in almost heavenly regard. Depicting the Kushites as being favored by the gods, tall, handsome, "blameless," "pious," and "'long lived." By most scholarly accounts, these observations were not based on race, but on the Kushites' political power and competency as rulers. Ancient Greeks knew much of Africa. Many of them went to Egypt to study history, science, philosophy, religion, and government. Foundational Greek scholars such as Thales, Solon, Herodotus, Plato, and the mathematician Eudoxus were educated in Memphis, Egypt, before Alexandria was founded. Sitting in the scholarly centers, or "Houses of Life," *per ankh*, where knowledge was taught. They studied from the papyrus scrolls that held the wisdom of ancient sages where scientific, literary, and religious works were produced.

Much Kush history has been recovered, but still less has been displayed. In 50 CE, a noble-born woman rose to power. Her name was Amanitore. One of a succession of ruling queens known as Kandake (often Latinized as "Candace"). The Kandake queens were figures of great historical significance, well known in the ancient world. Administering from her throne in Meroe, a city of fabulous wealth, she held meetings, read decrees, and hosted dignitaries. At its height, the Kush empire spanned an area of some nine hundred miles. I wonder how their society was stratified? Would our modern understanding of economic and social classes fit how they lived? We know that the royal family held the highest power and authority. Enslaved people were taken in battles with Egyptians, Canaanites, and Libyans, and likely formed a low servile class. As the entrusted guardians of all things sacred, priests were held in high regard. All things considered, laborers, craftspeople, farmers, soldiers, and others would've fallen somewhere or another in between. Or were they? We may never know, in terms of hierarchical structures, but there is also what is called a heterarchy. Many social organizations past and present operate horizontally rather than vertically. Within these more complex structures, many more people have the ability to exercise power.

Aside from that, the people of Kush lived in towns and small cities like Kerma and Napata. The city of Meroe was a hub for the transportation of gold, ebony, ivory, animal pelts, and wood bound for Egypt. Kushite horse experts actively trained and bred the animals for transportation and war.

"Ethiopia shall stretch forth her hands unto God"; so it says in the Psalms of the Bible, and it also mentions "Candace, queen of the Ethiopians" in that same book. So often in history we hear about males in battle and their inglorious conquests, but in Kush, women shared access to the ways of war, in this case access to the bow.

And it is in war that we see Queen Amanirenas burst onto the scene of history. Once upon a time, the Roman emperor Caesar Augustus conquered Egypt and ruled it as a vassal kingdom. He then had Marc Antony set up Romans in positions of prominence to collect Egyptian tribute. From there, Rome set its sights on Nubia. But Nubia was set to teach them a lesson in "the danger of hubris." In 24 BCE, flanked by her son Prince Akinidad, Amanirenas headed a force of thirty thousand soldiers to battle the Romans in Egypt, sword to sword and bow for bow. Using the element of surprise, she engaged the unsuspecting Roman army and sacked the Egyptian city of Aswan. Nubia for the Nubians, she was determined to remain unconquered.

The Kushite and Roman armies fought catastrophic battles. Blood flowed like the Nile, and the Black Queen held off the military might of the Roman republic for three grueling years. Irreverently, she pulled down the statues of Roman rulers in sacked cities, taking the bronze head of Emperor Augustus back to Nubia in an act of victory. Blinded in battle, Amanirenas earned the nickname one-eyed queen. But this wasn't simply a matter of war. This was a woman versed in the art of statecraft, with its government-to-government negotiations, foreign policy, and securing of national interests. Eventually a treaty was reached; the Kushites gave up no land and were forced to pay no dues to the Romans.

To explore gender is to see history lost within history. If we use our iceberg analogy, saying only 10 percent of African history is visible, how much or little of that is about women? Examples such as these, though exceptional, highlight real histories that show women as protagonists and not non-actors. But how difficult is it to locate, deconstruct, and reconstruct the lives of those mostly silenced in their own times? Kush gave way to Aksum, which was described by third-century Persian prophet Mani: "There are four great kingdoms on earth: the first is the Kingdom of Babylon and Persia; the second is the Kingdom of Rome; the third is the Kingdom of the Aksumites; the fourth is the kingdom of the Chinese." It was buoyed by a strong navy and its commercial activity stretched to Rome, India, Arabia, and even as far as China. Its banking, minted coins, contractual trade agreements, and active ports have been pointed to as having the elements of free market trade. There is so much more to learn, but one thing we do know—when archaeologists and scholars confronted facts contrary to a Eurocentric worldview, they left them ignored in the dirt.

Widespread Cultures

In 1943, tin miners working along the slopes of Jos Plateau, Nigeria, uncovered decaying human bodies, that is, sculpted bodies made of ceramic clay. These masterfully crafted terra-cotta sculptures unearthed evidence of one of the oldest civilizations in West Africa, the Nok culture, but without a comprehensive analysis of the site, it remains an enigma. We know their society ranged from around 500 BCE to 200 CE. They hunted but also cultivated millet and cowpeas. They mined the earth for iron ore using knowledge of heat and furnaces to transform the metal into workable tools. The origins of the Nok are shrouded in mystery. But their knowledge of metallurgy was not new in Africa. There is evidence of iron mining in Western Swaziland from at least twenty-eight thousand years ago. They built houses on stone foundations. Their artwork is so stunning it entices our curiosity. The figures boast elaborately detailed hairstyles and jewels. Abstract features add to the element of mystery surrounding who these people were. The heads were styled much larger than the bodies, which in later

African cultures signified intelligence. It is believed that the Nok influenced the masterful metalwork of the Ife people, who later lived in the same area of Nigeria from the eleventh to the fifteenth century.

Unsurprisingly, enlightenment thinkers weren't interested in these marvels of Black African culture and society. Georg Wilhelm Friedrich Hegel, the nineteenth-century German philosopher whose thoughts on history, society, and the state endure, said: "What we properly understand by Africa, is the Unhistorical, Undeveloped Spirit, still involved in the conditions of mere nature, and which had to be presented here only as on the threshold of the World's History." From the battle to wrest African history from such intellectual foolishness arose a Senegalese historian, anthropologist, and politician, Cheikh Anta Diop. A polymath with degrees in nuclear physics and chemistry, known for his infectious laughter and restless focus on restoring Black history, in 1966 he set up the first radiocarbon-dating laboratory in Africa. In his seminal 1974 book, *The African Origin of Civilization: Myth or Reality*, he relentlessly challenged those Eurocentric scholars who tried to whitewash Egypt out of Africa.

In Great Zimbabwe, a middle-age-era city, conical towers stretch high out of history, its winding stone walls carefully trimmed with decorative patterns. From around 1100 CE until the fifteenth century, when it was abandoned, it was a wealthy international trading network. The number of dwellings suggests a large urban development that was likely home to between ten thousand and twenty thousand people. It was a heavily militarized state with its armies outstretched to protect its highly lucrative trade routes and port settlements. Archaeologists discovered iron gongs, most likely used in ceremonies and finger rings and necklaces, as well as bronze bracelets with gold inlays. These medieval, Shona-speaking people traded gold for glazed Chinese stoneware and glass beads from India. With its unique architecture, twentieth-century Europeans thought it had to be non-Africans who built the site. Far from randomly constructed, Professor Ron Eglash suggests:

> In Europe and America, we often see cities laid out in a grid pattern of straight streets and right-angle corners. In contrast, traditional African

settlements tend to use fractal structures—circles of circles of circular dwellings, rectangular walls enclosing ever-smaller rectangles, and streets in
which broad avenues branch down to tiny footpaths with striking geometric
repetition. These indigenous fractals are not limited to architecture; their
recursive patterns echo throughout many disparate African designs and
knowledge systems.

Fractals, visually analogous to the recurring patterns in nature, might
tell us something about the nature of infinity. We see these nonuniform
patterns in clouds, rivers, leaves, snowflakes, and clustering galaxies. Traditional African mathematics are still poorly understood by those outside the
continent, but the contributors are numerous and complex. To organize a
body of knowledge on the subject would require stumbling through hundreds of languages, anthropology, ethnology, archaeology, economics, and
history. I also think about other expressive cultures like music. Not only the
talking drums but the lutes of all sizes, resonant harps, xylophones, lamel-
laphones (thumb pianos), reed pipes, bellowing trumpets, and stringed
lyres. "By day we saw nothing but woods," said the Carthaginian Hanno on
a fifth-century expedition to the west coast of Africa, "but by night we saw
many fires burning, and heard the sound of flutes and cymbals, and the
beating of drums, and an immense shouting. Fear therefore seized on us,
and the soothsayers bid us quit the island."

The ritualistic, the ceremonial, the joyous dance and music-making seem
to have always been a part of African culture. There is so much we have yet
to explore. And this could all be done, if there were more interest in Africa
beyond resources and missionary work, from outside the continent. African
empires cut across space and time from Carthage to Punt (known as the
land of the gods). The Kingdom of Alodia was a large, multicultural state in
Sudan with extensive cities and provincial governors. There was the Zulu
Nation, and the Kingdom of Mapungubwe in southern Africa. We could
spend this whole book rediscovering such places. Their histories have gotten
uneven attention, yet their contributions to humanity were anything but.

More powers emerged. The Mali Empire of West Africa, from around
1235 to 1670, is one of the best known. Its story began around 1235 CE,
with the Epic of Sundiata, the Lion King and founder of the Mali Empire.

Known for his military prowess and political dexterity, Sundiata Keita's journey is an adventurous tale of exile and redemption. Much of our oldest histories are told in epic form. Sundiata stands next to the epics of *Gilgamesh*, the *Iliad*, and the *Odyssey*. All of which close the enormous distance of time to give us enduring themes.

The *Epic of Sundiata* holds such expressions of truth as, "Yes, the day you are fortunate is also the day when you are the most unfortunate, for in good fortune you cannot imagine what suffering is." While many of the battles and locations are plausible, epic histories also inhabit fantastical worlds. Somewhere between fact and fiction is history. So, we might easily recognize the allegorical nature of the story when Sundiata, a boy, tears a massive baobab tree up from its roots and carries it effortlessly to his mother. The oral nature and mythic elements have caused many scholars to discard this as history. But others say we need to expand our definition. As Joseph Campbell once offered: "Mythology is poetry, it is metaphorical. It has been well said that mythology is the penultimate truth—penultimate because the ultimate cannot be put into words."

During its height, Malian cities like Niani and Timbuktu would have been a more desirable place to live than many European cities in the same time. Mali protected its borders with a military who could put a hundred thousand soldiers in the field, flanked by ten thousand skilled horsemen to form an adept cavalry. Its blacksmiths worked in an iron smelting tradition spanning 2,500 years. So skilled were these venerated artisans that when Moroccan invaders arrived in 1591, the Malian iron workers studied and replicated their firearms by hand. They had tremendous wealth, with gold as the most prized export and taxes levied on its rich commercial trade flowing into its imperial treasury. They were hunters with fantastic abilities in tracking and staying alive in the wilderness. They were monarchs, kings, and queens with the fate of nations at their fingertips. They were also musicians and cooks and mothers and fishermen and teachers, artisans, architects, and scholars.

According to the oral histories, it is out of Sundiata's reign that the "Kurukan Fuga Charter," also known as the "Manden Charter," was created. Once king, Sundiata consolidated the Mandingo Empire (also known as the Wassoulou Empire) and assembled his wisest advisors to create the charter. With the elements of a constitution—including the inalienable rights of human beings, a right to education, the integrity of the country, the abolition of slavery, and freedom of expression—it contains a preamble of seven chapters. Historians cite this document, not the Magna Carta, as the first declaration of human rights, but most people have never heard of it. Sundiata bridged the divide between religious worlds as well.

Nominally Muslim, he prayed to the then foreign God Allah while practicing the spiritual ways of his ancestors. African religion has been denigrated into so-called paganism, idolatry, fetishism, and heathenism. But we might look to late Kenyan philosopher John S. Mbiti for a different perspective. Of African religion, he said it is "as deeply rooted, and as legitimate, as Christianity, Islam, Judaism and Buddhism." Of course, African religions are far from uniform, but according to Mbiti, the missionaries filtering into Africa did not bring God with them; God was already there. An unchanging, infinite, transcendent spirit carried in the hearts and experiences of the people. A God incarnated in everything, dwelling in the smallest ant or thunderous storm. Existing in plants, air, and speech as an intrinsic life force. The Mande called it *nyama*—the mysterious, creative force; the vital or creative force indwelling in all organisms.

Mansa Musa, the tenth Musa and great nephew of Sundiata, was zealously dedicated to spreading Islam throughout Mali. He invested heavily in mosque building, Arabic education, and laid the groundwork for diplomatic success in dealing with Muslim nations. Well known as the wealthiest man in history, Musa lived a life of splendor. When holding court, people trotted in on Arabian horses. Young acrobats turned somersaults with elegance and skill as drums pounded and women performed with bows. Swordsmen put on shows with their weapons, a show of the skill and force from a powerhouse nation on a continent rarely invaded from the outside. All while Mansa walked slowly to his pavilion, ready to hold court and mediate tribal grievances. Maybe he thought about the lucrative trade routes under his control where a constant flow of camels moved across the world's third-largest desert, exporting gold across the brutal Sahara in exchange for salt from Northern Africa, silks from China, tools from Europe, and horses from Arabia. He had a lot of time to think.

The marketplaces in his country were bustling. Under his reign, he expanded Mali's standing as an international Islamic center for learning with multiple universities in Timbuktu. There, merchant-scholars could make a livelihood from selling books. Currently, about seven hundred thousand manuscripts have been recovered. Their pages documented every form of human activity. Local scientists calculated the distance to stars and pondered ways to circumnavigate the earth. Physicians wrote treatises on the uses of surgery for wounds. Astronomers documented a meteor shower in 1593. Religiously Muslim, many of the manuscripts were dedicated to Islamic law and the Koran. But there were also works on black magic, spells, and incantations.

Musa then set his sights on a hajj to Mecca—a pilgrimage every Muslim must make at least once in their lifetime. So, he set out across the blazing-hot desert with a caravan of sixty thousand men including his personal entourage of twelve thousand enslaved people. On horseback, Musa accompanied a baggage train of eighty camels, each carrying three hundred pounds of gold. If you consider that a baby elephant weighs three hundred pounds, you can get a scale of how much gold we're talking about here. One thing I think about is the logistical effort to mobilize such a massive amount of people and animals to travel months across the Sahara, the largest hot desert on the planet. It is a beautiful, cruel, and unforgiving landscape. Covering 3.6 million square miles, it swallows almost a third of the entire African continent. And they traveled on camels, which can be moody and dangerous if not properly trained. Can you imagine the potential problems? Thirst. The leading cause of death in the Sahara. The administration, planning, and management of it all must have been impeccable. This was a testament to a well-governed and relatively safe empire.

Foreign travelers said there was practically no crime. In America, it is difficult for us to imagine a society with no need for an active police force; where disputes and arguments are quickly settled personally, or, if necessary, by respected elders. This was also testament to an extraordinary trade network. At the end of the desert journey, the caravan entered Oualata, now southeast Mauritania and one of Musa's provinces where he would've been greeted by the governor, dignitaries, and armed guards. Then on to Cairo in 1324, and according to one observer he "flooded Cairo with his benefactions. He left no court emir nor holder of a royal office without the gift of a load of gold. The Cairenes made incalculable profits out of him and his suite in buying and selling and giving and taking. They exchanged gold until they depressed its value in Egypt and caused its price to fall."

In fact, he flooded the city with so much gold, the value dropped in Cairo for twelve years.

Beyond Empire

Using Mali as an example, we can also take a critical look at the African past and see what we overlooked when constructing a monumental history. Even when scholars have placed African empires in their rightful place among other notable historical empires, we might ask why we are so fixated on empires in the first place. Let's go back to those twelve thousand slaves. Remember, the ones enslaved by Mansa Musa? Here, it's important to pause and ask, why do humans enslave one another? I don't think a better cross-cultural study of slavery has been written than the masterful *Slavery and Social Death: A Comparative Study* (1982). The Harvard sociology professor Orlando Patterson examined sixty-six societies in the modern, premodern, ancient, and tribal worlds. His painstaking scholarship took him to Rome, Greece, China, Korea, the Islamic kingdoms, medieval Europe, the Caribbean islands, the American South, and Africa. He breaks his findings down to a simple premise: In the parasitic relationship between masters and slaves, the latter experiences natal alienation—in other words, estranged—from their traditions, history, cultural heritage, economic inheritance, and is rendered socially dead. That metamorphosis is achieved through recruitment, a push to the margins of society, and an eventual manumission or death. "There is nothing notably peculiar about the institution of slavery," Patterson wrote. "It has existed from before the dawn of human history . . . in the most primitive societies and also in the most advanced ones."

If we look back on such an all-pervasive human institution and assume we are incapable of committing such atrocities ourselves, we will fail to prevent it in the future. There were peculiarities to US slavery, mainly its racial nature and the juxtaposition of its republican ideals, but slavery was a wholly human institution. We always talk of nature's ruthlessness, but what about us? The only other creature on the planet we know to enslave its own species are ants, and out of approximately fifteen thousand known ant species, slave-making has been recorded in only fifty. We disparage nonhuman species but perhaps they are more humane than we, as Anthony Storr expressed so bluntly: "There is no parallel in nature to our savage treatment of each other. The sombre fact is that we are the cruellest and most ruthless species that has ever walked on earth; and that although we might recoil in horror when we read in the newspaper or history book of the atrocities committed by man upon man, we know in our hearts that each one of us harbours within himself those same savage impulses which lead to murder, to torture and to war."

If our humanity has the potential to connect us, then so does our inhumanity. On the road to African glory, royal regalia, and gold lies a trail of human suffering. Precolonial African slavery was not the same as transatlantic slavery, but powerful empires are rarely built and maintained with free and fair labor. Far more often, they succeed through war, kidnappings, and debt peonage. Sometimes the enslaved could chart a meritocratic rise to become kings, but this was the exception and not the rule. Some argue that chattel slavery in the Americas was worse than its African forms. Indeed, we should explore the Africanist viewpoint. Sometimes words are untranslatable and the word we use for *slavery* may not share the same reality with that practiced in Africa. But what then if we remove the word *chattel*? Indeed, it has been shown that across Africa, slavery varied. In some instances, slaves could own slaves and were treated as family. But these were societies with slaves, not slave societies. Sometimes people even sold themselves into slavery to escape poverty. But all of this still reeks of inequality and inhumanity.

Many Black scholars have bordered on African slavery apologists. As though African kings didn't trade in silks, gold, incense, and concubines. Caravans with hundreds of enslaved women bound for sale in Morocco are documented well before the transatlantic slave trade. They have overlooked those who died from exhaustion overworking in gold mines. Kings also enslaved family members to control the lineage, and the enslaved had no ownership in what they produced. I'm not arguing against the scale, impact, or uniqueness of the transatlantic slave trade—only that, we should be willing to submit to a study of the whole human institution no matter where it is found or in what degree.

Like Europeans, Mesoamericans, Asians, and the like, Africans typically enslaved the "other." The ones who found themselves in bondage were typically outside the ethnic or cultural group of the ones who placed them in that condition. Fascination with the concept of otherness stimulated the minds of many twentieth-century philosophers and psychoanalysts. The other is outside of self, apart and dissimilar. It is one who belongs to a socially subordinate group, those alienated from the center, reduced to labels, and placed on the margins. The other is a fly trapped in the amber of our reductive thoughts. They are defined by ethnicity, sex, sexual orientation, nationality, age, or any other arbitrary means that measures them less human. But the sword is accessible to all who can wield it. So, the marginalized, as a defense, use the same weapons as the oppressor, and so it continues. I am a proponent of self-defense, but remember, when two people wield a sword, someone must die. In this case, it is a perpetual death, as the other is kept outside of our race, our family, our gender, our sexual orientation, outside our nation. In them we refuse to see ourselves. A desire for sameness, fraternity, sorority, and exclusivity subordinates our common denominator—humanity.

Africa does not lie beyond the borders of critical history. So, when we bring a humanity ethic back, we remember the suffering of others who lived lives of subjugation, servitude, and captivity. The integrity required by those principles enables us to remember that those twelve thousand enslaved people carrying Mansa Musa's stuff surely didn't want to walk the almost two thousand miles across the scorching desert. They did it because they had no choice. The human spirit longs to be free.

But the Mansa Musa story also makes me wonder—have we valued wealth more than humanity? In our own time, material capital is so often placed above human capital. We work ourselves to death. We are a nation obsessed with wealth, which, I believe, is why Mansa Musa is the most famous African ruler ever, documented extensively in popular culture, even making a modern *Forbes* list as the richest man in history. If you asked me as a kid what I wanted to be when I grew up, likely I would've said "rich." Our modern world is defined by conspicuous consumption. We are magnetized by overt displays of power. Americans have a boundless respect for individual billionaires like Oprah, Bill Gates, and Elon Musk. As the most opulent, the wealthiest, and the most affluent ruler, Musa has also captured our attention. But when kings rule, someone is being ruled, and with great wealth comes great wealth inequality. The Arabic and European demand for chattel accelerated the African slave trade, but it didn't create it.

What have we missed with our hyper-focus on empire? Asking a different set of questions sends us off on some interesting tangents. For instance, wealth inequality correlates with violent crime, so what did that look like in Mali? Antagonistic tribes bordering the empire. Fugitives, landless wanderers, and tax dodgers roving the West African plain, raiding unsuspecting locals. Making off with their women and cattle.

I've always been interested in the study of social hierarchies. How do we divide labor and differentiate between the skilled and unskilled? How do we divide limited resources among our groups and decide who is in charge? Africa provides a great starting point to study a wide array of social structures and analyze the best ways to structure society. Many on the continent of Africa lived in stateless societies, structuring their interactions based on mutual aid and loose leadership with no kings or chieftains.

"The most distinctive contribution of Africa to human history," said French political scientist Jean-François Bayart, "has been precisely in the civilized art of living reasonably peacefully without a state (or government)." Run by the people, visibly absent any bureaucracy and aristocracy, many African social organizations managed very well. Africans who lived in stateless societies did not see their way of life as chaotic and unpredictable; rather, I suspect, they saw the state as chaotic and unpredictable.

There were federations, and some political organizations looked like republics. In our narrow view of monarchy, we forget that many precolonial African political systems, especially in smaller city-states, were participatory and representative. Dwelling primarily in southeastern Nigeria, the Igbo people have a warning for autocrats and monarchs: *ezebuilo*, meaning "a king is an enemy." America, too, rallied against the tyranny of kings, but with the rise of populist politicians who play to the ideas of the dominant group, many have abandoned the promise of democracy for what they deem as the stability of a single ruler. "Remember," said John Quincy Adams in

1814, "Democracy never lasts long. It soon wastes exhausts and murders itself. There never was a Democracy Yet, that did not commit suicide."

So, what then is the best form of government? Oligarchy, theocracy, socialism, communism, monarchy, colonialism, and military dictatorship, and all gray areas in between offer up examples to study. Is there only one fully legitimate way to select our leaders? I encourage you to look at the various forms of government and decide for yourself. In our own time there is a line being drawn between what some mistakenly see as zero influence democracy and absolute autocracy. But no single-ruler dictatorship is without challenge and no democracy is without influence. Political systems have always been challenged, tested, and strayed from their ideals. And through history, various parts of Africa have tinkered with these political structures with varying results. I'm not a fan of elite, repressive leadership, so if I'm crafting a monumental history, then I'm looking for egalitarian societies rather than empires. For that, Africa also has many examples.

Societies like the Dagaaba of northwestern Ghana, the Tiv of Nigeria, the Northern Somali, Nuer of Sudan, or Bedouin Arabs of North Africa. None of these societies were perfect, but they had the elements of communal rule and shared decision-making. Some still needed to forge centralized leadership in times of war, but they undoubtedly worked better in smaller and midsized populations with strong social bonds or kinship. Either way, they invite us to switch our telescopic view of historical empires to a wide-angle lens to see where people have shared the burden of work and acted on consensus, and where elders offered guidance and village councils offered structure and a space in which disputes could be mediated. Since no one person wielded power, it was less likely to be abused. "It was therefore in the societies without chiefs or kings," says Chancellor Williams, "where African democracy was born and where the concept that the people are sovereign was as natural as breathing. And this is why in traditional Africa, the rights of the individual never came before the rights of the community."

Africa deserves much more attention to gain a true understanding of its nuance and contributions to the world. Indeed, that's the only way to teach history honestly. Without seeing Africa at a finer resolution, past and present, the story of humanity will remain incomplete. Africa has produced great narrators to tell its history, but if no one is around to hear it, does history really make a sound? We will never know how much has been lost—how many scripts were never deciphered and how many libraries were burned, scattered, and looted? What would happen if we discontinued the use of uncritical and sweeping generalizations about entire countries and continents? I am a testament to the fact that we have much to gain. My spirit and mind are richer from my studies of Africa. I think about a book that once lit up my youth, *Why Mosquitoes Buzz in People's Ears*, a West African fable about the consequences of lying, by Leo Dillon, the first Black artist to receive the Caldecott Award for his illustrations. And I think about what we can gain by bringing the best of Africa forward to America. Its people, its stories, its culture, and its humanity in all its glory and flaws.

Coming to America

What if there had been an autonomous migration of Africans to the Americas by the free will of Africans? When speaking of his predecessor, Mansa Musa tells Ibn Amir Hijab, the governor of Cairo, how the Musa before him set out toward the Americas to find a land beyond the sea:

> We belong to a house which hands on the kingship by inheritance. The king who was my predecessor did not believe that it was impossible to discover the furthest limit of the Atlantic Ocean and wished vehemently to do so. So, he equipped 200 ships filled with men and the same number equipped with gold, water, and provisions enough to last them for years, and said to the man deputed to lead them: "Do not return until you reach the end of it or your provisions and water give out." They departed and a long time passed before anyone came back. Then one ship returned, and we asked the captain what news they brought. He said: "Yes, O Sultan, we traveled for a long time until there appeared in the open sea [as it were] a river with a powerful current. Mine was the last of those ships. The [other] ships went on ahead but when they reached that place they did not return and no more was seen of them and we do not know what became of them. As for me, I went about at once and did not enter that river." But the sultan

disbelieved him. Then that sultan got ready 2,000 ships, 1,000 for himself and the men whom he took with him and 1,000 for water and provisions. He left me to deputize for him and embarked on the Atlantic Ocean with his men. That was the last we saw of him and all those who were with him, and so I became king in my own right.

This is a fascinating story. An African ruler with the resources to send fleets West to explore beyond the known world. It is beyond possible that Africans could have made it to the Americas prior to Columbus. But just because something is plausible does not make it provable. I was floored when I read linguist Ivan Van Sertima's book *They Came Before Columbus* (1976), where he made the shocking claim that Africans established contact in the Americas twice. According to him, the ancient Egyptians arrived before Abu Bakri, and not only did they make it, but they also established extensive trading relationships, forming the basis of New World civilizations and cultures. Like Van Sertima, I, too, believed that intellectual racism undermined African contributions to the world. And I remain open to hard evidence, but Van Sertima did not present enough of it. Many have taken his work and replaced one form of mythmaking with another. For me, his research stands as a provocation for other scholars to look for proof where others have not, challenging a Eurocentric worldview that has, undoubtedly, had us overlook evidence that other societies did a lot more in history than we think they did.

As the keepers of Malian history, the griots are remarkably silent on the achievements of Mansa Musa and his predecessor. Perhaps this was a coincidence. Or maybe Musa's public approval took a deep dive. Perhaps Musa made new enemies with his relentless slaving campaigns. Maybe Malian historians found nothing praiseworthy about him and his predecessor. One who set out on an impractical discovery mission. The other who squandered state wealth to impress the Islamic outsiders, traveling to Cairo to worship a foreign God in which many of them didn't believe. Maybe Musa made even more enemies as he moved Mali further away from their original cults and religions. Rulers before him adopted Islam marginally in comparison. But for many, Musa's was a persistent and intrusive attempt to force an alien and undesired religion on the populace. This highlights the problems when we only have an unbalanced history to explore. Remember, the griots were praise singers, concerned with bringing only the best of the Mali Empire into the public sphere.

It's unlikely we will ever answer these questions. But, like the story of Louis Armstrong in the beginning of this chapter, we can name other concrete connections between Africa and America. Take for instance a man named Onesimus, kidnapped from the Akan region of modern Ghana in 1706, who ended up in Boston just as frequent smallpox epidemics tore through the city. It's a ghastly virus. It spread with merciless consistency through extended contact with an infected person or their bodily fluids, accompanied by fever, headache, abdominal pain, vomiting, and death. Small blisters swollen with pus appear on the face, arms, legs, and torso. By most accounts, it spread more easily than COVID-19. In areas with no preexisting immunity, it killed up to 30 percent of the population. We know with certainty that Onesimus introduced what was called inoculation to the colonies. His enslaver, prominent minister Cotton Mather, wrote down the process as Onesimus described it to him. After drawing fluid from a smallpox pustule it was then transferred into a cut made on a healthy person, reducing the rate of infection and conferring lifelong immunity. There were no medical schools. Physicians were physicians in name but still used home remedies. And the colonists were highly fearful of African medical knowledge.

Mather shared the procedure with Dr. Zabdiel Boylston, who conducted it with stunning success. In fact, the inscription on Boylston's headstone still reads, "First Introduced the Practice of Inoculation into America." There again, Anglocentrism renders Africa invisible. Like other American history, medical history has been written in connection with Britain, Germany, and other countries of Europe, as though they were the only people concerned with public wellness and human health. But if we look back to Africa and those who came from it, we will see that many of the stones in America's foundation come from the African continent.

6

Scattered Lives

I am black; I am in total fusion with the world, in sympathetic affinity with the earth, losing my id in the heart of the cosmos and the white man, however intelligent he may be, is incapable of understanding Louis Armstrong or songs from the Congo.

I am black, not because of a curse, but because my skin has been able to capture all the cosmic effluvia. I am truly a drop of sun under the earth.

—Frantz Fanon

In 1903, in the dark recesses of a cave in southwest England, the fragmented remains of a man were found. He lay 5'5" and weighed about 140 pounds. A great hunter, he was well fed, tracking wild game and gathering oysters by hand, then supplementing his diet with handfuls of fruits and berries. Now approximately ten thousand years old, he was in his twenties when he died. And judging by the huge hole in his skull, it was a violent death. Found in Somerset's Cheddar Gorge, they called him Cheddar Man. It's easy to imagine someone from England with dark brown hair and blue eyes, but in 2018 DNA models showed a 76 percent probability that he had "dark to black" skin. On the strength of this evidence, paleontological reconstructionists sculpted his likeness accordingly. Media outlets picked it up, and Cheddar Man went viral. In disbelief, many white Britons called for a secondary investigation. Some called it a hoax, saying he was an escaped slave. On the other hand, one organization put his face on a UK Black History Month poster alongside composer Ignatius Sancho and abolitionist Mary Prince.

Science pops up periodically to challenge our notions of race. Cheddar Man reminds us that the migration of African people began well before slavery and racism. But he also shows the near impossibility of discussing African migration absent slavery and racism. And while the discovery of Cheddar Man provoked goofy memes and racial bigotry, he also offers us a solution, that we might one day move beyond the dark call of prejudice and into our shared human history.

The Cradle of Humanity is the largest bridge to connect us all but is one that's seldom traveled. Origin stories are subject to change with new evidence, but complex research and penetrating scrutiny uphold simple facts. In this case, every human being comes from a single source, Africa. And experts, with job titles that compel you to grab the nearest dictionary, have spent the last several decades testing this hypothesis. Paleoanthropologists compared the anatomy and structure of fossilized remains. Geneticists independently sequenced genomes from participants all over the world, mapping our epic migration through DNA. Challengers occasionally arise with fresh evidence that Homo sapiens firsts evolved elsewhere, but thus far, their theories are unconvincing. Evolutionary biologists, archaeologists, forensic anthropologists, climatologists, and consistent findings in science laboratories all attest to this one simple fact: What would be recognizable as our modern human ancestors evolved in Africa some three hundred thousand years ago. Before these early humans, there were other variations of upright, bipedal, linguistically capable branches of hominid such as Neanderthals living side by side. But we are the ones who survived, Homo sapiens, dubbed the "wise" because of our brain size. It is a span of time of which we know painfully little, which, I think, is why it is such a difficult bridge to cross.

If we applied modern thoughts about life and intelligence, we would look back with prejudice and only see the ineptitude in the small bands of humans simply surviving and roaming at the mercy of nature. These same uncritical stigmas are still applied to indigenous people across the world who hunt, gather, and live close to the land. According to social scientists, we all generalize to make sense of the world for ourselves as we move about it from day to day. All politicians are bloodsuckers. Pit bulls are vicious. Atheists are overbearing about their nonbelief. Overgeneralizations live in the cave of ignorance morphing into stereotypes, and this is especially true of how we typically view early humans.

What if we looked at them as antecedents and ancestors, thus removing the separateness? What if we appreciated modern hunter-gatherers as connectors of our ancient past and present? They are the ones who will carry our oldest human practices into the future. Then we might bring the best of this history forward. It was difficult for me to create the clearest picture here, because the dates back this far shift with every new scientific discovery, but let's explore from what we have. Those early humans were survivors. Around seventy thousand years ago, they almost vanished. Details are sketchy. Some say their world got cold; others claim mass disease. But whatever it was, it almost rendered them—us—extinct. One study estimates fewer than two thousand reproductive adults survived the catastrophe. It was also around this time that they began to walk, scattering across the globe. We know this from the trail of bone tools, spearheads, and fossils they left behind. They split apart, cutting the umbilical cord from a proverbial mother Africa. Setting off to new lands, they hiked through unknown territory in Asia. Some settled while others kept going. They crossed the sea to Australia around fifty thousand years ago. Other groups left Africa and started their journey, spreading all over Europe around forty-six thousand years ago. They walked through modern-day Iran and trekked into India. Some credible studies estimate that the largest migration to the Americas occurred some fourteen thousand years ago. This might have been the first African diaspora, and it includes every single one of us. By all available evidence, we are all descendants of those intrepid explorers. People who braved the unknown in the first human migration off the African continent, never yielding to their hardscrabble existence. We survived because they survived. Our DNA contains the breadcrumbs that, time and time again, point us back to our common ancestral home.

We might wonder what the future will uncover about the first 150,000 years or more of human experience in Africa. This period is labeled prehistoric, and while that simply means before the written record, it makes it seem as though it has no value. Most histories choose to begin the human story within the last five thousand years with the advent of empires and statecraft. Despite these narrow views, with imagination, we can look back to see people with ancient skill and perseverance. If so, we might admire their strength. Modern-day scientists developed human athletic paleobiology to help them better understand how these ancestors could outperform an Olympic athlete in nearly any category. Early humans moved over long distances regularly, lifting, hunting, running, carrying, pushing, pulling, ducking, climbing, hurling, stretching, building, fighting, and even creating art.

In South Africa east of Cape Town, some seventy-three thousand years ago, there was art made with shell and ocher. On cave walls, they painted the symbols that would form the basis of science, words, and civilization. They saw things as they were, then imagined what they could be. Making axes from stones and blades from bones. They valued kinship. They bereaved the dead, then buried them. They formed complex social relationships based on communication and cooperation. They exchanged goods over hundreds of miles. The ones who planned settlements did so around the migrations of game. They started fires and cooked over them. They adorned themselves with beads and shells. These were our common ancestors, and they were the original founders. But what more is there to be discovered? It is astonishing that we have existed for so long but know strikingly little beyond the last five thousand years of our existence. We should recover what we can to understand everywhere that we have gone.

Into Antiquity

So far, we have argued that we can connect with one another by digging, sifting, and excavating our humanity to bridge our scattered existence. And we can still carry that humanism forward as we look at Africans exploding out of antiquity. By 1700 BCE, the African diaspora included a vast patchwork of people who looked, believed, and thought differently. Politically, within the continental borders of Africa, nations alternated between war and peace, welcoming and excluding immigrants. At times, they thought their cultures superior. Ancient Egypt was the envy of the ancient world. Purposefully and inadvertently, nations informed one another. Technology, culture, and religion spread through the world like fragrance molecules from a diffuser. And as Europeans and Asians entered Africa, Africans entered Europe and Asia. They entered Greece by way of Nubia and Egypt, where they were called *Aethiops*, a term applied to darker people, not to be confused with the state of Ethiopia.

The ancient world was so much more diverse than we imagine. The familiarity was so strong that Homer describes Zeus and the other Olympian gods feasting with Ethiopians. They fought under Xerxes in the Battle of Marathon (480–79 BCE) and in the Second Punic War (218–201 BCE), when Black Carthaginians were recorded fighting in the invasion of Italy, some serving atop war elephants. A fraction were enslaved in Greece and the multiethnic society of Rome, but many more went there for jobs, working as merchants, soldiers, gladiators, actors, boxers, laborers, craftspeople, and countless other occupations sustaining the Roman economy. Much of our curiosity about the African diaspora leads us to look at how Black people reacted to these new environments and how they were treated in them. And antiquity offers us some of the last images in which they were bridged by a global sense of human community.

Wars came and went. People worked and died. But African diasporic culture spread through cuisine, literature, music, and philosophy. I've always been fascinated by how the African diaspora cross-pollinated the ancient world, and one of the most profound examples of this is through spirituality. African beliefs took hold in ancient Rome, spreading through the cult of Isis, the birth-giving mother goddess. Depicted with her arms outstretched to the heavens, she was the antithesis of the male warrior gods, who crafted weapons to take human life. In contrast, Isis gave all life existence. She was the protector and loving wife who transcended all other deities. Born in Egypt, her cult gained a large following in Rome. And even when Romans converted to Christianity, Isis was reborn through the Orthodox Christian Virgin Mary. It was common to incorporate other deities into Christian worship as the religion spread. The rebirth of Isis is one of the most plausible explanations for the dark-skinned or so-called Black Madonnas that adorn the walls and, as statues, stand in some five hundred churches across Europe. Some scholars attribute the dark skin of these Black Madonnas to hundreds of years of smoke from the church's candles, as though the tone is merely an accumulation of grime over the centuries. But on close inspection, this smoke and accumulation are not uniform across the paintings. The reverence for a Holy Mother with dark skin may be difficult to comprehend when so many Black and Brown women have been denigrated throughout modern history, but it is a strongly backed possibility.

But in the early Middle Ages, theologians began associating the color black with spiritual darkness, and as the transatlantic slave trade began spewing this notion of Black racial inferiority, these images were developed less frequently. And yet, this Black icon of humility and motherly love has loomed large within Christian iconology. The fusion and the interconnectedness of different people have always inspired me. That is why I have tried to find the truth in our similarities, and the bridges go both ways. Ethiopia became a very early adopter of Christianity, and there we see major clements of Christianity in Africa. I couldn't imagine hiking up a mountain to attend church, but there you can find monasteries and places of worship carved into mountains piercing the clouds.

Let me say again that people literally carved churches into the side of mountains six hundred feet high. One is the Abuna Yemata Guh in Tigray, northeast of Ethiopia. Built in the fifth century, the holy structures sit 650 feet up, as if built to reach heaven itself. To get there, you must climb a sheer wall. Dedicated to Abuna Yemata (Abba Yem'ata), one of the Nine Saints who were key to the spread of Christianity in Ethiopia, these structures show us something all peoples have had in common—a longing for something divine, to somehow be closer to heaven and to the god(s).

Extraordinary individuals from the diaspora appear throughout premodern European history. One was a martyr. An archetype that always forces the question, would you die for a cause? Saint Maurice did. In records, he appears as a third-century Christian Egyptian military leader in charge of more than six thousand soldiers in the legendary Theban Legion of Rome. Sent to quash a rebellious group of Christian peasants in Gaul, Maurice faced a decision. Serve the orders of the future emperor Maximian or the orders of God in heaven. Maurice chose the latter. He refused to fight his spiritual siblings. According to the records of the church, he defied Rome and reportedly said, "We are your soldiers, but we are also servants of the true God. We owe you military service and obedience, but we cannot renounce God who is our creator and master. . . . We have arms in our hands, but we do not resist because we would rather die innocent than live by any sin." For this, his group faced decimation or "removal of the tenth," a terrifying military punishment where they summarily executed one of every ten soldiers at random. After this display, the men were threatened with total annihilation should they continue their refusal. "They made no resistance," says a later account, "but, dropping their arms, suffered themselves to be butchered like innocent sheep. The ground was covered with their dead bodies, and streams of blood flowed on every side."

For his sedation of fear, for his valor, and for his Christian piety, the church canonized Maurice as a saint. His main cathedral stands in Magdeburg, Germany. Maurice's act of resistance bridges him with other famous dissenters. What does it say about us that so many have put their lives and livelihood on the line as a matter of conscience, like Thích Quảng Đức, who burned himself alive, dying of self-immolation on a busy Saigon intersection in protest of the South Vietnamese government's persecution of Buddhists? Or how three years later, Muhammad Ali sacrificed title and reputation after his refusal to join the military and go to war in the same country. Albeit for different causes, all three made self-sacrifice a weapon of dissent.

Near the fortress ruins on Hadrian's Wall, at Burgh-by-Sands in England, there is an inscription that references "numerus of Aurelian Moors." Known in the third century by the Romans as Aballava, it is thought to be one of the first settlements of modern Africans in England. The Aurelian Moors were a specialist cavalry unit, so named for their African roots and after the Emperor Marcus Aurelius. These same so-called Moors, a word that generally meant Muslim or a person with skin darker than the average Englishman (Shakespeare described the character of Othello as Moor), ruled Spain for eight hundred years. Not everyone described as a Moor was from Africa, but many were. African people also discovered Europe and not just the other way around. The libraries of Moorish Spain attracted the brightest scholars and contained over one million manuscripts. It was a bookseller's dream. Comparably, the largest Christian libraries had at most two thousand volumes. Islamic knowledge laid the foundations for the Renaissance. Islamic religion and customs left an indelible stamp on the country, which is still visible in the great mosques that history left behind. Knowledge production was its own industry, like mining or banking, showing us that information is one of the most lasting elements of human history.

The Middle Ages in Europe are, without question, one of the most recognizable periods in human history. The folklore of Robin Hood and King Arthur comes to mind. Thoughts of knights clad in battle armor are easily recalled. Stone castles with moats, stained-glass-windowed monasteries, straw-roofed villages, and brilliantly green pastures capture our imaginations, along with kings, queens, ladies, lords, monks, friars, musketeers, and peasants. We see these images, and yet there is something that many of us are blindly unaware of—there were Black people in Europe. Not all enslaved people in Europe were African. Nor were all African people in Europe enslaved.

At the end of this period, John Blanke, a talented trumpeter in the royal court of Henry VII and Henry VIII, stands out among his pale Anglo counterparts on a sixty-foot-long manuscript because of his dark skin. We know little about him, but he seemed to live the life of a privileged musician whose music filled the halls of Tudor castles in England. He was paid twenty shillings a month in 1507, three times the rate of a servant. Finely dressed in gray and yellow livery, he played at a tournament in Westminster, and likely played at banquets, funerals, executions, weddings, and coronations. I wonder if he felt his difference as he pressed his cavalry trumpet against his lips. And John Blanke was ambitious when it came to his salary, boldly asking the king to double his pay when a senior trumpeter died. And he was far from the only African to appear in England. Described by the words *black*, *Ethiopian*, *Moor*, or *blackamoor*, these people lived lives in cities such as London, Plymouth, and Bristol, and in villages throughout England.

Anytime I mention the African presence in medieval Europe, I'm sure to mention an oil painting that I admire. In Portuguese it is called *Chafariz D'El Rey*, which translates in English to *The King's Fountain*. Painted around 1570 by an unknown Flemish man, it shows the oldest district in Lisbon, Alfama. The painting depicts a lively street scene. The busy atmosphere finds numerous people plying their trades and living their lives around the fountain of El Rei. Women emerge from windows to dry clothing. Constables are seen detaining a drunken man. Everywhere in small groups are people conversing. Boatmen unload grain and carry passengers. There appear jugglers, merchants, maids, and even a stray dog.

Many of those in the painting were Black. They were workers, merchants, and one appears as a knight on horseback. All expatriates from Africa, likely, many were from the Kingdom of Kongo. The visible goal of the painting is to explain what is happening in the moment. We might find this striking, but in the painting, they were not highlighted as anything less than ordinary. It is believed that as much as 10 percent of the population in Lisbon during this time was African, and they appeared within the highest and lowest rungs of society. This is the image of Black people so often obscured by the legacy of transatlantic slavery. One that has removed ordinary Black existence from a past where they interacted in infinitely dynamic ways. Even I was amazed by the Afro-Portuguese knight on horseback, draped in a garment officially endowed with the herald of the Order of Santiago. And the astonishment will continue, until the retelling of this history ingrains a new revolutionary understanding, that Black people have been self-conscious actors capable of adapting to and influencing any social situation in which they have found themselves.

Forced Migrations

We are now, finally, going to talk about the forced displacement that scattered millions of Black people across the globe. Nothing negatively impacted the African diaspora more than imperialism, colonialism, and slavery. Well, maybe the near human extinction mentioned earlier in this chapter, but nothing since then. The transatlantic slave trade dragged African people kicking and screaming through the Caribbean and Americas. Indeed, slavery was an old practice, but in the modern era its attachment to race gave it terrible new dimensions. This is an important breaking point in human history. If in the sixteenth century, race entered the lexicon of Europe, it was certainly fueled by navigation and increased encounters with strange people, plants, and animals, all of which they felt compelled to analyze. But before the explosion of the so-called discovery and consolidation of racial power, Europe was viewed as foreign and perhaps even as a backcountry to the rest of the world.

Times weren't all bad, but Europe experienced political turmoil, chaos, poverty, religious fanaticism with its crusades, and periods of scientific repression in the name of God, not to mention the Bubonic plague, which is believed to have been responsible for the death of millions in the fourteenth century and left rotting bodies in the streets. With no explanation for the plague, Christian leaders often targeted their Jewish neighbors as its source, using the plague as an excuse to reup their prosecution of a people long despised as the despicable other. Jewish families were barely tolerated, ostracized based on ethnic background and religion, and treated as outside of God in the ecclesiastical hierarchy. And throughout history, near and far, they were indiscriminately massacred. But here is where we also find foundations of anti-Black racism in America. Yale historian Paul Freedman connects this inhumanity to our own time and how this behavior escalates: "'Mexicans are lazy, or dirty, or unintelligent.' But when suddenly it's 'they are rapists, murderers, a danger to public order,' this elevates contempt to a different order of magnitude; they are an immediate danger." We will see this again in later chapters when we cover Black oppression in America.

The forced migration of Black Africans to America was not simply ethnic—not like the Italian history of enslaving people from Slavic countries (Armenia, Russia, Bulgaria) to sell in the Middle East—nor simply religious, neither was it captivity for prisoners of war. This time, it was systematically organized around profit and race. As historian Robin Blackburn argues:

> The powers that successfully colonized the Americas had their roots in medieval kingdoms, each of which displayed a propensity for intolerance and persecution, territorial expansion, colonial settlement, arrogant dispositions on subject peoples, and theological justification of slavery, racial exclusion, and sordid enterprise. Late Europeans were prone to stigmatize the infidel and the pagan and to entertain fanciful notions of 'wild' or 'monstrous' peoples. The mental habits of racism and colonialism were born out of the medieval world."

Global anti-Blackness acted as the glue of Black unity. If Black people didn't agree on much else, most understood the realities of globe-spanning racism and harbored a desire to triumph over it. Most understood that the sixteenth century saw Europeans cut up humanity into distinct colors and groups based on hair texture, lips, eyes, and other arbitrary features. And most still realize that this othering and placement of Black people on the bottom of a racial hierarchy haunts our current reality five centuries later. The European imagination of Black African people as barbarous, wild, and savage was projected all over the world, even in how Africans saw themselves.

The transatlantic slave trade accelerated this worldview—Blacks were looked at as commodities and described as "well fleshed," "strong-limbed," "lusty," "sickly," "robust," "healthy," "scrawny," and "unblemished." This justified the bodies fastened together two by two, thrown into the bowels of ships with irons riveted on their wrists and legs. Over more than four hundred years, millions of African people were pulled through the Atlantic. Bodies magnetized by the economic greed and avarice of the global ruling elite. The history of the Middle Passage is a story of unyielding moroseness. At least forty-one thousand individual slaving expeditions were documented between 1514 and 1866, making the Atlantic Ocean a heavily trafficked highway of human chattel.

The government coffers were overflowing with slave money in nations such as Portugal, England, Spain, France, Brandenburg-Prussia, and Denmark. But Africa has its own story to tell for its role in the slave trade. To meet the global demand for Black bodies, they sold their continental sons and daughters. As Britain became more aggressive on global abolition in the nineteenth century, King Ghezo of Dahomey, who grew wealthy from slavery, said in the 1840s that he would meet all British demands short of abolishing slavery: "The slave trade is the ruling principle of my people. It is the source and the glory of their wealth . . . the mother lulls the child to sleep with notes of triumph over an enemy reduced to slavery."

Descendants of those the kings enslaved still feel the pain of its history. Benin businessman Placide Ogoutade spoke for many in 2018 when he said, "Our anger at the families who sold our ancestors will never go away until the end of the world."

I wish we were, but we aren't done with forced migrations yet. A massive amount of study has been given to the transatlantic slave trade, but why have mainstream histories ignored slavery flowing in the other direction? We could successfully argue that the transatlantic chattel slave trade had more impact and scope, but go back and try telling that to victims of human trafficking in the slave societies of East Africa and Asia.

Bloody raids provided a steady stream of people from the East African coast for deportation across the Indian Ocean since the days of the ancient Egyptians, Greeks, and Babylonians. Overlooking the Indian Ocean slave trade in our study of forced migrations is like ignoring an elephant in your kitchen while you casually make your lunch. It lasted longer than thirteen centuries. Depopulation led to the demise of cities and whole civilizations. Africans from present-day Mozambique and the Sudan were unloaded on the docks bordering the Red Sea and Persian Gulf. Afro-Palestinians, Afro-Turks, Afro-Iranians, and various other groups trace their roots back to this history. The Afro-Iraqis were trafficked from Zanzibar to work the sugarcane plantations in Iraq. In 1869, they staged the fifteen-year-long Zanj revolt in a bid for freedom. Human bondage pushed the Black diaspora eastward over the Sahara, through East Africa, across the Red Sea into Asia. This slavery was older (800–1900 CE), lasted longer, and was no less malignant. Slavery in Mauritania wasn't outlawed until 2007.

No doubt much of American history is inward looking, but I must wonder if global slavery isn't spoken of more because activists felt it might undermine their position. On the other hand, the number one weapon of US slavery apologists is predictable: "Slavery has happened all over the world and is still happening, and it is an evil of humanity." This is true, but it isn't argued as a point of truth and universal inhumanity; it is an attempt to get Black people to stop talking about slavery in the United States and its lasting consequences. But here I am guided by the eloquent words of Aimé Césaire, French Martinican poet and politician, who said, "My mouth shall be the mouth of those calamities that have no mouth, my voice the freedom of those who break down in the prison holes of despair."

To get to the roots of human oppression, we must hear it wherever it speaks. Studying the Indian Ocean slave trade gives us a broader view of racism as a global phenomenon. The same theories of African inferiority used by Europeans were used as justification for the bloodletting and indiscriminate violence all over the world. At other points, Arabic enslavers worked Black Africans alongside white Christians who were seized every year to labor across the Middle East. Retired Ohio State University professor Robert Davis had his words and book, *Christian Slaves, Muslim Masters: White Slavery in the Mediterranean, the Barbary Coast, and Italy, 1500–1800*, summarized in an article that read: "Enslavement was a very real possibility for anyone who traveled in the Mediterranean, or who lived along the shores in places like Italy, France, Spain, and Portugal, and even as far north as England and Iceland. Pirates from cities along the Barbary Coast in North Africa . . . would raid ships in the Mediterranean and Atlantic, as well as seaside villages to capture men, women, and children. The impact of these attacks was devastating—France, England, and Spain each lost thousands of ships, and long stretches of the Spanish and Italian coasts were almost completely abandoned by their inhabitants. At its peak, the destruction and depopulation of some areas probably exceeded what European slavers would later inflict on the African interior." Imagine Brown- and Black-faced slave raiders capturing white cargo along the coasts of Britain, Ireland, Italy, and Iceland.

As European military power expanded, Arab Muslim nations looked to African regions below the Sahara for people to enslave. The island of Zanzibar, Tanzania, was home to one of the last highly visible international slave markets, which began around the seventeenth century and didn't end until 1873 when the British shut it down. Millions of Africans ended up in Eurasia. Curious, I looked to the farthest corners of Russia, wanting to know about the African diaspora there. And I found that the nation had no significant contact with the African slave trade. But there were isolated examples, such as the mixed-race Alexander Pushkin, father of Russian literature, known as the "Shakespeare of Russia." He boasted his African ancestry saying, "No Russian man of letters besides me may number a Negro among his ancestors." He again shows how normal it was for African-descended people to thrive anywhere given equal opportunity and privilege. There was also an enclaved group called the Afro-Abkhazians. There is little to go on other than the fact of their existence as most sources are in Russian, but almost anywhere you look for an African diasporic presence, you will find it.

Throughout history, many Africans went to Asia on religious pilgrimages, as part of the free labor market. Many Africans moved back and forth freely through Asia as the dynamics of slavery were different there. For instance, in India, Africans were largely needed for the military as more trade required more soldiers to protect the wealth. The earlier discussed slave markets continued stretching the African diaspora east. Ironically, in Sri Lanka, enslaved Africans fought on opposing sides. Some fought for the Portuguese who enslaved them; others fought for the Kandyan Kingdom.

According to one source, two Afro-Indian dynasties rose out of this history, the Sachin and Janjira. Though his reign was short-lived (1487–1489), former army commander Sayf al-Din traced his lineage back to Ethiopia. For the Middle East, it is important to remember that Arabs were not defined by race but by common language and the religion of Islam. Africans entered the Middle East, not only as enslaved people, but also as free men, interacting through solidarity of faith. We might also revel in exceptional examples of Africans in Japan like Yasuke, an African man, who arrived in Japan in the late sixteenth century alongside Jesuit missionary Alessandro Valignano. The story is sketchy, but several accounts record his arrival. It was said that he found favor with the *daimyō* Oda Nobunaga, a lord who controlled provinces and a towering figure in Japanese history, and became his retainer. But one part of the story that struck me was, when villagers saw this tall Black man, it is said they made him strip and rub his skin to ensure he wasn't covered with ink. And it leads us back to the curiosity and the Othering. One of the biggest considerations of a diaspora is how those migrating are treated and interact as they move about their new homes. Indeed, marginalization and acceptance are recurring themes that bridge the discussion.

The New World Order

The Age of Colonialism blended into the Age of Imperialism. Europeans ate up new lands like the mythical Wendigo, a malicious creature from First Nations' folklore who eats human flesh and only grows hungrier the more it eats. It has been said that the sun never set on the British Empire, because its territories were so expansive the light always shined on at least one of them. Europeans occupied 67 percent of the earth's surface by 1874, and by 1915,

Europeans gobbled territory at a rate of 240,000 square miles per year, holding 85 percent of the earth's surface under their control as colonies, protectorates, dependencies, dominions, and commonwealths. Time and time again, world military powers choose to rule directly, indirectly, or economically over other nations. The asphyxiating growth of European powers choked off the life and resources of those nations that could not industrialize quickly enough to offer major resistance. Here Aimé Césaire lends his voice again:

> Their wars of conquest were disguised as wars of liberation. What, fundamentally, is colonization? To agree on what it is not: neither evangelization, nor a philanthropic enterprise, nor a desire to push back the frontiers of ignorance, disease, and tyranny, nor a project undertaken for the greater glory of God, nor an attempt to extend the rule of law. To admit once for all, without flinching at the consequences, that the decisive actors here are the adventurer and the pirate, the wholesale grocer and the ship owner, the gold digger and the merchant, appetite and force, and behind them, the baleful projected shadow of a form of civilization which, at a certain point in its history, finds itself obliged, for internal reasons, to extend to a world scale the competition of its antagonistic economies.

The proliferation of white supremacist ideas traveled along with its ships and cargo, everywhere manifesting itself a little differently. Since 90 percent of enslaved people were taken to Latin America and the Caribbean Islands (only 4.6 percent came to the United States), they deserve special consideration. Now making up twenty-six distinct countries, known for sunny winters and endless hotels, the Caribbean has a brutal legacy of slavery. The islands were once home to the world's most profitable sugar plantations. There was a direct correlation between sugar production and a higher demand for enslaved Africans. Ironically, the sweetest stuff on Earth caused the most bitter brutality. And we might wonder how many people died so that European aristocrats could have sugar for their tea. Black people make up most of the population of these island nations, all harkening back to the slave trade. Some would stay while others would be seasoned before a destination in North America. In 2021, Barbados swore in Sandra Mason, its first president, to the sound of a twenty-one-gun salute, finally cutting its four-hundred-year-old colonial ties.

Though Latin America takes pride in its multiracial society and lack of Jim Crow, they enacted a racial hierarchy much more complex than Anglo colonies. The sex, sexual assault, and rape occurred at such a scale that it rendered a simple racial hierarchy impossible. There were Spanish aristocrats (born in Spain) at the top, then *creoles* (descendants of Spanish but born in the Americas), followed by *mestizos* (white European and indigenous), *mulattoes* (white European and African), indigenous people, then enslaved Africans at the bottom.

Lighter-skinned Latin and Hispanic people moved to the top of the social structure and darker-skinned to the bottom. Most people have never fathomed how subversive racism is. By 1795, in the Spanish empire, if you were a mulatto you could write to the Spanish crown and purchase whiteness. It was a process called the *gracias al sacar*, or "thanks for the pardon." Allowing one to erase "the defect that you suffer from birth and leave you able and capable as if you did not have it, repealing this time in your favor whatever laws, ordinances or constitutions speak otherwise." In other words, you were no longer barred from professions, could marry into white families, and enjoyed all the legal and social privileges of your new status. You got a white card. It was the legal version of skin bleaching.

These policies lay at the foundation of a Latin American and Caribbean anti-Black racism that is seldom discussed. Enduring racism in South American countries and islands like the Dominican Republic have caused many to distance themselves from their African roots. And it is in this era that the African diaspora has become synonymous with the Black diaspora. Not to be confused, I would argue that either of these are simply terms to suggest people who trace a common ancestry to Africa, recognize the pride and struggle of that circumstance, and find some political or ethnic solidarity in that fact. Many have confused the diaspora with a solidarity through slavery and victimization, but this is not true. The diaspora is older than modern racism. So, while there is shared oppression, we should remember it is not confined to that. It also represents an honoring of history and ancestors, an appreciation of that beauty, and a connectedness through political identity. It is a sense of connection and collaboration and recognition. It is Pan-Africanism.

The African diaspora is present everywhere. Not even tiny islands like Antigua (only thirteen miles across) were left untouched by slavery. And there were so many Africans enslaved in Brazil that the country now has the second largest Black population outside of Nigeria. There is not a single country in Central or South America that did not receive the children of Africa. People in Columbia, Nicaragua, Belize, Guatemala, Venezuela, and every other South American nation have those who trace their roots back to Africa. Many are surprised, for instance, that over one million people in Mexico track enslaved Africans as their ancestors and identify as Afro-Mexican. From the beginning of colonization, enslaved Africans resisted capture by establishing maroon communities of slavery fugitives living in the mountains and other far-off locations in Mexico. The formerly enslaved Gaspar Yanga established one of these communities and withstood almost forty years of Spanish assault. It was Afro-Mexican soldiers who also helped cast off Spanish rule in the 1810–1821 War of Independence. In Mexico, as in much of Latin America, African contributions to history have been ignored and forgotten. But rather than joining with the African diaspora, based on class or common ancestry, to challenge the racial structure, many Mexican and Latin advocacy groups tried blending into whiteness. In this way the caste system continues. There is even a phrase, *mejorar la raza*, which means to "better or whiten the race."

Due to its involvement in the Underground Railroad, Canada has often been seen as a historic beacon of equality, absent of raced-based discrimination. This, of course, is one of the great myths of Canadian history. They, too, saw enslaved people as less than human. Historians estimate there were around 4,200 enslaved people in Canada between 1671 and 1834, about a quarter of whom were African. The code noir, or Black code, adopted from France in 1743, was used to some extent in Canada, threatening hellish consequences on anyone heroic enough to run from the clutches of slave life, including but not limited to having their ears cut off and being branded with the *fleur-de-lis* as punishment. In the 1960s, an all-Black town called Africville in Nova Scotia was bulldozed and destroyed. Prior, the city of Halifax had refused to provide basic city services enjoyed elsewhere by white residents. Africville had no running water, sewage, garbage disposal, streetlights, or paved roads. It was the town dumping ground. Slaughter-houses, incinerators, an infectious disease hospital, and the prison were built there. All of this on top of the Black residents, who had been there since before Halifax was founded in 1749. But they had a sense of commu-nity until the city was demolished with little to no input from the residents. The centuries-long effort to censor this history still far outweighs the time and effort it will take to integrate it.

Full Circle

With Pan-African visions, Black people in the United States who were still fighting against legalized, de jure white supremacy joined with Africans fighting against European imperialism and anti-Black racism. The first ma-jor campaign on the African continent was Algeria's anti-colonial revolu-tion where more than one million French settlers (colons) lived. On November 1, 1954, after six years of fighting, more than seven hundred thousand colons fled Algeria for France after it achieved independence from France. In 1960, Kwame Nkrumah, a Pan-Africanist and the first president of Ghana, penned the book *I Speak of Freedom*. The words would inspire a generation of African revolutionaries to fight.

Twenty years later, on October 4, 1984, Thomas Sankara, the unpreten-tious but politically assertive president of Burkina Faso, stood at the United Nations General Assembly in New York City and gave a riling speech. He spoke with absolute clarity. Sankara's energetic eagerness for a strong revo-lutionary government made him a dangerous foe of the imperialist spirit, which he did more to extinguish and vanquish than any other man of his time. As a Pan-Africanist and Marxist, he was devoted to self-reliance and the power of workers. In *Thomas Sankara: An African Revolutionary*, biog-rapher Ernest Harsch describes Sankara as a populist champion of hard-working, rural-born Africans. He was a man of the people, often walking without an entourage or riding a bike around the capital. Through the Peo-ple Development Program, he initiated a nationwide literacy campaign, and nationalized land and mineral wealth, nullifying the power of the Interna-tional Monetary Fund and World Bank. He built roads and a railway to connect the nation without foreign aid. As a matter of fact, he loathed foreign aid, holding the motto that "he who feeds you controls you." Under Sankara, all public servants got a pay deduction, even his own salary. What's more, officials had to ditch luxury transport and fly coach. His stripped-down government approach infuriated the elite as he redistributed land from feudal landlords to the peasants. He also outlawed the deep traditions of forced marriage, polygamy, female genital mutilation, and appointed women to high government positions. He had goals to end corruption, repay government debt, build schools, offer scholarships to students from other poor countries, provide free healthcare for pregnant women and children, create camps where people could learn how to read, and eradicate homelessness. Sankara tried to liberate his country from the West, seeing a solution for third-world nations across the diaspora—complete independence in business, industry, and politics. As he said in his speech to the General Assembly of the United Nations in New York in 1984:

> We refuse simple survival. We want to ease the pressures, to free our countryside from medieval stagnation or regression. We want to democratize our society, to open up our minds to a universe of collective responsibility, so that we may be bold enough to invent the future . . . I speak not only on behalf of Burkina Faso . . . but also on behalf of all those who suffer . . . those millions of human beings who are in ghettos because their skin is black . . . those [indigenous Americans] who have been massacred, trampled on and . . . confined to reservations . . . women throughout the entire world who suffer from a system of exploitation imposed on them by men. . . . We wish to enjoy the inheritance of all the revolutions of the world, all the liberation struggles of third-world peoples.

Three years later, and only four years in power, he was assassinated with twelve others in the Burkina Faso capital of Ouagadougou. It was the familiar tale of "Judas and the Black Messiah." His right-hand man, Blaise Compaoré, sent a hit squad to kill him, assumed power, overturned the reforms, returned to foreign aid dependency, and ran the country as a dictator until he was overthrown by protest in 2014. As Africans roiled in the death throes of colonialism, there were mixed feelings on the part of Black

Americans. The African liberation struggle lasted until 1990, when Namibia won its independence, but the global movement began ninety years earlier. Alice Kinloch a South African activist, coined the term "Pan-African" at the first Pan-African Conference in 1900. A word used that embodied the worldwide pattern of anti-Black discrimination and calls for every Black person across the globe to join in a fight for freedom.

For decades, Pan-African energy was rich and vigorous. As African nations began to liberate themselves from colonial rule, it had the effect of debunking the myth of white supremacy. Not invincible, its power could be defeated. By the 1940s, the big five Black organizations (National Association for the Advancement of Colored People, National Urban League, National Negro Congress, National Council of Negro Women, and the March on Washington Movement) supported global Black solidarity. Mary McLeod Bethune warned that this new militancy among Blacks was not just an American phenomenon. And the National Negro Congress said that all Black people had a "responsibility to work for anti-Imperialism and anti-colonialism and to oppose obstructionist American foreign policy."

W. E. B. Du Bois was on the front lines of the struggle, but earlier the Pan-African movement took cues from leader Marcus Garvey who claimed he was able to grow his Universal Negro Improvement Association to upward of four million members in the early twentieth century. His vision was of Black people separating from the United States and looking out for self above all.

The 1945 Pan-African Congress was a major event in Black history. And the movement itself has resonated deeply in Black liberation consciousness. But with a new focus on communism and other challenges, the Pan-African movement began to fizzle out. The NAACP lost interest in campaigning for Africans while Black civil rights in America languished. As legalized racism broke down under the civil rights struggles of the 1950s and 1960s, differences in ideology were glaring. Many Black Americans championed liberal democracy, hoping to gain equality within the system. To the contrary, most African liberationists were committed to socialism, Marxism, and self-determination. Several prominent leaders still supported Pan-Africanism, such as civil rights leader Stokely Carmichael, who changed his name to Kwame Ture in 1968 in honor of two Pan-African leaders: Kwame Nkrumah and Sekou Touré. But the Black liberation movement splintered and fractured. With one group still finding hope in the struggle, and another believing that Black Americans had already put too much of their resources and muscle behind a global fight without getting the same support in return.

These cracks in the diasporic bridge continued to show, especially with the increase of African immigrants to the United States. In their study on African, Black American, and Afro-Caribbean relationships, researchers Jennifer V. Jackson and Mary E. Cothran drew an interesting conclusion about the relationship between the three groups in the United States, saying that although they share "similar interracial struggles that create some semblance of common bonds, they fail to appreciate their common heritage. . . . Communication problems are blamed on the history of slavery, its divisiveness, and the doctrine of divide and conquer. Black people were set up against each other and told not to associate with other Blacks because of negative attributes."

WE ARE IN A new era of the diaspora as the African immigrant population in the United States almost doubles each decade, and as all African-descended peoples now freely migrate across the world. African immigrant communities have flourished by taking advantage of employment and educational exchange programs. In theory, a shared heritage was supposed to forge a strong bond between native Africans and Black Americans. But such has not been the case. Native Africans harbor strong bonds to ethnicities Black Americans will never know—we share no food, dance, language, or worldview. And though anti-Black oppression is global, the vast differences in Black American culture—experiences during slavery, Jim Crow, and long-embedded racism in America—have made political unification more difficult to come by. And if trauma is the only thing around which to bond, well, those relationships never last long anyway. The argument is two-sided. On one hand, many Black Americans harbor a sentimental nostalgia about an ancient African homeland, but seldom connect to the plight of modern Africans on the continent now. On the other, native Africans have been slow to understand Black Americans' stance on racial injustice in America. The saddest reality, though, is that Black Americans and Africans have absorbed racist stereotypes and directed them at one another. Relationships are lost in a swirl of suspicion, distrust, and debased stereotypes. Myths and grudges form divisions, while mass incarceration, drug wars, anti-Black racism, and neo-colonialism continue without mass intercontinental Black resistance. The divided are conquered.

Could there be a coming together? Maybe the words of Audre Lorde, a Caribbean-born American writer and self-identified Black lesbian feminist revolutionary, might offer a way to regain a connectedness. Even though Lorde did not explicitly define herself or use the term *Black internationalism*, she did support the concept and espoused its tenets frequently in her work. She dreamed of us speaking across our separateness, even if we were so far, we had to scream. And she warned against diversionary tactics that take our eyes off self-determination and survival. For we cannot afford to be divided against one another anymore. A true diaspora is a bridge. That bridge was Audre Lorde when she went to Europe and worked with Afro-German women to find their voices, resulting in the 1986 book *Showing Our Colors: Afro-German Women Speak Out*. The best of the Black diaspora is when the Ghanaian government invited Black Americans, like activist and lawyer Pauli Murray, to the newly formed Ghana School of Law in Accra in 1960 where they served for sixteen months as a senior lecturer. It is the global Black people from Brazil all the way to Papua New Guinea saying "I can't breathe! I can't breathe!" to protest anti-Black racism and the killing of forty-six-year-old George Floyd at the hands of police in 2020. Across the diaspora, there still exists a wellspring of unity, a self-affirming resource waiting to be tapped by those Black people who recognize not only a globally shared oppression, but the honoring of a shared history.

7

Appropriate(d) Culture

All cultures learn from each other. The problem is that if the Beatles tell me that they learned everything they know from Blind Willie John, I want to know why Blind Willie John is still running an elevator in Jackson, Mississippi.
—**Amiri Baraka**

W hat is American culture? The bald eagle. Betsy Ross. Uncle Sam. The White House. Competitiveness. Republicanism. Apple pie. Christianity. These are all things associated with the American way of life. But wait, aren't there people from everywhere on Earth in America? Thus, every region around the globe has influenced American culture. So, to understand all the white ethnocentrism, we must look backward, which is the whole point here, isn't it? As the English began winning the European relay race in the 1600s to colonize North America, they became the de facto dominant culture. America cast itself in the mold of Europe, which is why you learned about ancient Greece and Shakespeare as a default. But make no mistake, people from all over the world have pollinated America with their ideas, influencing everything. The language of America. The traditions and rituals of America. What America eats. What it wears and how it is worn. All of this is passed down through a reservoir of history. Acknowledged or not, we are a nation built on intercultural metamorphosis rather than the stasis of white Americanism. We are a mosaic, but America would rather melt you in its pot until you're indistinguishable. So, the idea of pluralism, more than a century old, has never been fully embraced. But that doesn't change the fact that plurality is the biography of America. In denial, America forgets to cite its sources, especially when it comes to Black people.

Let us move to another question then: What is Black culture? Much of what has been given the name, isn't. American capitalism has so thoroughly wedded itself to the idea of "Black" that corporations would dig up the bones of James Brown and sell them if they thought it would make a profit. Far from naïve, many Black artists sought to get what they could from the tedious relationship between Black art and white dollars. "Being a Negro writer these days is a racket," said Harlem Renaissance novelist Wallace Thurman, "and I'm going to make the most of it while it lasts. About twice a year I sell a story. It is acclaimed. I am a genius in the making. Thank God for this Negro literary renaissance. Long may it flourish."

I don't blame him for capitalizing on the demand, but it is self-evident that Black culture is distorted by the toxins of commercialization. It is mutated for the masses. It becomes not what it once was, but what executives think might sell to the largest swath of the white demographic. So thorough is this concept that it has long been considered an achievement to cross over. This meant that your music, art, or writing made it past the racial borderlands to the embrace of white audiences. Black artists dodged stereotypes, but without power in the decision-making process and the need to sell to white executives and audiences, some fed into a myopic view of Blackness. How? By mimicking the same stereotypes that they thought "making it" would free them from. The global ubiquity of rap music has obliterated the notion of crossing over. But this just means that to do anything other than what is considered Black is not considered Black and thereby is invisible. What has been defined as Black culture is merely what fuels the pop culture machine, an apparatus that absorbs a predefined Black culture and discards Black people. What we end up with is what America thinks Black sounds like, walks like, and acts like.

In even more words, people think you can stand in a line for three hours to buy Blackness off a shoe rack. Or that the spirit of Blackness resides in the clenched-fisted Afro pick. Or that Blackness is a bite of golden, flaky, fried chicken. But therein lies the problem: America only bought into what it thought was Black. The man who designed and patented the enduring icon of Black hair, an Afro comb handle with a raised Black fist, was a white-Italian man named Anthony R. Romani. And the Scottish, not African-descended people, were the first to think of dipping the domesticated fowl into hot grease. What many assume to be Black culture is a set of assumptions about Black people.

So, again, what is Black culture? What is it when divorced from the commercial? What is its essence? My theory is that the best of the Black cultural tradition, the star stuff of Black existence, that has in kind powered American culture is contrasting creativity. It is the understanding that Black humanity will likely never be mainstream in a nation constructed on the bones of our ancestors. So long as America defines itself through white ethnocentrism, you will die trying to blend your unblendable skin, or you can still live and be and create in defiance of that reality. And within those pockets of creativity, in that space of contrast to the mainstream, that is where Black culture has been created throughout American history.

It happens when Black people are, as Toni Morrison defined it in one of her book titles, *Playing in the Dark* (1992). So, it is not limited to fried chicken generalizations and watermelon stereotypes. It reveals itself where Black creativity is forged in America's trial by fire. It is the coiled hairstyle antagonizing white social norms. It is the blues created in the landscape of Southern poverty and racial trauma. It is the soul bursting with love in the face of hate. It is the fight for democracy when they say you're not human, embedding that message in their laws and systems. It is turning food scraps into a forkful of the divine. It is the survival of the story, dance, and music after the brutality of the Middle Passage. It is fluid, reforming itself to meet the needs of every Black individual in America. It is creativity forged in the heat of fires so hot they're measured in kelvins. It is also Black at once unwelcomed and yet in synergy with the European. Like the musical compositions of Nina Simone. Or the patented inventiveness of Granville T. Woods. Or the plaster of Edmonia Lewis. Or the first feature-length film of Oscar Micheaux. Black culture is the spray can of Jean-Michel Basquiat. It is the brilliance of our souls manifested on Earth. Black history is the tattered fabric of America. Black culture is what threads that history into the present and future.

The problem is that the ways in which Black people have transformed the food, language, religion, beliefs, art, rituals, attitudes, and customs of America have very often gone uncredited. At times, it has been outright stolen and presented as blue-eyed soul. But the foundation of American culture is the interplay of African, indigenous, and European influences combined to create something unique. Though well understood, but less acknowledged, is how America has mined the products of Black culture while keeping Black humanity on the periphery, because America has embraced the brilliance of Black creativity but not the complex humanity from which it springs.

"The Music, Yearning Like a God in Pain"

Birthed on the African continent, the blue moans and guttural cries sharpened with the grueling labor of slavery. Samuel A. Floyd Jr., the founder of the Center for Black Music Research, devoted much of his life to writing about the origins of Black music. He paints a vivid picture of how the story of Africa traveled to America in the form of song and dance. He chronicles the evolution of Black music in the late nineteenth century. In fact, he puts us into the history, showing us how, after church or during periods of recreation, the stolen descendants of Nigeria, Senegal, Cameroon, Sierra Leone, Dahomey, Gabon, Gambia, and Guinea would gather in a circle to practice their melodic rituals.

One story is especially moving. In the late nineteenth century, a group would begin to dance, behind a cypress swamp, with muted repetitions, and then slow and measured movements, but the spirit gradually increased. Increased to a fevered pitch of rising energy. Every voice was lifted, some in response and others in competition. Men and women dancing into a frenzy, beating on their chests in absence of a drum. Dancing, shouting, clapping, and stomping rhythmically. Some moved to exhaustion and were dragged out by the arms, convulsing as though possessed by a spirit. Men and women danced in pairs birthing music through erotic gestures. Nothing was planned. The performance was a crescendo of improvisational intensity. This ritual was fueled by cultural memory. Traditional African beliefs are by no means monolithic, but in chapter five we mentioned the work of Kenyan philosopher John S. Mbiti, whose book *Introduction to African Religion* (1975) remains a worthy primer for the curious and uninformed. One thing we can say for certain is that a supreme, infinite, omnipotent African high god is believed to be present in all things. This god is an indweller in human beings, crossing the line between the material and immaterial, between the sacred and the profane. These rituals reinforced god, discipline, and community. God's presence was infused into the music and the dance.

Unable or perhaps unwilling to understand, white observers called it heathenish, and ragged "emphatic barbarism." They labeled it idolatrous and wild, then proceeded to stamp out the circle rituals across the colonies. Even drums were outlawed as enslavers recognized their power to communicate the signals of war. Floyd notes, as generations passed, even Black Christians began to look upon the rituals as beastly and savage. Was this out of their control? Maybe. When the dominant culture makes criminal all that is African, quickly assimilating is an act of survival. What is most striking, though, is how many of the negative attitudes toward African culture persist today.

But creativity is eternal. Surviving this age of prohibition, the music lived on in the banjo, the reed flute, and, when all else failed, rhythms constructed using sticks and bones. The lyric phrasings, the drums, the hums, grunts, and polyrhythms synchronized with European musical forms proliferated across America, only gaining some acceptance when cloaked in Christianity and transforming itself into the negro spiritual. Finally, and perhaps most important, Floyd shows us the African influences that continue to show up in ragtime, blues, jazz, gospel, rock 'n' roll, country, and every form of popular American music. He talks about the melodic utterances, the rough and sandy falsetto, and the ambiguous inflections. The shouts and wordless ad-libbing inserted as valuable contributors to musical composition. And the alternation between speaking and singing within a song. He then highlights the rhythmic hand clapping and beat making, foot tapping, and repetitive short rhythms. Finally, he points to the textual; the insertion of tales, folklore, ballads, metaphor, dialect, call-and-response. In this way, the memory of Africa survived.

Music is the universal language of humanity. Music needs no translation. It is recognized by the infant and the elder alike. It is a counselor, aiding in our recovery from stress and illness. As such, it has the potential to bring us together in a way nothing else can. And it brought America together in a way nothing else could, because it is humane. We all eat, dance, tell stories, enjoy music, crack jokes, and celebrate from time to time. Those things bring us together.

But American music could not escape the myth of white supremacy, resting on the ideals of Black inferiority. There may be no better case study to show the denigration of Black culture and humanity than the history of blackface. Until the 1960s, white men could make careers of blackening their faces with burnt cork, painting their lips white. They spoke in exaggerated accents, dancing, singing, and performing jokes, puns, gags, and ridiculous skits about lazy, stereotypical Black people. It was one of the most popular forms of American entertainment in the nineteenth and twentieth centuries. Troupes of white men toured city and countryside to sold-out crowds. They entertained Abraham Lincoln and Walt Whitman. In his history of blackface, Eric Lott described Samuel Clemens's (Mark Twain's) love for blackface minstrelsy. In his autobiography at the turn of the twentieth century, he described it as "the genuine nigger show, the extravagant nigger show. If I could have the nigger show back again, in its pristine purity and perfection," he said, "I should have but little further use for opera."

I'm imagining the most prominent white men of the era having a knee-slapping, gut-busting rollick of a time watching the most debased stereotypes play out onstage. It disgusted Black leaders like Frederick Douglass and Martin Delany, and it embodied the pathology behind the statement "the deeper the love the deeper the hate." In the minstrel show lay the juxtaposition of ridicule and respect, sympathy and revulsion. The psychological aspects of racism are wanting in research, but the minstrel show taps this underexplored area to show how white people have been deeply attracted to and even enthralled by Black culture. They were infatuated with the dark bodies they plundered and despised. Remember earlier we said that what is considered Black culture has often been the narrow definition of Blackness that white people consume.

The first minstrel show is believed to have begun in New York by a group of Irish performers. Eric Lott, in the book *Love and Theft: The Racial*

Unconscious of Blackface Minstrelsy, theorizes that this was a way for them to delineate themselves from Black people in the eyes of upper-class, white, Anglo elites. Lott goes on to say that the minstrel show defined what it was to be working class and white.

And this has created an environment where Black people feed into the stereotypes to ensure success, thus perpetuating the machine. In other words, "shuckin' and jiving for white folk." Eventually the cultural race boundaries were blurred further. Many white artists now are more open about their respect for the Black influences in their craft, but considering how Post Malone or Mick Jagger can perform without blackface shows the near absorption of Black into American culture. In his 2002 song "Without Me," Eminem, rapping in a silky do-rag, echoed the minstrel tradition while cleverly mocking it: "Though I'm not the first king of controversy / I am the worst thing since Elvis Presley / To do Black music so selfishly / And use it to get myself wealthy (Hey)."

All was not theft. In many instances, there was ethical, ethnic synergy. By nature of proximity, groups assimilated elements of the other. Sometimes brilliant bits of culture, perhaps a sound or a style was picked up and spread like wildfire through dry grass. Yet, America has constantly rebranded Black culture and sold it as its own. This is what record labels did, mining Black music for new gems and then stealing and packaging them as though they were originally white. Take the banjo, for instance, which started as a gourd. Thomas Jefferson noted, "The instrument proper to them [the enslaved] is the banjar, which they brought hither from Africa, and which is the original of the guitar, its chords being precisely the four lower chords of the guitar." The instrument was reformed and spread to white audiences, taking the form of bluegrass and country music. In this case, the whitewashing does not come from the omission of African tradition, but rather that the cultural history has gone unacknowledged.

To further the divide, in the 1920s, music publishers segregated music, selling what were called race records: music performed by Black performers sold exclusively to Black audiences. Racial discrimination abounded as white music companies withheld royalties from Black artists and even coerced them to give up their music rights. The artist Chuck Berry was plagiarized so often by white artists that they openly talked about it. The Beatles, Beach Boys, and Rod Stewart reproduced Berry's songs. You can hear Muddy Waters in the music of the Allman Brothers, and the familiar sounds of Motown Records' pioneering R&B soul in explosively popular groups like the Backstreet Boys and NSYNC. James Kennard Jr. understood the profound influence Black music played on American culture when he wrote in 1845:

> Who are our true rulers? The negro poets, to be sure! Do they not set the fashion, and give laws to the public taste? Let one of them, in the swamps of Carolina, compose a new song, and it no sooner reaches the ear of a white *amateur*, than it is written down, amended, (that is, almost spoilt,) printed, and than put upon a course of rapid dissemination, to cease only with the utmost bounds of Anglo-Saxondom, perhaps of the world.

Kennard looked to the future with trepidation. It was but the beginning of cultural appropriation through music, and the manifestation of white people claiming entitlement over Black artistic vision minus compensation or appreciation of the blood, sweat, and soul of those behind the art.

I was inclined to start another section here, but the music cannot be separated from the dance. Also born in Africa and characterized by sharp angular bends of the limbs and torso, the waterlike movement, the use of the whole body, dance was denigrated on slave ships, transformed from an act of total bodily freedom into a coerced act of exercise. A sailor explained that, after meals, kidnapped Africans were made to exercise. "This Exercise which is called Dancing consists in jumping up and rattling their Chains. It is done to the Beat of a Drum." I wonder if some took this as an opportunity to reconnect with the spirit world, but I'd imagine being forced to dance on those sunlit ship decks, to be made to do something so natural under the threat of punishment, smothered the fire inside. Thankfully, the spirit of movement survived. "The dance is strong magic," said American dancer Pearl Primus. "The dance is a spirit. It turns the body to liquid steel. It makes it vibrate like a guitar. The body can fly without wings. It can sing without a voice. The dance is strong magic. The dance is life." Dance has sustained us.

Cultural expression is strongly tied to societal values. As Black dance was perceived as hypersexual, it faced repression within repression. In colonial America, all that was sexual was only sanctioned in marriage, and the mythology of the oversexed Black male and female screeched against ideals of Puritan morality. Writing for *The Inquiries Journal,* a social sciences and humanities publication, scholar Rabah Omer leaves us with some useful questions:

The fact that Europe was just "discovering" the "liberating" elements of the erotic dance which it prohibited in its colonies as indication of savagery and backwardness is illuminating. It begs the question again about the meaning of "modernity" and "tradition" or to be more specific the modern and civilized" versus the "traditional and backward." How are they defined, by whom, and according to what premises.

And here again Black culture was seen through the fun house mirror, not for what it was about but for what society distorted it to be. And like the music, so, too, was the dance appropriated after going through the necessary reformations. African dance was fertile terrain for sexual expression, but the myopic view of this multifaceted art form obscures its prism-like complexity. African dance was also used in preparation for war, for shamanic spiritual rituals, for celebration, for royal processions, for the veneration of the ancestors, and an arrangement of other social purposes. Subjected to pernicious sexual stereotypes, dancers were under a heightened state of tension. Performers like Josephine Baker and Aida Walker found themselves wedged between free expression and primitive stereotypes in the early twentieth century. "I danced like the boys," said Jeni LeGon, the first female tap dancer to etch out a solo career, who often wore pants instead of skirts. Mastering the dance form, which originated from Irish and West African trading steps, she went on to say, "I could do the girls' splits, but I used the boys' splits because you could get up faster."

Dance had the power to break through the walls of gender, but it walled in many others.

On 142nd Street and Lenox Avenue, white patrons pushed through the doorframe of the Cotton Club. From 1923 to 1935, the venue hosted legendary performers like Duke Ellington, Lena Horne, and Cab Calloway. But the club was whites only with few exceptions. The nightclub was run by a mob member willing to break drug and prohibition laws with ease, while keeping the segregation laws fully entrenched. The club reinforced light-skin European beauty standards, hiring only scantily clad chorus girls no darker than tan. The venue was themed like a plantation, the menu like a jungle, complete with naked Black men and women dancing in the forest. Duke Ellington could only compose so-called jungle music. The venue launched the careers of comedians, dancers, musicians, variety acts, and caterers. But its monopoly put Black nightclubs out of business.

During the Civil Rights Movement in the 1960s, however, African American dance rose prominently as a form of cultural expression and was influential in integrating Black culture into American mainstream entertainment. But history rhymes with the present. In 2021, Black users on the video-sharing app TikTok went on strike, frustrated at the lack of credit given to them by the white users who were gaining lucrative social influencer careers by appropriating dances from Black creatives. What started as an app with silly but watchable short, lip-synced dance videos has turned into a media giant with a valuation stretching into hundreds of billions of dollars. What often begins as creative output by young Black performers picks up steam and is then repurposed by a white creator whose take goes viral. Then you see everyone from plastic surgeons to white suburban moms jumping in on the trends. Far from just social credit, creators are paid, gaining mainstream recognition and media opportunities for success on the app. Only after the boycott was there an acknowledgment by the company and a recommitment to diversity and inclusion. Even though the dances are in the public sphere, there is a blatant lack of cultural awareness. And unless there is more Black ownership, the neo-minstrel show will continue in new forms every generation.

How Culture Disappears

Born in 1904 (or so), in a small Black farming community in Brinkley, Arkansas, John L. Handcox etched out a living on the edge of poverty and the color line. In an era when poverty, disease, and landlessness plagued Black people and whites alike, Handcox was materially fortunate. His parents owned farmland, opening their home to needy strangers passing by, offering food and shelter. The family grew what it wanted when it wanted, so Hand-cox grew up watching his family feed needy whites and Blacks, and he could attend school for more than the standard two months out of the year that most sharecropping children could, many of whom picked up a hoe before picking up a schoolbook. In a land of scarcity, backbreaking work was plentiful. But it wasn't school that inspired John as much as his father's copy of a book by poet Paul Lawrence Dunbar. He may not have known it yet, but just like Dunbar, Handcox would one day use his words to change the world.

When Handcox was nineteen, his father was thrown from a wagon. The impact snapped his neck. The accident proved fatal. His family fell on terrible times and Handcox's dreams dwindled to survival. America as a nation wrestled with prohibition, immigration, and the aftershock of World War I. But Handcox navigated life under the crushing boot of plantation labor, all in the era of unchecked voter suppression and Ku Klux Klan race massacres. Cotton prices spiraled; drought worsened already horrid conditions. Losing his farm, Handcox became a tenant farmer under the old agrarian oligarchy.

During this economic misery, he joined the Southern Tenant Farmers Union, organized in 1934 as an interracial and gender-inclusive organiza-tion led by radicals and socialists. Sharecroppers, tenant farmers, and wage laborers flocked to its ranks. Of course, there were racial tensions, but in an era where so many Black people were expressly excluded from membership in unions, the Southern Tenant Farmers Union was unique. The numbers vary but the most reliable sources estimate around five million dues-paying members of the Ku Klux Klan in the 1920s. With this intensity of fear and hatred toward Black people, the Farmers Union was the lighthouse on a dark shore. It all started when twenty-seven sharecroppers, Black and white, met at a schoolhouse just south of Tyronza, Arkansas, where it was sug-gested that they form a union. "Are we going to have two unions," one per-son questioned, "one for whites and one for colored?" At that point, a Black sharecropper rose to his feet and said:

> We colored people can't organize without you and you white folks can't or-
> ganize without us. . . . We live under the same sun, eat the same food, wear

the same kind of clothing, work on the same land, raise the same crop for the same landlord who oppresses and cheats us both. For a long time now the white folks and the colored folks have been fighting each other and both of us have been getting whipped all the time. We don't have anything against one another, but we got plenty against the landlord . . . there ain't but one way for us to get him where he can't help himself and that's for us to get together and stay together.

While better known artists of the era such as Sister Rosetta Tharpe and Lonnie Johnson took their blues stories to the stage and studio, Handcox used Black blues culture to challenge income inequality. As a performer, songwriter, poet, and interpreter, he eulogized the nihilism of a sharecropper's existence. Available to stream, you can listen to his sharp voice crackle against resonant echoes on an archival album he recorded for the Library of Congress in 1937.

On "Mean Things Happening in This Land," he groans, then refrains: "There is mean things happening in this land / There is mean things happening in this land / But the union's going on and the union's growing strong / There is mean things happening in this land." Songs like "Roll the Union On" (1947) give dramatic, lyrical life to the spirit of labor organizing: "We're gonna roll / We're gonna roll, We're gonna roll the Union on," he says spritely. Then goes on to say, "If the planter's in the way we're gonna roll it over him," and, "If the boss is in the way we're gonna roll it over him." These songs were recorded in acoustic, but with soulful gospel influence. His voice is a beautiful instrument. He sang about what he thought was his inalienable right to land, shelter, food, and dignity. He also became one of the union's most outspoken leaders and successful recruiters. Through spoken word, poems, and blues, Handcox used musical storytelling to pass down the story of American poverty. He organized tenant farmers, sharecroppers, and day laborers to picket and strike for their rights, inspiring them by singing as they marched. His proletariat poetry brought together Black and white under the umbrella of unity, in the spirit of shared struggle.

Handcox and the Farmers Union rallied thousands of workers and put massive political pressure on planters. This activism came at great risk to

Handcox's life. Blacks organizing against their white employers were met with violence and terrorism. Local workers were attacked by police and vigilantes who raided the homes of union leaders and burned those homes to the ground. After a trip to represent the union with other local leaders in New York, Handcox came back to rejection. The union discontinued his small salary. He didn't take it well and went on the road, as a traveling orator singing his protest songs for socialist groups, preaching the gospel of the oppressed, and recalling the memories of the sharecropping masses.

Though Handcox fell into obscurity, his songs would not. Artist Lee Hays misappropriated "Roll the Union On," and Handcox's pioneering influence on American folk music was unmistakable but the credit was lost. Pete Seeger, one of the genre's most successful artists, rediscovered Handcox in the 1980s, and reintroduced him to the folk music circuit. For decades, Seeger had been singing, recording, and collecting royalties from songs created by Handcox. Though Seeger was a fan and, later on, acknowledged Handcox's influence, at a 1974 concert he reportedly said, "Plagiarism is the root of all culture." In the end, Seeger, not Handcox, would be credited as the "father" of folk music.

Toward the end of his life, Handcox, with his customary humor, joked about his empty pockets. In contrast, Seeger died a hugely successful music entrepreneur with millions. Such is the case with so many Black cultural originators, as their work was borrowed while they never saw a return. And as with Handcox, even when credited, they were not duly compensated.

A River of Words

Without our stories we wouldn't survive. Studies have shown that people sitting side by side unconsciously synchronize their heartbeats when captivated by a powerful tale. Like a smile or a tear, a story makes up the lexicon of the human soul. Black culture is anchored in the storytelling tradition. Orators carried the traditions of West African griots into churches and pulpits keeping their powerful elocution style alive. Black orators transformed and merged the art within their new environment, but what often got lost was the connection to Africa. Wherever we go, we end up back there. I think about the griots, a catch-all term for the indigenous storytellers of

West Africa whose role as oral historians and genealogists spans at least seven hundred years. They are the embodiment of Sankofa.

In the Manika language, the name *griot* is translated as *jali*, which literally means "blood." Griots and griottes were believed to be the lifeblood of the people, able to re-create history and carry on relationships with the ancestors. Without the transmission of stories, Black culture would not have survived the Middle Passage. Academics are recognizing the value of oral culture, but the widespread skepticism continues. Within Western scholarship, oral histories have been reduced to folklore and superstition. They have been described as prelogical remnants of a bygone era, and as such don't hold the value of written history.

We can better comprehend the subordination of African oral history by looking at a recent example. In April 2016, the US Army Corps of Engineers confirmed that an ancient human corpse located in 1996 near Kennewick, Washington, was indeed the "Kennewick Man" or "the Ancient One." A genetic ancestor of modern-day Native Americans, the remains were mired in legal, scientific, and ethical controversy from the moment they were discovered. Many believed it was the bones of a European trapper, but after carbon dating aged the remains between 8,340 and 9,200 years old, a court battle ensued. Five native tribes who sought repatriation of the remains for traditional burial went against scientists and anthropologists who wanted the remains for study. In the *Bonnichsen v. United States* decision in 2004, the court found that "the Kennewick Man was not Native American because there was no evidence he was related to a presently existing tribe, people, or culture." The courts also refused the native oral testimony on the Ancient One, saying "the value of such [oral tradition] accounts is limited by concerns of authenticity, reliability, and accuracy, and because the record . . . does not show where historical fact ends and mythic tale begins." Finally, twenty years later, science confirmed what the oral tradition already had when DNA testing matched modern Native Americans.

Of course, there are challenges to admitting oral traditions in court, but this has been a challenge America has been slow to resolve. We might wonder how many histories have been lost, forcefully transitioning indigenous populations into an unfamiliar system of literature. Black people held on to the spirit of their orations in the church and pulpit, but there was much lost through forced assimilation. But still the culture of stories lived on, representing an unbroken chain of transmission stretching back countless centuries. One case where that skepticism has been reversed is the case of Mamadou Kouyaté, a griot and oral historian of the Mali Empire:

> Other peoples use writing to record the past, but this invention has killed the faculty of memory among them. They do not feel the past any more, for writing lacks the warmth of the human voice. With them everybody thinks he knows, whereas learning should be a secret. The prophets did not write and their words have been all the more vivid as a result. What paltry learning is that which is congealed in dumb books!

I surround myself with books, so I got defensive when I first read those words. But he raises a valid question: Are spoken words a better transmission of the human spirit than words on a page? And in this way, the word survived. It survived the Middle Passage, that unending cycle of death where the red blood of millions mingled with blue seas, the disjointing and dislocating of five thousand voyages. The spoken word survived the violent terror, psychological torment, and brutality that hinged upon the production of labor, even when the oral tradition was called primitive, even when it was said to be unreliable, less than writing. It survived through orature, which Ugandan linguist Pio Zirimu says is its own form of communication, not subordinate to written literature. Folklore has become a cultural undercurrent, often overlooked because it was produced by the unlettered, uneducated, and spoken in dialect. So, we have to ask, as more Black people mastered Western speech and literacy, how could we cast off a history encapsulating the experiences of people with very different ties to dozens of countries? The stories that bound them together through shared interests and struggle, the stories that made a home in a foreign land. As author and activist Anna Julia Cooper once wrote, the worst possibility yet "is that the so-called educated Negro under the shadow of this overpowering Anglo-Saxon civilization, may become ashamed of his own distinctive features . . . and so all originality, all sincerity, all self-assertion would be lost to him."

I remember the tales of the Brothers Grimm, but the only African folk-tale I recall from my youth is the story of John Henry. There is no doubt that the seismic impact of the transcontinental railroad, completed on May 10, 1869, played a role in making the ballad of John Henry one of the most popular stories in American folklore. It speaks to the histories of some twenty thousand laborers, many enslaved, who laid portions of the 1,700-mile track that became the largest civil works project in American history. A legendary steel driver, Henry was part of a two-man team, using a nine-pound hammer to hand drill holes fourteen feet deep into solid rock, after which explosive charges would be placed. The work was brutal. Railroad laborers worked in extreme weather, laying tracks across rough rivers, grand canyons, high mountains, and scorching desert. Many died tragic, sometimes grisly deaths. One day John Henry was placed in a contest against a steam-powered drill. We can all understand the power of automation and its promise to free humans from dangerous or boring tasks. But many saw it as a threat to their livelihood, and Henry was one of them. So, he took on the drill, and he beat it. Then he died. The stress was too much to bear.

But there was also a real John Henry. A nineteen-year-old from New Jersey convicted of theft in 1866 and sentenced to years of hard labor on the Chesapeake and Ohio Railway. At the Lewis Tunnel, he and others worked alongside steam-powered drills, giving their lives while railroad bosses bathed in wealth and corruption. Forty-four million acres, $61 million in federal loans, and generous sums for every mile of track laid seeded a scandalous harvest of scams. One in which railroad companies would deliberately lay track over more treacherous terrain, killing more workers to get more money. So, the story of John Henry was a cautionary tale to avoid overwork at all costs, for the price is your life. This is embodied no better than with the Japanese word *karoshi*, which simply means "overwork death." It is when you exert yourself into a heart attack or stroke from stress. It is a universal truth, but especially for Black males, who have a lower life expectancy than any other group on the planet. Stressful jobs shorten lives. This one resonates deeply. Overwork is normal for me. Sometimes I rush to exhaustion. And I've thought about flying away to escape it all. Just like the legend of the flying Africans. Have you heard it?

The tale of those enslaved ancestors whose bodies became so featherlight, they up and flew back to the African motherland? The ones who knew magic and created invisible staircases ascending to the clouds. They got away, from the chains and the work and imprisonment. There was a Black man who did it, up in Jonesboro, Arkansas, I think it was. Well, he was being chased by police, and the faster they walked the faster he walked. They stepped once, he stepped twice. Until he stepped right into the air. He just spread his arms and sailed off, faster than the planes. Stories like these have been reconstructed in books like *The Annotated African American Folktales*, by historian Henry Louis Gates Jr. (If you study Black history enough, Gates will pop up around random corners, where you least expect him, smiling behind the small frames of his spectacles.)

I am grateful for the thousands of Black scholars who have felt the power of Sankofa and preserved those tales, so that we may know that the dreams of flying were connected to freedom. They were connected to the psychological exercise of free will. History and culture are intertwined, one impacting the other in a never-ending cycle. The people of a country and their culture are shaped by their history, while the history of a place is shaped by the culture of its people.

During the Harlem Renaissance, a mixture of folklore, orature, and American letters made up the raw material of Black literature. Black people were not new to writing, but during the 1920s and 1930s, they broke free from the genteel and realist literary styles of the previous era into the experimental and subversive. Writers such as Claude McKay, Jean Toomer, Alain LeRoy Locke, May Miller, Jessie Redmon Fauset, Rudolph Fisher, and others worked as playwrights, editors, philosophers, novelists, and poets. With rhetorical flame, they put bigotry on the barbeque and roasted racism with wit. Others sought out ways to differentiate their writing from white traditions. Even more simply, they hoped to accurately reflect the Black experience in America, while rejecting white standards of literature. In a time before civil rights, when Blacks were expected to be grateful for simply being American citizens, these writers celebrated their identity through both the spoken and written word. Black people not only mastered written English in a few generations, they transformed the language through contrasting creativity.

Langston Hughes said it plainly in his essay "The Negro Artist and the Racial Mountain" (1926). He wrote that individual Black artists intended to express themselves freely, no matter what the Black public or white public thought. Who else has defined the Black literary canon? Toni Morrison. Maya Angelou. James Baldwin. Alice Walker. Ralph Ellison. Octavia Butler. Zora Neale Hurston. All segregated from the white American canon with its Twain, Hemingway, Steinbeck, Woolf, Faulkner, London, and the like. The Black canon holds space for those who have best articulated race, identity, and culture in America. But I'm sure I can't be the only Black writer who has wondered if it is even possible to write a book in America as a Black person and not write about it? The Black experience is wedded to the American experience, making some writers obscured within obscurity.

Black women have very often faced a double erasure in Black history. Their stories are less likely to be valued and recorded. So, I was doubly joyed when I first came across the work of Pauline Hopkins. My eyes glinted across the pages of her 1902 novel, *Of One Blood: Or, the Hidden Self,* written one hundred years ahead of its time. The book explores a lost utopian civilization in Ethiopia, which she said had "all the arts and cunning inventions that make your modern glory." I bristled at the idea of a lost Black utopia. A place free of bigotry brimming with Black civilization. Then, I thought about how Black literary contributions to American science fiction writing have been long forgotten. Why? Raking in $631 million at the US box office by its sixth weekend in 2018, Marvel's *Black Panther* became the highest-grossing superhero movie at that point in US history . . . talking about a fictional Black utopia. A little different, I guess, when the story comes with superpowers. But before the story of Wakanda, there was another story about a lost African civilization.

I dig through the Black literary canon like vinyl collectors used to dig through crates at a record store. Iceberg Slim, Donald Goines, Sister Souljah, and Walter Mosley in crime fiction. Ah, the Black Arts Movement, the canon breakers: Ethridge Knight, Sonia Sanchez, Ntozake Shange, Amiri Baraka, and Angela Jackson. I look over to my bookshelf: Nikki Giovanni, Cornel West, Stanley Couch, Rita Dove. Black writers. Black words. Black ink. So many books—one life is simply not enough.

A Heaping of History

Pork chitlins washed and clean. Pig's feet cut in half lengthwise. Collard greens cooked with smoked turkey legs. Hog maws brought to a rapid boil, then cooked for hours until tender. Baked candied yams. Black-eyed peas. Every single bite thoroughly seasoned. Flavors sprout like spring after slow cooking. Patience. A watched pot never boils. The role of Black food culture warrants some discussion here, because food has been one of the greatest sources of sustenance and joy. I, too, stand in awe of the contrasting creativity that allowed Black people to render scraps into palatable dishes. From the forgotten corners of the African continent, *Citrullus lanatus*—the fat, green, striped fruit also known as watermelon—made its way across the Atlantic Ocean. Black-eyed peas, peanuts, okra, yams, and coffee also came with us. But so-called Black foods have been seasoned with racism. Seen as less nutritious, yielding less, and inferior to foods of other people who came from Europe. And yet, a cookbook titled *White House Cook Book*, written in 1887 by F. L. Gillette, which was used to cook for several presidents, included a recipe for watermelon rind pickles. Fannie Farmer's *1896 Boston Cooking-School Cookbook* contained watermelon recipes such as stewed watermelon rind and watermelon ice cream.

So, how did the food become associated with a racial stereotype? The racist and stereotypical references to Black people and watermelon really began proliferating in the 1860s, making their way into minstrel shows and other popular entertainment. But if we move beyond the stereotypes, we see how those foods sustained Black people and had a huge impact on American culture. Ham, turkey, fowl, beef, puddings, and jellies were served up to an enthusiastic George Washington. Brilliant Black cooks like Emmanuel Jones used his skills to transition out of slavery into a cooking career, while others working in kitchens and pantries nourished the nation.

Black food culture helped America survive. Sorghum, which came to America with colonists in the seventeenth century, has been Africa's culinary contribution to the world and is one of five plants that provide 85 percent of all human energy. Botanists believe that the peanut—which isn't a nut, it is a legume—made its way to Africa via the Portuguese, and then from Africa to North America on those slave ships. Now peanut butter, with its deep roasted aroma and flavor, is more American than apple pie, finding its way into 75 percent of American pantries.

In the Lowcountry of coastal South Carolina and Georgia, rice stalks shot up out of the fertile, swampy soil. From the 1750s to 1860s, rice was a dominant economic force, the massive wealth of the area created by a tiny grain. There are scholars who suggest that it was through Black knowledge and labor that America was able to eat and survive. Bringing over their knowledge of rice cultivation from the regions around Sierra Leone, they knew that rice required a lot of fresh water and periodic flooding to kill weeds and invasive plants. One can only imagine the longing as their new environment shared similarities with the mangrove swamps and riverain grasslands of their homeland. Sweating in the heat of the sun, they built earthen embankments, reservoirs, dikes, causeways, and handcrafted wooden floodgates to control the flow of water. They planted hundreds of thousands of acres of rice—the geographical evidence of their work can still be seen by plane if you know what to look for. There may have been no other group in the United States that hung on to more of their African heritage than the Gullah people (sometimes referred to as Gullah Geechee).

Today, the African-infused Lowcountry Gullah Geechee culture is being strangled out of existence—gripped by the slender, well-kept left hand of gentrification and the bony, leathery right hand of poverty. Now generations flee to big cities, trying to escape America's staggering racial wealth gap. Opportunity, now as then, is not equal for all US citizens. The Federal Reserve has shown that "Black families' median and mean wealth is less than 15 percent that of white families, at $24,100 and $142,500, respectively."

With a long history of exposure to mosquito-borne illnesses, planters retreated to Charleston mansions during warm months, to escape disease-infested swamps, leaving the enslaved alone for much of the year, which allowed them to retain their African culture. The Gullah Geechee people lived in relative isolation from white planters, who left them mostly unattended for fear of high humidity diseases. The law of unintended consequences reveals its truth here. Left alone, a unique hybrid culture blossomed, a Gullah Geechee dialect, beautiful handicrafts, foods, and customs. The serene lullaby "Kumbaya" was a musical gift given by the Gullah Geechee people, and their knowledge of food impacted American culture.

Black culinary traditions in America are an intersection of underappreciated cultural contribution, oppression, and liberation. Most people know that Coca-Cola once boasted cocaine as an ingredient, but lesser known is that the other half of the name represented an ingredient that came over as another import from Africa, the kola nut, with its caffeine and theobromine, which are also found in tea, coffee, and chocolate. It was used as a stimulant and a form of currency, as well as in religious ceremonies and to reinforce social contracts. Kola nuts were being shipped to the United States and Europe en masse in the nineteenth century as a staple of Coca-Cola, which touted "the combined active principles of Kola Nut and Coca Leaves." Mass consumption of culinary products such as rice, sugar, coffee, and Coca-Cola fueled the massive extraction of wealth and labor from the African continent.

There are many who have thought Black food culture has been stereotyped to represent only the barest of minimums. Associating those high-fat, high-sodium, high-sugar, and starch-laden foods with capitalism's inequality and the history of white control over the Black body. In 1948, food author Freda DeKnight argued against "a fallacy, long disproved, that Negro cooks, chefs, and caterers can adapt themselves only to the standard Southern dishes, such as fried chicken, greens, corn pone, hot breads, and so forth." With her influential cookbook, *A Date with a Dish: A Cook Book of American Negro Recipes,* she helped the formerly enslaved find foods that better nurtured their bodies and minds. The Black Power movement rejected poverty-necessitated foods in the 1960s, focusing on Black health as a form of liberation.

I have childhood memories of the old-style American poverty that put government cheese and powdered eggs on my menu, but my current position affords me higher quality food than neckbones and gizzards. And yet, my updated palate still craves the intestinal delights called chitlins that were lovingly placed next to the candied yams on my Thanksgiving plate. So, I try not to think about Black Power on that day, not unless I want to apply a tinge of shame with the Frank's RedHot (hot sauce). I'm only human.

There is a real trivialization of poverty, though. Dispossessed people ate these foods out of necessity and likely would've rather had steak, shrimp, and healthier foods if they were affordable. The irony is that the wealthy continuously "discover" foods deemed inferior, plate them nicely, and eat them with a silver spoon. This is especially relevant as racial health disparities run deep, and Black people wrestle with the fact that an old Southern diet is contributing to high cholesterol and hypertension. Even more if you're Black and poor, living in a neighborhood that struggles without a decent grocery store. But the creativity is at work as many Black people have turned back to their agricultural roots, planting community gardens and turning their roofs and windowsills into places to get fresh food. And in this way, Black culture, which is Black life, continues.

There were no limits to the contributions of Black American cultural influence on America, also no limits on how it has been co-opted, through carelessness, thoughtlessness, and borrowing with no intention of return. That is why, until recently, no one acknowledged that a Black man named Nathan Nearest Green created the recipe for the world's most famous whiskey, Jack Daniel's. Or that the so-called beatnik slang of the 1960s (*square, cool, dig it*) originated with Black people. Or that Tina Bell, a pioneer and co-creator of the 1980s Seattle grunge scene, helped to spark the genre. America has been content to strategically plunder and then distance itself from the gems created by Black people. But the best of Black cultural history is found, when we reach back to bring forward, paying homage to those brilliant expressions of Black life created in the contrast.

The Fabric
of America

Abused and scorned though we may be, our destiny is tied up with
the destiny of America. Before the Pilgrims landed at Plymouth,
we were here. Before the pen of Jefferson scratched across the pages
of history the majestic word of the Declaration of Independence,
we were here.
—Dr. Martin Luther King Jr.

It's easy to find historians who position the so-called discovery of the
Americas as the most important event in modern world history, wherein
European explorers—with their "guns, germs, and steel," a theory of conquest posited by geographer Jared Diamond—adventured over land and sea
and then decimated indigenous peoples. Though his theory has been wildly
critiqued, this story is hardwired into the framework of American history.
Scholars go further to conclude that colonization changed lives on both
sides of the Atlantic. I've always felt that this "changing" of lives spoke to
expansion of European civilization but distorted and concealed the steady
stream of indigenous death that occurred as a result. Like the later imperialism in Africa, the story of the Americas has been told in service to a monumental history of European discovery and progress, the inevitable thrust
of industrial democracy. In this telling, the Taíno men and women—half
naked and adorned with body paint, appearing from their villages to get a
better look at a strange-speaking Christopher Columbus—are presented as
almost ahistorical, existing outside of history. Like later colonial conquests

in Africa, people seldom asked just who these indigenous people were. What was their art, music, customs, spiritual practice, worldview, or social structure? In our history, they only die, gruesomely, as in the case of the Taíno, who greeted the Spaniards with water, gifts, and food. But most accounts assume they were powerless in the face of European war power, as Columbus later wrote an ominous passage that would define the European mindset in the so-called New World: "With fifty men all of them could be held in subjugation and can be made to do whatever one might wish."

Reading accounts like *A Short Account of the Destruction of the Indies* (1552), by Spanish friar Bartolomé de las Casas, has allowed many to at once empathize with, and reel in horror at, the mass slaughter of those like the Taíno, as he describes scenes like this one: "They took infants from their mothers' breasts, snatching them by the legs and pitching them headfirst against the crags or snatched them by the arms and threw them into the rivers, roaring with laughter and saying as the babies fell into the water, 'Boil there, you offspring of the devil!' . . . With my own eyes I saw Spaniards cut off the nose and ears of Indians, male and female, without provocation, merely because it pleased them to do it. . . . Likewise, I saw how they summoned the caciques and the chief rulers to come, assuring them safety, and when they peacefully came, they were taken captive and burned."

The book is a cluster of horrors, but remember we should always cross-reference and read multiple books. Las Casas presents a story of Spanish devils from the bowels of hell against pure, poor, and innocent indigenous people. *The Broken Spears: The Aztec Account of the Conquest of Mexico* (1962), by Mexican historian Miguel León-Portilla, offers another tale of the Spanish conquistadors like Hernán Cortés but from the perspective of the Aztec. According to León-Portilla, the indigenous didn't just bring gifts. They launched attacks, they raided, looted, and fought back.

But fighting and fighting back does not negate the colonial atrocities downplayed and whitewashed the world over. In 2017, Portland State University professor Bruce Gilley published his "Case for Colonialism" in *Third World Quarterly*, a respected and peer-reviewed academic journal. He argues that colonialism was a force for good. He invited mob-like outrage and the paper was retracted. But was the anger reactionary? Our history books are still written in ways that cry out manifest destiny. The technology, investment, and policies Europeans spread across the globe overshadow the glut of colonial crimes. But the question many scholars fail to ask is, if colonialism and the European way of existence were so much better than everyone else's, why did they always have to force it at gunpoint? And it is at gunpoint where we see Africans show up in the history of the Americas.

In 1502, a Spanish fleet of thirty ships arrived in Hispaniola with some hundred enslaved Africans. It didn't take a year for the governor to lobby a complaint to King Ferdinand about how they'd "fled among the Indians, taught them bad customs, and could not be captured." Enslaved Africans were escaping from the Spanish settlements to join the resistance army of the Taíno. The battle-hardened guerilla outfit harassed the Spanish for almost a decade. And according again to Las Casas, a cacique (chief) and resistance leader named Hatuey gave a riling speech rallying the newly formed alliance of Africans and natives. The purpose of this strategic alliance was to expel the invaders. After showing his group a basket of gold, he reportedly said:

> They tell us, these tyrants, that they adore a God of peace and equality, and yet they usurp our land and make us their slaves. They speak to us of an immortal soul and of their eternal rewards and punishments, and yet they rob our belongings, seduce our women, violate our daughters. Incapable of matching us in valour, these cowards cover themselves with iron that our weapons cannot break.

Hatuey was captured. Before he was executed by the Spaniards, he was asked to accept Christianity to go to heaven. He asked whether Spaniards go there, and the friar replied they do. Hatuey refused, saying he would rather go to hell, where he wouldn't dwell with such cruel people. No indigenous group on the planet was waiting to be colonized. Countless acts of resistance leave a trail of that evidence. The fabric of America begins, as it did in our study of Africa, with the lost histories of those who had their own complex systems of government, ranging from rural farms to city-states, their own languages, spirituality, and cultures. Cultures that have been cloaked in umbrella terms.

The Taíno do not nearly represent the unknown variation of peoples who lived across the Caribbean with their own distinct ways of life. Some cultures were likely as different as Philadelphians compared to New Yorkers or

New Yorkers to San Franciscans. Even more devastating was what has been termed "paper genocide." When identity is categorized by race, the dominant society gets to tell you what percentage of blood you need to be part of your ancestral tribe. How many indigenous or Afro-indigenous people were categorized simply as Black or mixed on the census? It is a heritage that may be lost forever.

Exploration and Settlement

It's common to begin the story of America at its declaration of independence from England in 1776, a view challenged by *The 1619 Project*, an ambitious effort in 2019 by Pulitzer Prizewinner Nikole Hannah-Jones and the *New York Times*, proposing a new American origin story. One that begins when a British ship landed at Port Comfort, near present-day Fort Monroe, Virginia, with "20 and odd Negroes."

Here is how the project describes the events: "[The ship] carried more than 20 enslaved Africans, who were sold to the colonists. No aspect of the country that would be formed here has been untouched by the years of slavery that followed." The project drew admiration for its "vital truth-telling" about slavery and cemented itself as a cultural zeitgeist. Not surprisingly, the project also drew a backlash, creating a firestorm with conservative media outlets, historians, and the Trump White House. They positioned it as a biased and racist view of American history. Historians disputed a sentence in one of the essays that suggested some of the colonists supported war efforts because they wanted to protect the institution of slavery.

But was the backlash simply over the facts? Another Pulitzer Prize winner, David McCullough, is one of the most popular history writers ever and a bestseller many times over with titles like *1776* (2005), *John Adams, The American Spirit: Who We Are and What We Stand For* (2017), and *Pioneers: The Heroic Story of the Settlers Who Brought the American Ideal West* (2020). Critiques of his books with accusations of mistakes and factual errors is a routine part of his book releases, but his condemnation amounts to a yard of crickets. Much of the backlash *The 1619 Project* received from critics was about the proposal of a monumental new history, a new interpretation that not only put Black people at the center of an expanding American democracy but explains why American democracy was never actually expanded upon to begin with. This version of history was a square challenge to its whitewashed opposite.

Now there are issues with both accounts. As we have already shown, so-called American history and Black history go back much further. There is a forgotten century. Even prior to 1619, thousands of Africans had already come to the Americas as slaves, servants, translators, aides, guides, and members of resistance movements. To start our story at 1619 or 1776 is to erase nearly a hundred years of remarkable Black and indigenous history. Even more so, a group of South Florida historians collaborated on an article that shows us just how dynamic things were before the seventh century in what would become their state: "Spaniards, Portuguese, Greeks, Italians, French, Flemish, Germans, two Irishmen, West Africans, sub-Saharan Africans, and a diverse group of Native Americans. In other words, early Florida reflected a population that resembled modern America. From the time of St. Augustine's founding in early September 1565, African descendants, both free and enslaved, played critical roles in the town's daily life." The forgotten century also allows us to understand the magnitude of racial slavery. European powers like Spain, the Netherlands, England, and Portugal were bitter intercolonial rivals who argued over many things, but the idea of white superiority was not one of them.

In 1526, Lucas Vázquez de Ayllón sent a scouting party sailing down the eastern seaboard of what is now the United States in search of a suitable location to establish an outpost. His expedition had embarked on what would become a relentless mission to colonize North America for the glory of the Spanish crown under the divine banner of an almighty God and angels. They found people at a place known by legend as Chicora, invited a group of them onto their ship, abducted, and enslaved them. After this, the conquistador ended his reconnaissance mission and returned to Spain. His report of the Americas was unreservedly positive, so much so that Ayllón was granted permission to return that same year. He left with five hundred settlers, a hundred enslaved Africans, livestock, and provisions. On August 9, 1526, they arrived in what is believed to be modern-day South Carolina and were immediately struck with disaster. Their largest ship sank. It was the one with all the food on it. Moving two hundred miles south around the Pee Dee River, the colonists forced the enslaved Africans to clear land for homes and a church. Too late to plant crops, many starved, and others were killed by the indigenous groups from whom they sought help. Even more met death from infectious microbes. We'd be mistaken to assume only people, ideas, and actions shape the past when disease has changed the course of history more than any of these. The colony dwindled to 150 people. We cannot be sure how many Africans survived; the Spanish dedicated little ink to the enslaved. But they seized freedom: "It happened that some of the Negro slaves independently set fire to [a leader's] house . . . and as the fire burnt, they all gathered to kill him; and in this way they managed to escape." They formed the weapon of their liberation out of fire, and the arsonists doomed the first attempt at a colony in North America.

Later, in a salt marsh north of St. Augustine, Florida, lay Fort Mose. It was part of Spanish Florida, a large area of land stretching from the Gulf of Mexico on the West up into modern Georgia and South Carolina. By 1738, there stood St. Augustine, America's first free Black settlement. By 1759, the community boasted twenty-two houses, fifteen women, seven boys, and eight girls. It was a diverse community, which Black people were among the earliest to settle, pushing for autonomy among the Spanish, and weaving their destinies with those native people who were already there. As English planters began to challenge Spanish territory, King Charles II of Spain exploited the rivalry, enacting a policy granting sanctuary to runaway slaves giving "liberty to all . . . the men as well as the women . . . so that by their example and by my liberality others will do the same."

There was a likely reason the lives of Africans in Spanish colonies were so fluid. Remember earlier we discussed the significant African presence in Spain and Portugal. For seven hundred years (711–1492 CE), they invaded and occupied most of Spain and Portugal. Education, arts, and sciences flourished there. Black Moors operated at all levels of society. Again, here we see how whitewashing works. The word *Moor* does not represent an ethnicity but was used by Europeans to describe Muslims living in Europe. The Latin term *Maurus* means "dark-skinned," but indeed many North Africans described as Moors were light-skinned, just darker than the typical European. The important thing to know, though, is that there were Black

Moors, many of whom, enslaved or free, began their lives in America as literate professionals interacting in North African and Spanish societies.

As a Black Moor exploring Southwest America alongside the Spanish, Estevanico found himself on the other side of resistance, not unlike Juan Garrido, a servant who participated in the conquest of the Aztec in Mexico. Originally named Mustafa and born in Azemmour, Morocco, Estevanico was only one of four castaways after a Spanish boat shipwrecked off the coast of Galveston, Texas, originally carrying three hundred people. Initially licensed to explore and settle in Florida, the fleet was lost. Violence marked both the weather conditions and their encounters with the indigenous people. In a reversal of fate, the small group were themselves enslaved by the natives. At some point, the "Arabic-speaking Black man" gained a reputation as a medicine man, which helped open his group's door to freedom. For almost eight years, they wandered. Estevanico must have been in awe as he moved over the thorny brush of the Southwest along the Rio Grande. His ability to learn languages came in handy as he was guided through different tribal territories by its people. He would have gathered information key to his survival. Like what wild plants, roots, and bulbs were edible. Or the hunting of white-tailed deer for skins and meat.

Then in 1539 his adventure turned to misfortune. As he eagerly scouted territory in northwestern New Mexico, he was killed by the natives of Hawikuh. In his extraordinary life, he'd traveled from Morocco to Spain and across the Atlantic to modern-day New Mexico. He was at once an intrepid explorer and a servile cog in the colonial settler machine, searching for rumored cities of great wealth and fortune for the glory of Spain. According to historian Christopher Schmidt-Nowara, "A servant/soldier/explorer like Estevanico . . . was perhaps a typical representative of slavery in sixteenth-century Spanish America: men of many talents and skills who were not reduced to the most brutal plantation conditions."

It is through these stories that we find out how people respond to power from various angles as it exerts itself over them. In each situation we see an adaptability and ingenuity applied to the creation of freedom. Our history of pioneers and settlers usually does not include Black people. But they, too, settled in America. It is impossible for any settlement story not to include the populations of people already here. Though Black people found themselves sometimes at odds and other times at peace with the indigenous population, their destinies were always intertwined. Under colonial rule, Native Americans were not only encouraged to enslave Africans, but were sold into slavery themselves. As a strategy, they were traded for enslaved Africans in the Caribbean to neutralize the threat of escape and resistance as they were familiar with the land.

"Between 1492 and 1880," says historian Linford D. Fisher, "between two and 5.5 million Native Americans were enslaved in the Americas in addition to 12.5 million African slaves." Here again I've seen people turn the critical lens to say that native people enslaved one another before Europeans arrived. This is seldom shared in a spirit of truth, but rather as a deflection to turn the conversation away from the lasting effects of racism at present. And indeed, just like Africans, indigenous populations did participate in slavery, as shown in books like *Bonds of Alliance: Indigenous and Atlantic Slaveries in New France* (2014) by historian Brett Rushforth. They even partnered with colonial powers to source, abduct, and enslave. But as we explored previously, it was the same process of othering the outgroup. Marginalizing the tribe different from your own, isolating its members for enslavement and natal alienation. We are not arguing here that Europeans were exceptional in their slavery practice. Rather, they oversaw the frightful acceleration of indigenous bondage to feed the global European slavery industry. And with it, they introduced an oppressive racial hierarchy that still affects every group they subjugated.

Yet even as the world was being rapidly remade, people still crafted lives. Seldom do we hear about Black pioneers and settlers like Jean Baptiste Point du Sable, a fugitive from slavery, and his Potawatomi wife, Kitihawa (also known as Catherine). Together, they built a prosperous farm on the northern banks of what was known as the Portage of Chicago in 1779, at the mouth of the river, trading furs with Native Americans and the French. It was the first permanent settlement there. Previously, Point du Sable had spent time with the Peorias, an Illinois tribe, who were descended from the great mound-building civilizations of precolonial times. Complete with a bakehouse, dairy farm, poultry house, mill, and smokehouse. Point du Sable facilitated intertribal and international trade, forming various alliances crucial to the foundation of Chicago.

Black families were not outliers on the American frontier; they also streamed West as refugees escaping antebellum slavery. Their relationship with Native Americans was a dynamic one—sometimes they were enslaved by sovereign tribes, fought them, intermarried, and formed alliances. An unintended consequence of Blacks fleeing their own destruction was the accelerated destruction of native territory. As the battle to maintain slavery expanded westward, Black people found themselves in the middle of bitter battles between territories seeking to either end or maintain the institution.

Untold and unseen settlement stories of Black people on the frontier thread the fabric of the United States. Officially, East to West movement in American history is still characterized by white European settlers carving out the landscape with the ever-present danger of hostile natives. The frontier myth is one of the most stubborn falsehoods of American history, but rather than analyze the inhumanity inherent in America's expansion, many would rather cling to the idea of John Wayne and bearded frontier heroes in coonskin caps.

Hoping to create an oasis in the desert, insulated from racism and away from the barren memories of enslavement, Black people continued West after the Civil War, erecting all-Black towns and municipalities. According to the Oklahoma Historical Society, between 1865 to 1920, Black people created more than fifty towns across the sprawling plains of Oklahoma. Human nature compelled them to find a space to belong, and unable to find it, they created it. Remaking themselves, shaking off the rigors and trauma of slavery. They created new borders and defined new land, and that land, in many ways, redefined them. Some of these Black towns still exist, like Eatonville, Florida, and thirteen Oklahoma towns. But many remain only in memory, now ghost towns of broken buildings and dreams. Like the town of Dearfield, Colorado, where nineteen settlers led by Oliver Toussaint Jackson built homes, planted crops, and carved lives. They grew the town to two hundred, with churches, brick manufacturing, schools, and a gas station. Their first crop raised $50,000. All was well until the 1920s, when the Dust Bowl blew it all away. As of this writing, a few wooden buildings, at risk of collapse, are all that remain. The ghosts of all Black towns still haunt the landscape of America.

So far, we have looked at the fabric of America through multiple frameworks. The critical, monumental, and empathetic, which animate the jazz-like analysis of American history, multiple cultures influencing one another under the outsized restraints of a white racial hierarchy and a budding global capitalism. We were able to push through the simple monumental narratives of heroes and villains and ask a different set of questions. What have we missed when exploring indigenous populations? When did Black people arrive in America? What were the international power dynamics that predicated their servitude and enslavement? How did Black people act in common with and in antagonism against indigenous populations already here? After all, these are the dynamics that lay the foundation for America as we know it.

War and Independence

America was a nation birthed in fire and blood. Black people joined every war fought by the United States. But in the beginning, their fight was not for the United States, but for the universal right to freedom. For the first time in its infant existence, the United States of America formally declared war in 1812. Politically, there are accounts that position the United States as aggressors who wanted to annex British-controlled Canada. But the United States listed Britain's interference with trade as the official grievance. This, and Britain's impressment of American seamen into the Royal Navy. British soldiers would, short of manpower, conscript men against their will into military service. Between 1793 and 1812, as many as fifteen thousand US seamen were impressed, many of whom were Black men. Like Elias Linch who implores a lawyer to help him in this letter:

Sir

I Rec'd youre letter on the 22nd & cording to youre Disire I forward my letter to youre office Hoping youre Goodness will remite it to Mr Lyman in London in wich I include my Protection Sir my Protection has been wet but I Dare to Say that youre goodness will take That in Consideration & Cleare me from this Serveis.

Unlike a more orderly draft, the British employed violent means to fill their naval labor shortage. Armed press gangs boarded merchant ships and then beat, kidnapped, and forced American men into service. Black mariners made up a significant part of the labor force on the docks of the Northeast. But mistrust, discrimination, and fear of Black people was almost universal in that era. And there is a gross misconception that free Blacks in the North enjoyed the same rights and social privileges as whites. They didn't. Writers spoke of "Free Negrodom" as a "grievous affliction," and a danger to the institution of slavery. "Jurists and legislators also characterized free Blacks as a class unworthy of envy, lazy and incapable of self-care, destined to live in a state of squalor and degeneracy far below the station of the slave, and fated to create a burden on society as a whole . . . a class of people who are neither freemen nor slaves, their presence at all times deleterious and often dangerous to the public welfare."

As we can now begin to see, overlooking the plight of free Black people has prevented us from understanding the origins of racial attitudes that traveled with westward expansion, and that are very much still in existence, especially regarding Black urban populations and the fear of a Black influx into suburbs, as this was the precursor to white flight. Even now I don't think it is a stretch to say that if one or two Black families move into a white suburb it is okay, but any more and it becomes a problem. Further ignored is the double burden. For instance, we are taught to empathize with the American Revolution idea that "taxation without representation is tyranny," but in an age of tax revolts, free Black people had to pay taxes for public institutions and services that they could not access. What we see with the examples of taxes and impressment is that at the same time Blacks faced outsized racial discrimination, they were no less affected by the most pressing issues of American history (no pun intended).

The War of 1812 raged on. A British fleet consisting of thirty frigates and bomb vessels sailed on the Atlantic Ocean and appeared at the mouth of the Patapsco River on Saturday, September 10, 1814. It was the Royal Navy. The most powerful in the world. Prepared to assault the city of Baltimore. We like to tell ourselves that the United States could never be invaded. But in a swaggering show of force, the British invaded Washington, DC, only weeks earlier, setting the capital on fire. They reduced all but one major building into a smoking pile of rubble. Back in Baltimore, five bomb vessels anchored in Chesapeake Bay, about two miles out from the Baltimore harbor. Unleashing a torrent of gunfire, they animated the sky with rockets throughout the night. Two-hundred-pound cannonballs burst overhead, bombs crumbled buildings, four American soldiers died, twenty-four were wounded. Under the command of Lieutenant Colonel George Armistead, the US soldiers fought back bravely. They fired round after round from their Springfield muskets, pushing back the British soldiers until they retreated. From this well-known battle in history comes a lesser-known fact. Of the thousand soldiers, one was a Black man. His name was Frederick Hall, who after escaping slavery, took the alias William Williams and joined the 38th US Infantry Regiment. Williams was a fugitive. For reasons unknown, his race was overlooked at his enlistment. But not long after, he was marching off to Fort McHenry, taking his place in the history of the War of 1812.

Black history is American history, often overlooked in America's most pivotal moments, but you shouldn't be surprised to find it once you begin to search. As 4,700 British troops marched on Baltimore, an American aboard one of their ships negotiated the release of his friend. The man was a young lawyer named Francis Scott Key. He was on board when the Royal Navy unleashed its bombs on Fort McHenry. As the United States fought its way to victory, Key witnessed the US flag, illuminated by the bombs bursting in air, with its fifteen stripes and stars, and it inspired him to write "The Star-Spangled Banner." You might be surprised to read this, but our national anthem has four verses, some of which you'll recognize:

> O say can you see, by the dawn's early light,
> What so proudly we hail'd at the twilight's last gleaming,
> Whose broad stripes and bright stars through the perilous fight
> O'er the ramparts we watched were so gallantly streaming?
> And the rocket's red glare, the bombs bursting in air,
> Gave proof through the night that our flag was still there,
> O say does that star-spangled banner yet wave
> O'er the land of the free and the home of the brave?

But you may not be as familiar with the other half:

And where is that band who so vauntingly swore,
That the havoc of war and the battle's confusion
A home and a Country should leave us no more?
Their blood has wash'd out their foul footstep's pollution.
No refuge could save the hireling and slave
From the terror of flight or the gloom of the grave,
And the star-spangled banner in triumph doth wave
O'er the land of the free and the home of the brave.

I could be wrong, but I don't think Diana Ross, Luther Vandross, or Beyoncé would've sung "The Star-Spangled Banner" at the Super Bowl if the lyrics "no refuge for slaves" had been included. Again, we find another whitewashed history. Was Key antagonizing the enslaved? We can't ask Key to verify the meaning of his lyrics, but it is likely he was referring to the Colonial Marines, units of enslaved Blacks who, promised their freedom, joined the British.

After the war, the British kept their promise by giving them land in Trinidad and Tobago. White colonists who sided with the British have been called loyalists, but I think the vast majority of Black people who picked up arms for either side were loyal to their own bid for freedom before any country or cause. I've noticed that people take pride in the vision of Black revolutionary patriots, and I hate to be the bubble buster, but how could there be Black patriots? I mean, since the United States claimed to be the land of freedom, many Black people sided with America. But patriots vigorously support their country and defend it against common enemies, so how could they be fighting to establish a country to which they could not belong, that repeatedly positioned Black people as the enemy? They were fighting on whatever side promised freedom.

Those like Key had no sympathy for Black liberation—he was himself a slaveholder from a wealthy Maryland plantation family. Viewing them as "a distinct and inferior race," Francis Scott Key would have had no sympathy for those like William Williams, the Black soldier who fought for the United States against the British. A man who was severely wounded, having his leg "blown off by a cannonball," and dying two months later. Those like Key would not have cared that American flags were being stitched by those like Grace Wisher, a Black indentured servant girl who, under the order of Mary Pickersgill, helped to craft those bold stars and stripes. Wisher labored for about seven weeks making the fabric—weaving and assembling, piecing together strips of loosely woven English wool bunting—until finally they assembled the 30' x 42' garrison flag that flew over Fort McHenry. So has been the story of Black people. If US history is like a textile, made by creating interlocking bundles of yarns and threads, then the Black experience is interwoven into every fiber of American history.

Building America

Black people built America. Frederick Douglass knew it, as he pondered Black equality during a speech in 1852, listing the ways in which Black labor fueled national growth:

> While we are plowing, planting, and reaping, using all kinds of mechanical tools, erecting houses, constructing bridges, building ships, working in metals of brass, iron, copper, silver, and gold; that while we are reading, writing, and ciphering, acting as clerks, merchants, and secretaries, having among us lawyers, doctors, ministers, poets, authors, editors, orators, and teachers; that we are engaged in all the enterprises common to other men—digging gold in California, capturing the whale in the Pacific, feeding sheep and cattle on the hillside, living, moving, acting, thinking, planning, living in families as husbands, wives, and children, and above all, confessing and worshipping the Christian God, and looking hopefully for life and immortality beyond the grave.

It is astonishing that while doing all of this, Black people still found time to agitate for freedom. Those like Prince Hall, a man who moved from bondage to poverty to become one of the most prominent men in Boston. By 1783, the judiciary of Massachusetts ruled enslavement unconstitutional, and Hall worked to assimilate with the Boston elite. Using the leatherworking skills he'd learned while enslaved (or indentured, depending on the history), he grew his business. But he was best known for catering. This contemporary account shows his esteem in the community:

"Prince Hall. A tall, lean Negro of great dignity, he always carried himself with the air of one who ruled many. Indeed, he did, for whenever a well-to-do person wished the best catering job in Eastern Massachusetts, he sent word to Prince Hall in Boston. . . . He appeared with a dozen of his black men, or two dozen, if necessary." A contemporary of John Adams, we might imagine Prince Hall passing him in the street wearing his waistcoat, stockings, and powdered wig. Hall was determined to make his way in colonial society, even forming his own Masonic lodge, after noting that some of the city's most prominent men were part of the organization.

But Hall was not only out for narrow success, as Professor Danielle Allen notes, he was a Black founding father. A man who pioneered the Black activist community and pioneered abolition through his brilliant use of the petition. Using the same language as the Declaration of Independence, only six months after it was written, Hall applied its truths to Black emancipation.

As Allen goes on to tell us: "Hall invokes the core concepts of social-contract theory, which grounded the American Revolution, to argue for an extension of the claim to equal rights to those who were enslaved. He acknowledged and adopted the intellectual framework of the new political arrangements, but also pointedly called out the original sin of enslavement itself."

Away from a few retellings by Black scholars, you will scarcely find the stories of those like Hall incorporated into the narrative of America's founding. Even though his many petitions expand our understanding of the fight to push the Constitution beyond its limitations. The problem with this sort of exclusion, other than the absence of Black colonial life, is that it plays to the myth of a perfect union. We hear about its brilliant articulation of power as an extension of the people, but not the cruelty of constitutional exclusion.

As Black people helped build lasting wealth in America, their own communities crumbled. White wealth and political power have almost always controlled who stays and who goes. As we mentioned in chapter six about Africville in Canada, development-induced displacement has forced people from their homes, and even desecrated burial sites to accommodate the construction of parks, dams, reservoirs, oil, and mining projects. In this way, Seneca Village, a settlement of predominantly Black property owners, was seized by New York City in 1853 to create Central Park. The neighborhood thrived with schools, churches, a cemetery, and the political power that came with property ownership, allowing those who lived there to vote. The Lyons family, part of the free Black elite, even ran a successful stop on the Underground Railroad, assisting countless fugitives. But as New York expanded with poor immigrants, wealthy whites created a vision of a grand park surrounded by wealthy homes. Claiming eminent domain, which allowed the government to seize private property for federal use, the 1,600 or so people living in Seneca Village were ousted. Dubbed "nigger village" in the papers, Black people were evicted along with their Irish and German neighbors. We can only imagine what America might look like if these neighborhoods had been left to thrive. Instead, we are left to reckon with the scars of their memory.

For more than a century, New Yorkers willfully forgot that their beloved Central Park was created by the displacement of the marginalized. This was a precursor to a long history of urban renewal, codified in the Housing Act of 1954 and lasting into the 1960s. The government shelled out billions to private interests to tear down blighted neighborhoods and replace them with affordable housing. But there was a net loss as developers expanded universities, hospitals, built shopping centers, and offices. Hundreds of thousands of homes fell at the swing of a wrecking ball. Some three hundred thousand people were displaced between 1955 and 1966.

As rents skyrocket and affordable housing decreases, architects and urban planners might do well to remember this history. For those who do not learn from the redevelopment plans of the past will be doomed to repeat them. But the burden of those mistakes falls mostly on poor and Black communities. Have we failed to connect the dots? At the vantage point from which I am currently writing, it all feels like manifest destiny 2.0. For most of American history, the ideal of development has played a major role in the devaluation of humanity, displacing people in the name of progress. So, even when Black communities have tried to build, they've been indiscriminately removed from their rental homes, private property, and businesses.

We've just shown the destruction of the Black fabric in America through the destruction of its buildings. But Black history also lies within the walls of buildings that still stand. The presidential palace at 1600 Pennsylvania Avenue represents American freedom though it was built by enslaved labor.

When construction began in 1793, they hauled materials, cut the trees, and sawed the lumber. They worked alongside immigrants from Ireland, Scotland, and other European nations. But the Black laborers didn't only do manual labor. They also worked in carpentry, ironworking, and bricklaying. The pure white limestone walls of the Capitol were cut by Black hands. They helped build the Capitol, the White House, the streets, and the building for the Treasury Department, which paid enslavers an average of fifty-five dollars a year for their labor. And while those European immigrants were paid a fair wage, the more than four hundred enslaved were only given clothing, food, and shacks to live in.

Up until 1855, the dome of the Capitol was inconspicuous. Congress wanted something magnificent to adorn its top, so they commissioned sculptor Thomas Crawford for the job. His original designs featured a graceful female figure wearing a liberty cap, the symbol from classical antiquity of manumitted slaves. Jefferson Davis, a slaveholder and future president of the Confederacy, wasn't fond of liberty caps. Saying that the cap "is the sign of a freedman," he added, "We were always free, not freedmen, not slaves just released." So, the symbolic liberty cap was replaced by a headdress featuring a wild-eyed eagle with its mouth open and its talons dangling on the side of her face.

But for all the disdain for the enslaved, it was a thirty-nine-year-old enslaved man named Philip Reed (variously spelled as Philip Reid) who saved the project. Once the statue made it to the Capitol, an Italian workman assembled it near the building to display what it would look like atop the Rotunda. However, when he was ordered to take it apart, he refused. As he alone "knew how to separate it," he would only do so under strict conditions, requesting a hefty increase in wages and guaranteed employment for years. It was mild extortion. But through Reed's brilliance, it would not be. Devising a pulley and tackle system, he was able to strain the rope in a way that revealed the joining of the top section, indicating where the bolts were located. In this way he continued until each of the five sections were disassembled. Reed eventually gained freedom, went into business for himself, and was "highly esteemed by all who knew him." His remains are in an unmarked mass grave. But in 2014, 134 years after his death, he finally received a placard to commemorate his overlooked contribution, which, not unlike the story of Robert Smalls (see chapter one), now sits on the ground in the dirt.

A History Overlooked

On the underside of that same Capitol Rotunda, suspended 180 feet above the floor, is a glorious fresco painting of George Washington rising to the heavens, surrounded by white female figures symbolizing liberty, fame, and victory. The painting is named "Apotheosis of Washington," *apotheosis* meaning the raising of a person to the rank of a god. The work, completed by artist Constantino Brumidi, an Italian immigrant, is astounding. Each carefully constructed scene tells the story of America's founding. One part, for instance, shows an armed goddess of Liberty flanked by an eagle defeating tyranny and kingship. And yet, even with all its cryptic symbology, the message is clear. White people won the American Revolutionary War and made America. They are the sole heirs of the great American founding. But a true picture would also show the Native American blood spilled in the war. A true telling would honor the manumitted slaves, for their participation in the Revolutionary War, who as stated by a Virginia legislator in 1783, "have thereby of course contributed toward the establishment of American liberty and independence."

Alas, absolute freedom would not come for all. When George Washington signed the Constitution, he forgot about those Black people whom he'd initially refused to admit to the Continental Armies, until a shortage of manpower changed his mind. America has had a difficult time seeing Black people as patriotic. When Crispus Attucks, a man believed to have African and Native American ancestry, was the first to die in the Boston Massacre, informally known as the first battle of the Revolutionary War, he was not uplifted as a hero. Then lawyer and future president John Adams called him a rabble-rouser. In paintings memorializing the event, the dead body of Attucks was painted white. Only later was he placed front and center by abolitionist artists. Fighting for America has never been enough to garner collective freedom for Black people, and it certainly was not enough to solve the constitutional dilemma of how natural rights could extend to end Black enslavement.

Some hundred years after, on July 4, 1965, Martin Luther King Jr. spoke from the pulpit at Ebenezer Baptist Church in Atlanta, Georgia, about making that American dream a reality. He was but one in a long line of Black people who helped build democracy. Some took a radical approach, others were more conservative, but many believed in the underlying principles of the Constitution and the Bill of Rights. All along, it has been Black people who held America up to its greatest ideals. Before the ink dried on the paper of the Constitution, Black people were trying to put into practice the essence of humanity's best hopes and intentions. Understanding King, "yes, the dream has been shattered, and I have had my nightmarish experiences, but I tell you this morning once more that I haven't lost the faith."

Many Black people search history and find defeat, alienation, and exclusion. Focused only on today and tomorrow, we forget that we are the progeny of those who shaped the American republic. The descendants of those who wove themselves into the fabric of America. The offspring of those who sought liberty through the courts, and carried democracy on their worn shoulders; of those who sought diplomacy and resorted to militancy; who formed eternal bonds in the name of freedom, endured racial hatred, and the oppression of enemies; and still later, who challenged immoral interpretations of the Constitution.

Black people, indigenous people, poor working people, and others who were marginalized get left out of the story. The great institutions have left off the names of those who helped to build them. But each generation has a responsibility to reinterpret the past, debunk the conspiracy of silence, and reclaim what was lost. Even now, we need a history to provide a space where true acknowledgment can be found. A true story of our history, one that gives insight into human behavior and lived experiences, illustrating patterns that might guide us along our never-ending journey of national transformation.

PART 3

Anti-Black American History

The people who dwell in the land of dimness, the people who could not see themselves except as formless shadows moving in a mist, the people who had gouged out their own eyes to keep from looking at themselves in the mirror, these people, these glorious people were none other than ourselves: The Americans.

—Henry Dumas

Resistance!
Resistance!
Resistance!

"Two hundred and twenty-seven years ago, the first of our injured race were brought to the shores of America. They came not with glad spirits to select their homes, in the New World. They came not with their own consent, to find an unmolested enjoyment of the blessings of this fruitful soil. The first dealings which they had with men calling themselves Christians, exhibited to them the worst features of corrupt and sordid hearts; and convinced them that no cruelty is too great, no villainy and no robbery too abhorrent for even enlightened men to perform, when influenced by avarice, and lust. . . . Let your motto be resistance! resistance! RESISTANCE! No oppressed people have ever secured their liberty without resistance. What kind of resistance you had better make, you must decide by the circumstances that surround you, and according to the suggestion of expediency."
—Henry Highland Garnett, 1843

I n 1730s South Carolina, an agrarian economy rapidly expanded into generational fortunes. Ocean-faring vessels kept the Charleston docks busy as bounties of rice and indigo were loaded for European markets. International trade, the wealth of nations, created sprawling coastal estates. Georgian-style plantation homes and Federal-style buildings welcomed monied, antebellum families through their mahogany entry doors. Chandeliers, floor-to-ceiling bookshelves, European paintings, and statues decorating sprawling thirty-room mansions. All of this was underpinned by a constant cycle of human chattel. As Native Americans were exported to the Caribbean, and Africans were imported into the Americas, the stage for this world of extravagance, cruel subjugation, and resistance was set nearly two centuries earlier. As we mentioned in chapter eight, in 1526 blood spilled on those Carolina sands, dooming the Spanish colony of Lucas Vásquez de Ayllón and eradicating slavery in North America for the first time in the history of European colonization. The writing was on the wall. The enslaved revolted again, again, and again.

As dawn approached on Sunday, September 9, 1739, a group of enslaved Kongolese people made their way to the Stono Bridge. They proceeded to kill all the whites in their path. The brutality of their enslavers was equally matched. No women or children were spared. They severed heads and placed them on pikes. It would have been strange and terrifying but not uncommon. A carryover from Europe, this tactic was used as a deterrent for unruly, enslaved people. As the group of rebels continued in hopes of making it to freedom in Spanish Florida, their numbers swelled. What started at around twenty soon approached one hundred defiant souls. Many relented, but others joined in "calling out liberty, marched on with colours displayed, and two drums beating, pursuing all the white people they met with." They fought with the bravery of seasoned soldiers, but the militia caught up and overwhelmed the enslaved warriors with force, hunted those who ran, chopped them down, and mutilated their corpses. There were countless revolts like this spanning the history of slavery. What might we conclude? Each illuminated the most desperate and violent response to the most tyrannical manifestation of white supremacy: race-based slavery.

The American public has been slow to open this Pandora's box of slavery, freedom, war, caste, and anti-Blackness. American history is drenched in blood and yet America has been all too willing to cover the stains. There are those who would skip right over this part of the past. Those who'd sum up America's anti-Black history in one paragraph. It usually goes something like this: The United States of America is by no means perfect, but the founding principles extinguished slavery, racism, equal rights violations, and evil itself from the law. And now we enjoy tremendous degrees of freedom, peace, and prosperity available to everyone.

The end. But not so fast, because we all know that this is not the end. In the here and now, people are pushing hard against this simplistic interpretation and coming to understand that injustice in America is rooted in our history. I've thought about how, in her 2010 book, *The New Jim Crow: Mass Incarceration in the Age of Colorblindness*, Michelle Alexander recovers the connection between slavery's past and present. Arguing that the spirit of slavery survived through Jim Crow, and now in the era of colorblindness, it survives through our system of mass incarceration, where:

> It is no longer socially permissible to use race, explicitly, as a justification for discrimination, exclusion, and social contempt. So, we don't. Rather than rely on race, we use our criminal justice system to label people of color "criminals" and then engage in all the practices we supposedly left behind. Today it is perfectly legal to discriminate against criminals in nearly all the ways that it was once legal to discriminate against African Americans.

I've thought about the conversations around reparations and how scholars have recovered the economic legacy of slavery. The numbers are staggering. According to Roger L. Ransom in his essay "The Economics of the Civil War": "In 1805 there were just over one million slaves worth about $300 million; fifty-five years later there were four million slaves worth close to $3 billion." And that doesn't even begin to account for the generated wealth or the residual value of buildings and infrastructure or the untraceable disappearance of intellectual property. I've thought about the studies of old-guard scholars like historian and Trinidad prime minister Eric Williams. In his phenomenal 1944 book, *Capitalism and Slavery*, he set out to prove the centrality of the triangular slave trade to the development of industrial capitalism. The connection between slavery and capitalism is now widely accepted, but in his own time Williams's work caused a seismic debate among labor historians. Meanwhile, his Marxist-inspired idea that race is secondary to class set off an infinite debate still ongoing among scholars. There is much to be said about the historic underdevelopment of the Black community and the exploitative tendrils of the US capitalist economy. The popular position today is that race and capitalism are inextricably linked, but Williams disagreed. "A racial twist has thereby been given to what is basically an economic phenomenon," he wrote. "Slavery was not born of racism: rather, racism was the consequence of slavery."

I agree that the obsessive quest of seafaring and militarily dominant countries to extract a wide range of resources was the parent of slavery and racism, but Williams pushed me to look at a range of factors when studying economic and labor history. Through his lens, we might see how industrialization factored into the end of slavery and examine the compatibility of morality and capitalism. The pendulum of history swings forward as we address the effects of rapidly shifting technology on Black people's economic plight in America. And Williams's view also reminded me about how far removed we are from the labor that produces our abstract commodities. Reports have come out about Starbucks repeatedly sourcing beans from Brazil coffee plantations that force slave labor from children. In Haiti people produced Rawlings baseballs for thirty cents an hour before the company closed its plant and moved to Costa Rica. None of that stopped anyone from getting a Caramel Cocoa Cluster Frappuccino or going to a great American baseball game. The modern separation between us and unethical sources of labor is easily understood with knowledge of the transatlantic slave trade.

In 2022, the *Washington Post* put together a chart titled "Who Owned Slaves in Congress," tracking more than 1,800 slave-owning Congress members. It dove into how they voted, the laws they shaped, and the states they represented. The patrolling, controlling, and surveilling of poor and Black communities in America are reminiscent of slave patrols. The use of dogs, the excessive force, the assumptions of Black criminality, the fear. I remember when people gained their perceptions of the police and poor and Black communities through shows like *Cops*. It is not surprising that those perceptions are highly distorted. I remember one episode in which a white officer in Kansas pried a Black man's mouth open with the butt of his flashlight before leaving the flashlight in the man's mouth while the officer searched for drugs. Such senseless violence also makes me think about the links recovered by scholars between slavery and Black health. How modern gynecology was founded on nonconsensual and unethical experimentation on enslaved Black women. How has the legacy of slavery affected negative stereotypes about Black health and pain? And how does the medical industry still exploit vulnerable populations like the elderly, the mentally disabled, the poor, and the orphans of all races. I think about all these things as directly tied to the history of slavery.

All those conversations are relevant, but there are a few key ideas that I tend to focus on when I recount the stories of racial slavery. One is global Black agency and resistance. Anti-Black history is not simply about what has been done to Black people, but how they leveraged what power they could muster from the depths of this new racial hierarchy. Two is empathy for the suffering. I always think about the heart of history. We can look to local headlines every year to see apathy on display. In 2019, teachers had students at a South Carolina elementary school recite a slave song and pick cotton on a class field trip. That same year, white students at a private school in Bronxville, New York, were encouraged to bid on their Black classmates. As I read stories like these, I wonder, does America have the heart to tell the truth about the centuries-long assault on Black humanity?

Because white power usually doesn't appear in a hood. It manifests in everyday settings like these. Even in professional settings, it is comfortable operating unbound from an expectation of reciprocal human dignity. How much more would young minds learn if they were introduced to slave narratives like Harriet Jacobs's *Incidents in the Life of a Slave Girl* (1861) and the autobiography *The Life and Times of Frederick Douglass* (1881), and then carefully walked through race and racism in America and what this history has meant for us all?

And finally, a deeper conversation about ethics. Does violence justify violence? How has a belief in the moral unworthiness of Black people shaped their disenfranchisement in America? What does American slavery have to teach us about current human struggles for existence and freedom? We live in a present where one in two hundred people are in some way enslaved. Why is the suffering of the enslaved ignored? How has racism halted the very attempts that would help us work through it? How can we construct a better moral philosophy out of this history? These are the themes and questions that will guide us through this chapter. The Black nations who acted in the rapidly changing world, and the survivors of American chattel slavery, have something to tell us about navigating this remade world. Billions of historic property, marriage, life, and death re-cords exist to bolster their narratives. Their stories alert us to the horrors of race-based slavery and why they resisted. Their stories need to be brought forward.

Our Country Is Being Completely Depopulated

In 1721, a ship docked at an estuary in Sierra Leone, or the Gold Coast, to load up human chattel for the long trip on the Middle Passage destined for Jamaica. This was a history almost three hundred years in the making. In 1441, a Portuguese captain sailing off the coast of Mauritania in West Af-rica thought it would be better to bring back human captives as a gift to the prince, in addition to seal skins and oils. One night, the men disembarked and followed a set of footprints leading to a man. They attacked him. He fought back and ran. But his wounds slowed him down and he was cap-tured. What began as a mission for one captive was escalated by greed. They moved farther inland capturing a woman. Then came across an encamp-ment of Africans they called Moors. A battle ensued, but the Portuguese javelins overwhelmed the men and their spears. They loaded the seal skins, oils, and captive humans onto the ship and sailed to Portugal.

This incident was no historical aberration; this pattern of strikes and surprise attacks began a seismic shift in the Old World balance of power as it tilted toward European domination. The unprovoked incursions by the Portuguese into places like Angola stimulated geopolitical shifts that were astounding in their global scale and velocity, and our world—reconstructed under the European racial world order—would never be the same. Many have bought into the idea that European domination equaled European superiority. But as economist and Stanford fellow Thomas Sowell observed:

> Europeans were able to cross the Atlantic Ocean in the first place because they could steer with rudders invented in China, calculate their position on the open sea through trigonometry invented in Egypt, using numbers cre-ated in India. The knowledge they had accumulated from around the world was preserved in letters written on paper invented in China. The military

power they brought with them increasingly depended on weapons using gunpowder, also invented in Asia.

The balance of power was shifting, but Afonso I, the ruler of the Kingdom of Kongo, who had first supported the slave trade, saw which way the winds were blowing and reversed his position. In 1526, through a series of thirty diplomatic correspondences, he implored the Portuguese crown to end the practice. "Our country is being completely depopulated, and Your Highness should not agree with this. . . . It is our will that in these Kingdoms there should not be any trade of slaves nor outlet for them." He learned a hard lesson, that enriching potential enemies to feed your mercantile interests is a quick way to compromise your defense. The more Africa fed the slave demand, the more powerful Europe became, and the less powerful they were to stop it. The Kongo was prone to oppose the Portuguese incursions for the same reasons most nations would, a mix of nationalism and desire for autonomy. They were prone to diplomacy for the same reason most nations are, to remain in economic, military, and political alliance with a more powerful nation and remain dominant in their own regional disputes. To restore the soul of history is to place nations like the Kongo back into history as agents, and not just passive observers. The Kongo offers a lesson in human geopolitics. It never turns out well when your national fate rests on the whims of one other nation. Portugal systematically exploited the imbalance of power with the Kongo at every turn.

Another leader drew a harder line. A woman who used a mix of diplomacy, strategic alliances, and aggressive military resistance to rebalance power back into her favor. Her name was Queen Njinga (sometimes spelled "Nzinga"). I don't mean to sound hyperbolic, but she became one of the most politically powerful women in the world in the sixteenth century, though it seems only Tudor women are candidates for that list. Born into the royal Ndongo Kingdom, a vassal state of the Kongo Kingdom, Njinga found herself sandwiched between enemy states and Portuguese encroachment. In her now famous meeting, she'd been dispatched by her brother, the king of Ndongo, to negotiate with the Portuguese. Making a huge showing, she appeared with a large retinue, draped in the finest traditional fabrics, covered in jewels and colorful feathers. Portuguese administrators refused her a chair. We might imagine that Njinga knew the consequences of deferring her authority by sitting on the ground, so she called an attendant to their hands and knees to act as her chair for the duration of the meeting. Becoming queen in 1626, she was a shrewd diplomat. Njinga secured trade in guns with the Portuguese, sourced, captured, and enslaved her enemies to avoid her own people becoming enslaved. Then she flipped and made friends of her enemies to fight against the Portuguese. It was not a relationship of military equals, but Njinga was astute in diversifying her alliances as a survival tactic. Pushed from the coast to the interior, she founded a new kingdom, Matamba, and strategically sided with the Dutch against the Portuguese.

Never timid in deploying hard power, Njinga led her battle-hardened troops into war well into her sixties. Her fierce pride and war stamina eventually tired the Portuguese, who signed a peace treaty and returned her original Kingdom of Ndongo. She died in in her early eighties in 1663. Why did Njinga resist? She was understandably angry at being treated disrespectfully by the Portuguese and clearly wanted to rule over a stable and autonomous nation free from Portuguese rule. Some have suggested that she saw the forms of slavery practiced by the Portuguese as unnaturally different from her own country's traditions, which were more like serfdom and bonded imprisonment. We know that slave exports from Angola dropped while she was in power, and at times her nation was a haven for the enslaved. At any rate, she was prudent and pragmatic not to set herself at the mercy of Portugal. Until recently, her complicated legacy was degraded in a cesspool of racism and sexism. Europeans labeled her as a "manly queen," and a Black savage cannibal who ate her victims. It was only through the work of resolute scholar Linda M. Heywood, who constructed the first full-length biography of her life titled *Njinga of Angola: Africa's Warrior Queen* (2017), that we have a more accurate depiction based on extensive records and oral histories.

When it comes to resistance in Africa, I sometimes go down the rabbit hole of "what ifs," wondering what history would have been like had a large coalition of West African polities combined forces to face off against European colonists. How would history be different if they could have set aside their disputes and united into a larger force to fight back, negotiate, and remain equals with the European powers? This sentiment is reflected by author Ngũgĩ wa Thiong'o in his novel *Wizard of the Crow* when he says:

> Why did Africa let Europe cart away millions of Africa's souls from the continent to the four corners of the wind? How could Europe lord over a continent ten times its size? Why does needy Africa continue to let its wealth meet the needs of those outside its borders and then follow behind with hands outstretched for a loan of the very wealth it let go? How did we arrive at this, that the best leader is the one that knows how to beg for a share of what he has already given away at the price of a broken tool? Where is the future of Africa?

This is a question that may have occurred to anyone studying the continent of Africa. There was no singular cause we can point to. The chain reaction was akin to dominoes. When the first domino falls, it impacts the next one with minimal force, but as the next tile falls, the game gains speed until the chain reaction has the tiles falling so fast you can barely register the velocity. Thus, the plight of Africa. An adventurous European merchant kidnaps a few Africans and entices his king with human cargo. More expeditions are funded, and this happens again and again, spread out over years. Europeans stoked the flames of age-old ethnic conflicts and poured accelerant on territorial fires among African polities. They enticed the African elite with flint, liquor, jewelry, and other material goods. The old weatherworn institution of slavery accelerated faster and faster and faster into a new global phenomenon. Then moved rapidly as transatlantic expansions to the Americas replicated the desire for cheap labor. Add in the racial, the ethnic, the colonial, and imperial ingredients, and you get a recipe for baked-in disaster. Massive wealth creation and advances in technology outpaced advances in morality. None of this was inevitable, but in hindsight it was predictable. Peace is seldom a match for unchecked power in a bid for resources. While ethics and cooperation are the paths to peace, greed accelerates warlike embers in dry brush on the edge of a forest.

Blood in the Water

Most of what we know about life and death on the Middle Passage comes from the accounts of white ship captains, sailors, and surgeons, along with merchants and planters. There is an eerie Black silence in their telling; we can barely hear their voices because they rarely shared their truths. So, when we look back, we can only imagine countless human figures. We cannot rescue them from their torment on those rat-infested ships, but we can reach back with outstretched arms to bring the nuance of their stories to the foreground.

Imagine the ring from a deafening crack. You're terrified. Men come and seize you and some of your people forcibly. You are then marched in coffles (groups of humans chained together) and passed off to other men with pale skin and a strange language, constantly shoved with their weapons. You don't know it yet, but if you're deemed fit enough, you'll end up in the hull of cargo ships specially built or converted for your transportation. They were not constructed for comfort. Your trip will last roughly eighty days. At times you're made to lie in your neighbor's feces, urine, and vomit. You'll be force-fed salty food, the English language, and Christianity. Some of those who share your destiny look like skeletons arisen from the grave, their eyes set back deeply into their skulls, their skin sagging and barely attached to the bone. They've refused to eat. Perhaps from despair. Perhaps from protest. How . . . could . . . anyone . . . endure such death, such decomposition, such decay, such demeaning violence? Lack of air circulation and ventilation causes a lingering stench and dampness. You'll fight for every breath. Or maybe you'll beg for death. And there were those who faced that choice and sacrificed themselves to the sea, hurling themselves over the side of the ships, mingling their fate with the waves of the ocean. This happened so often, netting was stretched out from the ship hull to catch those attempting to leap.

This fate awaited millions of people corralled like cattle, seized from their homes and marched to well-guarded barracoons. Perhaps they'd be there for days, maybe months. Then the ship would arrive and dock, and people quickly learned what it meant to lose all bodily autonomy. Like rejected goods, infants, the disabled, and the elderly were discarded if they weren't conducive to commercial profit. Teeth and gums were prodded to check age. Surgeons grabbed genitals, squeezed breasts, moved limbs, and tested bodies for a lifetime of forced labor, human breeding, and child-rearing.

Emerging from one of these barracoons was a man of "strong Make, and bold stern aspect." At the port when other captives submitted to these examinations, the man refused. He was whipped viciously with a "cutting Manatea strap" for his defiance. He took the blows with firm resilience, and a witness noted that he "shed a Tear or two, which he endeavored to hide as tho' ashamed of." They called him Captain Tomba. He had been the leader of a group of villages and was vehemently opposed to the slave trade. He and his group waged war on those who cooperated with the Europeans, burning huts and villages. For this he was hunted down. The man killed two of his attackers before he was subdued. Once on the slave ship he conspired to escape, partnering with an unidentified woman who slipped him a hammer through the ship's deck gratings, with which he immediately pounded off his fetters. Tomba killed two of the sailors with "single Strokes upon the temples," and when he killed the third, he woke the rest. Tomba was knocked out and subdued. It might say something about the disregard for human life and the parasitic greed of slavery that the life of the murderous Tomba was worth more than the three poor white sailors he killed; other enslaved humans were deemed less valuable and were brutally murdered. Tomba was whipped and scarified but spared. His perceived strength bought him immunity; he was viewed as too valuable to kill. He was sold in Jamaica along with 189 other enslaved people. Potential labor and profits are always worth more than humanity. But it is in these stories of inhumanity where we might find our own.

For almost two years, I lived in the historic city of Savannah, Georgia, where I'd heard the story of 1803, when, at Dunbar Creek near St. Simons Island in Georgia, some seventy-five enslaved Africans from present-day Nigeria, of Igbo descent, were packed in the belly of a small sailing vessel headed for a life of labor on one of the region's plantations. But it was also there that they rose to bear down on their captors. They had the element of surprise, so their enslavers leapt overboard and drowned in panic. What happened next was shocking. According to Pierce Butler, an overseer on a nearby plantation, they "took to the swamp." Some say they were led by their high chief, singing and drowning themselves, in an act of mass suicide. But as the oral traditions tell it, those precious souls flew over the water back to Africa.

I felt compelled to go there. One day I drove to find it. That was no easy task. There was no marker to memorialize the dead. But I puzzled it together from Google Maps and pulled over on a nondescript stretch of Georgia roadway. I was only greeted by cars whizzing by, and a couple of horns, most likely from people wondering what I was doing getting out at this seemingly random location. I walked down an embankment, plodded through mud, and stood surrounded by chest-level cordgrass. Looking out over the coppery brown water, I narrated their story in my head. I was moved to tears.

Then I recalled an old folktale. Have you ever heard it, the one about how a hurricane forms? Story goes that hurricanes begin around the African coast and follow the same path as the slave ships on the transatlantic slave trade. Sometimes, hurricanes form above the Cape Verde archipelago off the coast of West Africa, gathering colossal power in their transformation from tropical storm to hurricane. Some have said that those storms harbor the spirit of vengeance, an act of retribution from countless millions who died on the Middle Passage. Of course, this is a myth. Hurricanes bring death, destruction, loss, and suffering to all people, no matter what race. But then I thought, maybe by truly feeling these stories of violence, we'd want to move more quickly toward peace, toward justice, toward basic human dignity, as though running from a hurricane of human suffering.

Until Haiti Struck for Freedom

So far, we've shown how the winds of resistance drifted not only in America, but across the African diaspora. Transatlantic slavery and resistance were Pan-African affairs. Everywhere you look, you will find them. I often think about the insurgent maroon societies who escaped and formed war camps in mountainous interiors and deep woods, frequently raiding and pestering plantations. Most prominent in the Caribbean and South America, in Brazil these settlements were called *quilombos*. (They were known as *palenques* in Spanish-speaking countries. During the American

Civil War, similar camps created near Union lines were known as contraband camps.)

The largest one, founded by Ganga Zumba, was a self-sustaining community with 30,000 people and 1,500 homes. Descended from Kongolese royalty, he lived as a king on his compound complete with royal guards, ministers, subjects, officials, and intermediaries to negotiate with the Portuguese in between their many battles. It's almost unbelievable to think that there was a small city-state of African royalty in existence in South America in the seventeenth century. When I was reading about this history, I also came across a female warrior named Dandara, who was said to have mastered the techniques of capoeira, the cunning Afro-Brazilian mixture of dancing and fighting, replete with handstands, somersaults, kicks, sidesteps, dexterity, strength, taunting, bravado, and evasions. To see it is to see nothing like it.

It may be said that the most powerful event to spark the Black imagination with visions of liberation in America happened on an island 1,889 miles away. It was the Haitian Revolution. All the major slave revolts in the United States shared fatal similarities. They were mostly disorganized and destined for failure. Not complete failure, as the constant agitation caused the fear that kept the slavery question on the forefront, but they would've never resulted in some grand overthrow of the United States government. A war could not be won without a multiracial coalition, and most just wanted to escape. But Haiti was different.

Under the diplomatic brilliance of Toussaint Louverture (mentioned earlier in the prologue), and the fearlessness of Jean-Jacques Dessalines, untrained ex-slaves in Haiti were forged into a force capable not only of fighting but of gaining the leverage needed to negotiate advantageous deals with European powers. History is full of irony—by fighting for their own liberation from monarchial tyranny, the French had inspired the people they kidnapped and enslaved to fight for their own. When the French checked the bodies of deceased Haitians killed in the revolution, they found *Declaration of the Rights of Man and the Citizen* pamphlets in their pockets, which stated that all men are "born and remain free and equal in rights."

All wars are terrible. They plunder innocence and rob human life. But the one thing that can make its bitterness palatable is the fight for freedom.

The bare-bones ferocity and iron will of the people who fought in the early years of the Haitian Revolution give us insight into the revolts in America. Blacks were always outnumbered, undertrained, and ill-equipped. According to historian Laurent Dubois, what they lacked in resources, they achieved with what one observer called "ruse and ingenuity":

> [Quoting an observer] "They camouflaged traps, fabricated poisoned arrows, feigned cease-fires to lure the enemy into ambush, disguised tree trunks as cannons, and threw obstructions of one kind or another into the roads to hamper advancing troops." Some insurgents . . . stood firmly up to three volleys of shot, each of them "wearing a kind of light mattress stuffed with cotton as a vest to prevent the bullets from penetrating."

Britain and France sent huge armies against Haitians to quell their resistance. But Louverture rallied his troops and said, "For too long we have borne your chains without thinking of shaking them off, but any authority which is not founded on virtue and humanity, and which only tends to subject one's fellow man to slavery, must come to an end, and that end is yours." With astounding military prowess and the assistance of some nasty tropical diseases, the Haitians exorcised the demonic spirit of slavery from the island. Defeating France in 1804, they emerged as the first-ever Black republic. And before any European country, on the first day of its independence, Haiti was the first nation in the world to permanently ban slavery and the slave trade. We might call this the CliffsNotes version. I suggest the definitive book on the Haitian Revolution, *The Black Jacobins: Toussaint L'Ouverture and the San Domingo Revolution* (1938), by C. L. R. James. (Remember when we said that if you study Black history long enough, Henry Louis Gates Jr. will pop up periodically to lead you with a smile? Well, C. L. R. James will, too, but he's more likely to meet you with the stern face of Marxist analysis.) Other books like *Avengers of the New World* (2004) by Laurent Dubois offer a more balanced political perspective but are no less compelling.

The Haitian Revolution should be taught right alongside the American Revolution and the French, as Frederick Douglass reminded all of its magnitude and ripple effects throughout the Western Hemisphere in a riling speech:

Until she [Haiti] spoke no Christian nation had abolished Negro slavery. Until she spoke no Christian nation had given to the world an organized effort to abolish slavery. Until she spoke the slave ship, followed by hungry sharks, greedy to devour the dead and dying slaves flung overboard to feed them, ploughed in peace in the South Atlantic painting the sea with the Negro's blood. Until she spoke, the slave-trade was sanctioned by all the Christian nations of the world, and our land of liberty and light included. Men made fortunes by this infernal traffic, and were esteemed as good Christians, and the standing types and representations of the Savior of the World. Until Haiti spoke, the church was silent, and the pulpit was dumb. Slave-traders lived and slave-traders died. Funeral sermons were preached over them, and of them it was said that they died in the triumphs of the Christian faith and went to heaven among the just.

But in the new European world, ideologically steeped in anti-Blackness, there were limits to freedom. It was bittersweet. Haiti would never be dealt with on equal terms by European powers. And eventually, it was forced to pay reparations to France for its own value as slaves. Haiti's impending victory in 1803 was one of many reasons Napoleon sold off 827,000 square miles of Louisiana Territory so cheap you'd think America bought acres from a bargain-bin. But in history one thing affects another. More land equaled more native genocide. More land equaled more need for American enslaved labor.

How much did the Haitian Revolution inspire enslaved Black people in America? We may never know. There was the rare, recorded instance of angry, young Black Philadelphians taking to the streets in 1804, shouting "Give them Saint Domingue." But most reactions would've had to be cautious. White American planters spread fear and paranoia via the printing press and into the congressional halls, sensationalizing the Black combatants as bloodthirsty cannibals. They viewed an uprising of the slave class as a threat to their rights, property, and very lives. Inventively, they fabricated the image and motives of the enslaved to fit their own prejudices and economic aims, failing to comprehend that the main reason for the uprisings was simple: freedom.

A glimpse of this era allows us to see a nation careening toward the Civil War cataclysm. Of course, it would be six decades later, but in the span of history this represents but a moment. Other revolts surely accelerated the United States toward war. Some say Charles Deslondes drew inspiration from the wellspring of Haitian freedom. In 1811, on the eastern banks of the Mississippi River, about thirty-six miles from New Orleans, he divided his followers into companies, chose officers, and armed his "troops" with guns, swords, knives, and farm implements. Revolutionary suicide is what it was. But so was birth, as the average life expectancy of an enslaved person at birth was just twenty-two years. As they marched onward toward New Orleans, intent on forming a Black republic in coastal Louisiana, they rallied around the cry common to all revolutions, liberty or death. Whites, warned of their approach, fled in terror. Three plantations were burned to the ground and two whites were murdered. Militias massacred the rebels, a few fled, a few were let go, but ninety-five were killed. One witness testified that, "Charles [Deslondes] had his hands chopped off then shot in one thigh & then the other, until they were both broken—then shot in the body and before he had expired was put into a bundle of straw and roasted! The heads of the others executed decorated the levees as a morbid message to would-be rebels."

But these deathly consequences were not enough for Black people to abandon rebellion. And the fear of rebellion was palpable. When a Kentucky man was asked: "Are the masters afraid of insurrection?" He responded, "They live in constant fear upon this subject. The unusual noise at night alarms them greatly. They cry out, 'What is that. Are the boys all in?'" But most revolts were doomed before a conspiracy became a plan. We might wonder how many acts of betrayal took place by fearful captives. Or how many plots were foiled by those who cared more for their own personal safety than collective liberation. Yet still people tried.

Consider Denmark Vesey of South Carolina (mentioned in chapter one), who has a fascinating story. He bought a winning lottery ticket and purchased his own freedom for $600, but, unable to buy his wife and children, he plotted a revolt in 1822. The plan was to murder and torch their way to freedom and escape to the free nation of Haiti. Some say there were plans to enlist as many as nine thousand enslaved, but a Black house servant named George Wilson informed his enslaver of the pending revolt. Vesey was captured on June 22, tortured, and executed with thirty-five others. It surely wasn't a love of revolt that pushed them past the fear of brutal punishment, but the hatred of surrender. One book that has stood the test of time is from 1936, *American Negro Slave Revolts* by Herbert Aptheker, which posits that desperate struggles for freedom were not exceptions but rules. He traces at least 250 American slave revolts, where groups of ten or more people gathered, which leaves us to wonder, how many times did one, two, three, or four people think, *You know what, let's get free. But first, kill the masters.*

Everyday Survival

Let us remember John Berry Meachum, who, when Missouri made it illegal to educate Black people in 1847, anchored his own steamboat and turned it into a school, averting the law the same way boat casinos do, as navigable rivers are under federal jurisdiction. By establishing a floating school, he avoided state law. Let us remember Margaret Garner, an enslaved mother who completely unraveled, murdering her two-year-old daughter with a butcher knife rather than have her return to slavery. Infanticide was not unheard of as many parents believed they were sending their children to God, a far better option than a life of incomprehensible awfulness. Let us remember Henry "Box" Brown, who shut himself in a 3' × 2' wooden crate and had himself mailed as dry goods from Virginia to Philadelphia for freedom.

It is hard to generalize the totality of slavery. Everyone who went through it had a unique experience. Experiences that varied by generation and region. But in the fragmented portraits available to us, one thing seems conclusive—people continuously resisted. And yet, many did not. We can all sit in the safety of the present and say how much we would have fought back during slavery. But the human inclination to conform has been well documented by psychologists. In our social lives, we function as herd animals, constantly gauging the group, acting and nonacting based on fear, wishful thinking, and ignorance. To conform is to be human. And there have only been, in every generation, a few people who were willing and able

to stand up, leading the resistance against the psychopaths and warped ideologies that steered, and continue to steer, our world toward destruction.
Pressure to conform and adapt to slavery was tremendous, and that's what
makes these stories of resistance, even everyday resistance, truly remarkable.
For the better part of human history, slavery had been considered normal.
Imagine the societal pressure to wake up every day and do your job. Imagine
the daily coercion to keep you wedged in your place. Think about the carefully maintained environment of reward and punishment.

Compliance is an act of survival. It is easy to project a false sense of courage onto the past, but if we imagine slavery as being constantly at gunpoint
and told what to do, we might think twice. Revolt is much rarer than obedience. But it is important to remember that during this time people still
clung to life: They still built communities and fell in love. They formed
networks. They got married. They laughed. They joked. They played games.
They hoped and dreamed. They raised children. They showed inexhaustible
human fortitude and resiliency, a resiliency that is still part of Black culture.
Slavery was a normal fact of American life. Hard to resist. So normal that
between 1810 and 1860 there was an internal, forced migration, when one
million Black people were marched from the tobacco North to the cotton
South. It was a trail of tears. They marched by the hundreds, chained in
twos across the Virginia countryside, headed for the auction block in New
Orleans. This could only happen in a slave society.

We aren't just talking about a scattered system of belligerent overseers
and masters enacting day-to-day violence. This was a highly refined system
that relatively few white people fought against, more participated in, many
ignored, and from which the elite procured massive wealth. It was upheld
on a social structure of racism and fear. Imagine being at the bottom of a
labor system totally subjected to the will of another, where white authority
was elevated to such a level that a ten-year-old child could order another
enslaved person to whip your grandmother with little consequence. There
was a whole genre of juvenile literature instructing the children of enslavers
on how to be enslavers. Far from outsiders, white women tormented, intim-
idated, beat, tortured, and killed the enslaved right alongside their male
counterparts. This was all normal in America.

Most resistance was in small acts. Faking sickness and refusing medicine. Self-harming. Purposefully breaking farm implements and tools. Feigned ignorance, arson, back talk, sabotage, and theft. Some pretended to care for sick enslavers, then found relief when they died. Many donned the mask of conformity in public, "Yessuh" and "Massah," but when alone, cursed to hell those who enslaved them. At all times it seems they were conspiring to regain some of their power. What many whites viewed as "laziness" was just another form of resistance. Working slowly, sabotaging crops, and riling up animals on purpose, all to work less.

One observer reported:

> The overseer rode among them, on a horse, carrying in his hand a rawhide whip, constantly directing and encouraging them . . . as often as he visited one line of the operations, the hands at the other would discontinue their labor, until he turned to ride toward them again.

So often we look at the overall atrocity of slavery, but if we zoom in, we see how people not only survived, but resisted it in small, but no less significant, ways to maintain some degree of self-determination. There was an informal slave economy, some of which was clandestine, while other transactions were overlooked. After working sunup to sundown, some kept working elsewhere to earn wages after. Others used the small plots given by their enslavers to sell extra produce at market. Some hunted and fished and traded with poor whites. This so-called Black market was rooted in the soil of broken dreams and socioeconomic inequality, which still exists today. But the point is this: Every act, every breath, every day people chose to live can be seen as an act of resistance.

Self-Liberation

"The hardest days I have known have been in these years of freedom. I never knew what work nor what anxiety was when I had old master to provide for me and mine." These were the words of Susanna McGavock Carter, a small, graying Black woman, as she recounted her days at Belle Meade, one of the wealthiest plantations in Tennessee. But these were her words by the account of white people and under the surveillance of white people. A magnifying glass to her life tells another story, because after Emancipation she was absent from the place she supposedly loved. She shows up elsewhere, as a part-time worker, in control of her own labor, freedom, and destiny. Using baseless divine scripture and twisted "scientific" evidence, whites promoted the idea that Black people could not be happy in any other condition than enslavement. If a Black person ran away, they would be diagnosed, according to psychologist Samuel Cartwright in 1851, with "drapetomania," the mental diagnosis for slaves who ran away. "The cause, in the most of cases, that induces the negro to run away from service, is as much a disease of the mind as any other species of mental alienation, and much more curable," argued Cartwright. "With the advantages of proper medical advice, strictly followed, this troublesome practice that many negroes have of running away can be almost entirely prevented."

Few psychiatrists in the twenty-first century would assert racism as a socially acceptable behavior, but what does this say about how white racist attitudes, bunk science, and economic influences determined what is deviant and nondeviant, normal and abnormal, mentally ill and well, all based on the structure and values of the society they created? This is especially relevant as Black people are more likely to be misdiagnosed by mental health practitioners. Studies, such as one that "suggests a bias in misdiagnosing Blacks with major depression and schizophrenia," follow a trail leading back to this history. For a long time, Black escape was undervalued even in history. In the popular mind, the Underground Railroad has been presented as the story of abolitionists, mostly whites helping Black people to freedom. But this has separated us from a deliberate conversation about the truth of Black agency. Not only about the nature of freedom, but the continued social policy of belligerent police surveillance on poor, hyper-segregated Black communities always being viewed as against the law, leading to an unwarranted use of police power, despite dozens of studies since the early 1970s firmly establishing that most crime is committed by a small group of repeat offenders.

The Underground Railroad established the reality and idea of communities of Black fugitives. Most often, during slavery, resistance meant to flee.

But just because you escaped did not mean you were free, because you were never truly free. Self-liberating Black people were always at risk of being stopped, harassed, questioned, and recaptured by slave patrols and bounty hunters. It's thought that in 1831 an enslaver cursed an "underground railroad" when Tice Davids escaped from him in Kentucky making his way into neighboring Ohio. Aggressively pursued, Tice swam across the Ohio River. I've often thought about others who took this route. Intrepid souls risked getting swept up by the rapid undercurrent of the Ohio River—the river's width averages half a mile—rather than the deep and sinister undercurrent of enslavement. People walked, rowed, hid on steamboats, mailed themselves, ran, hid in wagons, swam, hid on trains, disguised themselves, and those who could, forged free papers. There was despair, fear, death, and anxiety on the Underground Railroad. There were people separated from families, shot down in cold blood, returned to poverty, and enslaved on the Underground Railroad. But there was hope and faith on the Underground Railroad, too. There were those who took a risk for freedom and carved out lives in the face of slavery. There were people who dreamed, loved, laughed, walked with dignity, and held on to their humanity.

When I was a kid, I thought the Underground Railroad was a subterranean train. Of course, this was untrue. But an Underground Railroad made up of fixed routes, secret agents, passwords, maps, and hidey-holes didn't exist either. And if you think it only existed because of benevolent white people saving downtrodden Black people, you'd be wrong. Until the 1960s, histories rarely referenced the efforts of Black people on the Underground Railroad. Levi Coffin, a white Quaker who carried the title "president of the Underground Railroad," said this about Black involvement: "Most of them were too careless, and a few were unworthy—they could be bribed by the slave-hunters to betray the hiding-places of the fugitives."

That sounds preposterous. Was there white collaboration? Of course—but *president*! The Underground Railroad was rooted in Black self-liberation. All the while, Black conductor William Still aided more than a thousand fugitives, detailed in the book titled, *The Underground Railroad: A Selection of Authentic Narratives* (1872). But freedom was no guarantee. Most people didn't make it. And it was worse for women, many of whom had to calculate the risk of bringing along children.

Stories are still coming to light. In the 2010s, Madeline Lewis, an undergraduate student at Columbia University, was digging through one of about eighty boxes in the Rare Book & Manuscript Library and stumbled on hundreds of firsthand accounts of Black fugitives that were previously unknown. They were stories taken down by a New York journalist named Sydney Howard Gay, who interviewed people as they arrived in New York City from 1855 to 1866. A Black man named Louis Napoleon is also in the records, as he met fugitives in the streets and directed them to Gay's office, then personally escorted them to their next destination after their interviews. The stories are harrowing; in just a few sentences, you can feel the heart of the history: "Mary Curtis, 19 yrs. of age, slave of Ben Gwyner of Chester Co. Maryland house-maid. Gwyner died recently and hearing that the slaves were to be sold, a free colored woman induced her to leave, and gave her money to pay her way to Philadelphia. Left father and mother behind her." This one story reveals a dictionary of information about the Underground Railroad and Black resistance. Black sisterhood, solidarity, and agency. But also, sacrifice.

In another story, a familiar name pops up:

Eliza Manokey, from Dorchester Co., Maryland. About 42 yrs. old. Ann Greaves, her owner, had hired her away so far from her husband (who is free) that she ran away rather than go. Has two children, son, and daughter. Mistress gave the son to her nephew, who took him to Missouri when he was 4 yrs. old. The boy clung frantically to his mother, begging her to save him, but in vain. Never heard from him since. The daughter is now sixteen or seventeen, belongs to the mother's mistress, and has four children. First ran away in January last, took refuge in the woods, alone. Free colored families aided her. Laid out in the woods till wheat harvest. Then came to Delaware. A brave earnest woman. (Came with Harriet Tubman.) Went to Canada. Sent her to Troy, needed no money.

I'm paraphrasing but I once heard that Harriet Tubman said that slavery is a descent into hell. And we cannot fail to mention the worst of what women were running from. Not all women were domestic workers. In many instances, they had to labor just as hard as men and at times keep that up through every stage of pregnancy until the moment of delivery, then get back out to work after a week; maybe they might get a month. And the ways they became pregnant could torture the imagination. The horrors of sexual violence were a fact of life as scholar Dorothy E. Roberts concretely depicts in her book *Killing the Black Body* (1997). Not only the perverted degradations of molestation and rape, but people were forced to breed. Think about the implications for motherhood, or sexually transmitted disease, or the utter lack of reproductive liberty. To resist was to face the most frequent punishment, scourging with a twisted bull's hide or a whipping with hemp cord that left indelible ridges and welts. If there were thoughts of a future sale, a paddle of heavy leather was preferable. This would only bruise instead of breaking the flesh, and be gone in weeks or months, for the enslaved who resisted frequently lost value. Resistance meant the shadowy cell of a plantation prison or torturing with an iron-horned collar. Black women were tortured by jealous and infuriated white wives. People enslaved their own children. Incest. Bloodhounds. The murky swamps of human depravity. All in the name of God's divine order.

There was also an Underground Railroad that ran south to Mexico where you could be free. That is because of the heroic deeds of Afro-Mexican president Vicente Guerrero. In 1829, thirty-four years before Abraham Lincoln, he abolished slavery. This was no small act—the wealthy classes of the recently independent Mexico were deeply tied to the institution of slavery. Infuriated, they deemed him mentally incapable of ruling, despite his numerous other successes, disposed of him, hunted, and killed him. Guerrero died for his egalitarian principles and commitment to justice. But his actions opened a door for fugitives. In 1937, an enslaved man named Felix Haywood was interviewed, offering, "Sometimes someone would come along and try to get us to run up north and be free. There was no reason to run up north. All we had to do was to walk but walk south, and we'd be free as soon as we crossed the Rio Grande."

There was no single method of escape. For some, to truly be free meant going where no one else dared, the dismal swamp. Known as a dreadful place, the inhospitable stretch of land originally covered more than a million acres between southeastern Virginia and northeastern North Carolina. Little of it was above water, with some speculators wanting to drain it, unsuccessfully. There were wild cattle, bears, wolves, deer, and snakes. There were bugs that bit, grass blades that cut, and spots so thick you might hardly work your way out. Some swore the gases rising from the water were so poisonous that even buzzards wouldn't go there. This foreboding environment was a perfect place for the Great Dismal Swamp maroons to make a life. By the time of the Civil War, generations had lived in the swamps for more than two hundred years. They were survivors who challenged the white power structure the whole time. The maroons stayed in huts on sparse land, and sometimes attacked plantations, taking resources. In other instances, they were employed by and traded with poor whites who resided near the swamp, but they would always be wary of betrayal.

Some escaped and disappeared into the free Black communities across the North and South, but to buy the myth of an all-pervasive Northern liberalism fogs centuries of racial exclusion and discrimination. To miss this is to miss an opportunity to witness the evolution of anti-Blackness as it relates to freeborn Black people, and how the US government abandoned the principles of human freedom to legalize racism and slavery. Northern lawmakers segregated public schools and housing while excluding Black people from higher education and employment. The Fugitive Slave Act of 1850 was revised out of the 1793 federal policy, and in free states, allowed enslavers to reclaim their "property," regardless of how long a person had been free. Free Northern Black people sprang into action to aid and protect the lives of those on the run from bondage. The New York City Committee of Vigilance helped a thousand people avoid enslavement. Through such vigilance committees, Northern Black women worked together to keep freeborn Black children out of the clutches of slavery and racism, escorting them to school and filing complaints about openly racist teachers.

With the Fugitive Slave Act of 1793, and later 1850, slave catchers prowled the streets of places like Manhattan before the Civil War, openly carrying whips, pistols, and manacles to reclaim "property." There was an epidemic of kidnapping and human trafficking. Illegal slave traders and murderers operated what was nicknamed "the reverse underground railroad," a nightmare of dehumanization. In cities like New York, organized, despotic street gangs worked sometimes with police in kidnapping rings. They "entered black churches during Sunday service looking for runaways and broke into homes and carried them off without legal proceedings." There was an epidemic of kidnapping. But we must remember the slave catchers, as vicious and terrible as they were, were part of a vicious and terrible system. It is not just the actions of one officer, or one judge, or one doctor, or one mob, or a few isolated incidents of racism.

Still they resisted. They resisted to remain autonomous nations. In Haiti their resistance resulted in the making of one. In America they revolted to follow in Haiti's footsteps, though their resistance only resulted in stricter repression. They resisted to be with family. At other times, older family members encouraged their sons and daughters to run and attain the freedom they never had. In one story, I read about a man who was whipped for breaking curfew, and when asked why he ran, he said that he resolved to go where a pass was not needed at night. Another murdered his enslaver because he could not go to a political convention. They resisted in small ways every day, just as the resistance to injustice in America continues. It is important to remember, where there is oppression, there is always resistance, and where there is resistance, there is life.

So, if someone is teaching you about US slavery and does not mention the resistance to it, that person should not be teaching you about US slavery. The whole story of Black humanity needs to be told, ringing with the word *resistance, resistance, resistance, resistance*! Black history offers tales of repeated opposition and also unending defiance. Slavery would not be allowed to have the last word. People defended children and family from the preying wolves intent on devouring life and liberty and truth and happiness. Then they emerged from the doorstep of death to find a ray of sunshine, and, finally, still having something to say about the highest principles of humanity, love, justice, and freedom.

10

Civil War

> The present SLAVEHOLDERS' WAR, as all know, would never
> have occurred, had the nation meted out justice to the colored man.
> It is this deviation from right which has brought a train of woes
> innumerable upon the land; and no one can now tell where or how
> the end will be.
> —**William C. Nell, 1862**

On the night of April 15, 1865, Joe Simms hurried to raise the curtain during a performance of *Our American Cousin* at Ford's Theatre in Washington, DC. As one of the few Black employees there, he might have stood out among the 1,700 people present to see one of the most popular plays in America. Two years into his job as a stagehand, he knew his way around a theater, and so, when he heard the crack of a pistol from the audience, he knew that it wasn't part of the script. Instead, he looked over to witness the assassination of President Abraham Lincoln by John Wilkes Booth.

"Nearly at the end of the third act I heard the report of a pistol, and immediately I looked across. I knew it was something strange for anything like that to occur in front of the stage among the people. I looked and saw a man jump down from the private box on the stage with a knife in his hand about a foot long. As he rose after the leap he turned his back on the private box and said something like 'revenge for the South' and made his escape across the stage and out at the back door." With the death of Lincoln, we might say that Simms witnessed the last shot fired in the Civil War. But his testimony along with thousands of other Civil War–era Black people have all but disappeared from the popular view. This was purposeful; the architects who built Civil War history constructed it this way.

Though most agree that those apocalyptic middle years of the nineteenth century had a greater impact on American society and politics than any other time in American history, many didn't think as much at first. So confident in Southern victory was the former US senator and Confederate James Chesnut Jr., he promised to drink any blood spilled. Many expected a quick victory. At the first field battle of Bull Run, men, women, and children came out with picnic baskets and opera glasses to watch what they thought would be a quick and decisive Union victory. But at the conclusion of the war in 1865; after some 750,000 bodies were buried, after some 470,000 lay mangled and wounded, after battles in backyards and muddy fields and on the Atlantic Ocean, after the gunpowder dissipated, the nation had to reconcile itself.

In turn, Civil War history was constructed as two siblings, who after a rivalry, got over their differences. Through a combination of mythmaking and record-righting, Southern chroniclers of the Civil War told a story to uphold the myth of white supremacy, stories that continue to live in the inflammatory bowels of our nation. As late military historian Edward Bonekemper summed it up:

> While history books call the slaughter that occurred from 1861 to 1865 the "American Civil War," it is often referred to as the "War to Preserve the Union," the "War of the Southern Rebellion," the "War to Make Men Free," the "War Between the States," or the "War of Northern Aggression," depending on the region of the country. What it is not called, but goes to the truth of the conflict, is the "Confederate War for the Preservation of Slavery."

The idea that Southerners seceded over states' rights is a notably persistent one. And yet, the strongest refutation of that argument are the words of the Southern politicians themselves. While Jefferson Davis and others were still drunk on secession and dreams of an outstretched slave empire, they made it clear that slavery was the reason they were breaking from the Union. In his now famous Cornerstone Speech in Savannah, Georgia, Alexander H. Stephens, vice president of the Confederate States of America, said in 1861 that slavery was "the immediate cause of the late rupture and the present revolution. The old confederation known as the United States had been founded on the false idea that all men are created equal." In contrast, he added, the Confederacy "is founded upon exactly the opposite idea; its foundations are laid, its cornerstone rests, upon the great truth that the negro is not equal to the white man; that slavery, subordination to the superior race, is his natural and moral condition. This, our new Government, is the first, in the history of the world, based on this great physical, philosophical, and moral truth."

When the Civil War ended, the nation was remade, and to take the position that chattel slavery was wrong became increasingly easy. So, to maintain respectability in a changing world, the Southern oligarchs shifted their language, saying it was not a war to preserve slavery, but rather about states' rights. Jefferson Davis crafted a new cause for the war, which was "the inalienable right of a people to change their government . . . to withdraw from a Union into which they had, as sovereign communities, voluntarily entered." The "existence of African servitude," he maintained, "was in no wise the cause of the conflict, but only an incident."

This idea has been the most enduring, that the act of secession wasn't about slavery, it was about autonomy, scrubbing Black people from the history of their liberation. This coded language, impartial to the cause of slavery and thus race neutral, has stalled discussions about the racial animus of the war into the present. We've forgotten the witness of those like Joe Simms at Ford's Theatre who had something to say about a nation reeling in turmoil, and a dead president who'd had premonitions of people weeping over a corpse at the White House days before his demise. If there is any pride to be found after surveying those bloodstained battlefields across America, it is seldom assigned to Black people. Not to those Black men and women who stood in utter defiance of the Confederacy's existence, the ones who buttoned up their blues, shouldered rifles, and made the very ideal of Black eternal bondage a lost cause. Three-fifths of all Black soldiers were formerly enslaved, knowing that their participation in the Civil War would make it far less likely that they would ever see that state of inhumanity again.

Whose Side Are You On

The nation was bitterly divided. Abraham Lincoln represented a threat to "the southern way of life," which was to keep, protect, and extend slavery, evidenced by the fact that Lincoln, a known opponent of the institution, survived more assassination attempts, plots, and schemes than any president until Obama. Followed by South Carolina, six states seceded from the Union in rapid succession mere months after Lincoln's inauguration. And they all made clear their primary reason for doing so. This declaration from Texas left no room for misinterpretation: "The servitude of the African race, as existing in these States, is mutually beneficial to both bond and free, and is abundantly authorized and justified by the experience of mankind, and the revealed will of the Almighty Creator, as recognized by all Christian nations."

Think about how an uncountable number of statements like that helped annihilate all the extraordinary and epic African history that we've learned so far from the written record. And how the statement "the experience of mankind" seeks to use a fabricated history as proof that racial inequality is natural and something to which Black people should gracefully submit. South Carolina made a similar assertion:

> Those [Union] States have assumed the right of deciding upon the propriety of our domestic institutions; and have denied the rights of property established in fifteen of the States and recognized by the Constitution; they have denounced as sinful the institution of slavery; they have permitted open establishment among them of societies, whose avowed object is to disturb the peace and to eloign the property of the citizens of other States.

So upset were powerful factions of Southerners about Lincoln's election that he almost didn't make it to the oval office. A white Southern Nationalist paramilitary group, called the Knights of the Golden Circle, nearly assassinated him on the way to his inauguration. The plot was only foiled when he switched trains. But the pen is mightier than the sword, and the narrative of Southern respectability in the war has been maintained. If designing a monumental history is about reconstructing our heroes from the rough stones of the past, then those choices were made based on racial politics rather than moral fortitude. The South chose to erect statues of Robert E. Lee, who, not satisfied with lashing the enslaved as punishment, had brine scrubbed into their festering wounds. A man who impressed the enslaved into service for the Confederate Army, threatened and made good the promise to indiscriminately execute Black Union troops, and who stood by as his officers kidnapped free Black people and sold them into slavery. I think about the continued veneration of those like Lee and then think about how history's narrators forgot those like Duncan Smith, a white Southerner who, according to his biography, "had opposed human slavery since long before John Brown's raid, and when the Civil War came on, his fiery opposition to it put him in bad odor with those who favored it, an abolitionist bitterly opposed to slavery. He was ready at the drop of a hat to die for the principle!"

He might have been the most hunted man in Louisiana during the war. In 1863, he had a bounty of $10,000 on his head hiding out in the marsh for a year to evade capture. But Southerners found no reason to sanctify any moral heroes, only those who shared their ideas of Black inferiority. The legacy is carried forward, as a symbol the Confederate flag still flies from homes and cars. Not once during the Civil War did that Confederate banner make it close to the United States Capitol, but on January 6, 2021, it was carried into the Capitol when white rioters violently stormed the building where electoral ballots were being counted.

The North also presented its narrative. After consoling the South by accepting its "lost cause" version of the Civil War, they set out to construct their own heroes. Abraham Lincoln, long revered in the Black community, was a shared hero with whites, who sanctified him as a prudent decision-maker and spotless savior. In the war, Black people were fought over, but only in the end did they participate in the fighting; it was mostly Northern whites who died for their freedom. Some abolitionists sanctified John Brown, the white radical abolitionist hanged in 1859, for his botched attempt to start a massive slave rebellion at Harper's Ferry. But most said he was a homicidal and suicidal maniac. Brown was not without crimes: In Kansas he massacred several pro-slavery men, some in front of their families. He was a guerrilla fighter who some called a terrorist. On the other hand, anti-Black terrorism has been so common in American history, we barely call it as such, so it is surreal to see a white man use terrorism as a force against it. For him it was inevitable, echoing darkly prophetic scripture, as he believed that the sins of the nation must be purged with blood. His words reverberate through history: "It is better that a whole generation of men, women, and children should pass away by a violent death than that slavery should live."

John Brown was not only antislavery but also anti-racist. One day in 1829, a group of white families asked if Brown would help drive off Native Americans who traveled to the area for an annual hunt. Brown retorted: "I will have nothing to do with so mean an act. I would sooner take my gun and help drive you out of the country." He met Black people on terms of equality in all spheres—met them at the dinner table, met in dignity, met them to politic, and met them to revolt. One of four Black men with Brown at the Harper's Ferry raid was Dangerfield Newby. He'd saved up enough money to purchase his wife's freedom, only to have her enslaver raise the price. He was the first to die after being shot in the throat. When they checked his body they found a letter from his wife, Harriet, telling him how difficult it was living enslaved without him. Here it is in part, and how she wrote it:

> Dear Husband . . . I want you to buy me as soon as possible for if you do not get me somebody else will the servents are very disagreeable thay do all thay can to set my mistress againt me Dear Husband you not the trouble I see the last two years has ben like a trouble dream to me it is said Master is in want of monney if so I know not what time he may sell me an then all my bright hops of the futer are blasted for there has ben one bright hope to cheer me in all my troubles that is to be with you.

That is why so many Black people gave their lives—so that their wives, husbands, and children would no longer be property. And with the momentum of centuries of slave resistance acting as gusts of wind at his back, John Brown struck the national conscience so hard that the path to Civil War was, from that moment forward, inevitable. Later, as the war faded from memory, so did John Brown. The Northerners, so many of whom were willing to tolerate an unseen slavery, would make no usable history from his memory. This is not so much a surprise. It might be easy to believe that white supremacist ideology was a Southern disease as Vermont abolished slavery in 1777, and every Northern state after followed. But it was the industrial economy that precipitated the rapid deletion of slavery from their laws. Morality played its part, but it was far from universal throughout the entire population. Northern whites had to be dragged into war.

The Union recruitment effort in 1863 sparked cataclysmic violence in Lower Manhattan dubbed the New York City draft riots. White men between twenty and forty-five years were eligible for draft into the Union Army, except for the wealthy, who could avoid war by paying $300 or hiring a substitute. This inflamed class tensions. Whites, mostly Irish and Irish-Americans, burned buildings, wrecked factories, looted homes, and attacked the Union recruiting office. Only three Gatling guns, placed on the roof and in windows, kept the *New York Times* from certain destruction. Black people bore the worst of it. The mob was incensed at the idea of newly Black freedmen coming up North to "take their jobs." Massive mobs bore down on the Black community with hurricane force and the "atrocities they perpetrated are so revolting that they are unfit for publication," said one contemporary.

Mutilated Black bodies were dangled from lampposts. James Costello, a shoemaker, was on an errand when he was chased down. Unable to escape, he turned and whipped out his revolver, killing one rioter in self-defense. But the mob was overwhelming. They "mangled his body and hanged it. Then cut it down and dragged it through the streets before burning it."

William Jones was murdered. "They instantly set upon and beat him and, after nearly killing him, hung him to a lamppost. His body was left suspended for several hours. A fire was made underneath him, and he was literally roasted as he hung, the mob reveling in their demoniac act." He was only identified by a loaf of bread he had gone out to purchase.

Even a Black orphanage was burned, with white men and women looting the supplies. Who knows what might have happened to the orphans had they not been removed to safety. It took the military and full weight of the police department to quell the riots. At a house on East 29th Street, a lookout said to a neighbor, "There is a nigger living here," and they were "going to bring him out, and hang him on the lamppost, and you stop and see the fun." The homeowner, Jeremiah Hamilton, had already escaped out the back of the house. As Wall Street's first Black millionaire, he cuts a fascinating figure across history. You've likely never heard of him, because he was not well liked. Black leaders thought he was brash and chastised him for a counterfeit scheme in Haiti where they said he undermined the world's first Black republic. He fit right into the odorous corruption of Wall Street, mirroring its practices and attitudes. But many of his dealings were aboveboard. He traded stocks, bought real estate, and made sound speculations, even as he also over-insured ships and then scuttled them to cash in on insurance claims, got into brawls, and punished his enemies. At one point, he went head-to-head in court with Cornelius Vanderbilt over a steamship line. But his notoriety and amassed millions couldn't stop the mob. Perhaps he was one of the first Black people in American history to discover that even the color of money can't buy your way out of anti-Black racism.

Eagle on Their Buttons, Muskets on Their Shoulders, Bullets in Their Pockets

The destiny of America was to be decided once and for all. The Union received its wake-up call in April 1861. On that day, all the discord between North and South exploded in the form of cannon fire from the Confederate Army. The first attack in the Civil War was on Union troops in Fort Sumter, the federal fort protecting Charleston, South Carolina. When America woke up on April 13, 1861, they knew that the war had started. Newspaper headlines read: "WAR!!! WAR!!! WAR!!!, CIVIL WAR COMMENCED., & WAR BEGUN." Instantaneous dispatches via telegraph made the Civil War a very modern one. In his nine-hundred-page, single-volume history of the Civil War, *Battle Cry of Freedom: The Civil War Era* (1988), historian James McPherson lays out the magnitude of the conflict:

> Most of the things that we consider important in this era of American history—the fate of slavery, the structure of society in both North and South, the direction of the American economy, the destiny of competing

nationalisms in North and South, the definition of freedom, the very survival of the United States—rested on the shoulders of those weary men in
blue and gray who fought it out during four years of ferocity unmatched in
the Western world between the Napoleonic Wars and World War I.

No one knew then if the United States would survive or if slavery would
survive. No one could speak of anything else but war. They died at Fort
Sumter, they died at Dry Wood Creek, they died at Glorieta Pass, at New
Orleans, and at Antietam. But even before Black men could legally enlist,
some men, like abolitionist and activist William Henry Johnson, a stalwart
of the Underground Railroad, decided to fight anyway. Johnson, who'd
long trained in an all-Black militia, had asked to fight with John Brown at
Harper's Ferry, but Brown declined because Johnson was expecting his first
child. There aren't many records for this early Black participation in the
Civil War, but estimates place thousands of men like Johnson who attached
themselves to Northern regiments, trained beside them, and took their
chance to fight. Johnson connected himself to the 8th Connecticut, his
being one of many groups who went by the "colored volunteers." But Johnson sent dispatches from the war front to Boston, and it is here we see his
powerful commentary and deep connection to a Union victory. At the Battle of Roanoke Island in North Carolina under General Burnside in February 1862, he wrote:

> Our armies will defeat the rebels, and hang slavery; a just Administration
> will execute the monster, and the good news and glad tidings will be borne
> by the many gallant ones to all parts of the Christian world; but the glory
> will belong to God! The abolition of slavery is rapidly progressing, South—it
> is in the natural course of events, and must be; for wherever the Federal
> Army goes, the so-called master dies, and the slaves, once chattels, are trans-
> formed into men!

He goes on to give us some colorful commentary for the day of March 14:

> Seven o'clock a.m.—We are engaging the rebels. They are behind water and
> sand batteries. The fight is waxing warm. Many brave souls have been sent

to their last account; and a larger number of traitors have been made to bite the dust. I forbear to name the locality. The fleet is also engaged.

Nine o'clock a.m.—The rebels are fighting like devils; they do not give an inch; their slaves are working their guns. I cannot stand that. This may be the last line from me; for now I go into the field armed with a revolver, and a sure rifle; and shall take my post to defend the colors of my regiment. We must win the day, though half our number are slain.

One o'clock p.m.—Thank God! the battle is ended; blood has ceased to flow. Victory perches on our banners, but we have paid dearly for it. . . . We have, for two days, fought them in their well-constructed batteries and rifle pits covering a space of twelve miles in a dense forest of tall pines and obstinate underbrush, on a poorly constructed railroad, and a turnpike which was covered with a slippery mud, and raining [all] the time. If it does not satisfy them that Uncles Sam is in earnest, and that Old Abe does not mean to split them like rails, we will give them another turn.

After suffering a horrendous defeat in the bloodiest single day of the war, and the largest surrender of Union troops, Lincoln issued the Preliminary Emancipation Proclamation on September 22, 1862, warning that if rebels refused to surrender and rejoin the Union by January 1, 1863, all slaves in the rebellious states would be free. With no surrender, he did what was promised, and while this did not free all the enslaved, it did officially allow Black people to enlist in the Union Army. What started as a Northern cause to save the Union gave way to a war to end chattel slavery. *Men of Color, to Arms!* was the banner of Frederick Douglass, who, in all his intellectual fervor and political intensity, knew that only if the Union could win the war would the promise made in that Emancipation Proclamation become a reality. Douglass had long advocated for Black troops:

I reproached the North that they fought the rebels with only one hand, when they might strike effectively with two—that they fought with their soft white hand, while they kept their black iron hand chained and helpless behind them—that they fought the effect, while they protected the cause, and that the Union Cause would never prosper till the war assumed an anti-slavery attitude, and the Negro was enlisted on the loyal side.

He'd long prophesized about the coming carnage. Back in 1852, Douglass had a powerful encounter with Sojourner Truth, the self-appointed traveler who told the truth about the horrors of slavery. She, too, was assisting with the war effort, collecting contributions to support Black regiments. They needed clothes, food, and blankets and she recruited men to join the Union. It wasn't always easy; not everyone was leaping into war. Many Black Northerners had never been slaves. And many didn't trust the whites in the Union Army. Her efforts aligned with those of Douglass, but at an antislavery convention in Salem, Ohio, he recalls her issuing a challenge. Douglass, who'd recently visited John Brown, whose stark visions of war influenced him, shifted from nonviolence to a militant ideology for slavery's end. Douglass was arguing that slavery could only be abolished by bloodshed when Truth sharply interrupted him, inviting complete silence to the room: "Frederick, *is God dead*?" Probing history shows us that many current attitudes aren't new. The same pessimism that pervades the conversation around pathological anti-Blackness, and the doubt that America will ever transcend it, has been part of Black racial discourse since the days of Douglass and Truth.

Far from unobtrusive assistants in the Civil War, Black infantry, nurses, cooks, guards, spies, surgeons, recruiters, laborers, steamboat pilots, and artillery turned the tide. Roughly 186,000 Black men enlisted to serve in the Union Army and another 29,000 in the Navy. Lincoln began to come around to their necessity, but at every turn, they had to prove not only their value as soldiers, but their humanity. We can look back to those estimated five thousand soldiers who fought in the American Revolutionary War to see a history of contempt and exclusion for Blacks seeking to enter the armed forces. It is true that there were white people who hated slavery for its repressive effect on other whites, or for how it tore up their country, but not because of any empathy for Black existence.

There was a gigantic depth of prejudice by Union generals about Black soldiering ability. One Sergeant William Pippey estimated that there wasn't one in one thousand abolitionists in the Union Army. One observer said that as Blacks set to hauling carts, building fortifications, digging latrines, and graves that they may as well have been slaves. If you read through first-hand accounts during this period of anti-Black history, you'll have to get used to hearing the word *nigger,* or should I say the n-word? I cannot. I will not. I use it here not gratuitously, but because we shouldn't perfume the fecal stench of its legacy. One Pennsylvania soldier wrote, "We don't want to fight side and by side the nigger. We think we are too superior a race for that." A Michigan corporal said he did not want to "get shot for a dead nigger."

I could go on much further, but the main point is how common these thoughts were. Criminology professor Jack Levin shared a thought-provoking point that speaks to prejudice in general, but especially applies to anti-Black history: "Crimes motivated by bigotry usually arise not out of the pathological rantings and ravings of a few deviant types in organized hate groups, but out of the very mainstream of society." Sometimes it is good to remember this context lest these examples stand out as exceptional. The bigotry that you are reading about in these chapters flowed from the mainstream.

But with all of this, they carried on. In the face of doubt, suspicion, and unequal pay and treatment, they carried on. I didn't learn much about Black Civil War soldiers growing up, but one thing I vividly remember was their daguerreotype photos. Some soldiers sat in portrait studios, while other images captured the frozen aftermath of battles. One image seared into my mind shows five Black men collecting the pale, ragged bones of soldiers killed during Ulysses S. Grant's 1864 Overland Campaign. One of the men kneels next to a pile of skulls and decaying limbs, his face frozen, like one that has seen too much death. "Only the dead have seen the end of war," said philosopher George Santayana, and that statement is felt in every shadow of the photograph. Others stood in their dark blue wool coats and forage caps with American flags draped behind them. They were young. I could see their character, their pride, their resilience, their self-control, and magnanimity. Some hold their pistols. Some are before and after photos that stand in striking contrast. Many photographers took photos of recruits right before enlistment, with their tattered clothing, then after in their uniforms. There's one like this of Private Hubbard Pryor of Georgia, who enlisted in the 44th United States Colored Infantry Regiment. Others gripped swords with hands in white gloves, like Lieutenant Peter Vogelsang, who served with the 54th Massachusetts Infantry Regiment. These were the faces that destroyed the Confederacy.

For a long time, everything I'd learned about the 54th was from random articles and the 1989 war drama *Glory*, with performances by Denzel Washington, Matthew Broderick, and Morgan Freeman. Indeed, there was glory. A parade of black men marching in synchronized rhythm off to liberate the enslaved. They stood confidently in their navy-blue uniforms, shouldering Enfield rifles, eyes full of determination. For eighteen months they risked their lives without wages, deciding that if they could not receive equal pay, they would accept no pay at all—until legislation finally corrected the pay disparity. The movie shows the heroic and haunting assault on Fort Wagner, South Carolina, by the 54th on July 18, 1863. In a charge, white officer Robert Gould Shaw eagerly led his men into battle, but they were severely outnumbered. Shaw was shot in the chest and killed, along with many others. But Sergeant William H. Carney, grievously injured, managed to save the 54th regiment's flag. For his valor, he became the first Black-American recipient of the Medal of Honor.

If the history of the 54th seems segregated from Civil War memory, there are others of which we hear even less. In Southern territory, enslaved fugitives emerged from the swamps and ran from plantations to join with Confederate deserters, draft resisters, and lawless white men, forming groups like the "Buffaloes," a pro-Union guerilla unit that raided and attacked Confederate troops and plantations.

Some women, like Cathay Williams, who changed her name to William Cathay, disregarded the constrictive norms of gender and presented as men so they could fight, too. Imagine the line they had to walk. But there is danger in constantly trying to prove yourself, especially in war, where it can push you over the line between bravery and recklessness.

Others fought to prove their manhood. Soldiering has always been associated with a masculine identity, and American manhood has been defined by competition, aggression, stoicism, courage, and independence. This was everything America said Black men were not. It is no surprise, then, that the psychological legacy of centuries-long stereotypes spurred many Black men to war. Imagine having to constantly prove your humanity. Black soldiers had to give outstanding performances for recognition, while a white soldier could give lackluster or mediocre effort and still be treated with dignity. The search for validation and approval from white people was a sad reality that drove many to war. Some simply fought for money and adventure. But poring through their letters, I saw a pattern—they consistently stated that they were fighting to end slavery. Not only that but for freedom, and more specifically, for all Black people to enjoy the full privileges and duties of citizenship. That was the deciding factor that spurred them to leave their families behind, many to fend for themselves, to go where they would be despised, because they saw themselves as a liberating army. "A double purpose induced me and most others to enlist," said Medal of Honor recipient Sergeant Major Christian A. Fleetwood, "to assist in abolishing slavery and to save the country from ruin."

They risked their lives for freedom. On June 2, 1863, when Harriet Tubman became the first woman in US history to lead a major military operation, she knew as she always had that she was fighting for freedom. Under the command of Colonel James Montgomery, she led 150 Union soldiers on the Combahee Ferry Raid. Tubman, already a spy for the Union Army, had gathered intelligence that several South Carolina rice plantations around the narrow river would be lightly guarded. On that information, they chased out enslavers and burned down the plantations. Over the course of the operation, some seven hundred enslaved people were freed from forced labor. It was so successful, the Union Army duplicated the strategy in future raids. Harriet Tubman was the mastermind. Tubman's only regret was that she ruined her green dress. The story, as reported in the Boston newspaper *The Commonwealth*, in 1863, offered:

> Colonel Montgomery and his gallant band of 300 black soldiers under the guidance of a black woman, dashed into the enemy's country, struck a bold and effective blow, destroying millions of dollars' worth of commissary stores, cotton and lordly dwellings, and striking terror into the heart of rebeldom, brought off nearly 800 slaves and thousands of dollars' worth of property, without losing a man or receiving a scratch. It was a glorious consummation. . . . The colonel was followed by a speech from the black woman who led the raid and under whose inspiration it was originated and

conducted. For sound sense and real native eloquence her address would do honor to any man, and it created a great sensation.

In that same year, Burt G. Wilder, one of the first white officers commissioned to the medical staff of the 55th Massachusetts, an all-Black regiment, captures the chaotic air and humbling effects of the operating table as soldiers were being treated for and dying from their wounds:

Thursday, May 7th, 7:45 p.m. As was anticipated the wounded, about fifty, came at 9:00 a.m. and everyone has been full of work all day. Many are bad cases; two or three shot through the lungs, one through the head, and many in the body or legs; one, shot through the knee, had his limb amputated at the thigh this afternoon; in this case, what has been done but once before in this hospital, I held the large artery with my fingers instead of using a tourniquet. Among the wounded are several rebels; one, from Virginia, is a perfect gentleman; all of them say they are tired of war. My work is as before. I take notes of special cases, and also act as Dr. Marsh's cadet for a dozen of the more severe cases.

In the next entry he writes:

This evening I have been working on my report and making the evening visit with Dr. Marsh. One of our men, shot through the chest and with some ribs broken, died this evening, and two died in other wards. Before breakfast my nurse called me to a man bleeding fast from a large artery at the shoulder where the arm had been amputated on the field; I opened the wound at once by cutting the stitches while the nurse controlled the artery as well as he could by pressure behind the collar bone; but we could not take up the end in the wound and tie it until Dr. Marsh and Dr. Badger came; then I controlled the artery, Dr. Marsh took up the artery and Dr. Badger put a ligature about it and the man was safe; had it not been discovered in season he would have bled to death.

We all love to watch movies but pay little attention to what goes on behind the scenes. Black Americans not only fought in the Civil War, but they were also involved in its production. They dug the trenches that protected soldiers from shrapnel and solid round shots, and then with the same shovels they dug the holes and buried the bodies of soldiers who died in those trenches, often unceremoniously in mass graves. They maintained ironclad steam vessels and readied them for battle on the seas or rivers. They served as surgeons and nurses. Music played a powerful role in the war, and young Black boys pounded drums as soldiers marched, and sang songs like "John Brown's Body" and "Battle Cry of Freedom." They cleaned the weapons and fit them for battle. But their battle was always twofold—fighting in the trenches and for equality.

Camps, Contraband, and Humanitarian Crisis

The desire to own other human beings caused bitter Southerners to purposefully create a humanitarian crisis as they thrust Black people toward death. Natchez, Mississippi, was the wealthiest town in America prior to the Civil War. During the war, planters stuffed their elaborate mansions with food and provisions while keeping the enslaved in what can be described as no less than concentration camps. The able bodied were impressed into menial service for the Confederate Army while others were pushed into Texas and Georgia and deeper into Confederate territory. They starved women, children, and the elderly, barely clothed them, and left them to wallow in disease, pushing them toward the Union lines. Author William Jewett Tenney described the scene:

> [Enslaved people] in many instances arrived sick, half-starved, and with only a few rags for clothing. It was obviously the duty of the Government to provide in part at least for these poor creatures, and to furnish employment for such of them as were able to work, that they might sustain themselves and their more helpless kindred . . . especially below Vicksburg, it was a matter of difficulty to obtain a sufficiency of rations for the soldiers, to say nothing for the 30,000 or 40,000 helpless colored people who looked to the Government for food . . . overcrowding, want of ventilation, malarious localities, prevalence of small-pox, want of medical attendance, poor and insufficient food, and lack of clothing. . . . At the camp at Natchez, where there had been

4,000 freedmen, the number was reduced to 2,100 by deaths, from fifty to seventy-five having died per day during July and August.

This instance has been dubbed "Devil's Punchbowl" and is still blamed on the Union, when it was the Confederate Army that was responsible. War is always bitter, but Southern hatred for Black people made it even more so. In 1864, showing a capacity for savagery, Confederate troops slaughtered Black Union soldiers in Fort Pillow, Tennessee, as they lay down their rifles in an attempted surrender. In the heap of three hundred corpses, roughly two hundred Black bodies lay in the bloody aftermath of the slaughter. An unmerciful Confederate field commander later boasted that his men had taught "the mongrel garrison of blacks" a lesson.

As I read deeper into this history, I was highly interested to learn about the firsthand accounts of camp aide Susie King Taylor. As a Black nurse whose grand uncles had fought in the Revolutionary War, she chronicled her Civil War experiences in her book, *Reminiscences of My Life in Camp with the 33rd Colored Troops, Late 1st South Carolina Volunteers* (1901). Born enslaved in South Carolina, she learned to read and write because of her grandmother's willingness to subvert the law and send her to a clandestine school for Black children.

"We went every day ... with our books wrapped in paper to prevent the police or white persons from seeing them," Taylor wrote. "I gave my service willingly for four years and three months without receiving a dollar. I was glad, however, to be allowed to go with the regiment, to care for the sick and afflicted comrades. . . . Many people do not know what some . . . colored women did during the war," Taylor journaled. "Hundreds of them assisted . . . Union soldiers by hiding them and helping them escape. Many [black women] were punished for taking food to the prison stockades for . . . [Union] prisoners. . . . The soldiers were starving, and these women did all they could toward relieving the men, though they knew the penalty, should they be caught. . . . These things should be kept in history before the people."

Black people fought and died, with regiments organized from Kansas, Massachusetts, Indiana, Michigan, New York, Iowa, Illinois, Pennsylvania, Connecticut, and Rhode Island. Bloody battle after battle. "It seems strange how our aversion to seeing suffering is overcome in war," said Susie King Taylor, who cared for many of these men, "how we are able to see the most sickening sights, such as men with their limbs blown off and mangled by the deadly shells, without a shudder; and instead of turning away, how we hurry to assist in alleviating their pain, bind up their wounds, and press cool water to their parched lips, with feelings of only sympathy and pity."

Life After Death

The Civil War is remembered sentimentally as armies on two sides making heroic sacrifices, both fighting valiantly down to the last soldier. Monuments were erected in the visage of men who soldiered with fortitude. All while undernourished, understaffed, underequipped, and under fire. In the narrow confines of this view, little is made of the ethical transgressions and moral wounds of war. The massacres. The carnage. Too little is said about the national tug-of-war between abolition and slavery, equality and racism, disenfranchisement and citizenship, repression and reconstruction. Most accounts place the first national Memorial Day celebration on May 30, 1868, when both Confederate and Union soldiers were buried together on the sprawling grounds of the Arlington National Cemetery as part of our national reconciliation. Stories are told about how white Southern women put flowers on graves before the Civil War's end, but Black people were already remembering.

On May 1, 1865, in Charleston, South Carolina, the recently freed Black community had organized a burial for the Union prisoners of the Civil War who'd died in a Confederate war prison. They erected an enclosure for the cemetery, exhumed the bodies, and buried them with dignity. On the archway at the entrance, they inscribed the words, "Martyrs of the Race Course." Then on May 1, some ten thousand Black mourners came out to mourn in a funeral procession led by schoolchildren holding roses and singing the Union anthem, "John Brown's Body." Black women carried wreaths, flowers, and crosses. Union soldiers followed along to give their comrades the respect in death that they didn't receive in life. This was the first Memorial Day. And for a long time, this one was buried with those Union soldiers alongside the rest of Black history:

The loved of many hearts is gone,
The light of many eyes;
His race on earth at last is run—
His home's beyond the skies.
No wife was near him when he died,
No friendly voice to cheer;
He fell the country's greatest pride—
A noble volunteer.
Twas hard for one so young and good;
But God had willed it so:
He fell, as every soldier should—
His face turned to the foe.
Short, truly, was his suffering-time;
How wondrous his reward!
His soul has gone to dwell above,
To stand before the Lord.

—"Obituary," by Mrs. E. Morris,
Frankford, September 26, 1864

Somewhere between Southern propaganda and Northern forgetting lies Black history. And in that space, we find two and a half years later, more than 250,000 enslaved individuals in Texas cashing in on the promise made in the Emancipation Proclamation for the very first time. Major General Gordon Granger of the Union Army, along with roughly two thousand Union soldiers, entered Texas to enforce the Proclamation.

In Galveston on June 19, General Granger publicly read General Order No. 3, which stated: "The people of Texas are informed that, in accordance with a proclamation from the Executive of the United States, all slaves are free." But we now know that freedom was conditional and still repressive in many ways. In fact, some states, like Kentucky, Delaware, and Mississippi, refused to ratify the Thirteenth Amendment until the twentieth century. Black freedom was, in so many ways, unattained. But this is the history. During despair, we see Black people coming out to find something to celebrate, grasping at joy. As the struggle for Black freedom in America continues, then it should be viewed as a marathon, and all marathon runners must stop at the water cooler at some point. We need to take a break in order to celebrate. Some people said that it was only symbolic when Juneteenth became a federal holiday on June 17, 2021, but symbolic for who? Black people have always celebrated freedom, even when they knew they had so much further to go.

Some groups celebrated emancipation on January 1 (also known as Freedom Day), the date of Abraham Lincoln's final Emancipation Proclamation; others chose to celebrate September 22, the date of the first Emancipation Proclamation; some people celebrated April 9, which was called "Surrender Day," the day General Robert E. Lee surrendered the Confederate Army. And New Yorkers celebrated July 5, the date slavery ended in their home state. But Juneteenth became the most popular day to celebrate. Despite the difficulties, we can never undervalue the impact and the importance of freedom. That is the story of Juneteenth. When the Black community came out with its Civil War veterans and their families to picnic, parade, smoke meat, eat red velvet cake, and play music, some laughed, and others cried. Some cut up a rope and each took a piece so that every time they looked at it, it would remind them they were free from bondage. That is the legacy.

These celebrations were the resolution to the question posed by Frederick Douglass, in his speech "What to the Slave Is 4th of July?" It so happened in Austin, Texas, in 1870 that some wanted to celebrate emancipation on June 19, while others chose July 4. Community leaders held a big meeting and debated their position. Juneteenth won out, as a newspaper said: "A mass meeting of the colored people was called at the courthouse and by large majority stuck to the 19th of June. They said that the fourth of July was a very good liberty day for the white man, but that it never brought their freedom. They knew that 'freedom come' on the 19th of June, through the order of General Granger, which date is indelibly fixed in the wards mind as the 19th of June."

11

Dawn to Dusk

And, instead of going to the Congress of the United States and saying there is no distinction made in Mississippi, because of color or previous condition of servitude, tell the truth, and say this: "We tried for many years to live in Mississippi, and share sovereignty and dominion with the Negro, and we saw our institutions crumbling. . . . We rose in the majesty and highest type of Anglo-Saxon manhood, and took the reins of government out of the hands of the carpet-bagger and the Negro, and, so help us God, from now on we will never share any sovereignty or dominion with him again."
—Governor James K. Vardaman, 1904

Robert E. Lee surrendered the Confederate military at Appomattox, Virginia, on April 9, 1865, after flying the South's thirteen-starred battle flag for the last time. The South had lost its bid to become an autonomous, slave-holding republic. Abraham Lincoln was dead. Chattel slavery, the great transgression of human existence, was mostly dead. The body politic of America lay only half-alive in the wasteland of the Civil War, looking down at its wounds and lacerations in agony, in desperate need of a surgical reconstruction. The Union victory had stopped the massive bleeding of battle, but not only did they fail to stitch the wound for optimal healing, it was still infected by the thoughts and sentiments of anti-Black racism. Freedom was far from absolute, and chattel slavery's final descendants had to grapple with an underlying anxiety, after looking forward to the long process of re-creating their very existence. Some fled the South in what was called "the scatter." Newspapers filled up with ads placed by those searching for lost family members. Reality set in as people needed homes, jobs, and food to feed their children. Out of desperation, threat, necessity, or even familiarity, some settled into a sharecropping system so close to slavery that a passive observer wouldn't recognize the difference. For me, the Reconstruction era was defined by the remarkable ways in which Black people carved paths to economic independence, citizenship, and then saw it dismantled in the blink of an eye. As Eric Foner, one of the foremost historians to write on the epoch, summed it up:

> Over a century ago, prodded by the demands of four million men and women just emerging from slavery, Americans made their first attempt to live up to the noble professions of their political creed—something few societies have ever done. The effort produced a sweeping redefinition of the nation's public life and a violent reaction that ultimately destroyed much, but by no means all, of what had been accomplished. From the enforcement of the rights of citizens to the stubborn problems of economic and racial justice, the issues central to Reconstruction are as old as the American republic, and as contemporary as the inequalities that still afflict our society.

Lines were drawn before the musket smoke cleared the air. Though chattel slavery was technically over, a shattered America had been, and will always be, shaped by it. Southern planters and Northern industrialists both had vast economic interests in reshaping the political landscape in the United States, and the country had spent some 5.2 billion dollars fighting the Civil War. Radical Republicans, moderate Republicans, Southern Democrats, and former Confederates argued, threatened, and compromised as they hammered out new state constitutions. Union soldiers occupied Southern towns and cities to enforce the new laws of freedom. Within a few years, Black people crawled, stood, walked, and then ran to political autonomy, the ballot, and elected office. Carpetbaggers descended from the North, working as teachers, merchants, businessmen, and the Freedmen's Bureau, a group created by Congress charged with coordinating the resettlement of the formerly enslaved. Scalawags, mostly made up of the pro-Union Southern white proletariat, supported Reconstruction policies and were called traitors for it. It was also the epoch that birthed the Ku Klux Klan and the race massacre. All of this wrapped in an era of rampant business and government corruption, where jobs were given as political favors and manipulators stole millions of taxpayer dollars.

This Is a White Man's Government

To understand the history of Reconstruction, we must first understand the forces that worked from the outset of the Civil War to undermine democracy and progress for Black people. The Union Army was not welcomed warmly in the South, and order had to be reestablished by the force of the federal government. But before questions could be answered around liberty and equality, there was first the question of the economy. It is not hyperbolic to say that the whole of the Southern *riche* amassed its wealth on the backs of the formerly enslaved, their invaluable labor seeding the bloom of unprecedented prosperity. An indisputable reality that brings us to an ever-embittered matter of restitution for slavery. The legendary forty acres and a mule story, where the US government was supposed to give land and a four-legged beast of burden to all emancipated Black people, has ballooned beyond the stratosphere of truth.

Here is what really happened: On January 16, 1865, General William T. Sherman issued Special Field Order No. 15, which set aside four hundred thousand acres of property seized from Confederate landowners for redistribution to Black families in forty-acre plots. Sherman was an avowed racist, but pragmatic enough to realize he faced a humanitarian crisis. According to historian Jim Downs in his book *Sick from Freedom* (2012), disease and starvation condemned to death one million of the four million formerly enslaved between 1862 and 1870. Smallpox, cholera, and mosquito-borne diseases wrought havoc on the contraband camps housing Black people. The conditions were so deplorable and the death so pronounced, there were Northerners who thought the Black population was on the verge of extinction. So, when a group of Black ministers in Savannah, Georgia, brought Sherman a plan to redistribute land to the formerly enslaved, he listened. They said, "The way we can best take care of ourselves is to have land and turn it and till it by our own labor."

Land has always been tied to freedom. Freedom to work the land, hunt the land, build, grow, get from, and give back to the land. And the United States had given reparations before . . . to slave owners. In 1862, a bill was signed to pay up to $300 for every enslaved person freed in the District of Columbia. The board reviewed some one thousand slaveholders' petitions in their claims on nearly three thousand enslaved people. So, by June 1865, forty thousand acres were distributed to some four million formerly enslaved. (Mules were not included in the order, but the Union Army did give some away as part of the effort.) Others received no land, and the Freedmen's Bureau was established to distribute food and clothing, to educate, and to provide medicine and medical care to thousands of the formerly enslaved.

The Freedmen's Bureau, with its policy of education, citizenship rights, and self-help, was an immense aid to Black people, and it also helped negotiate labor contracts used to force white employers to honor their end of employment bargains. Today, the bureau's records offer important clues about how the formerly enslaved reconstructed their lives. Women worked to obtain pensions for husbands who died in the war as their marriages during slavery were not legally valid. There were no marriage certificates or computers, so each of them had to give testimony in what must have been a painful retelling of their life's intimate details. The labor contracts tell us much about the work they had to do and the gendered division of labor. The vast majority of freed Black women had no upward mobility beyond domestic work: making clothes, soap, and candles, sewing, stitching, patching homes, cooking, washing, ironing, growing vegetables and healing herbs, raising cows and milking them, tending to pigs and slaughtering them, and collecting eggs from hens. All of these animals had to be fed, watered, and cared for, and often women did this while birthing, nursing, and raising children, and caring for the sick, disabled, and elderly. None of this labor was paid, and in addition to their day jobs, it was all in care of their families.

Black men found ceilings as well, relegated to agricultural labor; they typically had shot, fishing line, powder, hooks, and buckets among their belongings indicating that hunting and fishing were integral parts of supplementing a meager family income. Appreciating these inner worlds gives us perspective as we move into the bigger picture. And it gives us a glimpse into our own, as we all have toilets to clean, floors to sweep, and dishes to wash. When the focus of history is typically placed on major events, exploring the mundanity of daily life becomes extraordinary.

We will never know what Lincoln's vision for Reconstruction would've been, but following his assassination, Vice President Andrew Johnson was plunged into the highest seat of power to decide the direction of the postbellum South. Growing up poor in Tennessee, he was raised in politics as a champion of working-class whites, and while he harbored no love for the Southern oligarchy, being the only Southern senator that did not resign his Union seat, he crafted an identity cemented in his idea of superiority over Blacks. He was in no position to help deliver the nation from its contradictions; for him, states' rights took precedence over human rights. Plainly stated, Johnson wanted a white man's government. He overturned General Sherman's reparative order for forty acres and a mule, and began returning land to former Confederates who took a loyalty oath equivalent to a spit and a handshake. W. E. B. Du Bois wrote of this as a historic injustice when he said:

> [The Negro voter] had, then, but one clear economic ideal and that was his demand for land, his demand that the great plantations be subdivided and given to him as his right. This was a perfectly fair and natural demand and ought to have been an integral part of Emancipation. To emancipate four million laborers whose labor had been owned and separate them from the land upon which they had worked for nearly two and a half centuries, was an operation such as no modern country had for a moment attempted or contemplated.

President Johnson quickly granted pardons to ex-Confederates and looked away as Southern states reestablished the old racial order through draconian Black codes. Most formerly enslaved people were pushed back into a form of indentured servitude and near re-enslavement, having to sign yearly service contracts for plantation work, or pay a fine for not having one. Southern states used every tactic available to force undervalued Black labor and reignite their crumbling economy. In Mississippi, a law passed allowing the state to take control of Black orphans and wrest children from parents deemed unfit to "apprentice" them to white "masters or mistresses." Black people could not bear arms. Anti-miscegenation laws were facts of life. Black existence was criminalized with vagrancy laws. Landed Black people were illegally evicted from the soil that had been watered by their sweat, fertilized with their blood, and soaked with their tears.

It is not an exaggeration to say that freed Black people, with nothing but their tattered clothing and farm implements, performed economic miracles. They purchased every inch of affordable land whenever they could. By 1910, out of some four million formerly enslaved, 212,972 of them and their descendants owned 14 percent of all farmlands in America—about nineteen million acres. By the twenty-first century, they retained control of only 10 percent of it, as white tax assessors overvalued Black land, leaving residents with tax burdens they could not pay. By 1940, Thurgood Marshall, special counsel of the NAACP, pinpointed the white officials in the South who for years were "depriving Negroes of their property through subterfuge." President Andrew Johnson's lukewarm reconciliation policies helped restructure a system of white supremacy that acted as the machinery to crush Black wealth and dreams. He clashed with the Radical Republicans, a powerful faction of the Republican Party founded in 1854 as an antislavery party committed to passing racial justice legislation. This eventually led to him becoming the first president to be impeached. The party was led by the likes of Charles Sumner, who several years earlier was nearly beat to death by a pro-slavery senator for his antislavery views. And Thaddeus Stephens, a congressional representative who fought for Black freedom in life and refused to be buried in a whites-only cemetery in death.

"Strip the proud nobility of their bloated estates, reduce them to a level with plain Republicans, send forth to labor, and teach their children to enter the workshops or handle the plow, and you will thus humble proud traitors," said Stephens. And it was this stubborn opposition to the old racial order, with Black Republicans organizing on the ground and white radicals in Congress, that got the Civil Rights Act of 1866 passed, making Black Americans full citizens entitled to equality under the law. In response, Johnson turned to an old argument that asserted the federal government had no business overreaching its authority to promote social, political, and economic equality. This, of course, was a smoke screen; the real concern was that a landless class of Black citizens would have a say against former Confederates.

Extraordinary times called for extraordinary measures. Against recalcitrant Southern Democrats, the Republican Congress passed the sweeping

Reconstruction Acts of 1867, forcing military rule to edge ahead in the showdown for power. Before readmission to the Union, it was mandated that states must ratify the Fourteenth Amendment, which unlike the Civil Rights Act, prohibited discrimination against citizens and ensured equal protection under the law. Then the Fifteenth Amendment was passed, mandating that "the right of citizens of the United States to vote shall not be denied or abridged by the United States or by any State on account of race, color, or previous condition of servitude." We must note that it did not say gender, and while the Black male vote forever transformed American politics, the fight for Black women to gain the vote was just beginning.

A Moment in the Sun

After Andrew Johnson narrowly escaped conviction in an impeachment trial in 1868, former Civil War general Ulysses S. Grant was heralded into the presidency. The Fifteenth Amendment, guaranteeing voting rights, was ratified during his presidency and formed a Department of Justice whose first order was to protect Black voting rights. Like Lincoln, Grant was viewed favorably in the Black community, and it was said that "Lincoln issued the Emancipation Proclamation, but it was Grant who actually freed the slaves." Of course, he proposed flexing the muscle of empire and annexing Santo Domingo (modern-day Dominican Republic) to act as a safety valve for Black people experiencing persecution in the South, but on racial matters he was no Andrew Johnson. His actions continued paving the craggy road leading to full civil rights.

It is easy to think that the first Black people elected to Congress were in the 1960s. They weren't. In 1870, Hiram Revels won the Mississippi senate seat once held by the former president of the Confederacy, Jefferson Davis. Ninety-four years after the nation's founding, he became the first Black senator in US history. How could a Black man be elected to such a position in the South? American history has often overlooked all the gains made by the Black men who voted and were elected to office. Black men fought to get elected; women fought to vote. For a moment, there was hope of a new South. Black and white Americans stood together politically for the first time in US history.

After 1867, with the Reconstruction laws in place, Black Americans had significant political power in a land where only a year earlier, they had no political power at all. There were 1,400 Black men elected to state and federal office. They were a diverse group. More than half were formerly enslaved. The other half were free before the war. They were laborers, artisans, farmers, and professionals. And twenty-two of them, either through the purchase of family or by slipping through the cracks of unprincipled racial power, were former slave owners themselves. A few others were Black carpetbaggers, migrating down from the North to gain political positions. Some were quick to forgive former enslavers; others were not. They were the rapid response team who arose to craft political agendas, working to keep a balance between Black nationalist and integrationist reforms. By all available evidence, most worked in lockstep to better the conditions of the Black race, while uplifting policies beneficial to all working people. They were determined and effective political organizers and campaigners who used the church as a base of community and autonomy. They worked as lieutenant governors, sheriffs, and constables, tried cases as justices, and worked as clerks, county attorneys, commissioners, and registrars. They believed that education was central to democracy, and they used their newfound political power to open public schools, which scarcely existed before the Civil War. As a result of their newfound political power, virtually every Southern state boasted at least a rudimentary public school system by the end of Reconstruction.

George Teamoh, a formerly enslaved shipyard carpenter from Virginia, was dedicated to assisting all Black people. He focused his efforts on reforming his state's penal system, hoping to eradicate the punishment of whipping Black people as a consequence for their crimes. He was appalled by this vestige of slavery and sought its removal. The Union League, the first mass Black political organization in the United States, held major influence in the South. With the Union League growing in Mississippi and Alabama, the members pushed for free schools, free ballots, and agrarian reform. They petitioned for better wages, called strikes, and established towns. Black women thought about how they could gain enfranchisement and political power on their own terms, as Anna Julia Cooper so thoroughly represented in her argument that "only the BLACK WOMAN can say when and where

I enter, in the quiet, undisputed dignity of my womanhood, without violence and without suing or special patronage, then and there the whole Negro race enters with me." Black people were not only reconstructing but constructing from scratch.

In 1887, carrying on the unfulfilled dream of his father, Isaiah T. Montgomery and his cousin Benjamin T. Green purchased a patch of prime Mississippi real estate—840 acres of mosquito-ridden swamp surrounding thick hardwood forest. But it was not an unwise decision as the train ran through the area. The dream was a town where Black people could thrive, build, and own away from the woes of Southern racism, an autonomous, self-sufficient Black community. Montgomery led the first group to the land by train. "You see," he said, waving his hand in the direction of the forest, "this is a pretty wild place." He paused, and the men looked hesitatingly in the direction he had indicated but said nothing. "But this whole country," he continued, "was like this once. You have seen it change. You and your fathers have, for the most part, performed the work that has made it what it is. You and your fathers did this for someone else. Can't you do as much now for yourselves?"

Mound Bayou, the Black pride of Mississippi, thrived as a self-sustaining community. The enterprising group constructed "businesses, churches, a train depot, a newspaper, three cotton gins, a cottonseed oil mill, a zoo, a Carnegie library, bank, swimming pool, a sawmill, Farmers Cooperative and Mercantile company, and a hospital" with hard work and ambition. Meanwhile, in 1890, Isaiah Montgomery voted at the Mississippi constitutional convention in favor of sweeping measures that introduced poll taxes and literacy tests to disenfranchise Black voters. Why did he sell out to white authority? Or did he? "It did not wholly suit me," he said, "but it was the best that could be done. We had to take the best that we could get."

He found refuge in hope, thinking that in time Black people would become literate and with upright living, they could climb the political staircase to a fair and democratic vote. He lived long enough to see that his politics of accommodation didn't work against Southern authoritarians bent on reestablishing the traditional racial hierarchy. He was called a Judas and a traitor. The Black press didn't mourn his death. If he is remembered at all, it isn't for building an entire Black town from the ground up but as a disappointment. In private letters, he deeply regretted his decision. Will it profit a man if he gains the whole world but forfeits his soul? How much quarter should we give Montgomery considering historical context? The Ku Klux Klan was at its height during the 1920s. Extralegal violence, intimidation, and corruption made democracy a sham. But we are more likely to admire the Black people who formed militias for self-defense, even while outnumbered and entrenched. One thing is clear, in popular history, we only remember and respect the fighters, even if they lost. No one really remembers that King David built a small empire in Jerusalem, only that as a teenager, he slayed the giant Goliath with a slingshot. We take pride in those who stand up. Yet, the truth of history is that most people struggle just to get by. Not many of us would've pushed past the fear to boldly challenge such entrenched white power with a high likelihood of retaliation. And I think that's why we are so fascinated with the few who, unlike Montgomery, did.

Those like Josiah Walls, who was unafraid and said: "We demand that our lives, our liberties, and our property shall be protected by the strong arm of our government, that it gives us the same citizenship that it gives to those who it seems would . . . sink our every hope for peace, prosperity, and happiness into the great sea of oblivion." Born enslaved in Virginia and forced to serve in the Confederate Army during the Civil War, Walls later joined the 3rd United States Colored Infantry Regiment. He was the first Black man elected to the US Congress from Florida, and I found it tough to wrap my mind around the fact that he was the last Black representative from Florida until 1992. Or those like Robert Meacham, also from Florida, who was born enslaved, but knew he had to find a way to advance Black freedom. Using his limited education, he taught others by candlelight, was eventually freed, and went on to be one of Florida's first Black senators during Reconstruction, becoming instrumental in pushing for Florida's public school system. His body now likely lies under a parking lot in a mass unmarked grave in Tampa, Florida. The unyielding desire to build cemeteries on cemeteries, parking lots, and playgrounds over the remains of non-white peoples has obliterated so much of our culture and memory for all people.

Where is Robert Meachum? Quite literally, his grave is missing, just as the stories of those Black people who fought to transform American democracy are missing from the public imagination. Another Florida luminary, Zora Neale Hurston, was buried in an unmarked grave until novelist Alice Walker and literary scholar Charlotte Hunt sought, found, and marked it in 1973. Walker recollected their patient journey, and the depth of emotion as they rediscovered her history, offering reverence as they marked her grave: "Zora Neale Hurston, A Genius of the Southwest, Novelist, Folklorist, Anthropologist." The whole exercise of recovering Black history often feels like searching for unmarked graves, and there is always a frantic effort to unearth these legacies, etch the names, inscribe the epitaphs, and plant the flowers.

American Terrorists

As Black men were gaining the right to vote, and Black women were helping them to politically organize, those rights and privileges were being simultaneously and violently swept away. The Ku Klux Klan, an anonymous paramilitary group of white men, dressed up as the ghosts of dead Confederates, terrorized Black victims, and then vanished as though they never existed, other than the crosses still burning after their departure. At first, they hid in plain sight. Testifying before Congress in 1871, former Georgia representative John H. Christy gave an artificially apologetic statement. "Sometimes mischievous boys who want to have some fun go on a masquerading frolic to scare the negroes, but they do not interrupt them, do not hurt them in any way . . . stories are exaggerated, and it keeps up the impression among the negroes that there is really a Ku-Klux organization." But only a few years earlier, in 1868, a Klan who was already stripping, whipping, beating, murdering, tarring, feathering, and throwing fireballs into the houses of Black people evicted the newly elected multiracial Republican representatives from state governments. In Georgia, thirty-three Black men—thirty in the lower house, three in the state senate—were voted into the General Assembly. Those so-called "mischievous boys" known as the Klan forcibly expelled the so-called Original 33 with one quarter of them murdered, beaten, or jailed. The white governor Rufus Bullock, a Republican who advocated for Black rights, was run out of town under threat of his life.

White hate groups were hell-bent on keeping the government out of Black control via voter suppression and organized terror targeted at Blacks and their white allies. A clash was inevitable. Newspapers added fuel to the fire, writing about the scourge of "Negro Rule," "Negroes and Carpet-baggers," and "Negroes and Scalawags," with relentless ad hominem attacks. Philip Joiner, one of the expelled white officials, helped organize a march on the county seat in Camilla, Georgia, to protest with hundreds of Blacks. Nine Black people were massacred in cold blood, while others present that day were hunted like fugitives by bloodhounds, narrowly escaping.

One thing to remember when studying the countless massacres and murders of Black people in the United States is that these were not isolated incidents. They exist on a continuum, beginning with emancipation. These were premeditated racial cleansings, systemic uses of violence to disenfranchise Black voters. All in the spirit of upholding white supremacy. And while the vast majority of anti-Black massacres occurred in the South and Southwest, even in the North, Black electoral self-determination was viewed suspiciously. Republicans in the District of Columbia feared the Fifteenth Amendment would "Africanize the city," transforming DC into a "negro utopia." The harsh words of the South, "This is a white man's government," continued in word and deed.

While there is a vast untold history of Southern interracial tolerance, it only went so far. In most cases, poor whites shared similar economic interests with poor Blacks, an olive branch that might have united them in collective political action, but time and time again, racism wedged itself between large-scale efforts of class solidarity. Sympathetic to the Southern white oligarchs, the *New York Tribune* ran an article in 1871 that offered what was then a popular sentiment: "The most intelligent, the influential, the educated, the really useful men of the South, deprived of all political power, [are] taxed and swindled . . . by the ignorant class, which only yesterday hoed the fields and served in the kitchen." Unable to share a vision of an egalitarian democracy, wealthy whites convinced their poorer white constituents that the "lazy" Black people who'd overseen the government wanted nothing more than a redistribution of wealth. But they must have forgot, they wanted nothing more than "the proportion of those who will labour under all the hardships of life and secretly sign for a more equal distribution of its blessings." They were in lockstep with the words of James Madison.

The Making of a Modern America

The racial makeup of America stretches beyond the binary of Black and white. This is made clear as we look to another underexplored region in Reconstruction history, the West. In 1893 the United States invaded a sovereign and independent Hawaii. When a Southerner settled in the islands in the same era, he condescendingly sang, "You may call 'em Hawaiian, but they look like niggers to me." Though ethnically and culturally distinct with their own myths, customs, and cultural fabric, Hawaiian royalty from King Kamehameha to Queen Liliuokalani had the physical features of Black people and were treated as such. Blackness was weaponized against Hawaiians, and as a result, just like Black Southerners, they were deemed unfit to rule—dehumanized, and hanged, and on trips to America, they were subjected to anti-Black discrimination. On an earlier tour to the United States in the 1850s, sixteen-year-old Hawaiian prince Alexander Liholiho was leaving the White House as future head of state when the conductor told him to move to the back. "Just because I had a darker skin, he had taken me for someone's servant. What a fool," he journaled.

As the US global empire expanded into weakening Spanish territories, like the Philippines, Black people found themselves fighting there, too. Likely fed up with his racist treatment in the US Army, in 1899, David Fagen, a young Buffalo Soldier, deserted from the American Army and became a captain in the Philippine Revolutionary Army. Again, we see the world being reconstructed in the image of white supremacy; President William McKinley saw the racial inferiority of the Filipinos as justification to disregard their sovereignty. At least fifteen Buffalo Soldiers defected and decided to fight with the Filipinos rather than against them.

Back in the United States, Black people found themselves in a nation with rapidly changing borders, which included hundreds of thousands of new people, in what was formerly Mexico. They found themselves as cogs in the machine of the American empire, spilling blood in the Spanish–American War, all while railroads and telegraphs cut their way through the desert wilderness and through Native American territory where tens of millions of buffalo were slaughtered to starve the Plains tribes and solve the "Indian Problem." South Dakota, Wisconsin, and Washington gained statehood in this era, and starting guns were fired ceremoniously to begin land rushes where tens of thousands of settlers staked claims to some 1.92 million acres.

And it is here where we can pause to see the broad reach of white supremacy beyond the so-called Negro Problem. Looking toward the Pacific, we can see how prejudicial Reconstruction policies extended to other people on the margins who had been deemed unfit to commingle with the white race. There were Chinese exclusion acts, theft of Native land, massacres of Spanish-speaking peoples, and the reconstruction of a vast swath of our southern border. Like the days of old, missionaries spread out to Christianize, civilize, and assimilate the land and everyone on it. Capitalism stretched its arm to the West, reaching to expand the American economy into Asia and Europe by way of the port of San Francisco. Many of the tactics perfected during slavery were reapplied and duplicated on other marginalized groups who had their own communities to protect, but who also had to make a choice about how they would filter down oppression or collectively rise against it, in a rigid but ever morphing racial hierarchy. Black freed people moved along the deserts, rich pastures, pueblos, gold and silver fields and settled to work and live. They worked as cowboys, fur traders, miners, and in cavalry units on the Western frontier. The Black history of the West is equally rich in stories and omissions.

The compromise of 1877, one of the most forgotten and important moments in US history, spelled the end of the Reconstruction era. Compromises had always been made to solve the political crises facing America, but so often they were delivered at the expense of Black freedom. The same states that wanted the federal government to exert its authority to enact fugitive slave law now argued for states' rights, asking the federal government to pull away its troops stationed to protect Black votes and citizenship. The compromise was made in a clandestine backroom deal, to not anger the countless people who would oppose it. In exchange for a peaceful transition for incoming Republican president Rutherford B. Hayes, the South promised it would leave Black civil rights intact, if the government withdrew federal troops. Nicknamed "Rutherfraud" B. Hays because of his shady path to the oval office, he switched from a policy of force to withdrawal, to restoration instead of reconstruction. Few leaders were informed of this bargain, and the contract was never published. Federal troops who had protected Black voters were withdrawn, and the former Confederate Democrats regained power. Black voting rights were stripped away, and the Southern oligarchy returned to old tactics in order to place themselves back at the apex as the white aristocracy.

A new era was ushered in, which looked eerily like slavery. Well, perhaps because former slave owners regained power. Blood, violence, and terror brought a violent halt to the rapid progress of free Black people. White property owners vowed to never be ruled by Black people again. In 1890, Mississippi crafted a constitution that effectively eliminated the Black and poor vote with literacy tests and poll taxes. With the gains of Reconstruction nearly destroyed, another Black person was not appointed to the Senate to represent a Southern state until Tim Scott of South Carolina in 2013.

When the colossal Statue of Liberty was assembled on Bedloe's Island in 1886, it was not designed as a national symbol of immigration. While debated, some believe it was originally conceived as a celebration of the emancipation of enslaved people. Proposed by French abolitionist Édouard René de Laboulaye, it was sketched by sculptor Frédéric-Auguste Bartholdi, to have her holding broken shackles, as a nod to the end of slavery. The shackles ended up around her feet, barely visible, and so, too, has been the original meaning of the statue. But in 1886, with growing wealth inequality, deep labor disputes, women's suffrage struggles, immigration woes, and continued native removal, the statue may have seemed ill-timed as a symbol of liberty. With racial terrorism as the order of the day, the *Cleveland Gazette* summarized what seems to have represented a general feeling:

> Shove the Bartholdi statue, torch and all, into the ocean until the same "liberty" of this country is such as to make it possible for an industrious and inoffensive colored man in the south to earn a respectable living for himself and family, without being ku-kluxed, perhaps murdered, his daughter and wife outraged, and his property destroyed. The idea of the

"liberty" of this country "enlightening the world," or even Patagonia, is ridiculous in the extreme.

These sentiments reflect the frustration people feel when liberty is undermined by bigotry and extremism. Reconstruction shows us how fringe groups prepared for violence can be used as an arm of a government unwilling to bloody its own hands. And even how the noxious ideology of white supremacy was mainstreamed into the government, subverting democratic institutions and pushing Southern enclaves toward racial authoritarianism. We can look back and compare the successful coup in Wilmington, North Carolina, when a duly elected multiracial government was overturned by white supremacists who murdered sixty Black Americans on a rampage. And how the fire-breathing speeches and aggressive tactics of outright racists were able to shrink a Republican government into littleness, forcing its hand to appease, reconcile, capitulate, and abandon the cause of Black freedom, exchanging the gavel of the law for their wallets in the bid for global domination and westward expansion. Minus the murders, we only have to look at the attempted coup fueled by white extremism on January 6, 2021, which was an "organized, illegal attempt to intervene in the presidential transition by displacing the power of the Congress to certify the election," to see the historical similarities.

On the verge of world wars and depressions, it would take more than half a century for the nation to look closely at the cause of Black freedom again. Reconstruction was a success, but without federal protection, it was doomed to fail. Had it worked, we might have had a politically powerful class of Black people who, knowing the tyranny of slavery, could have helped make the nation a more free and fair society. Had the Reconstruction gains been protected, the South would have likely produced a large, economically, and politically powerful class of Black farmers. The Republicans would've dominated elections for the presidency and Congress. The South would've industrialized sooner, benefiting from immigration. Socially, the country would be much more integrated, comparable to a modern multiracial democracy. But that could not be. After reconciliation, Black people were blamed for the demise of Reconstruction. Senator Benjamin Tillman argued it this way:

In my State there were 135,000 negro voters, or negroes of voting age, and some 90,000 or 95,000 white voters. . . . Now, I want to ask you, with a free vote and a fair count, how are you going to beat 135,000 by 95,000? How are you going to do it? You had set us an impossible task. We did not disfranchise the negroes until 1895. Then we had a constitutional convention convened which took the matter up calmly, deliberately, and avowedly with the purpose of disfranchising as many of them as we could under the Fourteenth and Fifteenth Amendments. We adopted the educational qualification as the only means left to us, and the negro is as contented and as prosperous and as well protected in South Carolina to-day as in any State of the Union south of the Potomac. He is not meddling with politics, for he found that the more he meddled with them the worse off he got. As to his "rights"—I will not discuss them now. We of the South have never recognized the right of the negro to govern white men, and we never will. . . . I would to God the last one of them was in Africa and that none of them had ever been brought to our shores.

When I was looking through the Library of Congress archives for Black thoughts during the Reconstruction period, I came across a man named Henry Theodore Johnson. There was little information about him but in 1895 the minister wrote with the tragic hope that Black people, beset on all sides, could make it through this brutal period. His message is urgent. He asks if Black people have been forsaken in America, reflecting on how Black ballots were paid for in blood and cursing the human blight of ignorance at the root of racial power. But then he offers hope, asking Black people to remember where they've come from and all that they've overcome: "With every curse of adversity peculiar to our career since emancipation there are associate blessings and clouds of despondence should not be allowed to curtain them from our view. Faith and philosophy are the glasses which, if well adjusted, will enable us to discern a silver lining to these o'erhanging clouds." As I read these words, I couldn't help but see it as a message to our generation, as we fight our own daily battles to wrangle hope from despair.

12

A Portrait of Suffering

If we must die, let it not be like hogs
Hunted and penned in an inglorious spot,
While round us bark the mad and hungry dogs,
Making their mock at our accursèd lot.
If we must die, O let us nobly die,
So that our precious blood may not be shed
In vain; then even the monsters we defy
Shall be constrained to honor us though dead!
O kinsmen! we must meet the common foe!
Though far outnumbered let us show us brave,
And for their thousand blows deal one death-blow!
What though before us lies the open grave?
Like men we'll face the murderous, cowardly pack,
Pressed to the wall, dying, but fighting back!
—**Claude McKay, "If We Must Die," 1919**

They had a hunting season on the rabbit
If you shoot him you went to jail
Season was always open on me
Nobody needed no bail
—**Mavis Staples, _Down in Mississippi_**

T he use of force. Action taken on a body. A clash between bodies. Force in service of envy, in service of sloth, in service of lust, in service of pride, in service of gluttony, in service of hate, has violently transformed the world on a scale unimaginable . . . if we didn't have the photographs to prove it. Bodies lying in the ruins of force, from the stone-tipped spear to the nuclear warhead, that could indeed send us back to using stone-tipped spears. Force is constant, as old as time, present in the cosmic background of our existence. On a material level it is believed that the force of colliding particles precipitated the known universe. But the aftermath of violent force is always complicated. How do you rebuild a storm-battered home, a war-torn country, a bullet-riddled school? How do you recover from tragedy? The forceful violence of post-Reconstruction America left a trail of Black suffering.

This didn't escape the notice of historian Rayford Logan. When he was surveying Black history, he wanted to know when the nation had reached its lowest point, and when he published his findings in 1954, he coined the term "the nadir of American race relations," a period between 1887 and 1923 that was plagued by chronic violence. Depraved acts of racism butchered a bloody path through the Progressive Era, when sweeping reforms were bettering society. But by most accounts this is the era when America roared as a confident nation, awash in industrial riches, flappers in dance halls, dazzling scientific innovation, Hollywood empires, and men learning to soar through the sky. Social safety nets rapidly expanded to account for unemployment, illness, disability, death, and old age. Labor unions preached the gospel of fair wages, journalists slathered the newspaper with exposés of big business corruption, food and drug acts made eating a slice of bread less dangerous, laws were passed to protect vulnerable children from being exploited and maimed in factories, animal welfare was seen as equally important. It was as though democracy got a steroid injection of socialism.

In this era, America had a large and generous heart for all sorts of reforms, except anti-racist ones. And just like slavery, this part of US history is a time people do not want to look at; the contradictions are in such stark contrast with the national narrative of progress.

Because underneath all those shiny advancements was the force of white supremacy, which worked relentlessly to exclude and attack Chinese immigrants in 1882, place indigenous children in federal boarding schools to be beaten, abused, and stripped of their tribal culture, annex territory, and inspire so many anti-Black terror campaigns that the late 1870s through the 1930s could be dubbed the era of lynching and race massacres. It's hard to imagine living in a nation where mobs regularly form to enact public executions. But until recently this was America. Not only in the South but in the West and Midwest, and occasionally in the North, extrajudicial murder was common. But suffering is engaged myopically: non-white people—such as Louis Lundy, a Black man shot through the neck in Washington, DC, after allegedly cursing in front of a white woman (1908), and Marie Scott, a seventeen-year-old Black teenager dragged from her cell in Oklahoma and hanged from a telephone pole for stabbing a white man, an incident that the Associated Press said was self-defense for attempted rape (1914)—fall away from the pages of history. Believe it or not, so far in this book I have chosen to be restrained, offering straightforward descriptions of anti-Black violence, insinuating rather than going into the most horrific details. I never want to render violent force trivial, or intake so much as to grow numb, but in this chapter, we will fully engage the agony. We are going to expose and sit with the all-too-human brutality that bridges past and present, a force so common that for many of us it rarely registers any meaning.

And it is hard to balance. Pain is inextricably linked to the Black American experience, so to study this history is a constant recalibration between love and terror and beauty and war. And it makes my skin crawl to see those who have no true sympathy or love for the Black experience profit off Black pain. Black grief is bought, packaged, and sold to appease the same thrill-seeking sensibilities that put millions of eyes in front of horror films. I'm always reminded of a story about how, in 1852, Harriet Beecher Stowe, a white abolitionist from Connecticut, wrote a book that helped awaken the Northern consciousness to the horrors of slavery. Instantly controversial for its excessive depiction of anti-Black violence and crude stereotypes, this was probably the reason it was a bestseller. Below the Mason-Dixon line it was banned as abolitionist propaganda, but many Northern whites were shocked into moral awakening. Yet, Harriet Tubman was unamused. Invited by Stowe to see *Uncle Tom's Cabin* in a Philadelphia theater, she refused, "I haint got no heart to go and see the sufferings of my people played out on de stage," she said. "I've seen de real ting, and I don't want to see it on no stage or in no teater."

I understand her sentiment. Why watch someone play out the very real drama of your daily existence? Tubman was likely wrestling with the post-traumatic stress of slavery, and I think this leads us to an important question—are we engaging with the suffering of others as entertainment or empathy? I do think the stories must be told; if not, the suffering becomes invisible. Doctors used to perform surgery on infants without anesthesia, their crying and screaming inconsequential, because the medical community was certain their immature brain pathways didn't allow them to feel pain. Because infants could not speak about their pain. It wasn't deemed unethical by the American Academy of Pediatrics until 1987. So, here we will retell the stories as a way to confront the force of violence parallel to each and every one of our daily lives, something that if we don't talk about, and if we don't make it meaningful, it renders death and suffering as mere inconveniences.

Of Pain and Suffering

In 1898 letters flooded into the Department of Justice regarding a lynching that had recently taken place in South Carolina. On the morning of February 22, an angry white mob burned the home of Frazier Baker, and as his family fled from the fire, he and his infant daughter were shot, and left to burn in the flames. Outraged, citizens wrote the president, Congress, and the Department of Justice seeking federal protection. They decried the "bloody butchery, barbarism, and satanic majesty" of the white mobs who'd terrorized the Black citizens of South Carolina for the previous twenty-five years.

Two of the letters were drafted by Ida B. Wells-Barnett, and her story is deeply extraordinary, because she proves to be, from her beginnings, a fearless activist, fiery orator, political pragmatist, and woman of and ahead of her time. There were others standing up against villainous extrajudicial mob violence, but Wells-Barnett mustered the most heroic response. As a journalist, she emphasized two things: seeking truth and reporting it. She felt bound to the cause of anti-lynching victims. In 1884, when she was twenty-two years old, we see her show up in the centuries-long fight for desegregation. She'd bought a first-class ticket for a trip from Memphis to Woodstock, Tennessee. When the white train conductor came for her ticket, he demanded that she move to the men's only front car, which was reserved for smoking and drinking. Wells refused, saying she was in the ladies car, at which time the conductor

> tried to drag me out of the seat, but the moment he caught hold of my arm I fastened my teeth in the back of his hand. I had braced my feet against the seat in front and was holding onto the back, and as he had already been badly bitten, he didn't try it again by himself. He went forward and got the baggageman and another man to help him and of course they succeeded in dragging me out. I resisted all the time, and never consented to go. My dress was torn in the struggle, one sleve [sic] was almost torn off. Everybody in the car seemed to sympathize with the conductor, and were against me.

Why should she as a Black woman not get the same ladylike respect as a white one? She sued the train and won. It was taken to the Tennessee Supreme Court. She lost. Undeterred, she started the Memphis free speech newspaper where she investigated the causes of white violence against Black men and criticized the segregated educational system. Her writings were bold and militant. In 1891 she wrote a piece called "The Inequalities of the City's Segregated School System" that cost her a teaching job. This is one of the things that makes her exemplary; there is a sensible amount of self-doubt that comes along with the prospect of losing income that supports a family. Time and again people have refused to stand on a moral foundation and speak out publicly against an injustice for fear of retaliation, stigma, and even arrest. Not Wells-Barnett. And it was in Memphis where she became one of the foremost leaders of her time. It was a city modernizing with streetcars and telephones, but also being ravaged by yellow fever. A reporter in 1890 noted, "Efforts on the part of the Negroes to improvement of their condition morally, intellectually and physically will move away the cloud [of racial prejudice] now overshadowing [them], as the sun removes the morning dew."

Black businesspeople thrived in commerce and real estate. But in 1892, when a man named Thomas Moss opened a grocery store that threatened the success of a white rival, he was arrested on dubious charges. Black residents grabbed their guns and surrounded the jail to prevent what they were certain would become a lynching. But the sheriff deputized seventy-five men, dragged Moss and two others out of the jail to a railroad yard, and literally shot the men to pieces. Moss was a close friend of Wells-Barnett. "A finer, cleaner man than he never walked the streets of Memphis," she said. He was well liked, a favorite with everybody; yet he was murdered with no more consideration that if he had been a dog. She had had enough. In an edition of her paper, she declared that Blacks were being lynched on false charges, one of which is that they rape white women: "Nobody in this section of the country believes the old thread-bare lie that Negro men rape white women. If Southern white men are not careful, they will overreach themselves and public sentiment will have a reaction; a conclusion will then be reached which will be very damaging to the moral reputation of their women."

For Wells-Barnett to imply the chaste white woman might be interested in Black men infuriated white male Memphians, with their ideals of gallantry and chivalry. When in reality, it was many of their fathers who raped the enslaved Black women who birthed the very men they were accusing. The charge was so offensive that Nathan Bedford Forrest, first grand wizard of the Ku Klux Klan, incited a mob to storm her newspaper, destroy her equipment, and set it ablaze. But she was out of town in Philadelphia; if not, this very well might have been the end of her story.

We might pause and wonder how people could get away with such retaliation with impunity. I don't use the word *terrorism* as hyperbole, but these were more than hate crimes, protests, riots, and acts of civil unrest. If we situate this history in the present, it is more easily understood. Most people think about groups like Al-Qaeda, ISIS, and Boko-Haram when they think of religious terrorism, but we should broaden our definition. The most common terrorists can be religious, violent-far-right, violent-far-left, or ethnonationalist. If you look globally, people from all races and creeds use violent force in service to their beliefs, but in America, terrorism by far has been a constant tactic for white supremacy groups who conducted "67 percent of terrorist plots and attacks in the United States in 2020." According to terrorism historian Walter Laqueur, the "terrorist movements are usually small; some very small indeed, and while historians and sociologists can sometimes account for mass movements, the movements of small particles in politics as in physics often defy any explanation." The greatest tool of a terrorist is fear, and white supremacy instills the fear of random violence into the communities they target. So, what Wells-Barnett was facing never went away. It's bigger than the historic specter of the old traditional Ku Klux Klan, morphing into neo-Nazis, the alt-right, or whatever people call themselves who continue to pass down the same bigoted beliefs every generation; anti-immigration, debunked racial pseudoscience, anti-Semitism, pale-skinned superiority, fascism, and especially anti-Blackness.

In the twentieth century, white terrorist organizations worked as the arm of some state governments, documented from the FBI to local law enforcement. I wonder if Ida B. Wells-Barnett asked the question: When judges are white supremacists, sheriffs are white supremacists, and the whole justice system is full of white supremacists, who protects Black people?

While many in the federal government condemned racial terror, no federal legislation was passed to criminalize this behavior as a federal offense. The story of Wells-Barnett shows us that much of the Black fight for freedom has been rooted in not only civil rights and anti-racism, but anti-terrorism. She promoted self-defense, conducted surveillance of terrorist organizations like the Ku Klux Klan, and exposed their activities. She fought for federal anti-lynching policy, and garnered community support. Much of Black political history has been focused on the pacifist ideals of the late-stage Civil Rights Movement in the 1960s, but less attention has been paid to the long legacy of Black agitation.

Unable to return to Memphis, Wells-Barnett connected with T. Thomas Fortune and began writing for his publication, the *New York Age*. Fortune was a profound figure in his own right, mentor to Booker T. Washington and W. E. B. Du Bois, but his contribution to Black political thought is sorely overlooked. He was an agitator, even within his own community. One time he assailed Frederick Douglass, the most famous Black man in America, for his uncritical support of the Republican Party. Many of the ideas he first expressed are still debated in the Black community, like: 1) Do Black people need to stop looking for outside help and rely on themselves? 2) Is protesting racial discrimination a nonnegotiable? 3) Will we ever leverage the power of the sleeping giant—interracial worker solidarity? He covered politics, economics, education, leadership, and the intricacies of Black life, arguing that there were too many so-called race leaders but not enough community building to execute their ideals.

Wells-Barnett was surrounded by those who believed in the politics of agitation. Armed with perseverance and clear vision, she ignored obstacles and continued advocating for legal protection for Black people. She wrote *Southern Horrors: Lynch Law in All Its Phases* in 1892, and *A Red Record: Tabulated Statistics and Alleged Causes of Lynchings in the United States*, in 1894. Wells-Barnett armed herself with a pistol to tour the South and tell the horror stories, while tabulating the statistics of Black lynchings; she understood the weight of the tragedy; "It is with no pleasure that I have dipped my hands in the corruption here exposed." It is of no pleasure to recount those stories here either, but it is important to shed light on some of the most sadistic manifestations of racism.

You might imagine a bloodthirsty crowd gathering to mindlessly execute a warped sense of justice, but the latest research in crowd psychology tells us that there is much more rhyme and reason to collective violence. In crowd settings, people play to their chosen social identity, work within geographical boundaries, and agree on a legitimate target. That target is then rendered a thing to be feared, worthy of rage and savagery. Black people received the worst of this brazen vigilantism. Most lynched whites were kept clothed, hanged, and then buried. Black bodies were lynched and desecrated far more often. We may never get a clear picture on how many. But some estimates say at least 6,500 were murdered by white mobs between 1865 and 1950. And this isn't including assaults, attempted murder, and rape, or even the fact that so many witnessed all of this and did nothing. Southern elm trees harbor stories of the Black men and women who once hung from nooses on their branches. And the harsh glow of streetlamps illuminated the Black bodies dangling from them. The wicked flames of crosses burning in the darkness symbolized a fiery hatred. Punishments enacted in public not only to intimidate people, often forced to watch, but as spectacle. Sometimes as many as fifteen thousand came out to view the lynching of Black Americans in a carnival-like atmosphere.

After the death, whites would mutilate and dismember the necrotic bodies, then auction off their ears, noses, toes, crushed bones, and other parts as keepsakes. White families, some with small children, took photos with fetid Black corpses, then sent the pictures off to family members as postcards with a note wishing them a happy birthday. Violence was not spared on the youthful or the elderly. Nor did it care about the innocence held within expectant mothers. The magnitude of atrocity is evident in every individual instance. In 1899 it was normal for large swathes of Americans to view lynching as a form of entertainment. Two thousand of them came out to see Sam Holt stripped of his life. A firsthand account from a newspaper journalist describes how the Black farm laborer, charged with killing his white employer, was served a sadistic and warped justice:

> Sam Holt . . . was burned at the stake in a public road. . . . Before the torch was applied to the pyre, the Negro was deprived of his ears, fingers, and other portions of his body. . . . Before the body was cool, it was cut to pieces, the bones were crushed into small bits, and even the tree upon which the wretch met his fate were torn up and disposed of as souvenirs. The Negro's heart was cut in small pieces, as was also his liver. Those unable to obtain the ghastly relics directly paid more fortunate possessors extravagant sums for them. Small pieces of bone went for 25 cents and a bit of liver, crisply cooked, for 10 cents.

There is something deeply unnerving about the willingness of people to cannibalize another human for fun. Even more, to view lynching with the same enthusiasm of a baseball game or embrace excitement in its most forceful moments, like a home run smacking off a fastball. In our male-centered histories, the violence against Black women often goes unspoken and unacknowledged. As has often been the case with female lynching victims like Mary Turner, a pregnant black woman, hung in Georgia for publicly condemning her husband's lynching. I think the visceral description of Sam Holt was enough here, but books like *Lynching and Spectacle: Witnessing Racial Violence in America, 1890–1940* by Amy Louise Wood and *100 Years of Lynchings* by Ralph Ginzburg paint history in its darkest colors. Firsthand accounts, graphic details, dates, names, and locations bring a hideous reality to state-sanctioned violence and show how common it was for God-fearing Americans to embrace anti-Black terror campaigns.

So, the question becomes, when you see these lynching and massacres and murders, do you see yourself? When you hear about Michael Brown's lifeless body moldering in the unrelenting summer sun for four hours uncovered in Ferguson, Missouri, after the unarmed eighteen-year-old was shot six times by an officer who was acquitted in 2014, do you see the parallels with history? When you see the knee of police officer Derek Chauvin settle in on the neck of George Perry Floyd Jr. for eight minutes and forty-six seconds, while he called out for his mother, in that moment on May 25, 2020, do you sympathize with his suffering or identify with the officer? Do you condone such force at all, and if you do, you must ask yourself, who do you condone it for and against and under what circumstances? Do you see the carnage and mangled bodies as humans, and not just generic victims? Do you see the non-responsibility and nonaccountability of our most trusted officials? And do you understand how long this has been going on?

Dauntless in the face of such violence, Wells-Barnett urged Black people to fight on three fronts in the press, in the court, and if needed, in the streets. "A Winchester rifle should have a place of honor in every black home, and it should be used for that protection which the law refuses to give. When the white man who is always the aggressor knows he runs a great risk of biting the dust every time his Afro-American victim does, he will have greater respect for Afro-American life."

I picked up the Nicholas Johnson book *Negroes and the Gun: The Black Tradition of Arms* (2014), and one thing that stood out to me was how consistently Black people have embraced gun ownership as a matter of life-and-death self-defense, even though it was against the law during slavery up through the Civil Rights Movement. Black veterans and servicemen used their military training to protect their communities against state militias and mobs. They formed self-defense clubs. Sometimes they had to arm their kids to raise the odds from twenty against one to twenty against two. After the passage of the Thirteenth, Fourteenth, and Fifteenth Amendments, Black people looked to the Second Amendment, determined to exercise the right to bear arms and act in self-defense.

In 1909, Ida B. Wells-Barnett spoke at the National Negro Conference about three major points: First, that "lynching is color-line murder"; second, that "crime" against women is the excuse, not the cause"; and last, "that "it is a national crime and requires a national remedy." She implored Black people to leave the South, boycott white businesses in support of racist practices, and warned that wealth and social status alone would not protect them. While wealth might put excess food on the table, it could not prevent a white person from taking it away. Ever the pragmatist, she understood that without political agitation and action there would be no advancement. She was one of the cofounders of the NAACP and was highly active in religious groups. The legacy of Wells-Barnett intersects with the lives of other overlooked freedom fighters, like William Munroe Trotter. Trotter, whose name is not immediately recognizable on the pantheon of civil rights activists like Rosa Parks, Martin Luther King Jr., and Frederick Douglass, should also be a household name. He stands out in history for his use of the Black press to express seismic outrage. One generation removed from slavery, Trotter was recognizable for his radical politics and handlebar moustache. He was much too outspoken to be silenced in history.

One of the best ways to speak as a Black person in America was through one of the most democratic institutions in America, the free press. Across the United States, *Arizona Informant, Chicago Defender, Denver Urban Spectrum*, the *St. Louis American, The Guardian*, along with the other Black publications, circulated to millions of readers. From the barbershop or beauty salon you could read about every aspect of Black life, from entertainment to vacations. They ran satires and cartoons mocking Jim Crow, advertised Black businesses, identified sundown towns to avoid, jobs, and community events. But they were also the voices of activism. In one issue Trotter told his *Guardian* readers: "A paper must be known for what it does, not merely what it says. The *Guardian* is not like most colored weeklies, saying one thing and doing another. We 'do' for colored humanity what the world has conspired to deny us. We will not apologize, and we will not retreat—the *Guardian* makes itself responsible for our collective deliverance. None are free unless all are free." Historian Kerri K. Greenidge rescued Trotter's story from the archival depths with her book, *Black Radical: The Life and Times of William Monroe Trotter* (2019), but prior to her fantastic accounting, he was widely overlooked. It is curious to me that Trotter has faded so far into the background as an early-twentieth-century spearhead of the Civil Rights Movement. The nonviolent protests, sit-ins, arrests for civil disobedience and grassroots organizing, he set the stage for those who would come after him. His goals were clear: "Wage a crusade against lynching, disenfranchisement, peonage, public segregation, injustice, denial of service in public places for color, in war time and peace."

In 1913, he, along with other early civil rights leaders, met at the White House to discuss Jim Crow with President Woodrow Wilson. After the Civil War, Black Americans gained employment in the federal government, making up about 10 percent of its workforce. But as soon as Wilson got into office, his cabinet got to work segregating the employees by race. Trotter had supported President Woodrow Wilson in his 1912 presidential run, as did many Black Americans. But by the time Trotter could meet him at the White House, he was angry with the president. Confronting him for segregating Black federal workers, he offended the president so much that Wilson threw Trotter out of the Oval Office. Could it be because when the KKK-celebrating bestselling film *Birth of a Nation* came out in 1915, the president applauded and said, "It is like writing history with lightning"? Trotter led protests in Boston against the white supremacist film, which was part of the mythology that distorted the truth of the Civil War and Reconstruction.

Emblematic of his commitment to the poor and working class was Trotter's wealthy and well-educated background. He believed that the greatest power came from collective action. Along with Wells-Barnett, he pushed hard for anti-lynching legislation. With this pressure, in 1918, Congressman Leonidas Dyer of Missouri introduced the Dyer anti-lynching bill—known as the Dyer Bill—but it would be twelve more decades before lynching was made a federal hate crime, with the bill signed into law on May 29, 2022. Much too late to deter the force of racial violence when it mattered most. Trotter's life was rife with loss. He'd lost his wife to the Spanish Flu, and pouring every bit of his fortune into his newspaper and fight for civil rights, he lost countless connections and friends who he felt were too accommodating in their fight against racism. Trotter's life ended at sixty-five years old, when he fell three stories from the roof of his building in Boston; some say it was accidental; others, suicide.

From Suffering to Suffrage

Ida B. Wells-Barnett stood at the intersection of race and gender pursuing multiple social reforms. Unable to vote at the turn of the twentieth century, enduring forms of marriage slavery, unallowed to own private property, and institutionalized for little to no reason, women found themselves under a heap of real prejudice, and Wells-Barnett intended to do something about it. Though the Seneca Falls Convention in 1848 is considered the first gathering on women's rights, it was the 1837 Anti-Slavery Convention that was the first major instance of political organizing by American women, for American women. Black and white women converged to denounce the political, commercial, and domestic relations between North and South because of slavery. In a spirited debate, white abolitionist Angelina Grimké asked each woman to batter down gender barriers and, "to do all that she can by her voice, and her pen, and her purse, and the influence of her example, to overthrow the horrible system of American slavery." Though we have this very real example of interracial solidarity to look back on, the fight for suffrage was not a universal one. As poor women who lacked the resources to join in and go to the convention were excluded, the uneducated were excluded, and Black women were excluded.

Even in the earliest utterings of American feminism in the eighteenth century, there was a rift. While Abigail Adams reminded white men to "remember the ladies," Sojourner Truth was asking, "Ain't I a woman?" While white women were fighting for their equal place within humanity, Black women were still trying to prove theirs. *The History of Women's Suffrage* (1881), a tome of more than six thousand pages documenting the decades-long struggle to constitutionally enfranchise the women of the country, written by the movement's white founders, Elizabeth Cady Stanton and Susan B. Anthony, excluded Black women from its pages. White women controlled the feminist narrative. And, as a result, it has taken almost a century of study to fill in its holes. Mary Church Terrell, Black suffragist pioneer, surely knew that memory is often the terrain on which wars of interpretation are waged, and offered us this:

When Elizabeth Cady Stanton presented a resolution demanding equal political rights for Women in Seneca falls in 1848, the only person there willing to second it was Fredrick Douglass, . . . and it was his masterful arguments
and matchless eloquence that the resolution passed despite powerful opposition. Therefore, whenever the women of this country pause long enough to
think about the hard fight which had to be waged so as to enable them to
enjoy their rights as citizens . . . they should remember the great debt of
gratitude they owe to a colored man at a crucial occasion point when no
other man was willing to come to their aid.

Until recently, the lens looking into the toxic history of white women's
racism was a foggy one. But look closely and we see examples of women
who, well intentioned, embraced the ideals of fairness while stubbornly
clinging to the racial bigotry all too common of their time. At worst, they've
been eager partners in the murder and exploitation of other humans. There
are antebellum accounts of white women selling Black infants to buy horses,
dresses, and other luxuries. Even those like Jane Addams, the brilliant social
reformer, who penned the words, "The good we secure for ourselves is pre-
carious and uncertain until it is secured for all of us and incorporated into
our common life," found it difficult to find the good in lynching victims.
The famous peace advocate was openly against segregation, racism, and
worked with Wells-Barnett as one of the white people who took an outspoken stance against lynching. But, to Wells's annoyance, Addams believed
uncontrolled Black men often brought them on. Wells-Barnett mastered
the democratic necessity of embracing compromise, but never at the expense of her highest principles. She would not rest while Black women were
excluded from what they believed to be their God-given right to cast a ballot. Wells-Barnett said:

We were likely to have a restricted suffrage, and the white women of the
organization were working like beavers to bring it about, I made another
effort to get our women interested. With the assistance of one or two of my
suffrage friends, I organized what afterward became known as the Alpha
Suffrage Club. The women who joined were extremely interested when I

showed them that we could use our vote for the advantage of ourselves and our race.

In 1913, on the day before Woodrow Wilson's presidential inauguration, a massive suffrage parade began on Pennsylvania Avenue in the nation's capital. Lawyer Inez Milholland, a white woman, atop a white horse, in a white cape, led the procession. "Behind her stretched a long line with nine bands, four mounted brigades, three heralds, about twenty-four floats, and more than five thousand marchers." And somewhere at the end of all that were Black women, segregated. Alice Paul, a suffragist, and organizer, told an editor, "As far as I can see, we must have a white procession, or a Negro procession, or no procession at all."

Wells-Barnett refused. After waiting in the crowd, as the Chicago delegates marched by, she stepped right to the front, taking her place equally among the white marchers. "I am not taking this stand because I personally wish for recognition," she later said. "I am doing it for the future benefit of my whole race." Even with the passage of the Nineteenth Amendment, Black suffragist and civil rights leader Mary Church Terrell, who understood the inextricable link between race and gender, predicted that Black women would be denied the vote. "The colored women of the south will be shamefully treated, and will not be allowed to vote, I am sure," she said in 1920. She was right. Black voters were kept from registration offices under threat of violence.

War Cannot Bring Peace

There was no shortage of devious designs to keep Blacks from the ballot. What started as a minstrel character named Jim Crow, used by white performer Thomas Dartmouth Rice to mock and ridicule Black American culture, morphed into Jim Crow laws used to mock and ridicule justice for Black Americans. Through the 1960s, most states enacted a litany of laws and elaborate schemes to keep Black voters from the polls. Unnecessarily difficult literacy tests claimed to stop the uneducated from voting; even then, many educated Black people couldn't pass the tests, with their confusing questions and racist administrators. Racial gerrymandering diluted the

Black vote by packing them into one or two districts or spreading them over wider districts. In the case of *Gomillion v. Lightfoot* (1960), the United States Supreme Court ruled that the Alabama state legislature violated the Fifteenth Amendment in 1957. This is because they mapped the city boundaries into a twenty-eight-sided figure excluding almost all Black voters and no white ones.

Democracy is healthy when voters choose their representatives, but through gerrymandering, representatives choose them. Black voter registration plummeted. Jim Crow laws rendered Black politics invisible for nearly a century.

After some quiet, the years around 1919 ushered in what might be seen as the beginning of one of the darkest chapters of American history. World War I, otherwise known as the war to end all wars, claimed forty million lives, and involved the largest military powers in the world. The Central Powers, led by Germany and Austria-Hungary, fought against the Allied forces led by Britain, France, and Russia. By 1917, President Woodrow Wilson reluctantly thrust the United States into the war after abandoning his isolationist policies. Thousands of troops, tanks, guns, and provisions were sent to the European front. More than 380,000 Black soldiers served in that war. In fact, when it was declared, so many signed up that the War Department stopped accepting their applications. And arguably some of the most famous soldiers of the Western Front were the Harlem Hell Fighters.

> The famed 15th Infantry (now the 369th Coast Artillery) from Harlem stayed longer under fire (191 days) than any other regiment, yielded no prisoners, gave up no ground, suffered casualties of 40 percent. Negro veterans still grin delightedly when they recall the "Battle of Henry Johnson," in which a pint-size onetime Red Cap from Albany, N.Y. killed, wounded and routed a party of 25 Germans singlehanded.

Brave and fearless as they were, World War I has been romanticized in our national memory, but there is nothing ideal about international disputes being resolved over twenty million corpses. Black people were eager to work and keep the factories running, but their unemployment ballooned beyond any other group. They were hopeful to integrate yet remained segregated and hated. It is absurd to think about, but as the fate of the civilized world hung in the balance, US generals were strategizing on how to keep Black people from sitting too close. Some people describe racial progress like a fine bourbon, improving with age and gradual progression, but it's been more like grinding steel. Black people hoped, as they had in all wars, that fighting for the United States would prove their loyalty. But the irony of the Revolutionary War carried on—whether America was fighting for freedom or democracy, its highest values rang hollow when it came to Black people. I wonder what went through the minds of Black soldiers as they snatched leaflets out of the air titled "To the Colored Soldiers of the US Army." It read:

> Hallo boys, what are you doing over here? Fighting the Germans? Why? Have they ever done you any harm? Of course, some white folks and the lying English American press told you that the Germans ought to be wiped out for the sake of humanity and democracy. What is Democracy? Personal Freedom, all citizens enjoying the same rights socially and before the law! Do you enjoy the same rights as white people do in America? The land of Freedom and Democracy? Or aren't you rather treated over there as second-class citizens? Can you go into a restaurant where white people dine, can you get a seat in a theater where white people sit, can you get a Pullman seat or can you even ride . . . in the South, in the same streetcar with white people? And how about the law? Is lynching and the most horrible cruelties connected therewith a lawful proceeding in a democratic country?

The goal of such propaganda is always manipulative. But what makes it enticing is, sometimes it's true. Germany weaponized US racism while hiding its own. But they were right. Heroically fighting in wars never saved Black people from the war they fought on American soil. What some saw as hope, others saw as an ineffectual fantasy. Threatened that immigration and the social mobility of returning Black veterans would upend their way of life, white people reawakened the force of the Klan around 1918, just at the end of World War I. Far from just a Southern organization, the Klan boasted charters in every state, with 80,000 members in New York, 95,000 in Oklahoma, and 60,000 in Florida. These statistics don't even cover sympathizers, contributors, and associates. They came from all walks of life. Chiropractors, businessmen, salesmen, engineers, clerks, politicians, sheriffs, and teachers. Ministers prayed under crosses in the day and burned them at night. Vigilante justice was the order of the day. In the December cold of 1918, Charles Lewis was lynched in Kentucky. Only weeks after the conclusion of World War I, he was a recent veteran still wearing his uniform.

The next year, 1919, Ida B. Wells-Barnett was listed by the FBI as one of "the most dangerous negro agitators," for speaking out on lynchings like Lewis's. And that same year recorded the red summer. A year of anti-Black massacres. The crimson peak of American racism.

The Race Massacre

There have been hundreds of race massacres in American history. In fact, I once saw a viral post that dismissively said we need to pick one and "research it." But this misses the point. Research is not just an internet search. We aren't inherently born with investigative abilities. It is a skill that must be learned and improved over years. People need to be taught to research. And if I know, and you don't, and I want what's best for you, I will teach you. But to teach you, you must care. And the reason this history has stayed so hidden is because more people haven't cared enough to find it.

They haven't looked enough into places like St. Louis, when after two white plainclothes detectives were killed, mistaken for drive-by shooters that previously attacked the neighborhood, a three-day reign of retribution killed between 39 and 150 Black people from July 1 to July 3, 1917. Only after the one-week disruption of wartime industry, and more than one hundred buildings destroyed, did the government write a report. Carlos Hurd, a *St. Louis Post-Dispatch* reporter, wrote, "For an hour and a half last evening I saw the massacre of helpless negroes at Broadway and Fourth Street, in downtown East St. Louis, where black skin was a death warrant." A tactic of historical whitewashing lies in how we name things. There is a difference between a shriek and a whisper, a sprint and a stride, a bear and a chicken, as well as a riot and a massacre. The East St. Louis Race Riot, as it is still named, was a race massacre (an indiscriminate and brutal slaughter of people). Eyewitness accounts confirm this. As do contemporary newspaper accounts describing "negroes, shot, burned, clubbed to death," and white "manhunting mobs." To call it a riot is to erase history. These were massacres, the unnecessary, indiscriminate killing of Black human beings. At least twenty-five massacres took place in 1919, from Alabama to Omaha, and from West Virginia to Pennsylvania. Black people fought back in every instance; they even took some white souls with them as they were killed. Not only were they outnumbered, outmaneuvered, outflanked, and outgunned, but whole state governments and national guardsmen were in on the violence. They rarely stood a chance.

In Corbin, Kentucky, a white mob forced nearly all the town's two hundred Black residents onto a train with a one-way ticket; it was nothing less than a racial cleansing. On September 30, 1919, one hundred Black sharecroppers organized a union meeting at a local church to discuss cotton prices. They were protesting an unjust system keeping them in debt peonage to white farmers with untransparent accounting records. They'd hired white lawyers to help fight for better wages for themselves and Black women working in service positions. That night they were visited by a group of white men connected to law enforcement who opened fire on the church. Union workers returned fire. A white man lay dead. Then the mob descended to quell the "uprising." Hundreds of white men along with six hundred national guardsmen, murdered hundreds of Black people indiscriminately for the next three days. Many more were maimed and beaten. One white man was arrested—the union attorney's son—and 285 black men were arrested. Black newspapers called it mob violence; white papers labeled it a socialist conspiracy "established for the purpose of banding negroes together for the killing of white people."

The white lie cost Black lives. They were tortured to confession, and against all-white grand juries, 122 Black people were indicted for second-degree murder, 65 were sentenced, and 12 were sentenced to death. Scipio Africanus Jones, a powerhouse lawyer, and the wealthiest Black man in Arkansas, along with the NAACP, worked to free the Elaine 12, and in 1925 the last one was freed, but under threat of lynching, he was rushed from Arkansas. Black resistance and collective labor struggle were crushed out of existence. Ida B. Wells-Barnett wrote: "The terrible crime these men had committed was to organize their members into a union for the purpose of getting the market price for their cotton." There are too many massacres to name here. But it was always a question of force in service to white power, and it isn't difficult to see the patterns over a long span of history. We only need to look at who the power is being exerted over, and by whom.

When Black Suffering Is American Suffering

In 1893, Wells-Barnett sought to boycott the World's Columbian Exposition in Chicago with a coalition of Black leaders. A four-hundredth anniversary celebration of the so-called New World discovery by Christopher Columbus, the exhibition drew in visitors from across the globe, setting a world record for outdoor event attendance, attracting 751,026 people. After its design was completed by Fredrick Law Olmsted, America's most renowned landscape architect, 65,000 exhibits had been laid out by 40,000 skilled laborers over 630 acres. It was a spectacular sight, showcasing the newest in technology and the oldest in archaeology. There was a 250-foot Ferris wheel and a white city said to be inspired by *The Wizard of Oz*. The Aunt Jemima pancake brand was introduced there, which was retired more than a century later in 2021 for its caricature of a Black woman as a smiling, submissive mascot of self-effacing servitude. Sticking with her motto, "I'd rather go down in history as one lone Negro who dared to tell the government that it had done a dastardly thing than to save my skin by taking back what I said," Wells-Barnett and others charged the exposition committee with excluding Black Americans and promoting racial stereotypes. One of those accusers was Frederick Douglass, a mentor of Wells; he wrote the introduction to her pamphlet, "Why the Colored American Is Not at the World's Fair."

At seventy-five years old, Douglass was still advocating for Black people and fighting an emerging Jim Crow. He'd escaped from the razor-sharp claws of slavery and was still one of the loudest voices for freedom. Now he must fight Jim Crow. He has to stand and watch Black people be beaten back by laws and codes that restrict their freedoms. He witnesses domestic terrorism in the form of lynching, murder, and intimidation. The job title of freedom fighter doesn't come with a retirement plan. So, Douglass stands up in 1893 in front of 2,500 fairgoers, speaking on a dedicated Negro American day, for which Black people had to protest to even get a single day at the world's largest fair. Wells-Barnett refused to participate, knowing they were not wanted there. She cast a cold shoulder on what she saw as a shirking and symbolic concession. But Douglass saw it as an opportunity to lend his voice to Black freedom. He participated as a representative of Haiti, a country to which he had served as ambassador, and that had just gained its independence some ninety years earlier. As he began to speak, old man Douglass was heckled by a white audience member about the so-called negro problem. We're told he put aside his prepared notes, and we might imagine him as he straightens his back up, runs his hand over his thick gray mane of hair, sets aside his spectacles, and launches into this fiery impromptu speech:

> There is, in fact, no such problem. The real problem has been given a false name. It is called Negro for a purpose. It has substituted Negro for nation, because the one is despised and hated, and the other is loved and honored. The true problem is a national problem. Further, the problem is whether the American people have honesty enough, loyalty enough, honor enough, patriotism enough to live up to their own Constitution.

The thunderous voice of Douglass echoes throughout history. America does not, and never has, had a negro problem, a Black problem, or a race problem. America has had racial states of emergency, and far too often Black people have been visited with national disaster, under a government that has sometimes succeeded, but far too often failed, to enact policies for the protection of Black humans and citizens in the face of racist force. Black people have felt the moist heat of America's bloody history, then looked up to see those who did not bleed watch with cold indifference. We are taught to empathize and understand suffering very early. The Great Depression is taught in every school as the story of collective national trauma. Teachers zoom in on its central themes—credit, price supports, uneven distribution of income, stock market crashes, financial collapses, and the government policies enacted to lessen its effects. Then they focus on individual lives to talk about hardship and pain. K–12 students learn about death and the plight of Great Plains farmers, almost always white in the textbooks. We heard about how dust storms enveloped their homes. Then we learned how they had to stand in line at soup kitchens just to eat, discussing the psychological impacts of near famine. The Great Depression history frames suffering sympathetically. Americans went through hardship together. But the era of racial terror is not framed with such sympathy and understanding.

Violent force is as American as apple pie, yet it is not spoken of, as though we are incapable of dealing with suffering. Person after person confirms that anti-Black injustices happen; that they have happened; that they continue to happen; and that it is inseparable from the American story. We still live in a world—not merely with the fear of violence—but with the knowledge that the violence will come. But we are afraid to talk about it. There are centuries of denial, rationalization, and self-deception that must be dispelled if we are to emerge from our prisons of denial and onto our feet as one healed nation. But I think, unless we tell these stories, and until the humanity of Black people is loved and uplifted as much as the nation itself, we will never be whole.

13

Jim Crow Took
a Road Trip

If it may be said of the slavery era that the white man took the world
and gave the Negro Jesus, then it may be said of the Reconstruction
era that the southern aristocracy took the world and gave the poor
white man Jim Crow. He gave him Jim Crow. And when his wrinkled
stomach cried out for the food that his empty pockets could not
provide, he ate Jim Crow, a psychological bird that told him that no
matter how bad off he was, at least he was a white man, better than
the black man. And he ate Jim Crow. And when his undernourished
children cried out for the necessities that his low wages could not
provide, he showed them the Jim Crow signs on the buses and in the
stores, on the streets and in the public buildings.
—Martin Luther King Jr., speech at the conclusion
    of the Selma to Montgomery marches

L ooking to escape the South's oppressive racial hierarchy, in 1922
Mallie Robinson arrived with her five children to a new home in
Pasadena, California. In Grady County, Georgia, Mallie saw dark days.
She might have felt the loneliness and emotional neglect anyone would feel
spending years with a spouse who alternated between infidelity and abandonment. She'd worked hard to make the best of their sharecropping existence. Rising from neck bones and scraps to breeding their own chickens,
hogs, and turkeys, she grew sugarcane, corn, peanuts, potatoes, and a family. But despite this limited prosperity, the cheating was too much. She had
to leave. The rumble of the train screeched to a halt, and an emboldened

young Mallie wept, hugged her family, and left it all behind. Hoping for a new life without Jim Crow or her husband, Jerry. Mallie and her children were welcomed to the Golden State with a flaming cross in their front lawn. Not the warm welcome she was hoping for.

California wasn't much different than the South in its racial discrimination. The West Coast was more diverse than Georgia, but the color line was clear—there was white and everyone else. Black children attended segregated schools. Black parents lived in segregated housing. In the hot and arid Pasadena summers, they even segregated the pool, only allowing Black people into it on Tuesday, deemed "negro day." After that, they drained the water. Can you imagine how much money was wasted on stupidity like emptying and filling swimming pools to maintain segregation (someone should do a study on that). California had its sundown towns, along with the thousands that spread across the United States. They had written and unwritten rules stating that if you were non-white, you better leave by 6:00 p.m., or you'd be jailed. Maybe you'd never leave again.

In 2022, a Glendale, California, resident recalled a childhood story about a Black woman who was working there, sprinting toward a bus. When the children asked their mother, "Why is that woman running?" their mother said that she had to be out by 6:00 p.m. Think about this: You have a real and immediate need to find a job and support your family, so you scan the ads in the paper and find only one that might hire you. The pay is low and the hours are long but you'll survive, so the rational decision would be to apply and take it if it was offered, right? But here's the catch—the job is in a sundown town. You'd be crazy to take a job in a town where you'd very likely be harassed or threatened, potentially beaten, or possibly killed if you miss a bus after work. But if you have yourself and kids to feed, then the only sane choice would be to take it. These nuanced racial realities combined with the salient threat of violent force must have made Robinson feel like she was in Georgia with desert palms, minus the joys of her farm life.

Her son was Jackie Robinson, who would go on to integrate baseball on April 15, 1947, as the first Black player in the Major Leagues.

This story highlights a glaring myth, that Jim Crow laws, written and unwritten, were relegated to the South. As with Mallie Robinson, millions of other Black people migrated across the United States and Jim Crow went with them. This national history is the blueprint for the current construction of racial bigotry. We look back on the racist relics, jet-black lawn jockeys with lobster-red lips, Black children eating a watermelon, and Mammie saltshakers as though they are part of a not-so-distant past. But the spectral presence of Jim Crow ideology still shows up regularly enough to make himself felt. Like when a school served watermelon, fried chicken, and cornbread for Black history month in 2014. In 2020, sitting US senator Tom Cotton said slavery was a necessary evil on which the union was built. And in 2022, a Florida firefighter was fired after being discovered wearing blackface at a Halloween party. But there have also been those willing to give up on Jim Crow, under pressure. Movement for Black Lives activists pushed several brands to drop their old Jim Crow–era mascots like Uncle Ben, Aunt Jemima, and Mia, the Native American "butter maiden" from Land O'Lakes in 2021. In the grand ole American contradiction, there are those who want nothing to do with Jim Crow, and those who still cling to its caricatures.

The evidence of Jim Crow is all around us. If you search county demographics in your state and find a county with a non-white population of less than 2 percent, it might not have been a sundown town, but every single sundown town had a non-white population of less than 2 percent. There are a lot of those towns. Jim Crow's presence is everywhere, its racial ideology still leaks into white identity politics, and you can still see the color line just by looking up the racial demographics of your local zip codes. In politics, we see its history in the filibuster, a tactic used by members of the US Senate to prevent the passage of a piece of legislation. It was a favorite of Southern senators to stymie Civil Rights bills. Look to the history of drug prohibition, real estate, school testing, and the shaping of historical memory itself and you will find Jim Crow. Stripped from the racist past, some of these systems and practices seem common enough to be benign. In our final study on anti-Black history, we will see that bigotry is like bamboo. As the world's fastest growing plant there are species that can grow up to two feet per day. Jim Crow American racism was never torn up from its roots, and unless it is continually chopped down, it continues to grow.

Socially Segregated

Jim Crow was a racial caste system encroaching into every area of Black life. Into public schools and private universities, the state legislature and Congress; into the armed forces, hospitals, and prisons; into the press, corporations, and small businesses; into housing and the legal system; from the street officer on the beat to the Supreme Court; into banking and into finance. It blocked entrepreneurs from accessing loans and denied housing to the homeless. It outright stole land, derailing wealth for generations with the racist ideology that drove it, still operating on manual and autopilot today. Some actions were almost unbelievable. I remember reading about a civil rights swim-in in Florida, when in 1964, a young group of protesters tried to desegregate a swimming pool, and the owner of the pool poured muriatic acid into the water. This ideology even made it into churches. Jim Crow preachers stood under illustrations of a pale-skinned Jesus, rejecting dark-skinned people, contradicting the Christian love preached by a man, who, with any geographical accuracy, would've been somewhat swarthy.

Then there was all that paraphernalia of racism. All the signage and merchandise on display: "WHITES ONLY," "COLORED WAITING ROOM," "WE WANT WHITES ONLY IN OUR WHITE COMMUNITY," "PUBLIC SWIMMING POOL WHITE ONLY." In the army, side by side, signs read, "COLORED OFFICER SHOWER (arrow right), WHITE OFFICER SHOWER" (arrow left). "NO DOGS, NEGROS, OR MEXICANS." A pet cemetery with a sign, "NO NEGRO DOGS." Sometimes those signs were like oases in the desert, like ones that stated, "THE BEST SERVICE FOR COLORED ONLY." But the next town over another sign read, "NO COLORED RESTROOM."

With so many restrictions on where you could pee, an overactive bladder must have been one of the worst diagnoses. Thousands of Black motorists relied on *The Negro Travelers' Green Book*, self-published by the Black postal worker Victor Hugo Green. It was like a lighthouse on a darkened coastline. Indispensable to Black drivers navigating roads paved with asphalt, racism, and segregation, it helped Black people avoid the sundown towns that banned Blacks after dark. Places like Anna, Illinois, a town where white mobs expelled Black families in 1909, and that held the unofficial acronym

"Ain't No Niggers Allowed." In his book titled *Sundown Towns: A Hidden Dimension of American Racism* (2005), sociologist James Lowen estimates at least ten thousand of these towns. But people still walked the color line, and in some instances, stepped over it. One photo that has always struck me was of a Black man emerging from a bathroom at a courthouse in Clinton, Louisiana, labeled "WHITE MEN ONLY." In other instances artists used their talents to highlight the absurd contradictions of Black American life. Over his sixty-year career, "Ollie" Harrington used dark humor and a penetrating wit to attack Jim Crow racism, highlighting class divisions and social injustices. In a 1963 cartoon, he drew a middle-aged Black couple at a mass Jim Crow protest. The woman hunches down reaching in her purse with the caption, "Here Brother Bootsie, take this extra hammer I got here in case the gentlemens of the law decides that this demonstration is too peaceful!" In a 1969 cartoon for the *Daily World*, he illustrated two frail children in rags for clothes with outstretched hands, trying to grab bread and milk off a table, but it is a couple of feet out of reach, held up by US bombs for table legs. Humor and laughter have long been cultural components of the Black freedom struggle, and comedians like Moms Mabley, Sammy Davis Jr., Dick Gregory, and Redd Foxx not only offered the balm of humor, but many were directly involved in protests, fundraising, and campaigning against Jim Crow.

During the Jim Crow era, Blacks and whites were not supposed to share a meal or a drink together. In the rare instance they did, whites had to be served first. I read a story about how in Louisiana two musicians, friends from childhood, one Black and one white, shared jug wine onstage. The white musician drank first, then passed the bottle back, as it was against racial etiquette for him to drink after a Black man. But then they would just wait until the next song, and relying on the audience's forgetfulness, started the process over again, subverting Jim Crow rules onstage. In the study of anti-Black history, I'm always inspired by stories like this; even though the two men couldn't change the social rules, they wouldn't allow Jim Crow to have the last word. And there are others who grew up in the era that show us that the power of changing your perspective is crucial if you can't change your situation. Yemi Toure, a South Carolina migrant to California, still sought out the sources of good in his life:

I used to say that I was born and raised in Jim Crow South Carolina. I don't say that anymore. Now I say, I was born and raised in the loving arms of the Black community of South Carolina. I changed because, despite the harshness of the South of those years (I was born in 1948), lately I have come to realize that the true miracle was the care, protection, and Black love that surrounded me, protected me, and guided me in those years. Within the limits of Jim Crow, my family, my neighbors, and my teachers created a space in which I could feel safe and in which I could grow.

Psychologists are near unanimous in their suggestion that we are all wired for prejudice, holding negative stereotypes and attitudes about people from different groups to fulfill our need for quick decision-making. To be the gardener of your own mind is to question your deepest beliefs and assumptions, weeding out negative prejudices before they grow out of control. But during Jim Crow, racial prejudice continued its long relationship with white power, from court decisions, to segregated beaches, to the health and housing institutions that govern human survival. Now we are forced to ask how much these attitudes still exist, and since they have existed for so long, can they ever be eradicated? It seems there is always someone assigned the least value in society—the Dalits of India, the Roma (so-called gypsies) of Europe, the Aboriginals in Australia, the Hazaras of Afghanistan, and the darkest skinned have seen Jim Crow across the globe. To study the socially structured racism of Jim Crow in America allows us to understand the roots of prejudice and discrimination wherever we find it.

America Has a Prison Problem

The US criminal justice system is broken. With the highest incarceration rate in the world, you could compare almost any single state to any independent democracy on Earth and it imprisons more people per capita. Prisoners make license plates, gavels for judges, and body armor for pennies to buy overpriced Ramen noodles. In Angola, Louisiana, the prisoners still pick cotton at the 18,000-acre slave-plantation-turned-prison. But this overrepresentation of Black people in US prisons and jails goes back much further than the War on Drugs, the sweeping crime bill of the 1990s, or before the early 1980s when Ronald Reagan painted a dystopian picture by saying the only thing keeping back the barbaric hordes is "the thin blue line that holds back a jungle which threatens to reclaim this clearing we call civilization." It goes back to the earliest days of Jim Crow, after the Civil War, when Black men, women, and children were re-enslaved under the convict leasing system. The Emancipation Proclamation ended slavery, but only chattel slavery—states exploited the loophole in the Thirteenth Amendment, making an exception for those convicted of a crime. As author Douglas A. Blackmon, who wrote the book *Slavery by Another Name: The Re-Enslavement of Black Americans from the Civil War to World War II* (2008), described:

> It was a form of bondage distinctly different from that of the antebellum South in that for most men, and the relatively few women drawn in, this slavery did not last a lifetime and did not automatically extend from one generation to the next. But it was nonetheless slavery—a system in which armies of free men, guilty of no crimes and entitled by law to freedom, were compelled to labor without compensation, were repeatedly bought and sold, and were forced to do the bidding of white masters through the regular application of extraordinary physical coercion.

The system was sandwiched in between the Black codes, laws applied only to Black people, and the profit motive of private corporations. There was a financial incentive to arrest and convict Black people. When labor needs were high, arrests were higher. Inmates were worked to death. They were mass incarcerated for petty crimes such as vagrancy, breaking curfew, and not having proof of employment. Penal labor had been used before the Civil War, when many imprisoned whites, especially immigrants, were exploited for cheap and free labor. But after the war, race and prison became almost ubiquitous. The deliberate incarceration of Black people fueled the labor force that grew white wealth. A labor that built its roads and grew its crops, cut its bricks, then manufactured its textiles, forged its steel, and built its railroads.

Writer Marc N. Goodnow described camp in early twentieth-century Florida. Snake oil medicine was all the rage, and pine tar was a main ingredient. Physicians promised that their medicines would cure ailments from intestinal worms to depression, and customers lined up for the piney-flavored liquid. Thousands made their way into forests searching for longleaf pine, cutting boxed holes into the base of their trunks, spooning the tar gum into buckets, and carting load after load to stills. Goodnow described the convicts and their work as a "degraded, debased, sordid" existence, "worse than any exile, worse than any slum district.... No penitentiary in this country has ever equaled the sordidness of this or the other thirty camps in that State; no condition of servitude or savagery that I ever heard or read about has ever surpassed the state of inhumanity or hopelessness behind the whitewashed stockade of this camp." He goes on to explain how the state traded, bartered, and leased Black bodies for the sum of $281.60 per year, describing the profit of $100 per person for 1,500 people as *"easy money."* He describes how the prisoners were awakened at dusk, "astir in the fetid bunk- and mess-rooms of the stockade building some time before. A hurried 'bait' of salt meat and biscuit or corn pone breaks their fast; they file out of the stockade, hatless, coatless, bootless, and take their places in separate squads of ten to fifteen each . . . an armed guard or two on horseback and a couple of hound dogs trailing along behind."

Sometimes the history is almost unbelievable. In this same prison you'd often find Black people missing from their cells every week, taken out for what was called "the nigger chase," an exercise where guards would send inmates running into the woods for the sole purpose of training their dogs for real fugitives. Goodnow goes on to describe the conditions: "The work carries the men through infested swamps and marshes up to their waists; it holds them through rain or shine, hot or cold . . . the squad works rapidly and furiously, the men running back and forth, back and forth, between the trees and the barrels which hold the resinous gum and pitch. It is dark when these tired, silent, ghostlike wretches file back into the stockade."

The official convict leasing system was phased out by 1933, but many counties continued it for years later. The public outcry was loud, but it was only when Martin Tabert, a young white man from North Dakota, found himself arrested for vagrancy in Tallahassee, Florida, that the outcry get loud enough. While imprisoned, he was flogged to death by a whipping boss, and the resulting coverage earned the *New York World* newspaper a Pulitzer Prize. Outside of prison, Black labor was also undervalued. Sharecropping became the de facto system for poor farmers who worked a landowner's plot in exchange for a percentage of the harvest. Doesn't sound bad, right? Wrong, it was essentially serfdom, a form of economic misery. Black people farmed cotton, rice, and tobacco for practically nothing and under ever-increasing debt. In the 1930s a man named Henry Blake talked about how the system worked in Arkansas:

> When we worked on shares, we couldn't make nothing, just overalls and something to eat. Half went to the other man and you would destroy your half, if you weren't careful. A man that didn't know how to count would always lose. He might lose anyhow. They never give you no details. No matter how good account you kept, you had to go by their account, and now, Brother, I'm tellin' you the truth about this. It's been that way for a long time. You had to take the white man's work on note, and everything. Anything you wanted, you could git if you were a good hand. You could git anything you wanted as long as you worked. If you didn't make no money, that's all right; they would advance you more. But you better not leave him, you better not try to leave and get caught. They'd keep you in debt. They were sharp. Christmas come, you could take up twenty dollar, in somethin' to eat and as much as you wanted in whiskey. You could buy a gallon of whiskey. Anything that kept you a slave because he was always right, and you were always wrong if there was a difference.

Racial pay discrepancies remain yet a fact of life and come at a major cost to the entire nation. A 2020 report by two global economists for Citigroup analyzed wages, education, housing, and investment—and estimated $16 trillion could've been added to the US economy had the nation closed the racial wealth gap in the year 2000. Much of which stems from the lack of lending to Black entrepreneurs. Federal legislation barred Jim Crow discrimination, but people still failed to legislate their minds. And everyone has paid that tax.

Desperate Journeys

During the Great Migration, intermittent flash floods of humans flowed across the United States between 1916 and 1970, overflowing from the rural Southern United States to the urban Northeast, Midwest, and West. People moved like the wisp of the wind. Through history we have, as humans, consistently relocated. Moving from natural disasters. Fleeing war. Escaping poverty. Putting distance between ourselves and oppression. Sometimes we do it voluntarily; sometimes we are forced. Earthquakes don't care about your lease agreement. Sometimes we are simply magnetized toward the promise of better opportunity. Many of us have bid farewell to our hometowns in search of better jobs. Better resources. Better futures. Most times in history people don't have an attitude of sympathy toward migrants. And this was the case as six million Black people streamed across the country year after year. They faced exclusion rather than inclusion, unbelonging, and the continued status of foreigners in a nonforeign land. The magnitude cannot be understated; according to one historian, "it was one of the largest and most rapid internal movements in world history—and it may have been the most massive rapid movements of humans not caused by the immediate threat of war or starvation. In sheer numbers, it outranks the migration of any other ethnic group—Italians or Irish or Jews or Poles—to the United States."

It outranks the migrations out of ancient Egypt, and the migration of Asiatic peoples over the Bering Strait to the Americas. More migrated than the English who established the thirteen colonies, and it outsized the migrations of those war-torn peoples of Europe or the Middle East in sheer numbers. All these groups moved to escape oppression or to seek out resources.

Black Americans migrated to escape Jim Crow. I remember when I was a kid I thought Jim Crow was a cartoon character—the name obscures its pernicious nature, humanizing one of the most inhumane systems ever contrived. And, while this term is typically confined to state and local laws that enforced racial segregation, it was much, much more. It all goes back to the belief that non-whites are intellectually and culturally inferior, and if put in charge, if not in some way contained, will destroy America. Even worse was the constant fear of racial mixing—in other words, the mongrel-ization of the white race. The Black migrants left to pursue better educa-tion, acting on their belief that education was power. And Southern schools were purposefully kept inferior to keep the workforce ignorant. Senator James K. Vardaman once said, "Educating the black man simply renders him unfit for the work which white man has prescribed, and which he will be forced to perform . . . the only effect is to spoil a good field hand and make an insolent cook." So, they were no longer slaves, but not yet citizens, existing in some weird sunken place between citizen and slave. Between being physically alive and socially dead. This is what the Black Southerner was wrestling with. This is what they were running from. They stuffed themselves into train cars like Christmas stockings.

The puffing and hissing of a steam engine briefly interrupted a server taking an order on a Great Northern train departing from Chicago, Illinois, for Seattle. By the 1920s, 20,224 Black people scuttled up and down aisles working as Pullman porters and train service workers inside of unthinkably expensive railcars. A symbol of servility, Black workers were hired almost exclusively, making them the single largest Black workforce in the United States. The Pullman Palace cars exemplified Gilded Age luxury and aes-thetic excellence. Pullman cars were decked in audacious luxuries: dark walnut interior, wonderfully fine murals, plush carpet, brass fixtures, and glass chandeliers. The rolling hotels were the epitome of first class. Porters finessed wealthy clientele with excellent service, shining shoes, carrying baggage, hosting, maintaining sleeping berths, acting as an elite concierge fulfilling impossible requests. The job was a grind. Porters were married to their cars, rumbling over tracks coast to coast, working weeks away from home, sometimes in twenty-four-hour shifts, and three hundred to four hundred hours per month. On overnight stays at train stations, they piled into porterhouses swapping jokes, political news, and stories of the day hud-dled around large potbellied stoves. Joys, worries, and laughter were shared along with physical exhaustion. The public servants stood in the highest regard within the Black community, akin to doctors, teachers, and lawyers. It was one of the best jobs a Black person could get. But when we pull back the velvet veil, and look beyond the finery, we can clearly see de facto racism.

Porters had to answer to the name "George," after George Pullman, the industrialist owner of the Pullman sleeping cars, harkening back to the days when enslaved people answered to the first name of their enslavers. The men paid for their own uniforms, staying on call at every moment day or night, and it was common for passengers with a few drinks in them to let racist jokes come out. I'm imagining porters cursing those white passengers behind clenched-tooth smiles. Among the best paid in the Black community, they were still among the lowest paid of all train workers. Their wages weren't livable, and they worked off tips, an unthinkably common practice now, but in the past, it was the mark of second-class citizenship. The Oxford English dictionary of 1916 described tipping as "a small present of money given to an inferior," and one contemporary observer of the practice remarked:

> I had never known any but negro servants. Negroes take tips, of course; one expects that of them—it is a token of their inferiority. But to give money to a white man was embarrassing to me. I felt defiled by his debasement and servility. Indeed, I do not now comprehend how any native-born American could consent to take a tip. Tips go with servility, and no man who is a voter in this country by birthright is in the least justified in being servile.

It was possible to rake in good money, but it was completely inconsistent. People gained reputations for tipping or lack thereof; you could tell right off if a man would tip well, women not until the moment of. They said Jack Dempsey tipped well, while Calvin Coolidge tipped no more than fifteen cents. "We don't get no tips till the end of the run," said Daddy Joe, the legendary Pullman of sleeping car folklore.

No records exist of the first Pullman. When Chicago burned in 1871, the records of the first Pullman porters burned with it. But the story goes, once on the Yazoo Valley Railroad, Daddy Joe's car was almost swept away by a rising river. Inside the car, passengers panicked and screamed in horror. Without a thought, Daddy Joe rose heroically with his booming voice and delivered such a calming speech the passengers eased back into their seats. The water subsided and the train rolled into Memphis four hours and thirty minutes late, the exact length of his oration. There were dozens of tales about the exploits of Daddy Joe, always in control, always in service, never a tip until the job was done—his was the everyday life of a Pullman porter. But the porters saw tips as a form of exploitation, another indignity to suffer. And history seldom attends to the Pullman maids, seeing to every whim of white women and their children, carrying an extra burden. Don't forget there were no workplace sexual harassment laws—those weren't much of a thought until the Civil Rights Act of 1964 banned discrimination based on race, color, religion, national origin, or sex. And it was the Pullman porters who kept laying track in the century-long struggle for democratic citizenship.

In 1925, excluded from white unions, they boldly founded the Brotherhood of Sleeping Car Porters, a Black labor union of organizers who would later serve as the elders and unseen backbone of the last phase of the Civil Rights Movement in the 1950s and 1960s. They faced a mountainous uphill climb. Known to bust up unions, corporations used dubious tactics—legally with shark-toothed attorneys, covertly with infiltrating spies, publicly with smear campaigns, corruptly with bribery, and violently with weapon-wielding agitators. George Pullman would not budge easily. Organizer Eugene Debs said he was "as greedy as a horse leech, but that was unfair to leeches."

But they did it. After twelve long years, they signed a collective bargaining agreement with a top US corporation and were the first Black labor union to do so. The ripened fruits of their labor were pay increases, hour decreases, and job security. In April 2022, organized labor made a huge return to the national stage, when warehouse workers on Staten Island won the vote to unionize, defeating Goliath incarnate Amazon, one of the richest companies on Earth, with a campaign funded by GoFundMe; the porters did it with bake sales. Christian Smalls, a working-class Black man who led the movement, found himself linked to this long chain of Black labor history.

Back in the Jim Crow South, people took notice of all the Black people leaving for more lucrative pastures, by the ones, the twos, the hundreds, and the thousands. They noticed their fields emptying. Black people were literally disappearing. There are stories of churches having full congregations one Sunday, then the next week only a few people remained. Everyone else had left for the North or Midwest or West. White Southerners were upset. Not only because they needed the Black labor, but because of a love-hate pathology. Writer David L. Cohn said in 1935: "With all our crimes of omission and commission, we still retain a marked affection for the negro. It is inconceivable to us that we should be without him." Frederick Douglass, witnessing the precursor to the Great Migration in 1879, was disheartened and saw it as "a premature, disheartening surrender."

But those leaving the South might have told Douglass it wasn't them who were surrendering. It was the whites who had surrendered—to hatred, sadism, and inhumanity. Some of the most harrowing history comes from the many letters recovered from hopeful migrants sent to potential employers who'd sometimes send fare ahead to pull in Black labor. One from a man in Troy, Alabama, read:

> I am enclosing a clipping of a lynching again which speaks for itself. I do wish there could be sufficient pressure brought about to have federal investigation of such work. I wrote you a few days ago if you could furnish me with the addresses of some firms or corporations that needed common labor. So many of our people here are almost starving. The government is feeding quite a number here would go any where to better their conditions. If you can do any thing for us, write me as early as possible.

So, they left. Some ended up in the Filmore District of San Francisco, dubbed the Harlem of the West. They filled its vacant buildings with families, restaurants, pool halls, the sound of jazz at nightclubs like Bop City and the Champagne Supper Club, theaters, and stores left vacant by the Japanese forced out due to World War II internment. The irony: Black people vacated the South to escape Jim Crow, and filled homes vacated by the Japanese that Jim Crow threw out. The Black population skyrocketed there between 1940 and 1950 from 4,836 to 43,460. They moved to Phoenix, Arizona, the desert metropolis for farming and the expanding railroad industry; many of the sleeping car porters settled in the Southwest town as the South Pacific Railroad rerouted passenger cars there. They moved to Las Vegas, Nevada, for a new start processing metal at Basic Magnesium Incorporated.

In 1859, Oregon was the only state whose constitution explicitly denied Black people from living, working, or owning property. They could not even move there until 1926. That all changed during the Great Migration as the Black community in Portland expanded by 400 percent up to 9,529 residents between 1940 and 1950. They brought civil rights organizing and Black political influence to fight for antidiscrimination laws as they faced racial tension. The Pacific Northwest, Midwest, North, and Southwest hosted the streams of Black people. Many did find it better. One person interviewed for The Chicago Commission on Race Relations said: "I find it easier to live because I have more to live on. I was not counted at all in the south, colored people allowed no freedom at all in the south. Can vote; no lynching; no fear of mobs, can express my opinion. Can live without fear, no Jim Crow. The schools. The people. Opportunity to acquire something. Not held down." Others were glad they could vote freely, with more privileges, they could go to shows, didn't have to move off sidewalks for an oncoming white person, and were generally better respected.

Of course, these survey results were biased. Those who left the South likely did so because they were the worst treated, so they had biting commentary about Southern conditions. But by all available testimony the worst of the Jim Crow racial hierarchy landed on the backs of Black people in the Southern states. But even as they were trying to escape it, Jim Crow laws and practices spread across the nation like a noxious fog. State constitutions segregated schools and classrooms, like in New Mexico, where "separate rooms shall be provided for the teaching of pupils of African descent." Colorado, Nebraska, and Wyoming had limited segregation laws, not so much from an embrace of minorities, but because their populations were so small. And where Hispanic and Native populations were larger, they were Jim Crowed, too. Native reservations might be seen as the ultimate form of Jim Crow, as they were segregated onto separate lands under a misty notion of sovereignty. They, too, have been whitewashed, and I hope to show here that to mention their plight in no way invalidates the plight of Black Americans. Injustice is injustice, no matter who applies it or who it is applied to.

No Escape

The pages of US history held no space for places like Tulsa, Oklahoma. Indeed, the barbarity spread out West, and while hard work paid better, money can't buy life. In 2021, on the centennial of the massacre in the Greenwood District of Tulsa, many Americans were reminded of this timeless truth. As news of the Tulsa race massacre spread across social media and television screens, many were utterly shocked at the absence of justice and the untold horrors of one of the worst domestic attacks in US history, wondering why they had never heard of it. The history of Tulsa started when tribes were forcibly removed from the Southwest to Oklahoma, many of them Black Seminoles. Then in 1906 on a dusty patch of road, Ottowa W. Gurley built a grocery store. Like many Black men of the era, Ottowa went by his initials, O.W., as a form of protest to verbal emasculation. Social norms dictated that men call one another by surname. Mr. Smith, Mr. Johnson, or Mr. Gurley was a sign of respect and equality. First names were reserved for boys and Black men. So, using their initials helped Black men regain some dignity and circumvent this practice. Partnering with businessman John "the Baptist" Stradford (aka J.B.), who also resented the condescension of whites, they built up a mostly Black town. That distrust was not unfounded as white residents amassed on the south side of the tracks and tensions rose.

Bold Black wealth was radically at odds with Jim Crowism, which had expanded west with white migrants. And Black Tulsa had become amazingly prosperous. If you'd decided to move there, you could mingle among its ten thousand residents. If you decided to stay, you could reside in one of its beautiful wood and brick-built homes. Perhaps, you'd be lured in by the spiritual lullaby of a pipe organ, and the soft hum of a choir, then stumble into one of its many churches on a Sunday morning. That is, if you weren't too woozy drinking and jigging at one of its nightclubs on a Saturday night. You could send your child to a nationally renowned school supported by a book-lined library. Buildings everywhere built by Black hands. Hotels, salons, a pool hall, and restaurants packed with diners, a theater and banks, physicians, dentists, legal and real estate offices, and a printing press for the news. Tulsa was also transformed by innovation and productivity in the twenties. An era that brought us the airplane, the automobile, household electricity, and indoor plumbing. The city boasted a bus and cab service, and, with only two airports in the whole state of Oklahoma, six Black families owned private airplanes. Black dollars went back into the Black community recirculating to create more Black wealth. This could easily be a story about Black people bathing in the nouveaux riches of the early twentieth century but, like any American town, all wasn't equitable. There were several Black Tulsans living in thrown-together shanties. However, it is still a powerful example of what a strong sense of community and togetherness can build. We can look back with appreciation and say, look at the wonders that flowered out of a dirt road in Tulsa. We have the power to start the world over again. But money can't buy life. Though the strategy of isolationism cleared the path to Black ascent, it's difficult to keep to yourself when you have envious wealth, and your neighbors have more guns. So, when whites had a chance to act on all of the jealousy, they did what they always did. You guessed it, they accused a Black man of assaulting a white woman. When Dick Rowland, a Black teenager, was arrested on the morning of May 31, 1921, "charged with attempting to assault the seventeen-year-old white elevator girl in the Drexel building," all hell would break loose.

On June 1, a mob of more than a thousand white people overran the Greenwood district. Black people fought the attackers back for hours, but out of ammunition and vastly outnumbered, they were overrun. Machine guns were brought in and showered bullets on neighborhood homes with women and children inside. As we think more about the use of words in whitewashing, especially the difference between riots and massacres, we might even go a step further and call Tulsa a pogrom, a "violent riot incited with the aim of massacring or expelling an ethnic or religious group," a term typically reserved for Jews in the Holocaust. Until 2018, Tulsa was officially called a riot—a crime against historical truth.

In her book *Events of the Tulsa Disaster,* published in 1923, thirty-one-year-old eyewitness Mary E. Jones Parrish said her eyes welled with tears and her soul cried for justice recalling those terrifying two days. Historians still dispute eyewitness testimony, but Black residents who bore witness to the events swore they saw planes dropping bombs on Greenwood. If this is true, the Tulsa massacre would be the first time planes were used in an act of terrorism on American soil, predating the September 11, 2001, attack on the World Trade Center by eighty years. "The sidewalks were literally covered with burning turpentine balls, " said Buck Colbert Franklin (father of groundbreaking historian John Hope Franklin). "I knew all too well where they came from, and I knew all too well why every burning building first caught from the top," he continues. "I paused and waited for an opportune time to escape. 'Where oh where is our splendid fire department with its half dozen stations?' I asked myself. Is the city in conspiracy with the mob." The national guard was called in, but they arrested Black people instead of their attackers. The white segregated press dominated and was used as an instrument to control the narrative. With headlines like "Two Whites Dead in Race Riot," and "Many More Whites Are Shot," the newspapers blamed the Black men for arming themselves and going to the courthouse to defend Rowland from a lynching. "From a 10-room and basement modern brick home, I am now living in what was my coal barn," said resident C. L. Netherland. Dick Rowland was exonerated, but so was every white person involved. Reparations were paid to a white shop owner whose guns were taken from his shop.

In 2001, the Oklahoma Commission to Study the Tulsa Race Riot of 1921 concluded more than three and a half years of research, including interviews with the survivors. Investigators combed the autopsy reports in search of bodies, and forensic anthropologists searched for mass unmarked graves. Accountants assessed the property damage, $1.8 million lost at that time, or $28.6 million, in 2022 dollars. Tulsa may prove what so many already deem true, that there is no direct correlation between economic prosperity and racial equality. Testifying before members of a House Judiciary subcommittee in 2021, on the hundredth anniversary of the massacre, survivor Viola Fletcher said:

> I still see Black men being shot, Black bodies lying in the street. I still smell smoke and see fire. I still see Black businesses being burned. I still hear airplanes flying overhead. I hear the screams. I have lived through the massacre every day . . . I am 107 years old and have never seen justice. I pray that one day I will. I have been blessed with a long life—and have seen the best and worst of this country. I think about the terror inflicted upon Black people in this country every day. Our country may forget this history, but I cannot.

Jim Crow Strikes a New Deal, Goes to War, and Returns to the Ghetto

The years between 1929 and 1939 saw the American economy go from gilded age to gutted. When the stock market crashed in 1929, thousands of investors were ruined, and billions of dollars disappeared. The dominant figure of this era in American history was Franklin Delano Roosevelt, president from 1933 to 1945, and his presidency intersects with some very important moments, helping us to track the evolution of Jim Crow. Historians have shaped his legacy as the masterful World War II decision-maker and diplomat, Great Depression savior, and only president to ever serve four terms. A man who woke the sleeping giant of US military power to defeat Nazism and led the charge to save Europe, solidifying the US position as leader of the free world. Indeed, FDR's New Deal was one of the biggest decisions in all of US history, forever changing the US government's social contract with its citizens and putting together a program that offered Americans a basic social safety net. In a set of sweeping reforms, there were measures enacted to regulate banks and businesses, offer social security and unemployment insurance, provide aid to homeless and neglected children, and seed money toward public health services.

But even though some New Dealers like Eleanor Roosevelt, Harold Ickes, and Frances Perkins spoke out against racial discrimination, Jim Crow was at the negotiating table. Southern Democrats, who held veto power in Congress, were willing to negotiate on a lot of things, but strict racial discrimination was not one of them. Ironically, Southern Democrats were willing to engage with progressive politics, but only if it excluded Black people. And this isn't just a story of virulent Southern racism, but of well-meaning white liberals who readily acquiesced to them, just like during slavery, and just like during Reconstruction. Programs like the GI Bill and Social Security have been mislabeled as universal, and to whitewash them as such obscures the battles that it took to make them so. According to the 1930 census, 65 percent of employed Black people worked as agricultural laborers and domestic workers. Yet, one of the most excluded groups in the 1935 Social Security Act were agricultural and domestic workers.

Little did Southerners know, their progressive turn would backfire. The New Deal expanded the reach of the federal government, which opened the door for the King-era leaders of the Civil Rights Movement to walk through. Black leaders tapped federal power to enact change. On June 25, 1941, Roosevelt signed Executive Order 8802, prohibiting racial discrimination by government defense contractors. The armed forces were still segregated but ostensibly contractors could no longer discriminate based on race, creed, or national origin. But why did he sign it? A whitewashed history that time jumps Black people from slavery to the 1950s and 1960s Civil Rights Movement ignores nearly a century of history other than the Harlem Renaissance. Forgetting agitators like A. Phillip Randolph who planned a mass March on Washington. "Negroes mean business about getting their rights as American citizens," he wrote in a letter to the head of the NAACP. "To this end I have decided to undertake the organization of a march of ten thousand Negroes or more upon Washington." He met with Roosevelt, and seven days later, Order 8802 was signed. It was Randolph who'd organized the Pullman porters, and who got the Pullman Company to negotiate with the unionized group and reach a contract agreement in 1937. Before forcing the Pullman Company to negotiate, George Pullman sent Randolph a blank check, telling him to write in any number up to $1 million. Randolph refused.

World War II dominated the era. In studying it, many are shocked to find that the Third Reich in Nazi Germany looked to the Southern system in the United States to inform their white supremacism. The Germans studied "The American Model," for its policies on Native American decimation and removal, race-based apartheid, lynching, and ethnic-based control of immigration. They also worked closely with America in the development of eugenics, where scientists worked to create the perfect human race, by eliminating the mentally ill and targeting Black Americans and other minorities. This system of "racial hygiene" was implemented across America to bolster anti-miscegenation laws. State-mandated sterilization targeted the disabled, the criminally insane, the undesirable, the poor, but especially Black and Native women, many of whom were sterilized without knowledge or consent. In 1936, Adolf Hitler hosted the Berlin Olympics intent on showcasing what he believed was Aryan physical superiority. But runner

Jesse Owens crushed the competition winning four gold medals. In what could have doubled as an American blow against fascism and racism on the world stage, Owens's victory didn't earn him the status of National Hero. Roosevelt invited each white US Olympian to the White House, and excluded Owens.

Then, there was Roosevelt's decision to place more than a hundred thousand Japanese people, eighty thousand of whom were second-generation citizens, in desolate prison camps after the bombing of Pearl Harbor on December 7, 1941. It was later determined by a 1982 federal commission that this atrocity was "not driven by analysis of military conditions. The broad historical causes that shaped these decisions were race prejudice, war hysteria, and failure of political leadership." It is also a debate of whether he was a humanitarian or hero; as Nazis committed genocide against some six million European Jews, the US response was lukewarm. Roosevelt's private anti-Semitic remarks and curtailing Jewish immigration, during a time they needed it most, has shaded his legacy. Jim Crow came in more than Black and white, offering a nuanced history of racism with moments of solidarity between Black people and other ethnic groups who've found each other on the lower rungs of America's racially constructed ladder.

Only seventeen years old, a frail five foot six inches, 120-pound Sammy Davis Jr. was picked from the draft to fight in World War II. As part of the first integrated army unit, the horrific racism he endured was representative of the treatment of Black soldiers at that time. He recalled how he politely asked a white fellow soldier for directions and how, "He sized me up and down, reluctantly told me it is two buildings down followed by 'And I'm not your buddy, you black bastard!'" The other GIs painted him white and poured urine in his beer. He said, "They needed to say, 'Hey man, get that nigger now. Stop him.' I tried physically; I got my nose broke three times, man." On another television appearance, he talked about how he fought back: "And the guy said, 'Where I come from, niggers don't go in front of white people' . . . I turned and hit him . . . cat fell to the ground, his mouth was bleeding, and he looked up at me and he said, 'Well, you beat me but you still a nigger.'" Sammy Davis Jr. went on to become what many called the greatest living entertainer in the world, but God-given talent couldn't save him from Jim Crow. As he and countless other entertainers and wealthy

Black people would find, neither economic success nor celebrity have any correlation to racial justice.

World War II magnetized more migrants across the country. Lured by jobs in Northern defense plants, and employed in wartime production, this gave rise to the slums. Outposts in a concrete wilderness. Overcrowded buildings with scarce light, air, or sanitation, more akin to chicken coops than houses for humans. Finding housing was far less than fair. Real estate agents steered white tenants away from Black housing and excluded Black tenants from so-called white housing. Laws, requiring landlords to evict and exclude tenants who've had contact with the criminal justice system, disproportionately affected Black people. History is not old news; it was a similar desire for Black exclusion that infuriated white people enough to start a riot at the newly opened Sojourner Truth Homes in 1942. It took six thousand federal troops to stop the destruction and murder instigated by white people who refused to accept Blacks as their new neighbors.

Richard Wright, who was born on a plantation in Mississippi and then when he got older moved his mother and siblings to Chicago, expressed the fear of moving North: "Timidly, we get off the train. We hug our suitcases, fearful of pickpockets. . . . We are very reserved, for we have been warned not to act green. . . . We board our first Yankee streetcar to go to a cousins home. . . . We have been told that we can sit where we please, but we are still scared. We cannot shake off three hundred years of fear in three hours."

Prejudice plagued the Black community, too. First-generation poor Black Southerners were often treated terribly by established Northern Black people, who viewed the Southerners as culturally unsophisticated, unintelligent, and almost primitive.

In his book *Color of Law: The Re-Enslavement of Black Americans from the Civil War to World War II* (2017), Richard Rothstein laid out the history of what he termed the state-sanctioned system of segregation in the North. The Federal Housing Administration shattered homeownership dreams based on race. In the New Deal programs, communities were given arbitrary ratings based on race, and property values fluctuated based on skin pigmentation. Whole schemes were enacted to buy cheap and sell high as prime real estate was bought from Blacks at ridiculously low appraisal prices and sold to whites at a price tantamount to highway robbery. Jim Crow is the backdrop to our current racial canvas. Now in the twenty-first century, real estate agents have been caught racial steering, pushing Black people to Black neighborhoods and white to white.

Rats, roaches, asbestos, and peeling paint. So similar were these Northern slums to those of Europe, where swaths of ethnic Jews were segregated into walled-off parts of the city and discriminated against, they called them ghettos. Instead of legal segregation, more often Black people found themselves residentially segregated by federal rules, economic muscle, and civic policies just as rigid. White supremacy was the cloud that kept not only Blacks in their Harlems, but Latinos in their Barrios, and Chinese in their Chinatowns, while whites, even if poor, had the freedom of movement as far as their wallets could take them. This was not limited to the United States. In Britain, there was the color bar, a policy to keep Black and Asian people from pubs, bars, and restaurants; South Africa had its apartheid until 1994; in Brazil, Jim Crow racism keeps people segregated into favelas.

Back in the United States, landlords refused to rent to immigrants. Slumlords charged Black residents high rents for crumbling units, eviction was used as a tool of oppression, banks withheld mortgages and insurance payments from Black customers, and redlining dictated who could live where and how much their properties would be worth on the market. Developers built homes with the benefit of lower interest rates from the Federal Housing Authority, and received subsidies to build segregated housing. Crime festers in poverty and the urban ghettos marked an increase in lawlessness. In May 1939, the great American novelist Ralph Ellison, another son of the Great Migration, who was twenty-six and working for the Federal Writers Project, interviewed an old man hanging at a bar near 147th Street. He asked, "Do you like living in New York City?" The man said:

Ahm in New York, but New York ain't in me. You understand? Ahm in New York, but New York ain't in me. What do I mean? Listen. I'm from Jacksonville, Florida. Been in New York twenty-five years. I'm a New Yorker! Yuh understand? Naw, naw, yuh don't get me. What do they do; take Lenox Avenue. Take Seventh Avenue; take Sugar Hill! Pimps. Numbers. Cheating those poor people out a whut they got. Shooting, cutting, backbiting, all them things. Yuh see? Yuh see what Ah mean? I'm in New York, but New York ain't in me!

There was a stereotype that Black people living in ghettos were okay with crime. Or that the ways crime wedded itself to poverty was unique to Black people. A crime committed by a single Black person represented all Black people, where a crime committed by a lone white person is seldom representative of the race. Jim Crow lingers in these ideas, that young Black men are criminals prone to gun violence. Or that fatherless homes, definitely a problem, is solely to blame. Or that poor Black communities are cesspools of theft, extortion, drugs, prostitution, gambling, and graft. But violence is an all-American problem. America's gun homicide rate has been consistently double the average for all democratic countries. Black people in poor neighborhoods are astronomically more likely to become victims of gun violence than to perpetrate it. Yet, it's those same Black residents who are targeted by stop and frisk policies that harass rather than protect.

I'm all for looking back to see what works, and I often recommend the book *Bleeding Out: The Devastating Consequences of Urban Violence—and a Bold New Plan for Peace in the Streets* (2019) by Thomas Abt, which offers humane evidence-based strategies for the reduction of urban street violence. Most violent crimes are committed by less than 1 percent of a city's population. The same people over and over. At-risk behaviors of the perpetrators are predictable before the violence begins, posing opportunities for intervention in which America has failed to invest. Rather than getting tougher on crime, Abt suggests that we balance force with fairness. Catch the youth early when they go astray and offer them a choice for another path, connecting them with mentors and investing in robust social services, like cognitive behavioral therapy, job training, education, recreation programs, and healthcare. Balance police force with sympathy for the few individuals most at risk for violence. Implemented correctly, it has worked in several cities, like in Oakland, where homicides dropped by 50 percent over the seven years leading up to 2017.

The thing is, the only time there is national conversation about "Black on Black" violence is when it is used to deflect away from Black outrage and demands for a national response to the violence of police culture. When it comes to schools and mass shootings, people care deeply about stopping gun violence, but even with clearer solutions, everyday urban gun violence is almost looked at as an inevitability. It is a matter of will and morality, not policy. Policies fall on unhearing ears, are given up on too early, aren't implemented correctly, or are abandoned once they start working, and then violent crime increases again. This leaves us to wonder whose suffering gets counted; because the sad reality is that Jim Crow attitudes still criminalize Black poverty.

Any- and Everywhere

Jim Crow violence continued. Sgt. Isaac Woodard was maimed in Batesburg, South Carolina. He'd served honorably in World War II, only to be beaten and blinded for saying, "I'm a man just like you." All the way in Alaska, segregation reached the Black highway engineers and soldiers who built hundreds of miles of frozen highway in 1943. Jim Crow was a group of white teenagers, who shot thirteen-year-old Virgil Lamar Ware off the handlebars of his brother's bike in 1963. Jim Crow also murdered white allies, like William Lewis Moore, shot dead as he proceeded on a one-man march to deliver a letter to the Mississippi governor calling for an end to intolerance. It firebombed Black churches and killed young children in Alabama. It prevented interracial marriage in North Dakota. But the spirit of Jim Crow also showed up in the white women who stood by to witness racial injustices, screamed obscenities at children on their way to desegregated schools, and falsely accused countless Black men of rape. Jim Crow was a doctor, janitor, and shopkeeper. Jim Crow was not only a father, brother, husband, uncle, and grandfather, but a mother, sister, wife, aunt, and grandmother. And sometimes, even at its most insidious, Jim Crow was silent. You didn't know it was there, but it always was.

It had been eighty-two years since federal legislation was passed to protect Black rights, when Dwight Eisenhower signed the Civil Rights Act of 1957. It was an effort worthy of critique and commendation. Eisenhower had not infrequently sympathized with white supremacist Southerners and ardent segregationists, keeping an icy distance between

Civil Rights leaders. "Mr. President! Mr. President!" yelled Alice Dunnigan, the first Black-accredited White House reporter, trying to get Eisenhower's attention in press conferences. Known for reporting on issues important to Black Americans, after she asked Eisenhower hard questions on civil rights, he ignored her for two years. But a Black coalition that was transforming into a burgeoning Southern Christian Leadership Conference applied consistent political pressure to his administration.

When a young, energetic Martin Luther King Jr. burst on the scene in the 1950s, he stood tall on the shoulders of nearly one hundred years of modern civil rights organizing. He worked with the guidance of civil rights stalwarts like A. Phillip Randolph and was mentored by those like Nannie Helen Burroughs, a seasoned civil rights activist who traveled and organized with Black women all over the United States from my hometown in Louisville, Kentucky.

Generations of struggle came before that moment on August 6, 1965, when President Lyndon B. Johnson signed the Voting Rights Act, and other sweeping political reforms. The Voting Rights Act, Medicare and Medicaid, War on Poverty, immigration reforms, and environmental protections. But Johnson's actions raise the question, is an act only morally right if it was done for a morally right reason? "Let's face it," said Johnson. "Our ass is in a crack. We're gonna have to let this nigger bill pass." But to simply say Johnson was a racist is shallow analysis. I think he was playing right out of the Machiavellian politics playbook, when the sixteenth-century philosopher advised the prince to adjust his agenda according to political necessity, even if it meant abandoning morality.

Johnson wasn't some singular force wielding legislative power like Thor's hammer. It was the lightning rods of the Civil Rights Movement that put those bills on the table. It was political pressure that got Democrat and Republican legislators to craft these bills in back rooms over bourbon. Legalized Jim Crow was only ended by negotiating with it, prodding, and poking it, and pushing it. A chilling observation from German sociologist Max Weber crosses my mind when he says to engage with politics is to contract with "diabolical powers and . . . it is not true that good can follow only from good and evil only from evil, but that often the opposite is true. Anyone who fails to see this is, indeed, a political infant."

I'm sure all those who were morally inspired to fight for change didn't want to deal with the monster, but the monster faced them every day, and they had no choice. Civil rights legislation didn't just end Jim Crow; the law had to be applied in thousands of situations. Like in Houston, Texas, in 1979, when a group of Black homeowners fought a bitter battle to keep the Whispering Pines Sanitary Landfill from being placed a mere 1,500 feet from a local school. Black residents made up 27 percent of the population, but all of Houston's five city-owned landfills, six of eight incinerators, and three of six private landfills were in poor Black neighborhoods. It was the first time civil rights legislation was used for such a cause. They lost but kicked off the environmental justice movement that acknowledges that poor and predominantly Black communities breathe more toxic air, live nearer to more chemical and coal-burning plants billowing smoke plumes, and reside in more flood zones than any other group. The larger environmentalist movement has only recently begun to accept that the legacy of Jim Crow is in the water of Flint, Michigan, and choking the oxygen out of inner-city neighborhoods. Jim Crow is not entirely dead; his fingers still twitch from time to time.

Many Americans are still tormented by Jim Crow's legacy, while others refuse to look at the autopsy report. His stench hovers in the form of ideological bigotry. I always find it interesting when the argument is proposed that the overt racism in America's anti-Black history was just a sign of the times. And I think about how Samuel Bowers lived from 1924–2006; Fred Rogers lived from 1928–2003. Samuel Bowers was a cofounder and imperial wizard in the Ku Klux Klan, who fatally bombed a civil rights leader. Fred Rogers was "Mr. Rogers," a humanitarian educator awarded for compassion, who consistently promoted racial equality on his television show. So, the 1920s did not produce racism; some people were just racist.

But remember, racial bias, a basic psychological process, can grow like bamboo if not rooted out. Most often it does not appear in open hostility or hatred. Instead, aversive racism typically shows up in everyday interactions. When people let their discomfort, anxiety, or fear about another race guide their actions toward that group. But on any level, especially institutionally, extracting this deep-seated ideology can be like separating sand from cement. Once we understand that we all harbor prejudice—often unconscious, negative feelings and beliefs about others—a greater human-ity ethic might emerge, helping us to cut down the invasive bamboo in our own minds. We can all change our attitudes about others, rough stones smoothed by water.

But, when we look at its record, it is important to remember the legacy to which Jim Crow and its ideologies belong, not only to the South, but across America. In that sense, the record is still incomplete, lost, and unex-amined. As the Great Migration entered its final years in 1967, a Black man in Alabama spoke about why he never left: "It was a hoax if you ask me . . . they're packed tight into the buildings, and can't do anything, not even dream of going North, the way I do when it gets rough." Perhaps he was right—there was nowhere to run. It is now becoming an acknowledged fact that Jim Crow has maintained a lasting impact, but the biggest myth about Jim Crow was that it only existed in the South, during a specific period of time, when in fact it existed everywhere and for all time.

PART 4

Let's Speak of Possibilities

In the bigger scheme of things the universe is not asking us to do something, the universe is asking us to be something. And that's a whole different thing.

—Lucille Clifton

14

Excellence
or Equality

Really, I don't know what you, my people, want. You have everything.
You have Jesse Owens, the fastest track man of all times; Joe Louis,
the greatest fighter in the world. You even have God—Father Divine
Peace, it's wonderful! Now you have the Jones Brothers with one of
the finest stores in the world. Patronize them and do everything you
can to be satisfied.

—Bill "Bojangles" Robinson, at the opening of the world's first
   Black-owned department store in 1930s Chicago (Bronzeville),
   Illinois

If you stick a knife in my back nine inches, and pull it out six inches,
there's no progress. If you pull it all the way out that's not progress.
Progress is healing the wound that the blow made. And they haven't
even pulled the knife out much less heal the wound. They won't even
admit the knife is there.

—Malcom X

n America, the prevailing concept of excellence is like climbing a mountain. We each start off lower than we want to be in some regard, but with
the application of talent, genius, and skill we can all reach the summit. This
resonates in theory, that anyone, regardless of social class, race, or any other
factor, has a chance to rise by giving it their best effort and going from plateau
to plateau to the top. We look back and see others who have done it. In this
way, those who have forged themselves in the fires of adversity inspire us.
Looking over our shoulders we can find this sort of Black excellence wherever

we look: John Rice Green, an enslaved man trained as an artisan in early nineteenth-century North Carolina, who hired himself out, purchased his own freedom, and attained some economic equality and standing; Bessie Smith who sang on street corners to make a living as a youth after her parents died, then filled the air with her remarkable voice, paving the way for what it meant to be a Black superstar; Jackie Joyner-Kersee, six-time Olympic medalist from East St. Louis who overcame severe asthma to compete in the 1980s and 1990s; Travers J. Bell Jr., who in 1971 founded the only Black-owned investment firm on the New York Stock Exchange—he grew up in the housing projects of Chicago's South Side, earned degrees in finance, worked as a messenger, and grew a company from $175,000 to $15 million. Historically Black universities like Howard and Spelman pump out engineers, biologists, geologists, actors and actresses, pianists, pageant queens, poets, news anchors, Pulitzer Prize winners, judges, vice presidents, Nobel laureates, generals, and other Black superachievers. We marvel at their achievements and say to ourselves, I, too, can climb that mountain. But the question remains, do we want a meritocratic society that only celebrates excellence?

The truth is hard work doesn't always pay off. You don't always get what you deserve, and wealth disparity still exists for the millions who work exhaustively every day. There are those who've had all the frugality, work ethic, and talent who never could move on from poverty lines and dilapidated housing to suburbs, comfortable retirements, and black-tie affairs. Limited class mobility remains widespread among those who hustle, regardless of individual work ethic. Shout out to those trying their best and working hard daily but are still in the struggle. We applaud noble efforts of community members making it their mission to "give back," but the truth is, philanthropy has never purchased equality. When I began writing this chapter, I intended it as a story on "Black excellence," where I was going to tell tales of Black people who made it. I desperately wanted to offer a triumphant Black story after dealing with so much painful history.

But that is not what this book is about, and so I reframed the chapter as a question to myself. What is the trade-off between excellence and equality? Where does the line between personal responsibility end and the social contract begin? Not only as Black people or Americans, but as human beings?

The answers to these questions reveal the very heart and soul of who we are, what we care about, and who we value. How do we unleash the best of every human being? And who told us that excellence was a debt, something we owe our ancestors to do better than they did? Who told you that you had to work until exhaustion and sacrifice your family, time, and sanity to fulfill your dreams? These notions originated in the twentieth century when Black people felt they had to prove themselves to earn legitimacy in a white-run society. Those who thought that success through assimilation would fulfill the democratic promise. A self-help book from 1919 titled *How to Succeed* offers some of the same practical advice you might find in any entrepreneurial self-help book published today:

> There is no royal road to success, the road that leads to success lies through fields of hard, earnest, and patient labor, it calls on the young man and woman to put forward all energy . . . the most successful men oftener have the most failures . . . poverty does more, perhaps than anything to develop the energetic self-reliant trait of character . . . the greatest misfortune of all is not to be able to bear misfortune.

This is still sound advice for one in a quest for wealth, but here we will move beyond this to reimagine Black excellence, looking for it in unexpected places. And looking to the best of Black history to see how it is bound up not only in the quest for excellence, but in the fight for equality and the common good. A community where those rewarded through talent and merit provided for those with average or less-than-average abilities and skills.

Rags to Riches

Bridget "Biddy" Mason embarked on a tedious journey far, far away from the cotton kingdom. We are peering now into the life of a woman, bought and sold across state lines from Georgia to South Carolina, then trafficked with Robert and Rebecca Smith to Franklin County, Mississippi, before the enslavers dragged her West behind a caravan of Mormons escaping religious persecution in 1847. She labored as part of Robert Smith's ever-increasing estate with thirteen other enslaved women and children, working alongside indigenous people forced into indentured servitude.

She was forced to walk behind the members of the Church of Jesus Christ of Latter-day Saints as they sought a promised land on the western plains. Not much is known about her journey, but Jane Manning James, an early Mormon convert, and first Black woman to set foot into Utah a year earlier, described her journey West: "We walked until our shoes were worn out, and our feet became sore and cracked open and bled until you could see the whole print of our feet with blood on the ground." Indeed, Biddy Mason, who by then had three small children, faced travails slogging behind that caravan of three hundred covered wagons, while her enslavers were carried by horses. Along with her children and nine other enslaved, they would have walked in sun, darkness, rain, hail, and snow. Facing disease, mountain lions, copperheads, coyotes, fatigue, and death. In addition to tending to her own children, she worked as a midwife, cooked the meals, and tended cattle. The land offered hope and salvation for the Mormons and their pro-slavery, theocratic founder, Brigham Young. They called their new home the Great Salt Lake City or the "City of the Saints" and commenced to plow, plant, build, displace, and enslave the Shoshone, Goshute, Ute, Paiute, and Navajo, who had lived on the land for centuries.

For Mason, it was paradise lost. But she wouldn't be in Salt Lake long. She was transported to California as part of the Mormon expansion to San Bernardino, a land that only a few years earlier was part of Mexico. Now she could hope. Adopted in 1849, the first constitution of California stated: "Neither slavery, nor involuntary servitude, unless for the punishment of crimes, shall ever be tolerated in this State." But a non-slaveholding state was at odds with a nation that still permitted slaveholding. The slaveholders who moved West brought slavery with them. In California, Mason entered a rapidly changing world, where Mexicans, indigenous people, and Afro-Latinos were forced off their land by the so-called settlers, who squatted on the land they had lived on.

It was there that Mason met Don Pío de Jesús Pico, California's last governor under Mexican rule. He was from a prominent Afro-Mexican family, wealthy and powerful in Mexican-era California. He built Los Angeles's first prominent hotel and was reportedly so rich that, when entertaining guests, he circulated trays full of coins so they wouldn't have to gamble with their own money.

Many in California harbored open hostility to slavery, so when Robert Smith lost much of his land to a bad real estate deal, he decided to move to pro-slavery Texas. The details are obscure, but evidence points to the free Black community alerting the sheriff to Smith's plans to move Mason and the others out of state. Since an 1850 statute dictated that no Native American or Black person could testify in court against a white one, some suggest Elizabeth "Lizzy" Flake Rowan, a Black woman who'd befriended Mason, was the complainant. The sheriff's posse surrounded Smith's camp in the Santa Monica Mountains, served him with a writ of habeas corpus, an action used by many free states to determine if a person has been unlawfully imprisoned, and took Biddy and the other enslaved into protective custody. It was there she sued for her freedom.

In the 1856 landmark case *Mason v. Smith*, Biddy Mason was brought before Judge Benjamin Hayes, an unlikely ally given his brief stint as an enslaver in his home state of Maryland. But it was an era when white Americans faced mounting abolitionist pressure. Freedom was in the air. That same year, in May 1856, the militant abolitionist John Brown and his sons murdered slavery supporters in the Pottawatomie massacre, in retaliation for the sacking of Lawrence, Kansas, by pro-slavery forces. On a smaller scale, this national battle played out in a Los Angeles courtroom. Smith immediately started to intimidate Mason and the Black community. He bribed Mason's lawyer for $200, who then withdrew from the case. He attempted to bribe the jailers with liquor to release those still in protective custody. He convinced a witness to lie on the stand. Judge Hayes was outraged. He interviewed Mason in his chambers with two observers to circumvent testimony laws, and eventually ruled in favor of freedom:

> And it further appearing by satisfactory proof to the judge here, that all of the said persons of color are entitled to their freedom and are free and cannot be held in slavery or involuntary servitude, it is therefore argued that they are entitled to their freedom and are free forever.

Smith fled the state before the case concluded. Judge Benjamin Hayes was ostracized by slavery sympathizers in Los Angeles but said he never regretted his decision. Biddy Mason finally tasted freedom. She was hindered by illiteracy and on the razor's edge of poverty, but she blended with the Spanish-speaking community by becoming fluent in Spanish. There was also a long multiethnic history between Black people and Mexicans in California. By all available evidence, in 1781, forty-four people founded the city of Los Angeles, with twenty-six of them being of African descent. The city and the people in it would change Biddy Mason's life. As a midwife, nurse, and healer using herbal remedies passed down by her grandmother, Mason gained a positive reputation and befriended those like Pío Pico and Robert Owens, a successful Black landowner, who'd helped her in her emancipation struggle.

Undeterred by the dramatic disparity of opportunities facing her, she took up work as a nurse midwife alongside Dr. John S. Griffin, helping women through the labor, physical, and psychological challenges of childbirth. She also risked her life treating those who'd contracted smallpox in the devastating outbreaks of the late 1800s. Biddy navigated her uninviting financial landscape with independence and skill. And it is here where we see the secret ingredient to success not spoken of enough—a network. Mason's excellence was not only predicated on hard work and skill but her connections among the Black and Mexican elite. But so many aren't born into the privilege of a wealthy network and are never accepted into one. So, what does it say about personal responsibility when today some 80 percent of jobs are attained through networking and hiring discrimination has remained unchanged for decades? White people get 36 percent more callbacks than Black people followed by 24 percent for Latinos. Mason's success was predicated on her network and the mentorship of Robert Owens, who offered her three practical words of financial advice: Buy real estate. With his advice and example, she planned.

In 1866, at age forty-eight and after six years of monetary prudence, she bought two lots on 331 Spring Street in downtown Los Angeles. She was the first Black woman in that city to do so. Intentional about managing what she had and savvy in commerce, she rented space on her property for people to rest their horses and carriages. Then she invested in more property, compounding her interest until she amassed unprecedented wealth.

Not stopping there, she vigorously pulled together with the community and voluntarily redistributed her wealth, investing in projects that helped Californians in the long term. She invested in schools and hospitals, and financed the first AME (African Methodist Episcopal) Church in California. As people look to history and study the rise of philanthropy, we are left to wonder why those like Biddy Mason have been left out of the conversation. Only recently have Black entrepreneurs like Madam C. J. Walker come into the national consciousness. But perhaps it was California, with its shaky diversity and earlier journey to freedom, that showed some of the greatest Black economic energy. William Leidesdorff, believed to be the nation's first Black millionaire, was a founder of San Francisco. Mary Ellen Pleasant boldly labeled herself on the 1890 census a "capitalist by profession." Her legacy is obscured because she does not fit the mold of blameless hero, but nonetheless saw possibilities in chasing million-dollar dreams. When her white husband died, she gained a significant $45,000 inheritance, moved to California, and opened a string of laundry businesses, then gained the trust of rich businessmen by presiding over society dinner parties where she gleaned information about how to invest her money. In doing so, she became a millionaire. Her life is shrouded in mystery—some say she was a madam, a queen of voodoo, and she said that she funded John Brown's raid on Harper's Ferry. When he died, there was a note in his pocket that read: "The ax is laid at the foot of the tree. When the first blow is struck, there will be more money to help" and signed "M. P." She was a fierce anti-slavery advocate and ran a station of the Underground Railroad out of her home, helped young women get a start, and fought for Black civil rights in court. It is in these Black entrepreneurial examples where we see that Black capitalism, like all capitalism, is not always clean and that a network is a prerequisite for success. There are a handful of winners who submit to relentless work and hit the lottery of success, but if your identity is tied into economic production, it will never be excellence. Success builds networks for self-interest, and excellence builds networks for community. The best of economic success, then, has been in using what one has built for the common good.

Excellence Overlooked

As we continue to look at excellence and equality, I want to take a minute to recover examples of excellence overlooked. So often we look to the success stories in Black entertainment and arts, and maybe that is because that is where people see the most opportunity. But the most unsung chapter in all Black history may be what we can only call an age of invention. Despite tremendous struggles and obstacles, Black people found ways to contribute their genius to the Industrial Revolution. Between 1870 and 1940, Black Americans filed some fifty thousand patents, second only to English and German immigrants. Most recorded patents were from free people in the North, but the fact that many of these breakthroughs were conceived while some were enslaved or held very little education speaks to the human capacity for rapid intellectual progress. Thomas Jennings, a freeman from New York City, patented a process called "dry scouring" in 1821 to remove dirt and grease from clothing. With his method, clothes could be cleaned without damage from water soaking the fibers.

This effectively laid the foundations for modern dry cleaning. He went on to own one of New York City's largest clothing stores, purchased his family from enslavement, and funded the abolitionist movement. Yet the process of gaining patents was difficult even for the free. When we think about how Black existence is threaded into the fabric of America, think about all the untold stories of lost and stolen Black intellectual capital. Which again, when we talk about equality, we look back to a US Patent and Trademark Office, which was created in an age where it was thought that Black people were intellectually inferior. But after emancipation, we see how a Virginian woman named Martha Jones, of Amelia County, Virginia, rose from the pages of history to obtain US patent No. 77,494 in 1869 for her "Improvement to the Corn Husker, Sheller," a machine that husked, shelled, cut up, and separated the husks from the corn in one operation. Silent in the record, we will never know her rationale for the improvement.

Other stories like that of mechanical engineer Elijah McCoy are illustrated more clearly. McCoy found himself underemployed as what was then called a railway fireman, shoveling coal into the furnace of a steam engine, and maintaining railway facilities as well as the cranks, pumps, connecting rods, pistons, and other various components so the train didn't explode, a frighteningly common occurrence. Overall, he produced some fifty patents, mostly related to his expertise in lubrication. He also patented an ironing board and lawn sprinkler. But even with all his ability, he lacked capital to manufacture his creations. In later life, after selling the rights to several inventions to investors, he finally opened his own shop.

In 1899, Dr. George F. Grant, a dentist from Boston and golf lover, was the first to patent the golf tee. Lewis Latimer was a self-taught drafter, who helped Alexander Graham Bell develop the telephone, and as part of Thomas Edison's research team, developed a light bulb superior to Edison's. "Learn to do common things uncommonly well," said George Washington Carver. More than just finding three hundred uses for peanuts, George Washington Carver saved Southern agriculture. After cotton farmers abused the soil in Alabama, the region faced a highly eroded landscape. Families were starving. Carver found different crops to restore the soil and educated farmers on up-to-date methods of crop rotation. He also helped Henry Ford by developing synthetic rubber for tires during wartime rubber shortages. And just like the ancestors before him, he believed in a spiritual connection to nature and its synergy with science, writing: "Anything will give up its secrets if you love it enough." He intimately believed in a direct line from nature to God and would electrify audiences when he spoke at universities with his intellect. "I love to think of nature as an unlimited broadcasting station, through which God speaks to us every hour, if we will only tune in."

Black people in science have spanned neurosurgery, physics, mathematics, computer science, and chemistry. Dr. Matilda Evans was a surgeon and public health pioneer in South Carolina who earned her degree in 1897. She treated Black and white patients, founded a hospital, published a book, and was a lifelong advocate and practitioner of healthcare as a universal right. In her white lab coat, PhD chemist Marie M. Daly helped us understand how foods and diet affect heart health and the circulatory system. After earning her PhD in mathematics from Yale in 1949, Evelyn Boyd Granville developed computer programs at IBM. Not widely known today, she then lent her brilliant mind to NASA before heading back to IBM as a senior mathematician. Black scientists like Ernest Wilkins, Carolyn B. Parker, and George Warren Reed worked on the Manhattan Project, the scientific enterprise that split the nucleus of atoms with uranium to create the H-bomb.

The moon landing offers us snapshots within a larger national narrative, regarded as one of the most important moments in American history. Bridging past and present, Katherine Johnson was one of the brilliant mathematicians who, along with Mary Jackson, Dorothy Vaughn, and a group of other Black women, calculated the trajectory for a moon flight and return. It was a beautiful moment to see her get a standing ovation at the Oscars in 2017, at ninety-eight years old, with the cast of *Hidden Figures*, the 2016 movie celebrating her group's veiled but crucial work in American space exploration. Taking on the challenge of President John F. Kennedy, the women worked as an unlikely collaboration of scientists to put two American pilots, Neil Armstrong and Buzz Aldrin, on the craggy surface of the moon on July 20, 1969. The star-spangled banner planted in its crust after the landing of Apollo 11 was the biggest spectacle the world had ever seen and a technological feat of cosmic proportions wrapped in themes of humanity, nation, earth, and the universe. The United States had won its technological, propaganda, and culture war against the Soviet Union. It only cost $28 billion. This moment catapulted NASA into a beloved brand, worthy of inspiring anyone who has ever looked to the stars. There is humanity within that story, one that has defined American heroes.

But a Black man was also set to take "one step for mankind," and make history, almost. Ed Dwight had the credentials, was an aeronautical engineering graduate, and a US Air Force pilot. He had the experience, piloting an F-104 Starfighter in 1962. An aircraft conceived during the Korean War, the radical design was called "a missile with a man in it," for its stubby wings and supersonic speed. Dwight had logged some nine thousand hours in the air. And in terms of strength of character, he'd literally served as a Catholic altar boy who grew into a man of great moral character. For these reasons he was picked by JFK to be America's Black astronaut, and potentially the first man on the moon. And though he made it to training camp, he would not be selected. There were fewer people pushing for a qualified Black space candidate than there were trying to push one out.

When Kennedy died, so did Dwight's dreams of going to space. He had the ability, but NASA was not separate from the battle of race and gender inclusion being waged across the country. NASA employed fewer people of color and fewer women than any other agency in the federal government until the early 1970s. Most of their facilities were in the Jim Crow South—Alabama, Texas, Louisiana, Florida, and Mississippi—and the attitudes were reflected. Unfortunately for Ed Dwight, it seemed that NASA was more interested in space missions than people missions. Often, we ignore the social history of monolithic organizations such as NASA in favor of a triumphant one, thus ignoring the history of exclusion of those who otherwise might have reached their fullest potential.

Black Status Versus Black Power

The Black aristocracy of Washington, DC, sat in a class above what one might think possible in the late nineteenth and early twentieth century as many were formerly enslaved. One of the most prominent, Blanche K. Bruce, was the first to serve a full term in the US Senate during Reconstruction. After becoming a wealthy landowner in Mississippi, he moved to Washington for its cultural opportunities. He and his wife threw lavish parties, representing a Black upper-middle class who sought status and consumed conspicuously. They lived in material comfort and wealth, while some had country homes where they could spend their summers and sent their kids to camp at the nation's first Black YMCA. They were physicians, attorneys, government employees with a foothold in the DC political sphere, caterers, entrepreneurs, and others who worked at the prestigious Howard University.

As the saying went, men had to wear ties and women white gloves to walk down the famed U Street, a thriving Black business hub. They might have been barred from white businesses, but in the Shaw neighborhood, Black people rested at Black hotels, shopped at Black department stores, read the news from the Black paper—the *Washington Bee*—picked up medicine from their own pharmacies, food from their own grocery stores, and were entertained at one of many theaters, cabarets, billiards halls, jazz clubs, and casinos in their neighborhoods. It was a city within a city. Those who lived there sent their children to M Street, a school that boasted some of the most well-educated Black minds in the country. Mary Jane Patterson—the first Black woman in America to earn a bachelor's degree when she graduated from Oberlin College in 1862—was an early leader of the school and worked feverishly to grow it. Richard T. Greener, the first Black graduate of Harvard, was acting principal in 1873. Mary Church Terrell, famed racial justice and women's rights activist, taught math and science at M Street, serving as principal from 1899 until 1901. In 1899, there were four public high schools in DC, three white and one Black. That Black school was M Street, and in that same year, they outscored all but one of the white schools on standardized tests. Anna J. Cooper should be a household name for her push toward educational progress, civil rights activism, and contributions to feminist philosophy. And in 1902, she was also a principal of M Street High School. She was instrumental in M Street's success, and it might say something of her indomitable spirit that she somehow juggled her professional excellence while raising five adoptive children. She always wanted to do more and go beyond what was possible. "I constantly felt as I suppose as many an ambitious girl has felt, a thumping from within unanswered by a beckoning from without."

Cooper wasn't interested in playing by any rules but her own; she was deeply suspicious of white people who focused on vocational training for Black students. When she disagreed with the Washington, DC, school board, who supported the push toward vocational training, she resigned. The school taught low-income and middle-class Black students, boasted low absenteeism, and had a staff so motivated they came back to work after retirement. Rapidly closing achievement gaps, M Street pumped out a slew of "Black firsts." The first full Black professor at a major university, the first West Point and Annapolis graduates, the first Black federal judge, general, and cabinet member. After 1916, M Street was renamed Dunbar High School, but though the name changed, their remarkable performance remained the same through the mid-1950s. The Shaw neighborhood continued to thrive, even boasting Black banks lending to Black businesses, churches, and homeowners. But there were cracks in the foundation of equality. Elitism and colorism were visible, and many of the wealthiest had light skin and integrationist views. Nannie Helen Burroughs, who graduated from the illustrious M Street High School, was denied a teaching position at the same school for being too Black.

In his 1957 book, *Black Bourgeoisie*, E. Franklin Frazier put forth a toothy and dismissive analysis of upper-middle-class America, and more specifically the Black upper-middle class, that nonetheless held nuggets of timeless truth. "The old upper class in the Negro community erected an impenetrable barrier between themselves and Negroes who represented the 'sporting' and criminal world," he said, pointing out a glaring class division. He goes all the way back to slavery to show how there has always been a middle class of Black people within the context of American capitalism, and while the ticket for entry was once lightness of skin, it later shifted to financial status. He went on to argue that a carbon copy of European success—conspicuous consumption, materialism, laissez-fare business practices, and concentrated wealth for a small contingent of Black elites—would not provide knowledge, freedom, or equality to the poor Black masses.

Our current world of make-believe is even more convincing as our screens light up with Real Housewives and Husbands, lifestyle bloggers, and the new elite flexing wealth in 1080-by-1080 pixel squares and endorphin-spiking thirty- to sixty-second videos on social media. Not much has changed—the rich get richer, wealth follows wealth. After desegregation, the Black elite largely fled to white suburbs, taking their talents to white businesses, enjoying better schools, opportunities, and amenities. In recent years the median white family has reported up to ten times the wealth of the median Black family. For me, it is hard to study the history of Black economics without remembering that no matter the generation or the circumstances, a disproportionate amount of Black people have always lived in poverty.

As the Black and privileged removed themselves, poor Black people continued to migrate from Southern states, and many came in from Virginia and the Carolinas. By 1970, 71 percent of Washington, DC's population was Black, and after the murder of Dr. Martin Luther King Jr., the nationwide riots, and murder of El-Hajj Malik El-Shabazz (Malcom X) in 1965, the city bristled with resentment and rebellion. Young activists from across the country saw it as Ground Zero for a Black city built on revolutionary power. Moderate civil rights stalwarts, the Nation of Islam, Pan-Africanists, Socialists, Black Panthers, Marxists, Nationalists, and others came together under the umbrella of Black Power. Like an elder shaking his finger at the youth, civil rights statesman Bayard Rustin called the Black Power movement a guise to "elect Negroes to office in proportion to Negro strength within the population." He went even further to say, "'Black power' not only lacks any real value for the civil-rights movement, but that its propagation is positively harmful. It diverts the movement from a meaningful debate over strategy and tactics, it isolates the Negro community."

The Black Power era was brief, yet the movement burned like a blazing star. Most histories are dismissive of this era of Black history, but perhaps they just don't know what to do with the 1970s, 1980s, and 1990s. The rejection of integration, anti-capitalist rhetoric, blistering attacks on imperialism, the embrace of violence as a liberating tactic, and aggressive imagery put Black Power proponents at odds with their civil rights parents. But much has been missed in this narrow view. Black Power expanded visions of Black democracy to reinvigorate the conversation about the global diaspora, transforming what democracy looks like for Black people on a local, regional, national, and global scale. Gary, Indiana; Cleveland; Atlanta; Newark; and Detroit established political machines to elect Black mayors. Not a monolith, some factions formed multiethnic coalitions, while others called for separate schools, communities, and even a separate Black state as an escape from institutionalized racism. Women, so often silenced in the Civil Rights Movement, joined the vocal energy of the crusade, pronouncing the boldest feminist visions up until that point in Black history. The movement galvanized public housing tenants into bona fide organizers fighting for better wages, living conditions, and social services. But instead, this nuanced history of the Black Power era has been replaced with images of violence, black fists, and the wanted poster of Angela Davis.

In DC, a wide array of groups crowded the city. The Blackman's Volunteer Army of Liberation had an initial goal to train an army for a liberation war in Africa. An impractical plan, they instead began treatment programs for heroin addicts as the drug epidemic of the 1980s ravaged Black communities. Right around this time the federal government released more than $2 billion to fight an unconditional war on poverty. Millions of dollars made it into the hands of activists, who founded arts and community centers, schools, and youth centers, redefining Black life. They focused less on equal opportunity and more on resources for the poor. According to historian George Derek Musgrove, "By the late 1970s, Black Power activists dominated the newly created local government and had begun to build institutional power in national politics. Many street activists and insurgents became elected officials, non-profit directors, and lobbyists." As government officials with constituencies, the talk of revolution and anti-imperialism waned, and the leaders focused on more institutional programing like multicultural education and equal representation. The young radicals started growing up and many grabbed on to the same power they once railed against. Tensions festered over movement integrity infused with so many federal dollars. But with the election of Ronald Reagan, social service money was slashed, and the nation suffered a devastating recession; the new Black political class became entangled in corruption and bureaucracy.

Within the last few years, I've driven through the Shaw neighborhood, where Dunbar High School sits as a new building in Washington, DC. It is now home to all the signs of gentrification—hipster enclaves, variety craft beer bars, electric scooter rentals, dog parks, luxury condos, bed-and-breakfasts, rowhouses in various phases of gutting or remodeling, affluent white people, and displaced Black people. All within blocks of historian Carter G. Woodson's historic home, which sits out of sorts, an unintentional piece of Black culture branding. And so it is no wonder that so many Black people have seen Black entertainment culture as the only way out.

Black Power has been summed up in the words of James Brown, who said, "I used to shine shoes in front of a radio station. Now I own radio stations. You know what that is? That's Black Power." Like so many, he conflated Black capitalism with Black Power. Stokely Carmichael (later known as Kwame Toure) offered another definition resonating with both excellence and equality. For him, Black Power gave Black people love of self. The dashiki, the cowrie shells, the ankh bead necklace, the prideful kinky hair, the swaggering confidence, the freedom to express the Black identity without shame, that is the legacy of Black Power. The best of the Black Power tradition lies in the spirit of agitation, which reinforced all Black freedom struggles. It stands against anything preventing Black people from actualizing their fullest capabilities and potential as individuals and as a group. Black Power was an affirmation of Black might and autonomy in the face of what America was predicting would be a dark future for Black people.

It was during this time that those in the Bureau of Labor, like then–secretary of labor Willard Wirtz, said that Black people were part of the "the human scrap heap," left behind by technological development, mired in educational failure and poverty, and unable to make it in a skilled economy without assistance. So, Carmichael was calling for Black people to set aside differences to come together, find common ground, and put forth an agenda for the common good of all Black people. Not to the exclusion of other groups, but to say the only way for Black people to gain economic and political power is to find unity in a shared culture and heritage, and work through differences as a constituency to create opportunities for Black people in America.

Perhaps the war on poverty failed because society didn't really change. Government programs aren't the end-all, be-all when kids still live in broken single-parent homes, are stuck in inferior schools, and grow up with the absence of jobs offering a decent wage. To truly attack poverty would mean societal values would need to shift. "Reorientation means an emphasis on the dignity of man," said Carmichael, "not on the sanctity of property. It means the creation of a society where human misery and poverty are repugnant to that society, not an indication of laziness or lack of initiative. The creation of new values means the establishment of a society based on free people, not free enterprise."

To Stand on Principles

When Shirley Chisholm ran for president as the first Black woman in America on a major party ticket in 1972, she knew she would lose. Not because she lacked personal qualities (competence, honesty, integrity, empathy, courage) but because of resources. As the first Black woman elected to Congress, she then emerged as the second woman to run for a big-ticket presidential nomination. Campaigns are expensive, and to win over delegates takes extensive traveling, rallying, marketing, and other ventures that smolder the fire of small-donor grassroots movements like Chisholm's.

There was no way she would dethrone her democratic contender, Hubert Humphrey, heavily connected to wealthy donors, who contributed 90 percent of his $838,715 campaign funds.

Chisholm was an unlikely candidate, not only as a Black woman, but as a former daycare worker with no political background. Yet she worked her way into the New York political landscape volunteering for political organizations, serving on boards, and campaigning for other candidates. Eventually she won a New York State Assembly seat in 1964, galvanizing a female voting base undoubtedly tired of their own underrepresentation. In the 1960s, women took a sledgehammer to gender inequity, chipping away at the walls of sexism, double standards, and the age-old edict to stay in a kitchen. For centuries, the face of a politics had a beard, and Chisholm thought it time for politicians to better reflect the diversity of the people voting for them. Then, after an envelope with $9.62 and the encouragement from a neighbor to use it toward a campaign for Congress, Chisholm reached for the stars and moved the goalpost, becoming the first Black woman elected to the US Congress. Chisholm faced death threats, hate mail, and racist slur attacks but said she got more hate for her gender than her race. Her male constituents took a sexist approach, and she retained little support from men, some of whom called her the "*castrator*," and "the little black matriarch who goes around messing things up."

But the excellence was in the attempt. The excellence was in her platform: to be a woman running on a promise of humane leadership in a world of political ruthlessness. But when inhumanity is the norm, humane policies are radical. In a policy that still resonates in our own time, she said, "One bill that I introduced should become law in every state, but unfortunately it did not succeed even in New York. It would have made it mandatory for policemen to successfully complete courses in civil rights, civil liberties, minority problems, and race relations before they are appointed to a police department." Running on a platform that was the antithesis of how the government was operating at the time, her slogan was, "unbought and unbossed." Because where there is government, there is corruption.

"Who will govern the governors?" said Thomas Jefferson. "There is only one force in the nation that can be depended upon to keep the government pure and the governors honest, and that is the people themselves. They alone, if well informed, are capable of preventing the corruption of power, and of restoring the nation to its rightful course if it should go astray. They alone are the safest depository of the ultimate powers of government." In 1972, the White House was withering from constitutional lawlessness and executive decay. Only a year earlier, COINTELPRO, the FBI's clandestine war on political freedom, was exposed. While FBI agents were distracted watching the blockbuster boxing match between Muhammad Ali and Joe Frazier, activists broke into the field office in Media, Pennsylvania, stealing more than a thousand documents that revealed the spectacular fraud in America's most powerful law enforcement agency. Ironically, Ali was a COINTELPRO target.

Security must have been lax in those years, because in 1972, burglars also broke into the Democratic National Committee headquarters at the Watergate complex in Washington, DC, leading to one of the worst presidential scandals in US history. "I am not a crook," said President Richard Nixon, nervously addressing the public as the salacious information was made public, but it turns out that he was. Awash in corruption, Nixon treated campaign financiers and donors as his personal bank account, colluding with the milk lobby to raise prices in exchange for $2 million in campaign contributions, resulting in $500 to $700 million in additional costs to consumers. During the Watergate investigation, federal investigators found that in a bid to crush political rivals, Nixon's operatives "followed members of Democratic candidates' families and assembling dossiers on their personal lives; forging letters and distributing them under the candidates' letterheads; leaking false and manufactured items to the press; throwing campaign schedules into disarray; seizing confidential campaign files; and investigating the lives of dozens of Democratic campaign workers."

Shirley Chisholm was one of those candidates. The Nixon campaign fabricated a fake news release using the official stationery of candidate Hubert Humphrey, accusing Chisholm of mental illness and sexual deviancy. It was then sent to *Ebony* magazine, *Jet*, and the Associated Press. Despite this, Chisholm stayed the course, forming what she called a "union of the disenfranchised." "I am not the candidate of Black America, although I am

Black and proud. I am not the candidate of the women's movement of this country, although I am a woman, and I am equally proud of that . . . I am the candidate of the people of America. And my presence before you now symbolizes a new era in American political history."

One paper called her campaign "quixotic," but she did not deter. With little funding and a small team, she pushed her progressive causes, running as a connector of responsive women, minorities, the poor, and the young, who she hoped would see a promise in her for a new government. Fluent in Spanish, she appealed to the growing Hispanic population. She assured all underrepresented groups that they might barely be heard alone, but together they would make a mighty roar. Regardless of political perception, she worked alongside and was endorsed by the Black Panthers in support of their survival programs. She was criticized for working with radical organizations, but she asked what have been the conditions in America that made a group like the Panthers necessary in the first place?

Chisholm knew she couldn't win the presidency. But she could set an example. She was unafraid and was serious about rallying people and awakening them to new possibilities. She knew she was a face against racism, like that of George Corley Wallace, the fierce opponent of the Civil Rights Movement, who had stood at the door of the University of Alabama to block the entrance of two Black students, offering the infamous quote, "Segregation now, segregation tomorrow, segregation forever!" But she also had moral integrity, so when Wallace was gunned down in an attempted assassination, Chisolm went to visit him. Wallace reportedly exclaimed, "Shirley Chisholm! What are you doing here? What will your people say?" To which she replied, "I know what they are going to say. But I wouldn't want what happened to you to happen to anyone." Wallace wept as they held hands and prayed. She later said, "The next time a woman runs, or a black, or a Jew or anyone from a group that the country is 'not ready' to elect to its highest office, I believe that he or she will be taken seriously from the start . . . I ran because somebody had to do it first."

Other than a reprinting of her own self-written biography, and a couple of television cameos, there has been little scholarly interest in telling the story of the woman who opened the door for Obama and so many other

Black politicians. Perhaps she knew, excellence is not only about winning, it's putting forth the best effort in the pursuit of a goal. Excellence is when someone tells you that you have a place and you must stay there, but you move out of it. It's about setting your own bar, and if you meet it, that is excellence.

What It Means to Rise Again

He woke up at 5:50 a.m. As the sun quietly crept above the horizon, on Earth was the sound of a rhythmic patter, shoes hitting the asphalt. His name was Muhammad Ali, and he'd just started his daily six-mile run. When most people think of Ali's excellence, they recall his three heavyweight titles won three separate times; how he defended his titles nineteen times, but I think about the hunger. Ali was serious about his workouts and his runs, cultivating a routine he stuck to with the religiousness of a high priest. This was no ordinary run, it was "roadwork," involving all the grueling aspects of a high-endurance marathon, but with things like push-ups and suicide dashes added into it. It was designed as deliberate practice to mimic the movements and strength needed in a boxing ring. Ali had been doubted his whole life. Hated even, for his conversion to the Nation of Islam, and his refusal to fight in the Vietnam War. But Ali kept going.

On that bright morning, Ali started running at a steady pace as a traditional marathon runner would, then suddenly, as if possessed, he burst into a high-intensity sprint. Steadying the pace again, he turned onto a familiar street with a steep incline, a conscious choice to match the resistance he'd face moving toward an aggressive opponent. The average onlooker would've been befuddled as he dropped down from a full sprint into one hundred push-ups. Finally, in the last mile, he turned and ran backward. Sometimes, you must retreat in a fight, give up ground for better positioning. Every movement, every exercise, every training method was deliberate practice to meet the performance demands of a heavyweight brawl. Few under the sun mastered boxing to the level of Muhammad Ali. A sport requiring speed, strength, explosiveness, endurance, intelligence, and cunning. Skills gifted to him by deliberate practice. A conscious daily routine helped make him one of the greatest boxers in history.

"No one starts out on top," Ali offered. "You have to work your way up. Some mountains are higher than others, some roads steeper than the next. There are hardships and setbacks, but you can't let them stop you. Even on the steepest road, you must not turn back. You must keep going up. To reach the top of the mountain, you have to climb every rock." The inner motivation of Ali reminds us that no form of excellence can come from without; it always begins from within. As one of the loudest voices for civil rights, especially during the later years of the 1960s, we might wonder if Ali believed in a balance of equality and excellence, in other words, that we do not want people to have to run uphill backward while so many others walk downhill.

In 1967, he was convicted of draft evasion and stripped of his title for opposition to the Vietnam War. But under the glimmer of the moon in Kinshasa, Zaire, seven years later, on October 30, 1974, Ali did the impossible. The then-thirty-two-year-old sent a younger and far more powerful George Foreman thundering to the ground in the eighth round in front of sixty thousand people. The lore of the Phoenix, thought to have originated in Egyptian mythology, and transferred to the West 2,500 years ago by Greek historian Herodotus, comes down to us as the story of a mysterious and magical bird. According to legend, the life span of a Phoenix was five hundred years, and only one of the majestic birds could live at a time. What is most fascinating is, just before its death, the Phoenix carefully constructed a nest and set itself ablaze. After which, a new bird ascended in a glorious rise from the ashes.

Resilience has been thrown around as a leadership buzzword associated with "warrior wisdom," and a way to navigate life's rough patches. But the resilience I mean here, and the wonder of Black history, is how, after going toe-to-toe with adversity, trauma, tragedy, threats, and astronomical stress, Black Americans evaded extinction. That is the spirit of Black history that has been passed down through the culture, the will to survive. I think about how the Black residents of Tulsa, Oklahoma, were nearly bombed out of existence. But despair was not the result in Tulsa. That story does not end with that devastating massacre on June 1, 1921. Excellence had the last word, and for a time, Tulsa residents bounced back. The massacre rivaled a natural disaster in its destruction. But in fixating on the disaster and lack of justice, we forgot something. The city of Tulsa turned its back on displaced

Black residents, offering little aid or recovery help. Insurance companies didn't honor their policies, and through all this, Black people rebuilt. Living in tents provided by the Red Cross for the next year, they rebuilt. Surviving the Tulsa winters that go below freezing, they rebuilt. When the Kansas & Texas Railway Co. offered 50 percent discounts on one-way tickets out of Tulsa to rid the city of them, they rebuilt. Some eight hundred structures were rebuilt by the end of 1921. Black families, landowners, and entrepreneurs paved a road to recovery. They assessed the 314 looted homes and rummaged through the 1,200 destroyed. They might not have found much, but they found the indomitable will of their human spirit. To be sure, many drifted away, unwilling to stay, unable to deal with the anxiety, disruption, and uncertainty of displacement. Those who stayed faced obstacles seemingly insurmountable. Like, when white commercial speculators tried to remove them from their land by enacting an arbitrary fire zone, which would have made it illegal for them to reconstruct houses. Those same residents fought back legally. Black lawyers argued all the way to the Oklahoma Supreme Court, challenging Tulsa's plan to thwart property rights for the commercial interests of land speculators as unconstitutional. They won. They filed 1,400 lawsuits to recover some $4 million in damages, but the city of Tulsa claimed it was not responsible for the actions of the mob.

Despite the injustice, we can pause to appreciate the excellence of a community coming together to rebuild. Because people pursuing greatness despite their hardships is excellence defined.

15

Are We a Democracy Yet?

> Where you see wrong or inequality or injustice, speak out, because this is your country. This is your democracy. Make it. Protect it. Pass it on.
> —Thurgood Marshall

O n July 4, 1776, the Second Continental Congress convened and adopted the Declaration of Independence, declaring: "We hold these truths to be self-evident, that all men are created equal, that they are endowed by their Creator with certain unalienable rights, that among these are Life, Liberty and the Pursuit of Happiness." Then, in 1787, those ideals were crystalized in the Constitution of the United States. It was an imperfect document, very much influenced by its time, but no one can argue against its omnipresence and influence in world history. As we have seen, egalitarian ideals were not new, but for much of recorded history, the average person labored under the rigid hierarchy and ironclad rule of kings, queens, dictators, barons, emperors, lords, czars, and pharaohs. But then General George Washington, after a seven-year war of attrition, and nine years away from home and family, organized a paltry force of loosely organized militias, and defeated the juggernaut Kingdom of Great Britain, the most militarily powerful nation on Earth. He attains the heights of power and then gives it up. And thus began our experiment in democracy with its separation of powers, checks and balances, and protection of individual rights derived from a voting population it termed "the people." And perhaps the failures of modern democracy are not so much the ideal itself, but the fundamental question that is yet to be answered: Who are the American people?

One of the greatest things about the founding documents is their flexibility, but instead of moving the conversation forward to address our twenty-first-century concerns, they have become the unquestionable bible of our civic religion. The Declaration of Independence, the Bill of Rights, and the Constitution sit under the Rotunda of the National Archives in Washington, DC, encased in moisture-proof and bulletproof glass, with two armed guards standing watch before being lowered into a fifty-five-ton steel-and-concrete bomb-proof vault every night. It's worth noting, though, that there are those who might set those documents on fire because they were written by slaveholders, forgetting how many people have fought to bring America closer to its highest ideals, the ones pronounced in those same documents.

One of my favorite paintings, *Self-Evidence* (2011) by Titus Kaphar, brings clarity to the remainder of the narrative. In this brilliant piece, Kaphar references the iconic photo of Muhammad Ali towering over a knocked-down Sonny Liston in their 1965 title fight. Ali stands there full of fire and unbridled passion and raw physicality and piercing wit. Challenging Liston, "Get up." But instead of Ali standing over Liston, Kaphar paints him standing on a table over the founding fathers as they sign the founding documents. And they are looking up at him as he looks down over them menacingly, as if to say, where am I? Taunting them through history for excluding Black humanity.

America has always been a grand contradiction; for the first few decades of independence, free Black people and women in the United States could vote in some colonies, but those rights were legally torn away, and by 1807, the vote was gone. Democracy was killed in plain sight. We know the definition of the word *people* was much narrower when our country was founded. Women were viewed as property, indigenous people savages, Black people slaves, and landless whites as servants. But what our nation likes to tell itself is that we cannot judge the founders by their contemporary moral and political standards, that they wanted to free the enslaved, but it was impractical. But then I picture Ali standing over those documents again.

They knew slavery was morally wrong, that there were two clear choices, and yet gave in to its evils, siding with a forgotten founder like Charles Pinckney of South Carolina who was pro-slavery to the core, rather than Robert Carter III, who worked out a plan to slowly free all his enslaved people, a total of 450, all manumitted seventy years before the Emancipation Proclamation, saying that slavery was "contrary to the true principles of Religion & justice." He did what other founders claimed they could not, and we must wonder if they were so energized, whether the extinction of chattel slavery might have come much sooner.

Frederick Douglass called the Constitution "a glorious liberty document," and praised its principles, which, "if properly understood, gave slavery no permanent protection." But he also knew it left the door open for future states to pass laws sanctioning the institution. And they did, either banishing Black freedom, or severely limiting it. And so Black history became linked to the fight for liberation, with every generation producing handfuls of heroic souls with full disregard for the risk to their lives, mustering the courage and fight for the promise of freedom. Once they stood up, others joined, and the rising tide of Black democracy has lifted all boats. People are afraid of true freedom. We settle into the false security that comes from routine. We are more likely to conform to societal norms. But nonparticipation—legalized, coerced, forced, or chosen—is a death sentence to democracy, and in America, it was political death for the millions unable to participate for 189 years, the time between the signing of the Constitution and the Voting Rights Act of 1965. As of this writing, America has been a democracy for less than six decades.

The fact that America was founded with the narrow vision of the people has made many deeply distrustful and certainly cynical about US government, politics, and leadership, but the government is not a democracy any more than the car is its driver. There have been drivers who have taken us dangerously close to the cliff to near destruction, while others have used it to explore all of America's possibilities for freedom. And trust me, I get it. The electoral college is a strange political device of government that was designed to protect the voices of slave states and slaveholders. The filibuster is linked to a racist history of shutting down civil rights bills, and gerrymandering, where politicians pick their districts, is still rampant. I've seen working-class Black people be unable to vote, because they can't be late to work, or the polling places are too far away. I've seen intelligent people fall under the spell of demagogues, populists, and conspiracy theories. With social media, the gap between rhetoric, true virtue, hollow babbling, or problem-solving is ever wider. And I've seen corporations co-opt social justice causes. We are in the age of activist influencers who vie for corporate dollars from corporations like State Farm who promise to build safer communities, or Gillette razors in their bid to take on toxic masculinity.

We all know that our two-party system has become old and decrepit. The Republican Party has made a mockery of democracy; their policies pander to the wealthiest among us at the expense of everyone else, and they've relied on populism, racism, and intolerance to keep their electoral base happy and voting. They talk about America as though those who vote against them aren't even a part of it. Under the right, military budgets balloon while education budgets deflate. But the Democratic Party has also made a mockery of democracy. They have paid lip service to poor and working people while their policies similarly pander to the very wealthiest among us. Citizens are seen as consumers, our choices best exercised by buying and selling. With its "let the market decide" approach, equality is measured only through productivity. The amount of money allowed to flow into political campaigns by the power elite makes our nation almost indistinguishable from an oligarchy or plutocracy, and who can really tell the difference anyway? So, insulated by personal troubles, and overwhelmed by the larger issues, every generation has a portion of the population who act as if politics do not exist. Those who just go through their everyday lives and try to etch out an individual existence within their circumstances. But an analysis of Black history shows us that, even when it seems hopeless, political participation is the fertilizer of freedom. If not used, it will surely wither away.

The Many Degrees of Black Political Fire

Black politics in America have always been linked to freedom, citizenship, economic and political rights, and the fight against ever looming threats of American racism. But Black politics has also become associated with an undying loyalty to the Democratic Party and a history of nonviolent struggle cloaked in the moral blanket of Christianity. And while it is true that Black spirituality and political ideology have been inextricably linked, the story has been told with monotonous predictability. Before Black people figured out how to shape the words of the Bible into a political instrument, many were still praying to Ogun, the Yoruba God of iron and war, deity of creation and destruction, to protect them during their rebellions. As humans have long looked to the sky to worship God(s), male, female, or genderless, to make sense of life and the hereafter, Black political organizing didn't begin with Christ. Before the first Black churches were constructed, Black Muslims had been in America even before the Jamestown settlement. They came with the Spanish since 1503. Many were Moors, converted in North Africa, descended from those African and Arab Muslims who'd conquered a large swath of the Iberian Peninsula and ruled for eight centuries leaving an indelible influence on Spanish culture. Charles Ball, an enslaved man who broke away and wrote his narrative in 1837, said:

> I knew several [people] who must have been, from what I have since learned, Mohamedans [Muslims]; though at that time, I had never heard of the religion of Mohamed. There was one man on this plantation . . . who prayed five times every day, always turning his face to the east, when in the performance of his devotion.

While in Virginia campaigning for religious freedom, Thomas Jefferson demanded "recognition of the religious rights of the Mahamdan, the Jew and the pagan." Black American Muslims, more likely to be literate, used their religion as a political tool for liberation. In October of 1807, Jefferson found himself unable to read two Arabic manuscripts, sent to him by two enslaved fugitives, who'd just been captured in rural Kentucky, asking him to intervene and secure their freedom. By the nineteenth century the Muslim faith had almost all been stamped out of the population of enslaved people. But spirituality survived in the hush harbors, places where enslaved people conducted spiritual practices in secret. Whites feared Black gatherings, not because of a simple worship service, but because spirituality was bound up in the politics of liberation. And still, in those hush harbors, we find syncretism, or the blending of Christianity with African Traditional

Religions. Many now are rediscovering the truth through the spiritual traditions practiced by distant ancestors in Africa. Without a written book like a Bible, these spiritual systems were living and breathing, and the enslavers did not have access to them. They were a way for the enslaved to humanize and politically organize themselves, under the nose of white authority.

With the Great Awakening, Christianity spread through America like wildfire. On the Middle Passage and within plantation life, Black people were introduced to a God who sided with the institution of slavery. Justifications for this institution were cherry-picked from the Bible and used as evidence for a divine order of inequality. It is here in the early days of colonial America that Black people faced one of their starkest religious realities. In the Bible, many found hope, faith, and salvation in Jesus Christ. But even if Christianity saved your soul, it could not save your body; the colonies made it clear that spiritual conversion didn't mean freedom. In 1667, Virginia passed a law declaring "baptisme of slaves doth not exempt them from bondage." Other states followed suit. In the land of religious freedom, Black people had to worship in secret. Unable to attend white churches and prayer meetings, they congregated deep in the woods, ravines, and gullies. Scholars have labeled the Black church as the social center of the Black community and central to Black life. But what we know of as the "Black Church," that venerable institution that served as the base of political organizing into the 1960s, can be glimpsed by looking back to the First Baptist Church in Williamsburg, Virginia, formed in 1776. Indeed, the church has been a source of comfort, and a place where people have gone to "Lift Every Voice and Sing."

Fiery orations, lawsuits, abolitionist organizing, and petitioning have been the preferred political tools in the struggle for Black freedom. Free Black people submitted petition after petition arguing that America should end the hideous practice of slavery, but the legislature denied one after another. They wrote them anyway, from at least 1773. Abolitionist Prince Hall wrote a petition using the same language as the Declaration of Independence, where he petitioned for freedom only months after the Revolution in 1777, which said: "The petition of A Great Number of Blackes detained in a State of slavery in the bowels of a free & Christian County

Humbly sheweth that your Petitioners apprehend that they have in Common with all other men a Natural and Unalienable Right to that freedom which the Gr[e]at Parent of the Universe that Bestowed equally on all mankind." Black politics prior to emancipation had to be informed by the crises of slavery, for there could be no other political fight until the one to gain the fundamental human right to freedom was won. In the early twentieth century, Pauline Hopkins penned a line that feels like it could have been written yesterday: "Even today it is erroneously believed that all racial development among colored people has taken place since emancipation. It is impossible to believe for some, that little circles of educated men and women of color have existed since the Revolutionary War." Hopkins was referring to groups like the Free African Society (FAS) of Philadelphia, cofounded in 1787 by free abolitionist ministers Richard Allen and Absalom Jones. It was an early organization where concerns for Black freedom transcended religious affiliation. From different denominations, Allen and Jones knew they needed to come together to challenge the powerful institutional structures upholding slavery. United against a common struggle, they formed FAS as a mutual aid organization to assist the newly freed, rather than leave them to fend for themselves.

Based on the moral principles of their faith, they got to work stridently organizing, attacking racism, and meeting the real needs of the Black community where the government would not. They, along with countless other men and women, nursed the sick, taught literacy, and provided financial support, including burials. They offered emotional support, spiritual guidance, and leadership training. It is no understatement to call Richard Allen one of the most brilliant Americans of his generation. Disillusioned by the segregation in the church that saw his friend Absalom Jones physically removed from his knees while praying, Allen led one of the first major nonviolent protests in Black American History. He also successfully sued in the Pennsylvania courts in 1807 and 1815 to form the first organized Black denomination in US history, the African Methodist Episcopal Church. There is no question that this political history ties directly into the currents of democratic activism leading to the later Civil Rights Movement, which on the surface seemed like a very long mass protest movement, but was a long political one, based directly in building coalitions, compromise, transforming political parties, and utilizing the force of law to remake the nation into a true democracy.

In Black politics religion has played an outsized role. Kongolese Catholics and West African Muslims were among the first Black people to land on the shores of North America. They used their literacy to interpret ideas of salvation from the Koran and the Bible, avoiding menial labor; they worked in skilled trades as bookkeepers, personal servants, and coachmen. African Traditional Religions incorporated Akan philosophies and the Yoruban high gods operating under a supreme creator spirit to which we will all one day return. Subordinate spirits formed pantheons and the ancestors were active in everyday life. Spiritual practice made its way into medicine, cosmology, building, agriculture, and art.

Religious diversity is vastly understudied in Black history, but we cannot discount the Black church as the social center of the Black community and central to Black life, as well as the backbone of activism. Benjamin Elijah Mays pointed out the power of Black religion, used to "endure suffering and survive as it helped blacks get through heartache with the music of the soil and the soul." But it was not without shortcomings; its patriarchal structure was not reflective of the same democracy it was fighting for. In mid-nineteenth-century Philadelphia, Jarena Lee was one of the few to crack the glass ceiling of misogyny to become the first woman authorized to preach in the A.M.E. Church. Gender-based discrimination in American religious institutions has gone relatively unchanged. It has never been uncommon for religious institutions to use the Bible to inform the societal roles of men and women, but women have often found themselves on the bottom of a divine social order. It was the desire for an egalitarian spirituality that made Lee ask the fundamental question: "If the man may preach, because the Saviour died for him, why not the woman? Seeing he died for her also. Is he not a whole Saviour, instead of a half one?"

How often do we stop and ask, have women's voices been heard? How have Black women shown up and been prevented from showing up in our history? What issues are unique to their experiences with power and how would they like those experiences to be shaped for the betterment of themselves? Not out of some narrow politics of identity, but because if we apply a humanity ethic, these are important questions to ask. To see humanity is to understand how different people and groups have issues unique unto themselves. That they have shared issues with white women—suffrage, battery, domestic service, obligatory childbearing, and the like—but have never stood on equal social standing with them, so often excluded from their movements. And while they have shared in the struggles of freedom and heritage with Black men, there have been gross deficits in terms of their labor and voices within male-dominated organizations.

The women of the Combahee River Collective, a small organization that included those like Audre Lorde, Barbara Smith, and Demetia Frazier, began their own group as an escape from the homophobia and misogyny within the Civil Rights Movement, and the racism and a lack of racial awareness in the mainstream feminist movement, writing, "I want to situate black lesbian and gay life in its appropriate context of Black social, political and cultural experience."

They saw their liberation as a nonnegotiable and struggled for personal autonomy. Of course, there were also those like activist Fannie Lou Hamer who joked, "I got a black husband, six feet three, 240 pounds, with a 14 shoe, that I don't want to be liberated from." She also connected abortion with eugenic attempts to exterminate people of color, because she knew the wound of such racist machinations personally. In 1961, Hamer became one of the thousands of Black women who suffered a forced sterilization. As Lorraine Hansberry wrestled with her own identity, she hoped that one day America would look back and truly recognize what women had contributed to democracy, and that there have always been remarkable men and women willing to die and protect the rights of women, but that sexism and heteronormative ideologies excluded many voices from being heard.

Much of Black history connects to the politics of revolution. David Walker, the Black American abolitionist, activist, and political writer, was one of the most fearless and harshest critics of American slavery. His 1830 manifesto, *David Walker's Appeal, in Four Articles; Together with a Preamble, to the Coloured Citizens of the World, but in Particular, and Very Expressly, to Those of the United States of America,* was meant to inspire action. It was immortalized in Black political thought up until the Civil Rights Movement in the 1960s. It has been believed that in the political interest of democracy, there must be those who speak the truth and expose lies. The

Greeks termed this nonviolent political act *Parrhesia*, meaning "to tell the truth," or "to speak freely," or "to speak boldly." Indeed, it is a form of speech that takes courage, for speaking truth to power entails great risk. It is one unafraid to speak in critique of themselves or of popular opinion, if they believe there is a fundamental wrong. It is a tool of the less against the more powerful. Or as philosopher Michel Foucault pronounced:

> Parrhesia is a verbal activity in which a speaker expresses his personal relationship to truth and risks his life because he recognizes truth-telling as a duty to improve or help other people (as well as himself). In parrhesia, the speaker uses his freedom and chooses frankness instead of persuasion, truth instead of falsehood or silence, the risk of death instead of life and security, criticism instead of flattery, and moral duty instead of self-interest and moral apathy.

David Walker's *Appeal* was an act of parrhesia. A devout Christian, he plunged a spiritual knife into the underbelly of America. As an evangelical, he might have believed he was a conduit channeling the electric wrath of God. His plan was contemptuous and unlikely, but his words were so full of fire that we can still see the smoke rising from 1830. America must immediately end slavery, or else, he warned. If not, Black people should take their freedom by any means available to them:

> Having travelled over a considerable portion of these United States, and having, in the course of my travels, taken the most accurate observations of things as they exist—the result of my observations has warranted the full and unshaken conviction, that we, (coloured people of these United States,) are the most degraded, wretched, and abject set of beings that ever lived since the world began; and I pray God that none like us ever may live again until time shall be no more.

As if anticipating the argument that "America didn't invent slavery," he goes on to ask his audience to prove a time in history where any enslaved people were ever considered beneath the status of a human being. Then he asks:

> Can a man of colour buy a piece of land and keep it peaceably? Will not some white man try to get it from him, even if it is in a mud hole? I need not

comment any farther on a subject which all, both black and white, will readily admit. But I must, really, observe that in this very city [Boston], when a man of colour dies, if he owned any real estate, it most generally falls into the hands of some white person. The wife and children of the deceased may weep and lament if they please, but the estate will be kept snug enough by its white possessor.

He is bold in his call to arms when he says:

It is no more harm for you to kill a man, who is trying to kill you, than it is for you to take a drink of water when thirsty." And he lays stake to a claim in America paid for by blood, sweat, and tears. "Will any of us leave our homes and go to Africa? I hope not. . . . Let no man of us budge one step and let slaveholders come to beat us from our country. America is more our country, than it is the whites—we have enriched it with our blood and tears. The greatest riches in all America have arisen from our blood and tears:—and will they drive us from our property and homes, which we have earned with our blood? They must look sharp or this very thing will bring swift destruction upon them. The Americans have got so fat on our blood and groans, that they have almost forgotten the God of armies. But let them go on."

He then brings up the contradiction perhaps for the first time that will be used over and over as a political critique of America all the way into modern history:

See your Declaration Americans!!! Do you understand your own language? Hear your language, proclaimed to the world, July 4th, 1776—"We hold these truths to be self-evident—that ALL MEN ARE CREATED EQUAL!! that they are endowed by their Creator with certain unalienable rights; that among these are life, liberty, and the pursuit of happiness!!" Compare your own language above, extracted from your Declaration of Independence, with your cruelties and murders inflicted by your cruel and unmerciful fathers and yourselves on our fathers and on us—men who have never given your fathers or you the least provocation!!!!!!

The unapologetic demands of the appeal resonated powerfully with some, while others shuddered in fear. Walker mysteriously died in 1830, the same year he published the third volume of his appeal. Though available sources concluded his death was natural, many in the Black community believed he was murdered, which could not be ruled out. They say his body was found slumped on his doorstep. Once the appeal spread through the colonies, it raised so much fear that white Southern planters and political leaders acted, and the governor of Georgia offered a cash reward of an exorbitant $10,000 for his capture. Walker knew the risk he was taking publishing his documents, concluding that he would be imprisoned or killed; he was a man marked for death. He spent his last days stalked by bounty hunters eager for the reward.

The revolutionary energy of Walker never left. During the first Red Scare of the early twentieth century, Americans were already deep into the Cold War with the Soviet Union, and deeply suspicious of communism. Communism is most associated with collectivized control of production, Chinese famine, Russian gulags, and millions of dead under authoritarian regimes. But like democracy, it has also attracted numbers of Black people, not because of its worst realities but because of its best promises.

Far from victims of communist propaganda, many were jaded by the slow progress of democracy and were drawn to the sunnier promises of racial ambivalence and working-class solidarity. Many Black political movements and organizations like the NAACP had lost focus on the poor. Black elites and the middle class garnered oversized attention. From the early 1920s and 1930s, the communist party left a footprint in Black history. It was they who gave the Scottsboro case international attention, where nine Black boys were falsely accused and imprisoned for raping a white woman in 1931. In 1932, nineteen-year-old communist Angelo Herndon was arrested under "servile insurrection law," for organizing a peaceful demonstration of unemployed workers in Atlanta, an arrest that sparked protests and exposed Black people to the race-conscious militancy of the communist party.

Black citizens like Robert F. Williams affirmed his Second Amendment right of the people to keep and bear arms, outlining his ideas in the 1962 manifesto *Negroes with Guns*. A tenacious defender of Black life, the

World War II veteran formed a rifle club determined to "meet violence with violence." Similar groups like the Deacons for Defense and Justice sprang up in Louisiana, Arkansas, Mississippi, and Alabama, not in the spirit of aggression but in self-defense. The passage of time often obscures historical connections. But it'd be hard to argue that the same desire for security, self-assurance, and lack of trust in police protection isn't what drove Black gun ownership up 58.2 percent in 2020. *This Nonviolent Stuff'll Get You Killed: How Guns Made the Civil Rights Movement Possible* (2014), by Charles E. Cobb Jr., is a fascinating read. Cobb makes the case that self-defense was a much larger part of the Black freedom struggle than we tend to think. Spearheaded by returning world war veterans, the practical and firm use of firearms against white terrorist groups wasn't a fringe occurrence in a remote corner of the Civil Rights Movement; it was a deliberate and well-thought-out part of it. Nonviolence is the key memory in Martin Luther King Jr.'s story, but according to his advisor Glenn Smiley, considering the real and present danger to himself and his family in the 1950s, King's home was "an arsenal." Only when he placed the fear driving him to keep a gun within the framework of his Christian faith did he leave his life to God, determining that he would walk in the shadow of death without firearms.

But it was from this little-known corner of the Civil Rights Movement, the one that advocated armed self-reliance, that the Black radicals talking Black Power, wearing black leather jackets, and carrying black rifles showed up on the national stage. The most visible group was called the Black Panther Party for Self-Defense. Most known for militance, they were a product of history. The militant groups of the Civil Rights Movement before them are rarely discussed. But the Panthers were directly inspired by those in Lowndes County, Alabama, where there was so much anti-Black violence and voter suppression that the county was nicknamed "Bloody Lowndes." This was also the title of a fascinating book by Hasan Kwame Jefferies, who calls on us to view the struggle for civil rights as a continuous and unbroken struggle beginning in the dusk of the Civil War.

One of the Panthers' most charismatic leaders, Fred Hampton, leader of the Chicago Black Panther Party, formed the Rainbow Coalition in 1969, an anti-racist, class-conscious, multiracial movement. Only a few years prior

to his death, Hampton graduated with honors from Proviso East High
School in Maywood, Illinois, where he had been the youth director of the
NAACP, growing its membership to five hundred members in a town of
only twenty-seven thousand. In high school, he registered people to vote
and led walkouts protesting Black students' exclusion from nominating a
Black homecoming queen.

Hampton was murdered eight months after forming the Rainbow Coalition, as he slept next to his partner, who was nine months pregnant. It
was a concerted effort of the Chicago Police Department and organized by
the FBI. A 1978 book by the National Lawyers Guild called *Counterintelligence: A Documentary Look at America's Secret Police* details how the US
government worked to discredit Black leaders in their own communities.
Blackmailing, intimidating, entrapping, infiltrating, surveilling, and attempting to subvert movements. People were wiretapped. Fake letters were
sent to opposing groups forcing rifts where there were potential coalitions.
All of this helped to shape a historic narrative that painted the civil rights
and radical movement as an inherently disruptive threat, which could only
be controlled through militarized police, law, and order.

There is a long list of assassinated civil rights leaders, which fulfilled the
ominous mission of FBI director J. Edgar Hoover to prevent "the rise of a
black messiah." Overarching everything is the salient truth that, in the telling of American history, you can be white and revolutionary but not Black
and revolutionary. And so the phrase "Give me liberty, or give me death!"
by orator Patrick Henry is considered a quintessential revolutionary phrase
in American history, while Malcolm X, who said it's "the ballot or the bullet," is viewed as menacing.

Notwithstanding the scant attention Black conservative history has received, a fair and open-minded survey of history must make room for this
school of political thought. For as much as they are summarily dismissed as
race traitors—found guilty in the court of Black opinion (and Black Twitter) as disloyal—and then rejected with the egregious Jim Crow–era label
of *coon*, taking a conservative political stance does not make one any less
Black. Even if the majority sees them as acting outside the best interests of
Black people.

One of the earliest was C. H. J. Taylor, or Charles Henry James Taylor, a formerly enslaved man turned successful lawyer, whose pamphlet, *Whites and Blacks, or The Question Settled*, was published in 1889. It ideologically linked him with the Democratic Party, who, as the party of segregation and disenfranchisement at the time, was loathed by most Black people. He urged Black people to move beyond the dead past of slavery, criticized the loyalty of African Americans to the Republican Party, and said that Blacks in the South would only achieve civil liberty by fostering a better relationship with white Southerners.

Taylor harbored a rare sympathy toward white people, writing of slavery, essentially saying, hey if you were white, you would have done the same thing. "Prove to the south that you understand individual responsibility as a citizen," he said, "and that you are not filled with prejudice toward them, then will come your political emancipation and with it all that any other citizen enjoys." Some of Taylor's thoughts landed on common ground. He believed the Republican Party, who'd allied themselves to Black progress during Reconstruction, had now taken their vote for granted. He thought that the party cared more about Black votes than Black people.

Overlooked by the modern feminist thinkers who invoke her name is the fact that much of Zora Neale Hurston's professed thoughts and views were unapologetically conservative. But this was during the Harlem Renaissance when, during the 1920s and 1930s, democratic debate thrived from the comfort of living rooms to the more structured settings of Black universities. Hundreds of writers, artists, musicians, and intellectuals produced vast amounts of work, seeking and finding themselves, crafting ideas about everything from politics to what it means to be Black.

Anticipating the ad hominem attacks, Hurston challenged Black people to drop the pejoratives of "uncle tom" and "sell-out," and look at her thoughts on their own merit. When speaking on *Brown v. Board of Education*, she looked at the US Supreme Court decision not as an honor but as an insult. Daring to ask, why should Black Americans trade their dignity to forcibly associate with the white people who hated them? Weary with the notion of Black racial pessimism, she went on:

I am not tragically colored. There is no great sorrow dammed up in my soul, nor lurking behind my eyes. I do not mind at all. I do not belong to the sobbing school of Negrohood who hold that nature somehow has given them a lowdown dirty deal and whose feelings are all hurt about it. Even in the helter-skelter skirmish that is my life, I have seen that the world is to the strong regardless of a little pigmentation. No, I do not weep at the world—I am too busy sharpening my oyster knife.

Hurston unsettles the narrow view of Blackness. The view of how those abundant in melanin are supposed to act or think. Here is a woman from the heart of the South, in Notasulga, Alabama, who moved to the first incorporated Black town in America, Eatonville, Florida, and whose fearless voice clashed with the racial politics of her era. At a time when it was expected that everyone who was Black not only talk about the race problem but talk about it the same way. Here is someone who shared her own perspective, no matter if it was a circle in the square hole of Black politics. If the drama of Black history has played out through oppression, Hurston was unafraid to improvise and go off script. Projecting a humanistic intellect, she went on, "My interest lies in what makes a man or a woman do such-and-so, regardless of his color."

Perhaps no one presented the complexity of thought, feeling, and spirit more than journalist George Schuyler. If he is recognized at all, it is not on the list of canonical Black writers. He is better known for controversy, merciless wit, and the ultraconservative views he held in the second half of his life. But Schuyler negotiated two identities in stark contrast. In his early life, he was a member of the Socialist Party of America and Friends of Negro Freedom, the latter group founded by A. Philip Randolph and radical writer Chandler Owen. An active member of the NAACP through the 1930s and early 1940s, he penned articles like "The Caucasian Problem," "Battering Down the Barriers of Prejudice," and "Scripture for Lynchers." But Schuyler was always an insurgent critic. With a penchant for frustrating Black liberals, he took the position that Blacks were essentially white, saying a Black man "is merely a lampblacked Anglo-Saxon.... Aside from his color, which ranges from very dark brown to pink, your American Negro is just plain American. Negroes and Whites from the same localities in this country talk, think, and act about the same." He went on to say that the idea of Blackness was sold by the media, and that every single Black person in America, no matter how Black they claimed to be, was educated in white institutions, developed under white influence, studied from the same books, and participated in the same market economy as white people. With a penchant for pestering Marcus Garvey and his brand of Black nationalism, he called the political activist a "Master Megalomaniac," saying, "all Garvey ever freed Negroes from was their hard-earned cash."

A true Jekyll-and-Hyde persona, Schuyler also wrote some sixty-eight articles from 1928 to 1938 under the pseudonym Samuel I. Brooks, a Black militant who shared Garvey's vision. Around the same time, he was criticizing Garvey. Then George Schuyler criticized his own alter ego. Later he debated Malcolm X, railed against Martin Luther King Jr. winning the Nobel Peace Prize, and held little appreciation for the Civil Rights Movement, saying it legally forced race relations. Schuyler praised American progress and its "capacity for change and adjustment inherent in the system of individual initiative and decentralized authority to which we must attribute the unprecedented economic, social, and educational progress of the Negroes in the United States."

In later life, Schuyler fell into tragic obscurity. Very little has been written about Black moderates and conservatives. Historians, scholars, and journalists focus almost exclusively on the liberal left, progressive, radical left, and Black nationalist strains of political thought. But this neglect has left us with an incomplete and one-sided view of history. Buoyed on the self-help agenda of Booker T. Washington, Black conservatism saw a resurgence in the Reagan era in the 1980s and again under Bush in the early 2000s. Thomas Sowell, a liberal and Marxist economics scholar in his twenties, morphed into a free-market capitalist conservative thinker. As the modern patron of Black conservatism, he has produced dozens of books since the 1970s ranging from *Discrimination and Disparities* to *A Conflict of Visions: Ideological Origins of Political Struggles*. Though not a stand-in for all conservative thought, there are common themes threading his positions: Superiority of free-market capitalism, the destruction of the Black nuclear family, trickle-down economics, the immeasurability of systemic racism, the ineptitude of government, decreased spending, the welfare state, rational thinking, incentivizing big business, and that crime is the biggest issue facing the Black community are the common talking points of conservatism. Compare this with the progressive platform: Medicare and a living wage for all, investment in communities of color, embeddedness of racism, workers' rights, ineptitude of business, increased government oversight and taxes on big business, visionary thinking, mass incarceration as the biggest Black community issue, and the tear between the two platforms sounds like a crisp piece of paper ripping down the middle.

Other Black conservatives run the gamut from Ben Carson, Walter E. Williams, Glenn Loury, Condoleezza Rice, the late Herman Cain, and Robert Woodson of the Woodson Center and 1776 Unites initiative. Like all political debate, verbal sparring is a constant between the Black right and left, but there is a big reason I think Black conservatism has failed to convert more followers. Aside from policy, there is the refusal of the white-dominated party to allow any internal dissent or criticism from its minority of Black members. I'm leery of any group that demands complete mirroring and non-dissent to maintain respectability. A true accounting, and indeed a democratic one, would hold space for all voices, however unpopular, even if the majority disagrees.

As Black frustration mounted in the 1960s, radical voices like those of Malcolm X resonated more with Black youth. Malcolm, later known as El-Hajj Malik El-Shabazz, was the ideological opposite of Black conservatives and much farther to the left of most progressives:

> No, I'm not an American. I'm one of the 22 million black people who are the victims of Americanism. One of the 22 million black people who are the victims of democracy, nothing but disguised hypocrisy. So, I'm not standing here speaking to you as an American, or a patriot, or a flag-saluter, or a flag-waver—no, not I. I'm speaking as a victim of this American system. And I see America through the eyes of the victim. I don't see any American dream; I see an American nightmare.

After an eight-year term in prison for burglary, Malcolm joined the extremist Nation of Islam, founded in Detroit in 1930 by a shadowy figure named Wallace Dodd Fard. The nation stood on the fringes, with a theology pronouncing that white people are literally "devils." Observers of Malcolm X tend to focus on these bitter notes, and his subscription to the white devil's ideology, and his militancy. He is associated with the phrase "the ballot or the bullet." Many dismiss his tactics as apocalyptic, but militance, though it falls within starker edges of democracy, is as American as apple pie. Take what Abraham Lincoln had to say in his first inaugural address: "If by the mere force of numbers, a majority should deprive a minority of any clearly written constitutional right, it might, in any moral point of view justify revolution."

Malcolm embraced the diaspora and made his movement a global one, this global consciousness reflecting movements into the 1970s, linking the struggle against imperialism in Africa, the Pacific Islands, Asia, and South American countries with the oppression and exploitation of Black people in America. While some Black radicals stood on the edge of democracy, others stood completely outside it. The fight for democracy was much more revolutionary than is typically acknowledged. People have seen possibilities ranging from nationalist to conservative, and liberal to radical. They've shifted from Bookerism to Garveyism, between assimilationist to separatist politics, from liberalism to neoliberalism, and occupied all the gray area in between. Some of us have been fully participatory while others are politically apathetic. Some have sought greener grasses in socialism, Marxism, and communism, though I haven't heard too many votes on monarchy or totalitarian governments. We might disagree on a lot but having a king or political party with zero limitations on their power is not one of them. But by and large Black people have never given up on the promise of democracy.

Our Highest Ideals

In a message that turned out to be prophetic, Ella Josephine Baker, architect of the Civil Rights Movement, consistently called for a divestment away from messianic leaders. Innovatively calling for a horizontal, rather than a top-down vertical style of leadership, Baker knew that if you attack the head then the body will follow. And Baker also knew that you can't kill a headless movement, one that fanned out through cooperative ideas, organizing, and consensus-building. Reflecting on her long activist career for a 1980 biography, Baker said: "You didn't see me on television, you didn't see news stories about me. The kind of role that I tried to play was to pick up pieces or put together pieces out of which I hoped organization might come. My theory is, strong people don't need strong leaders."

Over her fifty-year career, going back to 1930, she spearheaded several of the most venerated Black political groups of her time, such as the Student Nonviolent Coordinating Committee, along with so many other unacknowledged women of the movement like Fannie Lou Hammer and Septima Clark, all who brought their own fire to the fight for equal rights. As I survey Black American history, I am reminded of the words of Baker when I think about how she wanted to pick up the pieces and organize them. That has always been a critical question—how do we come together? There is no one singular Black history or Black nation or American nation as a monolithic whole; we are more like a Russian nesting doll of politics and ideas, similar in so many ways but with many variations. American democracy has overpromised and under-delivered, and if it fails, it will be because it failed to unite people as equals. But a grasp on Black history shows us how it might be reenvisioned. A future where one faction does not seek domination over the other because there is always a humanity ethic that prioritizes solidarity. That is the only reason Black people have been able to push forward democracy in America. Black history was always rooted in the acknowledgment of a common humanity, no matter what religion or how radical or conservative the ideology.

Back in 1968, America walked in the valley of the shadow of the death of Dr. Martin Luther King Jr., who, just after 6:00 p.m. on April 4, was shot and killed by a sniper, firing from a bathroom window in a rooming house across from the Lorraine Motel. Looting, burglarizing, and flames followed. American cities were burning. Pittsburgh, Baltimore, Chicago, Washington, DC. Thousands of national guardsmen poured into cities across the country. King would've understood the riots that broke out after his death.

He remained unshakably committed to nonviolent protest, but also toed the blurry line to sympathize with Black radical anger. But I think he touched the main nerve of Black people when he said: "We are here also because of our love for democracy because of our deep-seated belief that democracy transformed from thin paper to thick action (Yes) is the greatest form of government on earth."

Democracy is not universally loved, but it remains steadfast as one of the worthiest ideals in human history, an idea that can be found in various fragments deep into the past. It is the idea from ancient Athens, *demokratia,* meaning the people hold the power. It has been the communal assemblies in Africa predicated on collective decision-making. Like the precolonial Mossi people, where each social class was represented in the election of a constitutional monarch from eligible candidates, one without absolute power, and accountable to a council of ministers.

It is the idea that people can and should have a direct say and an ongoing stake in the political process. A democracy where a diverse group of citizens come together to solve collective problems. It is the idea of participatory democracy, or some form of it, where politics bring people from isolation and into community, where every major decision is voted on by the people, perhaps through technology, and a solution-based democracy not predicated on the unattainable promises of a few representatives. In this way democracy is not abstract; it is human. Everyday people involved in running the affairs of the community. The best of the Black contribution to democracy was not rooted in material culture or market concerns, but in the ethical, civic, social, and spiritual. It has been the desire to make decisions, to listen to one another, to be accountable to one another, and to strive for justice and the common good.

16

The Crossroads of History

We must go on struggling to be human.
—**Robert Hayden,** *Words in the Mourning Time*

This final chapter ends back at the beginning—with me in the library—searching. I am there again looking for the truth, except this time I'm in the library of my mind. It's not so organized in there, but shuffling through the mess of thoughts I remember my days as a gauche gap-toothed teenager, and it reminds me again of why this all started. In class we were taught a neuron-melting number of historical facts. I remembered none of it. Do any of us really need to memorize the date the Stamp Act was passed or what Civil War battle suffered the most casualties in a single day? What I do remember, however, was how that lack of substance and soul in history sent me on a self-directed quest for meaning. I hoped that by studying the history of Black people I could find something worthwhile about who I was. Only after that did I realize a lack of historical awareness is why we don't collectively understand who we are as humans.

Throughout the book we've explored history as a yin-yang alternation of whitewashed atrocities and a record of progress. We've visited the sunken graves of our ancestors and shown their spirits reanimated through the generations. We've shown history as an anchor, a chain, a tragedy, and a triumph. We've traveled the world together, surveyed lives ranging from militants and coolheaded leaders to ordinary people. We've tested the atmosphere of Black thought and culture, all leading us back to the present. Fears

of nearsightedness and bias typically keep academic historians away from
the last forty or so years—but then again, I am not a historian so let's talk
about the last forty or so years. The way I see it, history lies at the intersections on the map of memory. Since I also believe that history becomes especially meaningful when it crosses into our individual recollections, it seems
fitting to explore how the last several decades of history have overlapped
mine.

History for me began in 1983, the year I was born as the second of three
boys into the loving arms of my mother and father. My parents worked as
educators in the Louisville, Kentucky, public schools, salaries that afforded
us a cramped apartment in a poor neighborhood until my adolescence. Some
of my earliest childhood memories, other than the black Toyota hatchback
that got us around, shopping trips at K-Mart, or a Halloween costume of the
TV character Alf, were informed by Black American culture. Michael Jordan proved that humans could indeed defy gravity, a well-read copy of *The
Color Purple* (1985) sat on our shelf, and with *Thriller* (1982), Michael Jackson outsold anyone who has ever recorded an album. Ever. Though, it was
David Ruffin and the Temptations' bittersweet melodies, lingering with the
smell of fried bacon, that I remember the most. But not long after taking my
first steps, Black America, or rather how it was portrayed, took a turn, standing on the precipice of crack, a cheaper and more powerful variant of cocaine.
Occasionally, I think about the friends I've lost to the despair of dilapidated
houses turned narcotized drug dens, or anti-crack laws that set penalties for
crack possession a hundred times harsher than that of powdered cocaine.
They might as well have been dubbed the anti-Black laws as Nixon advisor
John Ehrlichman later admitted:

> By getting the public to associate the hippies with marijuana and blacks with
> heroin, and then criminalizing both heavily, we could disrupt those commu-
> nities. We could arrest their leaders, raid their homes, break up their meet-
> ings, and vilify them night after night on the evening news. Did we know
> we were lying about the drugs? Of course, we did.

These policies continued into the Ronald Reagan era. And so, we had
police come to our schools as part of the D.A.R.E (Drug Abuse Resistance

Education) program to pass out T-shirts and warn us about the dangers of controlled substances, while some of my classmates were witnessing first-hand the devastating effects those same substances were wielding upon their parents and loved ones. Known as the man who won the Cold War and ended Soviet communism, Reagan championed supply-side economics, forever known as "Reaganomics." His policies advocated economic deregulation, tax reduction on businesses, and a decrease in government spending, except on the military. Massive cuts to education swelled classroom sizes, shrank school lunch portions, kept obsolete books in classrooms, and yet he pushed for tax incentives to accelerate the growth of private schools. It would seem that his administration took the advice of economist Milton Friedman, who described public education as an "island of socialism in a free-market sea." The Republican Party platform in the 1980s was laid out as such: "We affirm our deep commitment to the fulfillment of the hopes and aspirations of all Americans—blacks and whites, women and men, the young and old, rural and urban." But Reagan was against the Civil Rights Act of 1964, and the Voting Rights Act of 1965, because they were "humiliating to the south." I'm not here to argue Reagan's achievements, or lack thereof, but in his last year in office, the Black poverty rate was at 31.6 percent, about three times that of white people .

It is from here that we can see how the pendulum of history swings from the 1980s into the next century. In many ways, Donald Trump did a roundabout to the policies and attitudes of Reagan, taking Reagan's "Let's Make America Great Again" slogan and running with it to the presidential finish line. Both used all manner of white power telepathy and divisive rhetoric to stoke the fires of fear, picking at the unhealed scabs of race relations in America. Democrats pandered to these same racial fears, but under Reagan and Trump, Black people found little reprieve. They flattened the Black identity under a set of overly simplistic myths: Black moral deficiency and welfare dependency was the result of a "culture of poverty." Black lawlessness could be contained with "tough on crime" bills targeting "thugs." And the "dysfunctional Black family" was the main culprit for Black problems. Immigration issues could be resolved by keeping non-white people out who come from African nations and other "shithole countries."

We had seen that same roundabout in a different direction with Trump's predecessor, Barack Obama, whose multiethnic democratic coalition could be sourced back to the organizing efforts of Jesse Jackson, who, in a bid to oust Reagan, vied to be the candidate for the Democratic Party in 1984. Even before Jackson, it was the uncredited efforts of Shirley Chisholm and Black Panther Fred Hampton that proved Blacks, working-class whites, Latinos, and other marginalized groups could ally under a single banner to ignite change. But a Black radical talking about self-determination for the Black community and a Black woman running on an anti-corruption platform were obscured by Jesse Jackson's more popular and liberal Rainbow PUSH Coalition in his bid for president, who in turn inspired the type of organizing that got Barack Obama elected president in 2009.

But back in the 1980s, I had little awareness about the rhythms of politics or how ideas flow in and out of generations. And I certainly didn't understand how the great acts of the past intersected with the smallness of my present. History reveals itself in specs of memory, like when I'd visit my grandparents and flip through the latest *Jet* and *Ebony* magazines that sat on the side table right next to the gray sleeper sofa. It showed up in the memories of World War II service lingering over my grandfather's head like a cloudy envelope, though he seldom spoke on the horrors of war. It was the slices of luscious butter pound cake my paternal grandmother made from a decades-old recipe. It was the goodness of my maternal grandmother, who came north from Alabama during the Great Migration and stood in the tradition of the Black church. She had little but gave much.

Then came the 1990s. Barely taller than four feet, I hugged my father's desert camouflage trouser leg as he went off to join a US-led coalition of more than nine hundred thousand troops to storm the sand on the borderlands of Iraq. The next year, I saw California burn after a jury acquitted the Los Angeles police officers who beat Rodney King for ninety seconds on videotape. Cell phone footage of Black murders and police brutality have become so common now we often forget that the grainy footage of King getting clobbered with billy clubs was the precursor to nationally syndicated anti-Black violence.

Back in my world, the hard basslines of rap music detonated in my headphone speakers as I tried to buffer out the scratch on my Outkast *ATLiens*

CD with the underside of my T-shirt. That rebellious, fun, and fearless music born in the South Bronx, filled with streetwise rhymes, set to brisk beats, provided the soundtrack to my life then. Well before rap folded every other genre into itself, skyrocketing past rock, and eventually fusing with pop to become the commercial behemoth that it now is, there was a golden age. Between the 1980s and mid-1990s, the genre sat comfortably between gangsterism and conscious self-awareness. My immersion into hip-hop culture was complete and total. I never could dance well, but the tone, the attitude, the dress, the parties—I was all in. The music spoke to what I saw and often felt but didn't have the words to express. It wasn't long before the mainstream became obsessed, and the genre superimposed itself into all things American. But when I think of it, like the jazz and R&B before it, America has always been infatuated with Black creative brilliance, but has still failed to prioritize the contrasting social suffering and political wellspring from which it flows.

The years went on. I remember how surreal it felt as I sat in my high school art class. I was painting a papier-mâché tiger I'd sculpted when I glued my eyes to the television screen. My teacher had turned it on in time for us to see the second Boeing 767 crash into the South Tower skyscraper on September 11, 2001, live in real time. The panic. The horror. It was heartbreaking and terrifying. Somehow, then, in a moment of crisis, a divided nation banded together in patriotic sentiment born of trauma. For a flicker in time, we were all Americans.

One of the first firefighters who surged forward into the collapsing tower to evacuate office workers was fifty-two-year-old Ronnie Lee Henderson of Engine Co. 279, Ladder 131, in Brooklyn. The former marine's decision to fight fires was shaped by his determination to see Black people better represented in public service. The Sunday before the tragedy, his wife, Shirley, had an ambiguous nightmare that turned out to be prophetic. It began in a cave with several caverns; she was deliberately digging into the ground. Then she looked around to see others doing the same before being beckoned by a blinding light, and at its end she finds her son crying. So, when she heard about the towers going down, she said she knew Ronnie would not be coming back out. To this day scientists are still working diligently to identify and match the body parts dug out of the charred rubble.

More than a thousand of the 2,753 Ground Zero victims have yet to be found or identified.

A war on terror, an ocean dropping its contents on New Orleans in 2005 during Hurricane Katrina, a financial implosion in 2007. There are frequent crashes at the intersection of historic struggles. Then came hope. "Obama! Obama!" the crowd cheered as Barak Obama gave a speech in 2008. He didn't make it far into his opening before an audience member interrupted: "We love you, Barack." "You know I love you back," he replied with his customarily cool demeanor. And yet, his attitude was not always so glacier, nor his persona so unfazed. Out of all of his books, it is *Dreams from My Father: A Story of Race and Inheritance* (1995) that I found to be the most revealing, perhaps because it was written when he was fresh out of law school, before his meteoric political rise to senator, before his presidency, before he was transformed from a mere human into a symbol onto which the American people projected their hope, love, hate, and fear.

In his first book, we get an unfiltered glimpse of a young American man born to a white mother and Kenyan father, raised by white grandparents struggling with his mixed-race identity in a nation that only sees him as Black. The book deals with the universal themes of compassion, abandonment, and dreams. As he tries to find himself, he realizes the vast ocean of difference between African and Black-American culture. And it is this recurring theme in the book, the struggle for identity, that hits with the weight of an anvil. In the end he reconciles his identity as a Black man and offers this statement: "To be black was to be the beneficiary of a great inheritance, a special destiny, glorious burdens that only we were strong enough to bear."

And then we come back to that historic presidential campaign. Black history was on full display as Martin Luther King Jr. signs sat in juxtaposition to Obama's banners, reading "Change We Can Believe In." Obama gave riling speeches to crowds so big, they could make the NFL Super Bowl jealous. Crowds of forty thousand, seventy thousand, one hundred thousand people flooded in to see him at a rally in Denver. On November 4, 2008, he did the unthinkable. After enough votes were tallied to confirm a decisive victory over Senator John McCain, Barack Obama was elected as the forty-fourth president of the United States. I watched the election from inside a noisy hole-in-the-wall sports bar and leapt up from my seat as the results were confirmed, yelling out with the joy of a Fisk Jubilee Singer. Obama won 95 percent of the Black vote. We didn't know him, but we loved him. It wasn't something spoken so much as felt—in the centuries-long struggle to be at once Black and American—and seen in the tears trickling down our grandparents' faces who could scarcely vote much less envision a Black man as the head of state in the White House with a Black family. Maybe, just maybe, King's dream was realized.

For a moment, we all felt as though we'd soared into the clouds of Black progress. A competent, intelligent Black man with a Swahili first name had become the nation's first Black president. Obama's idealism made us forget that political wings are made of wax, and one can never fly too high or too low. Democracy does not act with the swiftness of a revolution; it only works with compromise and splitting the differences between disparate groups. So, like the Greek myth of Icarus, whose wings melted when he flew too close to the sun, two wars in the Middle East, and an economic recession sent Obama tumbling back down to earth. The headlines were clear as they read, "Obama's team tries to temper expectations."

All good things come to an end. Obama's presidency was the biggest crossroad in Black history since the Voting Rights Act, and that can never be denied, but Black history does not end with his election. As the reality set in that sweeping transformational change was nigh, Obama was flanked by a Republican establishment determined to thwart his policy changes and a growing far left progressive sentiment echoed by those like moral philosopher Cornel West who said Obama was "a black mascot of Wall Street oligarchs and a black puppet of corporate plutocrats. And now he has become head of the American killing machine and is proud of it." I think I fell more into an idea, or rather an open-ended question that was, how much could a Black president, or any other president, really do on his or her own to fix all the problems of Black people in America?

What was clear, though, is that King's dream was only partially realized. Yes, we moved the needle on achieving a multiracial democracy, but when it came time to eliminate what King described as the "sickness that has been lurking within our body politic from its very beginning . . . the sickness of racism, excessive materialism, and militarism," we were far from the goal. If human history shows us anything, it is that human nature will always necessitate a battle between our better angels and darkest demons. Corporate dollars will continue to attract the bribable into positions of power, spirited toward the abuse of power. Financial tyrants on Wall Street will be rewarded for greed, and many of us ordinary folk will continue to worship at the feet of totem gods like Maybach and Gucci. Black value will continue to be determined by its proximity to wealth and status as opposed to a common humanity and shared destiny. Racism will live on in America. And our misadventures in empire will carry us into outer space looking for places to colonize. But history also reveals that we must continue to fight against all of this anyway. If we don't, it only gets worse. The center must hold.

The movement of Black history continued as we came to another crossroads. In 2013, George Zimmerman was acquitted of shooting and killing seventeen-year-old Trayvon Martin after following Martin through a gated community as he walked home from the store with his cell phone, iced tea, and candy. From this came the hashtag #BlackLivesMatter. An online conversation snowballed into a movement that redefined what the fight for racial justice would look like in the twenty-first century. Founded by Alicia Garza, Patrisse Cullors, and Opal Tometi—three radical Black organizers—the movement merged the aggressive strategy of the Black Power movement and elements of the Black feminist movements of the late 1960s and 1970s. What started as a hashtag and a network of committed local organizers turned into a national movement in 2015 as thousands of activists from across the nation converged in Cleveland to "strategize ways for the Movement for Black Lives to hold law enforcement accountable for their actions on a national level."

It has now become one of the largest Black mass movements since the 1960s, born of the people, not from the direction of a single leader, but out of a merging of minds focused on transformational change. The nascent movement began with a focus on police brutality but grew to incorporate groups focusing on everything from bail-bond reform to Black creative joy. But personal joy and national optimism are two different things, and the movement framed Black existence in apocalyptic terms. Black people were besieged in a war. Not just a political battle, but a war on drugs. A war on Black communities. A war on Black youth. A war on Black bodies. There is power in such unwavering resolve as seen in the radical movements before it, but unlike them, BLM has constituted the most racial, ethnic, gender, sexual, and globally diverse coalition of people the nation has ever seen. As a political force, they exercised enough leverage to sway policy, push establishment Democrats off the fence, at least when it comes to naming racial injustice, and sway a large part of the party to become more progressive. As a cultural force it has awakened many who comfortably slept through America's history of racism like the noxious fumes of a smelling salt to the nostrils. They changed the conversation and the way we both publicly and privately talk about race in America.

There has been vicious backlash from those who might've preferred to stay asleep, but the dissent has not only come from white Republicans. As we've studied the history of Black mass movements, it is no surprise that Black activists have not only held America to account but have never been afraid to scrutinize their own ranks. For some, the lack of transparency, diluted leadership, and concerns about how multimillion-dollar donation money has been spent, or where it has come from, have made the debate about the present fight for racial equity more complicated. Ten local chapters broke away from the global Black Lives Matter network in a public statement in 2021, claiming that the national organization abandoned the democratic consensus-style approach that allowed all voices to be heard: "With a willingness to do hard work that would put us at risk, we expected that the central organizational entity . . . would support us chapters in our efforts to build communally." The discovery of a $6 million property purchased by one of the original leaders, Patrice Cullors, only fanned the flames. The stakes were huge—after the death of George Floyd, some $90 million flooded into the National BLM coffers. All three founders have since resigned, though the local grassroots movements and global foundation live on.

It is a strange time for racial justice in the age of mass social media and activist influencers. Surreal events like "BreonnaCon," complete with barbeques and school supply giveaways in honor of the twenty-six-year-old emergency room technician killed by narcotics officers in Louisville, Kentucky in 2020, seemed like it could've existed alongside a comic book convention. I tend to believe that the majority of grassroots activist groups are well intentioned, but it has become harder to differentiate opportunistic grift and a principled desire for racial justice. Even the mothers of slain police brutality victims accused attorneys of swindling and "ambulance chasing," and well-known activists of running after movie and book deals, profiting off the death of their loved ones. This history will be much easier to analyze by a more detached and analytical historian of the future, but as of now, the emotions still run raw. In the present, it is easy to lose sight of the forest for the trees.

All that happened in 2020, a year that seemed to be in contempt of humanity. People wonder how we got there, but that year intersected with the long narrative of Black history we have explored up until now. When I think about the officer Derick Chauvin kneeling on a distressed and restrained George Floyd's neck for nine minutes and twenty-nine seconds, I can't help but connect it to centuries of uninterrupted struggle. For instance, the great-great-grandfather of George Floyd cultivated a hard-earned fortune with his family after the Civil War by diligently working the land, only to have it stripped away by the fraud, racism, and corruption that robbed millions of acres from Black landowners and their descendants, leading to Floyd and his family spiraling into an impoverished existence.

When this past is whitewashed, we are unable to connect it to the present. Movements fade in and out, infight, metamorphose, transform, and change, but the intersections of American history are like déjà vu. The whitewashing of Black humanity and the unresolved issues come with the surreal feeling that we've been here before. The social and economic weight of being Black in a country dominated by white power has lessened, but the burden took a power-lifter's effort to begin with. One thing is certain, even after the gains of the Civil Rights and Black Power Movements, the racial estrangement felt by Black Americans has not gone away, as they continue to see themselves as the recipients of the worst American outcomes within everything from criminal justice to healthcare to the global pandemic.

The crossroads of history can seem invisible as we zoom past them year after year. I feel like I should be absorbing it more, but I can't be alone in thinking that it's moving so quickly that I can't keep up. Human interactions have been reduced to mouse clicks, thumb swipes, and banal thoughts posted in social worlds built to feed on our most vulnerable emotions. In the last few years, the present has flown past like a wave of vehicles at an intersection, and then the COVID-19 pandemic swerved and crashed into all of us, and everything went in so many different directions that my head spun in the divergent chaos. Social isolation, mask mandates, vaccinations, mass misinformation, and six-foot distances. Then there was the presidency of Donald Trump, a man whose civic duty to protect our national electoral process was betrayed by his narcissism, ending his single-term presidency with a catastrophic threat to our democracy that still fogs the future of every American, as we wonder if democracy will survive another flirtation with authoritarianism. Claiming that the 2020 election was stolen, despite American institutions giving no credence to these claims, he fanned the flames of destruction that sent a wave of angry white people storming into the Capitol, holding up the inauguration of President-elect Joe Biden and threatening the integrity of voting rights that people fought centuries to attain. So, when I look to history unfolding, and if the past gives us a sort of map, we can see we have been on these roads before, and perhaps, this time, we can find the right way forward.

I am quite certain we are at another crossroads. One we've been at before and one that we will surely come to again, and that is, who have we been as a nation and what do we want to become? And we can only answer that question by keeping an unwavering commitment to telling the truth about our history. The paradox seems clear, at least to me: America is more interested in Black history than ever before. The beauty of the National Museum of African American History and Culture now shares space in the National Mall with the Washington Monument, while the Lincoln Memorial statue casts the everlasting gaze of the sixteenth president in their direction. Dr. Martin Luther King Jr. has made it into the canon of American heroes during the last forty years. And Carter G. Woodson himself might not have imagined a future where so many Black history books are international bestsellers. But on the other hand (there's always another hand), the progression of Black history has been fought for inch by painstaking inch.

Black people petitioned decade after decade for an African American history museum, and Dr. King was only coronated when his family rescued his legacy from a vicious FBI smear campaign to discredit him. Yes, there is more Black history available than ever before, but we are still wrestling with its whitewashing. History has never been told by being quiet. As Harlem Renaissance writer Gwendolyn Bennett once wrote, "Silence is a sounding thing, to one who listens hungrily." But silences are ear-splitting in our watered-down history books. Silences are thunderous in the Black absence from 1776 commissions and in the stories of America's founding "fathers." Silences blare when we don't acknowledge that America's global cultural footprint is imbedded with the grooves of the Black spirit. Silences are noisy during Black history month celebrations where octogenarian civil rights survivors are given attention once a year, trotted out like trophies of progress. And silences are deafening when we fail to realize that Black people have balanced America's cosmic ledger with their moral vibrancy, its economic ledger with their labor, and its mental register with their intellectual vitality.

Even more, we are still dealing with outright hatred. We can never forget. At a Kroger in Louisville, Kentucky, one I've frequented, a white man killed two Black shoppers after a failed attempt to shoot up a Black church. The congregant members had remembered to lock the doors behind themselves that evening. As I write this, a mass shooting at a Tops Friendly Markets store in Buffalo, New York, is dominating headlines as an anti-Black hate crime. Since 2008, the historical markers placed along the banks of the Tallahatchie River to commemorate Emmett Till, the young boy who was lynched after allegedly whistling at a white woman, have been destroyed. Some were thrown into the same river where his body, tied to a cotton gin fan with barbed wire, was found. One removed marker was riddled with 317 bullet holes, so the latest one is bulletproof. Another one was soaked in acid.

I have come to a stark truth, because of instances like this, that we will never live in some post-racial world. There are those who will never see the stains on the pages of American history. There are those who will never reckon with the horrors of the past. Engagement with history ranges from nostalgic whitewashing to those mining the American myth for examples that maintain their idea of white supremacy. I have come to accept that there are those who will never see America as anything more than an exceptional nation built by and for white people. I don't believe most people harbor such ill intent. Hoaxed into believing that history's sole objective is to foster nationalism or pride, we end up engaging history only as a balm for our fragile feelings or as evidence of our greatness. To the contrary, the real purpose of history should be to find the truth. History should tell us something about the human condition, those things that transcend time and space to help us understand who we are. History provides an opportunity for us to get to the root of things.

The biggest crossroad in that search for truth, at least for me, was when I realized that my heroes had to die. They never existed. Malcolm X pimped. Maya Angelou prostituted. Martin King plagiarized. Frederick Douglass disparaged Native Americans. Billie Holiday was a heroin addict. The Civil Rights Movement was rife with misogyny. Alain Locke internalized racism. James Baldwin chain-smoked and died of cancer. Gwendolyn Brooks conformed her poems to "white norms." All flawed. But they still move us. Still inspire us. All were human. And like most of us should not be pulverized by critique, nor escape it. When we acknowledge the flaws, it makes the fact that so many rose above them all the greater. There are no uncomplicated stories.

And here is another thing: No single narrative has a monopoly on truth. But America has not been so willing to uncover the truth of its own heroes. Behind the star-spangled cloak of patriotism we find much more than flawed individuals, but centuries-old conditions continuously feeding monstrous violence, gaping inequality, and structural racism. Only with truth comes reconciliation, and to keep a light on the truth of American injustice would force a level of transformation and accountability that the nation has never been ready for.

But I fear that Black humanity is often lost in the single narrative of American oppression. The gains made by departed freedom fighters are lost to a defeatism that says everything is so structural and unbeatable that there has been no progress. I have made it a point in this book to highlight the dark cruelty of America's anti-Black history, to point the finger at its perpetrators, and to show its current effects. But the triumphs show the true soul of Black history, not the instances of people who tried to kill it. I remember the words of Earl Hines, the jazz impresario who died in 1983, the same year I was born. In an interview, he talked about how he holds it together in the roughest moments. "I get out in deep water," he said, "and

I always try to get back. But I get hung up. The audience never knows, but that's when I smile the most, when I show the most ivory." I've been inspired by the smiles. I look around and I see a new generation focused on health, community, and always trying to get back as the struggle continues. Joy and happiness are no less important than resilience and tenacity.

So, in the same way, we should not forget to carry the best of Black history forward. Once, there was a journalist for the *Philadelphia Times* who'd heard about such a person, about a man who lived on the top floor of an unremarkable rowhouse, preserving a massive amount of Black history in his apartment. When the journalist went to visit, he discovered the most remarkable Black history collection he'd ever seen. In that building lived William Henry Dorsey, a second-generation Philadelphian whose father escaped to the North in the late nineteenth century by way of William Still on the Underground Railroad. Dorsey transformed his cavernous home into a miniature museum. There were books from floorboard to ceiling. Everywhere lay relics of humanity, with themes resting on American slavery, emancipation, and Black achievement. Fine paintings from obscure but accomplished local artists hung on the walls. Some 388 scrapbooks contained more than thirty thousand carefully assembled pages. A meticulous recordkeeper, Dorsey carefully pasted newspaper clippings to what are now yellowing and frayed pages. The collection housed newspaper clippings on such prominent figures as Marcus Garvey and speeches of Frederick Douglass. He kept a well-preserved volume of Phillis Wheatley Peters poems from 1789, as well as letters by Sojourner Truth. There were volumes out of print even in that time with titles such as *The Literature of Negroes,* and *Tribute for the Negro.* He organized the materials into categories such as politics, the economy, popular culture, art, and religion. There were theological treatises, biographies, family portraits, and articles concerning the desegregation victories happening at various public schools.

In that interview session, Dorsey provided his personal ethos: "It has been my continual aim, as I have journeyed along, to gather every fragment of published matter concerning the colored race. . . . My portraits, books and letters are simply priceless, and nothing gives me more pleasure than to show and explain them to anyone feeling sufficient interest in them to visit me." Dorsey's story inspires me. He was not a professional historian, something we share, but he reminds me that history is preserved anytime someone has passion enough and integrity enough to bring the past forward. Dorsey had the spirit of Sankofa, and a heart to preserve the legacy of Black life and potential.

Rereading James Baldwin, an astute observer of how the past intersects the present, I came across this quote "To accept one's past—one's history—is not the same thing as drowning it; it is learning how to use it. An invented past can never be used; it cracks and crumbles under the pressures of life like clay in a season of drought." We certainly shouldn't drown in our turbulent past, but we should always be mindful of the truth, too—easy stories of endless glory are almost always fabricated. One of the greatest uses of history is to understand the present as an effect caused by the past. Black history is denied because of the racial disparities that manifest themselves in healthcare, education, employment, and housing, and our social discontents trace backward from slavery and Jim Crow forward. But if we are to stay afloat, we must navigate all of this without allowing ourselves to succumb to a wave of struggle or a pool of trauma to be waded in ad infinitum. In other words, if history is only used to confirm our impending tragedy, the soul dies with nothing to aspire to.

Most important, at least for me, is that history is a map in the search for the truth of who we are. I'm certain I'll never find *the truth*, but I have found some truth. Ironically, it always seems to be the things that transcend history—love, death, purpose, inequality, the search for God, you know, the simple things. It's not easy. Questions that penetrate our deepest problems seldom have final answers, but that doesn't negate our ethical responsibility to ask them.

One final word before I leave you here: *ubuntu*. It is a word said in different variations among the Bantu-speaking people across South Africa, but in Zulu it is called *ubuntu*, meaning "humanity," "I am because we are," or "I am what I am because of who we all are." It is the recognition of our interconnectedness. It is the feeling you get when you truly see yourself in the eyes of another. It is the mirror of humanity, which allows us to see in common, regardless of difference. Through the study of Black history, I found my own humanity, and then was able to find that same humanity in others. Because I reckoned with the worst of Black history, I could reckon with the worst of human history, and by bringing forth the best of Black history, I could bring forth the best of being human. And finally, in bringing forth the triumphs of Black American history, I brought forward the truth of the American myth—or, at least, I have tried to. Studying history in this spirit of *sankofa* and *ubuntu* allows us to duplicate that process for other peoples. We could write a book about Native American, Japanese, Irish, Pakistani, or any other group across race, class, ethnicity, gender, or anything else with this same humanity framework and find out something about who we all are.

Despite all this, to find the gems, we must dig through the dirt. The brute reality is that those in power will always seek to control the historical narrative, which in America has typically fallen somewhere on a scale of white-washed to white supremacy, depending on the era. We aren't surprised anymore when they tell us the history of justified wars when millions died in them. Or that slavery was benign. Or that down is up. Or any other manner of historical rubbish. And we have to remember there are impressionable young minds who believe this stuff; I was once one of them. So, we will always have to contest these narratives, and tell our stories, or it only gets worse.

While writing this, I came across an article in the Lafayette, Louisiana, newspaper the *Daily Advertiser* about a mysterious enslaved teenager from New Orleans. He stands in a painting behind three white children. They all smile, but he leans against a tree in the background, arms crossed, looking out into the distance, jaded. His name was Bélizaire. He was enslaved by the Freys, a prominent New Orleans family. It was the passage of time that introduced us to Bélizaire; he'd been painted over on purpose. Only after the painting was sold at an auction in 2005 was he revealed during the painting's restoration. Prior to that moment, he had been erased from history. Perhaps he was an illegitimate child, or the family just wanted to hide their enslaving past. But the story reminds me that the truth will always come to light. They can ban the books. They can paint over us. They can subordinate the oral history of our ancestors, who had a spiritual connection with the stories and didn't write them down. But the rocks cry out. And the graves cry out. The paint chips off. And humanity is revealed.

In a world where people draw a line between their group and everyone else, I have come to the unavoidable conclusion that I must go on searching for the common cause. Nothing is perfect, but the best of Black history for me is the story of people trying to hang on to love and fight for the greater good. It is the story of those who reconciled the irreconcilable, and built the unbuildable, and who fought the monsters head-on but didn't become them. Despite all the attempts to obscure it, and in the face of unspeakable tragedy, Black humanity has never been in question. That is my conclusion. I'll leave you now to draw your own. Never stop learning or walking in the shoes of another. Look to your history and you will find yourself. Then look to another's history and you will find yourself there, too. Now I bid you farewell. I'm off to archive more humanity.

ACKNOWLEDGMENTS

FOR THOSE WHOM I LOVE: my wife, children, mother, father, brothers, family, and friends. For those who saw something in me and gave me a chance. But most importantly for you, my dear reader, for if it weren't for you, they'd be the only ones with this book. I didn't know until I started, but I'd been writing this my entire life, and I hope that you saw yourself within its pages.

BIBLIOGRAPHY

Author's Note

Knowledge is one of the most important things one can possess—and yet, even more important, is where to find it. *The Humanity Archive: Recovering the Soul of Black History from a Whitewashed American Myth* has been my lifelong journey into a labyrinth of libraries, an abyss of archives, and the boundlessness of bookstores. I pulled the first source for this book back in 1995 (well, maybe). Shaking loose my memories can be like smacking a snack machine and waiting for a hanging bag of chips to come out, but if I had to guess, I was about twelve years old. I wouldn't have called myself a scholar then, just a kid stumbling around a library, defying the limits of my limited worldview.

Now, to be sure, this point marks a series of endings and beginnings: the beginning of a decades-long discovery of Black history, the end of this book, and a transition into a broad bibliography spanning the full spectrum of the Black experience. It is a scattered array of sources representing a life of research. For those who read further, I hope the remaining pages act as a guidebook for your further exploration of Black history and also a road map of my thoughts and conclusions. I chose every newspaper, every book, every periodical, and every digital source with care. These sources trace the long and winding path I took to bring you every bit of knowledge presented in these pages.

While many academic research papers are funded with public money, they are not always open to the public, so I hope these remaining pages make history more accessible. I was fortunate enough to fund my research, but with a limited budget, I erred on the side of thrift. I searched the internet for as many free and low-budget resources as possible. For instance, a free website called Freedom on the Move strains under the weight of thousands of "fugitive ads," all of which combine to give a visceral picture of what self-liberation looked like during slavery. And, speaking of pictures, the National Museum of African American History and Culture has a trove of images and artifacts available free to view on the internet. I'm forever indebted to the Internet Archive, which offers millions of free digital books. I hope listing these resources might act as a wrecking ball to the paywall blocking someone from accessing their cultural heritage. So, too, have I listed countless contemporary Black scholars, so if their work is supported, the cycle of Black scholarly life continues. This book sits squarely on the shoulders of the giants of Black historical scholarship that came before me, and I hope their work takes you further into the complexity and dignity of Black humanity.

For a free digital workbook, author insights, and other research resources, head over to https://www.thehumanityarchive.com/book-notes, or just scan the QR code below:

Prologue

CBS Los Angeles. "High School Under Fire for Project Reenacting Slavery." CBSLA, 18 September 2017. https://losangeles.cbslocal.com/2017/09/18/high-school-under-fire-for-project-reenacting-slavery.

Hipkins III, Julian, and David Busch. "Transportation Protests: 1841 to 1992." Civil Rights Teaching. https://www.civilrightsteaching.org/desegregation/transportation-protests.

Jensen, Latisha. "A Portland Parent Found Her Daughter's Textbook Racist. Her Teacher Has a Contract That Says He Could Use It Anyway." *Willamette Week*, 3 March 2021. https://www.wweek.com/news/schools/2021/03/03/a-portland-parent-found-her-daughters-textbook-racist-her-teacher-has-a-contract-that-says-he-could-use-it-anyway/.

Kenworthy, E. W. "200,000 March for Civil Rights in Orderly Washington Rally; President Sees Gain for Negro; Action Asked Now." *New York Times*, 29 August 1963. https://www.nytimes.com/1963/08/29/archives/200000-march-for-civil-rights-in-orderly-washington-rally-president.html.

National Park Service. "Carter G. Woodson." New River Gorge National Park and Preserve, 26 January 2021. https://www.nps.gov/neri/learn/historyculture/carter-g-woodson.htm.

Parks, Rosa, and Jim Haskins. *Rosa Parks: My Story*. Reprint ed. New York: Puffin Books, 1999.

Ruane, Michael. "'I Wanted to See Him Kill a Ku-Kluxer': Artifacts Show a Rosa Parks Steeped in Freedom Struggle from Childhood." *Sydney Morning Herald*, 5 February 2015. https://

www.smh.com.au/world/i-wanted-to-see-him-kill-a-kukluxer-artifacts-show-a-rosa-parks
-steeped-in-freedom-struggle-from-childhood-20150203-1353r9.html.

Sinnette, Elinor Des Verney. *Arthur Alfonso Schomburg: Black Bibliophile & Collector.* African American Life. Illustrated ed. Detroit: Wayne State University Press, 1989.

Theoharis, Jeanne. "How History Got the Rosa Parks Story Wrong." *Washington Post,* 1 December 2015. https://www.washingtonpost.com/posteverything/wp/2015/12/01/how -history-got-the-rosa-parks-story-wrong/.

Chapter One: Whitewashing American History

American Institute of Architects. "2017 Gold Medal: Paul Revere Williams, FAIA." https:// www.aia.org/showcases/23066-paul-revere-williams-faia.

Bancroft, George, et al. *History of the Colonization of the United States.* Vol. I. 17th ed. Boston: Charles C. Little and James Brown. Boston, 1859: 3.

Bayoumi, Moustafa. "They Are 'Civilised' and 'Look Like Us': The Racist Coverage of Ukraine." *Guardian,* 2 March 2022. https://www.theguardian.com/commentisfree/2022/mar/02 /civilised-european-look-like-us-racist-coverage-ukraine.

Carroll, Charlotte. "Report: DNA Evidence Traces Muhammad Ali Ancestry to Heroic Slave Archer Alexander." *Sports Illustrated,* 2 October 2018. https://www.si.com/boxing/2018/10 /02/muhammad-ali-ancestry-archer-alexander-civil-war-slave-dna-evidence.

Case, Sarah H. "The Historical Ideology of Mildred Lewis Rutherford: A Confederate Historian's New South Creed." *Journal of Southern History* 68, no. 3 (August 2002): 599–628. https://doi.org/10.2307/3070160.

Dixon, Thomas, Jr. *The Clansman: A Historical Romance of The Ku Klux Klan.* New York: Doubleday, Page & Co., 1905: 292.

Douglass, Frederick. "'A Suggestion.' (April 19, 1875)." *Encyclopedia Virginia.* https:// encyclopediavirginia.org/entries/a-suggestion-april-19-1876/.

Ellison, Ralph. *Invisible Man.* 2nd ed. New York: Random House, Inc., 1952: 151–55.

Finkelman, Paul. "Master John Marshall and the Problem of Slavery." *University of Chicago Law Review Online,* 1 September 2020. https://lawreviewblog.uchicago.edu/2020/08/31 /marshall-slavery-pt1/.

Flower, Harriet I. *The Art of Forgetting: Disgrace and Oblivion in Roman Political Culture.* Studies in the History of Greece and Rome. Chapel Hill: University of North Carolina Press, 2011: 5.

Foner, Eric. *The Second Founding: How the Civil War and Reconstruction Remade the Constitution.* New York: W. W. Norton & Company, 2020.

Hudson, Gossie Harold. "William Florville: Lincoln's Barber and Friend." *Negro History Bulletin* 37, no. 5, 1974: 279–81. http://www.jstor.org/stable/44176232.

Kunhardt McGee Productions. "Robert Smalls: A Daring Escape." *The African Americans: Many Rivers to Cross* (video series). Episode 3: "Into the Fire." PBS, 2013. https://www.pbs .org/wnet/african-americans-many-rivers-to-cross/video/robert-smalls-a-daring-escape/.

Kytle, Ethan. J., and Blain Roberts. "Robert Smalls's Great Escape." *New York Times,* 12 May 2012. https://opinionator.blogs.nytimes.com/2012/05/12/robert-smallss-great-escape/.

LegiScan. South Carolina House of Representatives House Resolution 5023, 2022. https:// legiscan.com/SC/text/H5023/2021.

Lincoln, Abraham, and Don Fehrenbacher. *Abraham Lincoln: Speeches and Writings 1832–1858*. New York: Library of America, 1989: 205.

Lineberry, Cate. *Be Free or Die: The Amazing Story of Robert Smalls' Escape from Slavery to Union Hero*. New York: St. Martin's Press, 2017.

Lowcountry Digital History Initiative. "Establishing Slavery in the Lowcountry." *African Passages, Lowcountry Adaptations*. https://ldhi.library.cofc.edu/exhibits/show /africanpassageslowcountryadapt/sectionii_introduction.

Maffly-Kipp, Laurie. "The True Story of the Freed Slave Kneeling at Lincoln's Feet." *New Republic*, 1 July 2020. https://newrepublic.com/article/158334/true-story-freed-slave -kneeling-lincolns-feet.

Marbury v. Madison. 5 U.S. 137 (1803). Justia Law. https://supreme.justia.com/cases/federal /us/5/137/.

McRae, Elizabeth Gillespie. *Mothers of Massive Resistance: White Women and the Politics of White Supremacy*. New York: Oxford University Press, 2020: 60.

Multiculturalism: Roots and Realities. Edited by C. James Trotman. Bloomington: Indiana University Press, 2002.

New King James Version Bible. Bible Gateway. https://www.biblegateway.com/versions/New -King-James-Version-NKJV-Bible/

Parker, Adam. "International African American Struggles with Turnover, Morale, Memo Alleges." *Post and Courier*, 20 December 2021. https://www.postandcourier.com /news/local_state_news/international-african-american-museum-struggles-with-turnover -morale-memo-alleges/article_9765351c-5de8-11ec-b78e-37262bb48789.html.

Pennington, James W. C. *A Text Book of the Origin and History, etc. of the Colored People*. Detroit: L. Skinner, printer, 1841. The full text is downloadable from https://books .google.com/books?id=gnZ2AAAAMAAJ.

Poole, Alex. "The Strange Career of Jim Crow Archives: Race, Space, and History in the Mid-Twentieth-Century American South." *American Archivist* 77, no. 1 (Spring/Summer 2014): 23–63. https://doi.org/10.17723/aarc.77.1.g621m3701g821442.

Riddick, M. "Review: The 'Boy' Who Became a Man" Review of *Captain of the Planter. The Story of Robert Smalls*, by Dorothy Sterling. *Phylon Quarterly* 19, no. 4 (1958): 442–43. https://doi.org/10.2307/273121.

Sterling, Dorothy. *Captain of the Planter: The Story of Robert Smalls*. Garden City, NY: Doubleday & Company, 1958.

Taylor, Tony. *Denial: History Betrayed*. Melbourne, Australia: Melbourne University Press, 2008.

US House of Representatives: History, Art & Archives. "Smalls, Robert, 1839–1915." https:// history.house.gov/People/Detail/21764.

Weicksel, Sarah, and James Grossman. "Racist Histories and the AHA." *Perspectives on History*, February 2021. American Historical Association. https://www.historians.org/publications -and-directories/perspectives-on-history/february-2021/racist-histories-and-the-aha.

York, Geoffrey. "Tigray War Has Seen Up to Half a Million Dead from Violence and Starvation, Say Researchers." *Globe and Mail*, 14 March 2022. https://www .theglobeandmail.com/world/article-tigray-war-has-seen-up-to-half-a-million-dead-from -violence-and/.

Chapter Two: Who Are You?

Arthur, Adelaide. "Africa's Naming Traditions: Nine Ways to Name Your Child." BBC News, 30 December 2016. https://www.bbc.com/news/world-africa-37912748.

Bishop, Joseph Bucklin. *Theodore Roosevelt and His Time Shown in His Own Letters,* Vol. II. Gallaher Press, 2010.

Delany, Martin Robinson. *The Condition, Elevation, Emigration, and Destiny of the Colored People of the United States, and Official Report of the Niger Valley Exploring Party.* Introduction by Toyin Falola. London: Humanities Press, 2004.

Douglass, Frederick. "(1869) Frederick Douglass Describes the 'Composite Nation.'" Black Past. https://www.blackpast.org/african-american-history/1869-frederick-douglass -describes-composite-nation/.

Dupree-Wilson, Teisha. "Phenotypic Proximity: Colorism and Intraracial Discrimination Among Blacks in the United States and Brazil, 1928 to 1988." *Journal of Black Studies* 52, no. 5 (15 June 2021): 528–46. https://doi.org/10.1177/00219347211021088.

Durkin, Hannah. "Finding Last Middle Passage Survivor Sally 'Redoshi' Smith on the Page and Screen." *Slavery & Abolition* 40 no. 4, 2018: 631–58. https://doi.org/10.1080/01440 39x.2019.1596397.

Durkin, Hannah. (2020). "Uncovering the Hidden Lives of Last *Clotilda* Survivor Matilda McCrear and Her Family." *Slavery & Abolition* 41, no. 3 (2020): 431–57. https://doi .org/10.1080/0144039x.2020.1741833.

Fanon, Frantz. *Black Skin White Masks: The Experiences of a Black Man in a White World.* Translated by Charles Markmann. New York: Grove Press, 1967.

Freedom on the Move. *The Daily Picayune* 1846.

Garvey, Marcus. "'Look for Me in the Whirlwind,' Freedom speech - (circa) 1924." Speakola. https://speakola.com/political/marcus-garvey-look-for-me-in-the-whirlwind-1924.

Gates, Henry Louis, Jr., and Meaghan Gomez, Michael A. "Muslims in Early America." *Journal of Southern History* 60 no. 4 (1994): 671–710. https://doi.org/10.2307/2211064.

Hiatt, Brian. "Slash Speaks! Inside the Guns N' Roses Reunion and His New Album." *Rolling Stone,* 14 August 2018. https://www.rollingstone.com/music/music-features/slash-speaks -inside-the-guns-n-roses-reunion-and-his-new-album-710144/.

Hurston, Zora Neale, Deborah G. Plant, and Alice Walker. *Barracoon: The Story of the Last "Black Cargo."* New York: HarperLuxe, 2018.

Joiner, Lottie. "'Barracoon': The Story of the Last Slave Cargo, in the Words of a Survivor." *USA Today,* 29 March 2019. https://eu.usatoday.com/story/news/investigations/2019 /03/29/black-history-barracoon-first-person-account-slave-trade/2807580002/.

Jones, Janelle M., and Michaela Hynie. "Similarly Torn, Differentially Shorn? The Experience and Management of Conflict Between Multiple Roles, Relationships, and Social Categories." *Frontiers in Psychology,* 5 October 2017: 8. https://doi.org/10.3389/fpsyg.2017.01732.

Kharem, Haroon. "Chapter Four: The American Colonization Society." *Counterpoints.* 208 (2006): 208, 75–101. http://www.jstor.org/stable/42980005.

Kruglanski, Arie W., and Shira Fishman. "The Need for Cognitive Closure." In *Handbook of Individual Differences in Social Behavior.* New York: Guilford Press, 2009: 343–53.

Library of Congress. "The African-American Mosaic: Colonization." Exhibition (n.d.). https:// www.loc.gov/exhibits/african/afam002.html.

Long, Karen R. "Sociologist Orlando Patterson on African-Americans' Profound Cultural Influence: 'America Is Indelibly Blackish.'" Anisfield-Wolf Book Awards, 17 October 2016. https://www.anisfield-wolf.org/2016/10/sociologist-orlando-patterson-on-the-influence-of -african-americans-america-is-indelibly-blackish/.

Markowitz, G., and Rosner, D. *Children, Race, and Power: Kenneth and Mamie Clark's Northside Center*. Charlottesville: University of Virginia Press, 1996.

Morrison, Toni. *Playing in the Dark: Whiteness and the Literary Imagination*. Reprint ed. New York: Vintage Books, 1993: 47.

Murray, Ch. J. (1854). *People v. Hall*, 4 Cal. 399 (1854). Harvard Law School Library. https:// cite.case.law/cal/4/399/.

National Archives. "Slave Manifests for Charleston: Slave Owner William H. Davis." 2016. https://www.archives.gov/atlanta/finding-aids/slave-manifests/charleston/davis.html.

Raines, Ben. *The Last Slave Ship: The True Story of How* Clotilda *Was Found, Her Descendants, and an Extraordinary Reckoning*. New York: Simon & Schuster, 2022: 130.

Rambaran-Olm, Mary, and Erik Wade. "The Many Myths of the Term 'Anglo-Saxon.'" *Smithsonian Magazine*, 14 July 2021. https://www.smithsonianmag.com/history/many -myths-term-anglo-saxon-180978169/.

Rogers, Joel Augustus. *Sex and Race: Negro-Caucasian Mixing in All Ages and All Lands—The Old World*. 2nd vol. Illustrated ed. Middletown, CT: Wesleyan University Press, 2014: 367.

Rule, Sheila. "Fredi Washington, 90, Actress; Broke Ground for Black Artists." *New York Times*, 30 June 1994. https://www.nytimes.com/1994/06/30/obituaries/fredi-washington -90-actress-broke-ground-for-black-artists.html.

Siekman. "The Brick Wall: Where Was My Black Ancestor Before 1880?" *The Root*, 8 July 2016. https://www.theroot.com/the-brick-wall-where-was-my-black-ancestor-before-1880 -1790855930.

Taney, Roger B. "The Dred Scott Decision," 1857. Digital History. http://www.digitalhistory .uh.edu/disp_textbook.cfm?smtid=3&psid=293.

The Grio staff. "Former American Slaves Played Oppressive Role in Liberia's Past." *The Grio*, 1 February 2010. https://thegrio.com/2010/02/01/former-american-slaves-played-oppressive -role-in-liberias-past/.

Thompson, Mary. V. "Islam at Mount Vernon." George Washington's Mount Vernon. https:// www.mountvernon.org/library/digitalhistory/digital-encyclopedia/article/islam-at-mount -vernon/.

Trust, C. O. T. Z. N. H. (2018). "The Last Slave." *Vulture*. https://www.vulture.com/2018/04 /zora-neale-hurston-barracoon-excerpt.html.

Wolfe, Brendan. "Racial Integrity Laws (1924–1930)." *Encyclopedia Virginia*. https:// encyclopediavirginia.org/entries/racial-integrity-laws-1924-1930/.

Yong, Ed. "How African Americans Use DNA Testing to Connect with Their Past." *The Atlantic*, 27 June 2017. https://www.theatlantic.com/science/archive/2017/06/how-african -americans-use-dna-testing-to-connect-with-their-past/531834/.

Zucchino, David. *Myth of the Welfare Queen: A Pulitzer Prize–Winning Journalist's Portrait of Women on the Line*. New York: Simon & Schuster, 1999.

Chapter Three: Miseducated

"Dr. B. T. Washington, Negro Leader, Dead." *New York Times*, 15 November 1915. https://archive.nytimes.com/www.nytimes.com/learning/general/onthisday/bday/0405 .html

African American Registry. "Tue., 06.27.1905—Ruby M. Forsythe, Educator Born." https:// aaregistry.org/story/a-teacher-in-its-truest-sense-ruby-forsythe/.

Anderson, Erik. "Buried Secrets: Study of Skeletal Remains May Hold Key to Slave History." *Frederick News Post*, 12 April 2015. https://www.fredericknewspost.com/news/human _interest/buried-secrets-study-of-skeletal-remains-may-hold-key-to-slave-history/article _587f3e81-55c3-52ef-b2e0-96ab11990f76.html.

Anderson, J. D. *Education of Blacks in the South, 1860–1935*. Chapel Hill: University of North Carolina Press, 1988: 6.

Bedini, Silvio A. *The Life of Benjamin Banneker: The First African-American Man of Science*. 2nd ed. Baltimore: Maryland Historical Society (now the Maryland Center for History and Culture), 1999.

Brooks, Joanna. "Our Phillis, Ourselves." *American Literature* 82, no. 1, 2010: 1–28. https:// doi.org/10.1215/00029831-2009-067.

Carleton, David. "Old Deluder Satan Act of 1647." *The First Amendment Encyclopedia*. https:// www.mtsu.edu/first-amendment/article/1032/old-deluder-satan-act-of-1647.

Child, Lydia Maria. "Charity Bowery, 1839." The Nat Turner Project. https://www .natturnerproject.org/charity-bower.

Cornelius, Janet. "'We Slipped and Learned to Read': Slave Accounts of the Literacy Process, 1830–1865." *Phylon* 44, no. 3, 1960: 171. https://doi.org/10.2307/274930.

Dalton, Karen C. Chambers. "'The Alphabet Is an Abolitionist.' Literacy and African Americans in the Emancipation Era." *Massachusetts Review* 32, no. 4, winter 1991: 545–80. http://www.jstor.org/stable/25090304.

Dayton, Cornelia H. "Lost Years Recovered John Peters and Phillis Wheatley Peters in Middleton." *New England Quarterly*, 94, no. 3, 2021: 309–51. https://doi.org/10.1162 /tneq_a_00901.

Donohue, John J., James J. Heckman, and Petra Todd. "The Schooling of Southern Blacks: The Roles of Legal Activism and Private Philanthropy, 1910–1960." *SSRN* (electronic journal), April 2000. https://doi.org/10.2139/ssrn.232549.

Du Bois, W. E. B. *The Education of Black People: Ten Critiques, 1906–1960*. New York: Monthly Review Press, 2002: 26.

Du Bois, W. E. B., and B. H. Edwards. *The Souls of Black Folk*. Oxford World's Classics. Reissue ed. London: Oxford University Press, 2009: 38.

Founders Online. "From Thomas Jefferson to Benjamin Banneker, 30 August 1791." National Archives. https://founders.archives.gov/?q=thomas%20jefferson%20to%20benjamin%20 banneker&s=1111311111&sa=&r=3&sr=.

Founders Online. "To Thomas Jefferson from Benjamin Banneker, 19 August 1791." National Archives. https://founders.archives.gov/documents/Jefferson/01-22-02-0049.

Gates, Henry Louis, Jr. *The Trials of Phillis Wheatley: America's First Black Poet and Her Encounters with the Founding Fathers*. Reprint ed. New York: Basic Books, 2010: 8.

Grantham, Dewey W. "Dinner at the White House: Theodore Roosevelt, Booker T. Washington, and the South." *Tennessee Historical Quarterly* 17, no. 2, June 1958: 112–30. http://www.jstor.org/stable/42621372.

Hammond, James Henry. *"Mud Sill" Speech*. 4 March 1858. Teaching American History. Edited and introduced by Jason W. Stevens. https://teachingamericanhistory.org/document /mud-sill-speech/.

Hanson, Melanie. "Education Attainment Statistics." Education Data Initiative. EducationDate .org, 22 November 2021. https://educationdata.org/education-attainment-statistics.

"History of African-American Education in Montgomery County." Montgomery County Historical Society. Retrieved January 20, 2022, from https://montgomeryhistory.org/history -of-african-american-education-in-moco.

Holan, A. D. "In Context: Donald Trump's 'Very Fine People on Both Sides' Remarks (Transcript)." Politifact, 26 April 2019. https://www.politifact.com/article/2019/apr/26 /context-trumps-very-fine-people-both-sides-remarks/.

Irons, P. *Jim Crow's Children: The Broken Promise of the Brown Decision*. Reprint ed. New York: Penguin Books, 2004.

Irons, Peter. *Jim Crow's Children: The Broken Promise of the Brown Decision*. New York: Penguin, 2024.

Johnson, Whittington B. "Free African-American Women in Savannah, 1800–1860: Affluence and Autonomy Amid Adversity." *Georgia Historical Quarterly*, 76, no. 2, 1992: 260–83. http://www.jstor.org/stable/40582536.

Massachusetts Historical Society. "1848: Sarah C. Roberts vs. the City of Boston." Long Road to Justice. http://www.longroadtojustice.org/topics/education/sarah-roberts.php.

Moses, Robert P., and Charles E. Cobb. *Radical Equations: Civil Rights from Mississippi to the Algebra Project*. Illustrated ed. Boston: Beacon Press, 2002.

Noel, J. *Developing Multicultural Educators*. 3rd ed. Long Grove, IL: Waveland Press, Inc., 2017: 122.

Pazzanese, C. "Harvard Sociology Conference to Give W. E. B. Du Bois His Due." *Harvard Gazette*, October 2018. https://news.harvard.edu/gazette/story/2018/10/harvard-sociology -conference-to-give-web-du-bois-his-due.

Pildes, Richard. H. "Democracy, Anti-Democracy, and the Canon." *SSRN* (electronic journal), 13 July 2000. https://doi.org/10.2139/ssrn.224731.

Rochester, Shawn D. *The Black Tax: The Cost of Being Black in America*. Published by Shawn D. Rochester, 2018.

Salmon, Emily Jones, and John Salmon. "Tobacco in Colonial Virginia." *Encyclopedia Virginia*. https://encyclopediavirginia.org/entries/tobacco-in-colonial-virginia/.

Scribner, C. F. "Surveying the Destruction of African American Schoolhouses in the South, 1864–1876." *Journal of the Civil War Era*, 10, no. 4, 469–94. https://www.jstor.org/stable /26977402.

Taylor, K. A. "Mary S. Peake and Charlotte L. Forten: Black Teachers During the Civil War and Reconstruction." *Journal of Negro Education*. 74, no. 2, 2005: 124–37. http://www .jstor.org/stable/40034538.

Tomlins, Christopher. "Reconsidering Indentured Servitude: European Migration and the Early American Labor Force, 1600–1775." *Labor History* 42, no. 1, 19 August 2010: 5–43. https://doi.org/10.1080/00236560123269.

Torrey, Jesse. *American Slave Trade; Or, an Account of the Manner in Which the Slave Dealers Take Free People from Some of the United States of America, and Carry Them Away, and Sell Them as Slaves in Other of the States.* London: J. M. Cobbett Collection, 1822. https://archive.org/details/americanslavetr00torrgoog/page/n118/mode/2up.

Turner, C. "The Burden on Black Teachers: 'I Don't Belong At Your Table.'" NPR, 4 November 2016. https://choice.npr.org/index.html?origin=https://www.npr.org/sections/ed/2016/11/04/500247228/the-burden-on-black-teachers-i-dont-belong-at-your-table.

Tuskegee University. "Dr. Booker Taliaferro Washington." Retrieved January 20, 2022, from https://www.tuskegee.edu/discover-tu/tu-presidents/booker-t-washington.

US National Park Service. "The Sarah Roberts Case." Boston African American National Historic Site. https://www.nps.gov/articles/the-sarah-roberts-case.htm.

Washington, Booker T. "Booker T. Washington Delivers the 1895 Atlanta Compromise Speech." 18 September 1895. In *The Booker T. Washington Papers*, Vol. 3. Edited by Louis R. Harlan. Urbana: University of Illinois Press, 1974: 583–87. http://historymatters.gmu.edu/d/39/.

Washington, Booker T., and W. E. B. Du Bois. *The Negro in the South, His Economic Progress in Relation to His Moral and Religious Development: Being the William Levi Bull Lectures for the Year 1907.* New York: Palala Press, 2015.

Wilgoren, Jodi. "Algebra Project: Bob Moses Empowers Students." *New York Times,* 7 January 2001. https://www.nytimes.com/2001/01/07/education/algebra-project-bob-moses-empowers-students.html.

Williams, H. A. *Self-Taught: African American Education in Slavery and Freedom (The John Hope Franklin Series in African American History and Culture).* Chapel Hill: University of North Carolina Press, 2007: 69.

Chapter Four: The Search for Truth

Adorno, Theodor. "Theodor W. Adorno." *Stanford Encyclopedia of Philosophy*, 26 October 2015. https://plato.stanford.edu/entries/adorno/.

Ballard, Allen. *The Education of Black Folk: The Afro-American Struggle for Knowledge in White America.* New York: iUniverse, 2004: 26.

Barker, Colin. "Some Reflections on Student Movements of the 1960s and Early 1970s." *Revista Crítica de Ciências Sociais*, 81, 2008: 43–91. https://doi.org/10.4000/rccs.646.

Biondi, Martha. *The Black Revolution on Campus.* Berkeley: University of California Press, 2014: 16.

Chapman, A. *Black Voices.* Kolkata, India: Signet Press, 2001: 302.

Chervinsky, Lindsay M. "Vietnam War Protests at the White House." White House Historical Association, 15 June 2020. https://www.whitehousehistory.org/vietnam-war-protests-at-the-white-house.

Clark, Kenneth B., and Mamie P. Clark. "Emotional Factors in Racial Identification and Preference in Negro Children." *Journal of Negro Education* 19, no. 3, 1950: 341. https://doi.org/10.2307/2966491.

Clifton, Lucille. *The Book of Light.* Port Townsend, WA: Copper Canyon Press, 1992: 62.

Danieli, Yael, Fran H. Norris, Jutta Lindert, Vera Paisner, Brian Engdahl, and Julia Richter. "The Danieli Inventory of Multigenerational Legacies of Trauma, Part I: Survivors'

Posttrauma Adaptational Styles in Their Children's Eyes." *Journal of Psychiatric Research* 68, 2015: 167–75. https://doi.org/10.1016/j.jpsychires.2015.06.011.

DeAngelis, Tori. "The Legacy of Trauma." American Psychological Association, *Monitor on Psychology* 50, no. 2, February 2019: 36. https://www.apa.org/monitor/2019/02/legacy -trauma.

Edwards, J. A. "Black Pathways: Examining the History of Race Considerations in College Admissions at Highly Selective Campuses." *Journal of Critical Thought and Praxis*, 10, no. 2, 2021. https://doi.org/10.31274/jctp.11607.

Ferreira, Jason. "From College Readiness to Ready for Revolution! Third World Student Activism at a Northern California Community College, 1965–1969." *Kalfou: A Journal of Comparative and Relational Ethnic Studies*, 20 May 2014: 117–44. https://doi.org/10 .15367/kf.v1i1.12.

Geiling, Natasha. "The Evolution of American Barbecue." *Smithsonian Magazine*, 18 July 2013. https://www.smithsonianmag.com/arts-culture/the-evolution-of-american-barbecue -13770775/.

Gordon-Reed, A. *Thomas Jefferson and Sally Hemings: An American Controversy.* Updated ed. Charlottesville: University of Virginia Press, 1998.

Hunter, Charlayne. "Confusion Fear in Black Studies." *New York Times*, 8 March 1970. https://www.nytimes.com/1970/03/08/archives/confusion-feared-in-black-studies-group -seeks-more-stress-on.html.

James, C. L. R. "The Black Scholar Interviews: C. L. R. James." *Black Scholar* 2, no. 1, 1970: 35–43. http://www.jstor.org/stable/41202957.

New York Times. "The Inauguration; Maya Angelou: 'On the Pulse of Morning.'" *New York Times*, 21 January 1993. https://www.nytimes.com/1993/01/21/us/the-inauguration-maya -angelou-on-the-pulse-of-morning.html.

Nietzsche, Friedrich, and Adrian Collins. *The Use and Abuse of History.* Reprint ed. Mineola, NY: Dover Publications, 2019.

Parks, Gordon. *Gordon Parks: Collected Works.* The Gordon Parks Foundation. Göttingen, Germany: Steidl Verlag, 2012.

Porter, Lavelle. "Should Walt Whitman Be #Cancelled?" JSTOR Daily, 17 April 2019. https:// daily.jstor.org/should-walt-whitman-be-cancelled/?fbclid=IwAR0DnLwJ7nFb694ZHps ImniiQol-X-MLcGATK2CUNmBkfhIrokMjC1kf4m0.

Prosser, Jay. *Light in the Dark Room: Photography and Loss.* Minneapolis: University of Minnesota Press, 2004: 118.

Riland, John. *Memoirs of a West-India Planter.* London: Hamilton, Adams, 1827: 22–23.

Sandefur, Sean. "Photographer Gordon Parks' Work Was Weapon Against 'Racism, Intolerance and Poverty.'" KMUW, 25 January 2016. https://www.kmuw.org/arts/2016-01 -25/photographer-gordon-parks-work-was-weapon-against-racism-intolerance-and-poverty.

Schevitz, Tanya. "S.F. State to Mark 40th Anniversary of Strike." *SFGATE*, 26 October 2008. https://www.sfgate.com/bayarea/article/S-F-State-to-mark-40th-anniversary-of-strike -3264418.php.

Temple, C. N. "The Emergence of Sankofa Practice in the United States." *Journal of Black Studies* 41, no. 1, 2009: 127–50. https://doi.org/10.1177/0021934709332464.

Van Niekerken, Bill. "How SF State's Bloody Strikes Changed Academia and Nation 50 Years Ago." *San Francisco Chronicle*, 6 November 2018. https://www.sfchronicle.com/chronicle_vault/article/How-SF-State-s-bloody-strikes-changed-academia-13362709.php.

Chapter Five: Into Africa

Adams, William Y., "Medieval Nubia: Another Golden Age." *Expedition* magazine, 35, no. 2, 1993. Penn Museum, posted on web 12 January 2022. http://www.penn.museum/sites/expedition/?p=4479.

Aronson, Elliot. *The Social Animal*. 9th ed. New York: Worth Publishers, 2003: 204.

Ayittey, G. B. N. *Indigenous African Institutions*. Ardsley, NY: Transnational Publishers, 1991.

Bai, Haihua, et al. "Whole-Genome Sequencing of 175 Mongolians Uncovers Population-Specific Genetic Architecture and Gene Flow Throughout North and East Asia." *Nature Genetics* 50, no. 12, 2018: 1696–1704. https://doi.org/10.1038/s41588-018-0250-5.

Bayart, J. *The State in Africa: The Politics of the Belly*. Cambridge, UK: Polity, 2009: 59.

Bentley, Amy R., Shawneequa Callier, and Charles Rotimi. "The Emergence of Genomic Research in Africa and New Frameworks for Equity in Biomedical Research." *Ethnicity & Disease*, 29 (Suppl 1), 2019: 179–86. https://doi.org/10.18865/ed.29.S1.179.

Britannica, The Editors of Encyclopedia. "African Music: Musical Instruments." *Encyclopedia Britannica*. https://www.britannica.com/art/African-music/Musical-instruments.

Britannica, The Editors of Encyclopedia. "Zabdiel Boylston: American Physician." *Encyclopedia Britannica*, 5 March 2020. https://www.britannica.com/biography/Zabdiel-Boylston.

Bullock, Alan, Stephen Trombley, and Alf Lawrie. *The New Fontana Dictionary of Modern Thought*. 3rd ed. London: HarperCollins Publishers, 1999: 620.

Campbell, Joseph, and Bill Moyers. *The Power of Myth*. New York: Anchor, 1991: 206.

D'Souza, Aruna. "African History, Written in Africa." African Humanities Program, 4 April 2019. Carnegie Corporation of New York. https://www.carnegie.org/our-work/article/african-history-written-africa/.

Davidson, B. *The African Genius*. 2nd ed. Athens: Ohio University Press, 2005: 101.

Department of the Arts of Africa, Oceania, and the Americas. "Nok Terracottas (500 B.C.–200 A.D.)." Metropolitan Museum of Art, October 2000. http://www.metmuseum.org/toah/hd/nok/hd_nok.htm.

Deutsche Welle. "Cheikh Anta Diop, Visionary Scholar." Deutsche Welle, 16 March 2018. https://www.dw.com/en/cheikh-anta-diop-visionary-scholar/a-43013082#:%7E:text=Cheikh%20Anta%20Diop%20had%20degrees,the%20independence%20of%20African%20countries.

Eglash, R. *African Fractals: Modern Computing and Indigenous Design*. Brunswick, NJ: Rutgers University Press, 1999.

Emberling, G., and B. Williams. *The Oxford Handbook of Ancient Nubia*. Oxford Handbooks Series, London: Oxford University Press, 2021.

Ezeanya-Esiobu, Chika. *Indigenous Knowledge and Education in Africa*. Singapore: Springer Nature, 2019: 69.

Falola, Toyin, and Mohammed Bashir Salau. *Africa in Global History: A Handbook*. Berlin, Germany: de Gruyter Oldenbourg, 2021.

Fauvelle, F., and T. Tice. *The Golden Rhinoceros: Histories of the African Middle Ages*. Reprint ed. Princeton, NJ: Princeton University Press, 162.

Founders Online. "From John Adams to John Taylor, 17 December 1814." National Archives. https://founders.archives.gov/documents/Adams/99-02-02-6371.

Gates, Henry Louis, Jr., Evelyn Brook Higginbotham. *African American Lives*. London: Oxford University Press, 2004: 641.

Graeber, D., and D. Wengrow. *The Dawn of Everything: A New History of Humanity*. New York: Farrar, Straus and Giroux, 2018: 29.

Henze, B. Paul. "The Aksumite Empire. Ethiopia as a World Power." Layers of Time, 2000: 22–43. https://doi.org/10.1007/978-1-137-11786-1_2.

Keita, L. "Two Philosophies of African History: Hegel and Diop." *Présence Africaine*, 91, 1974: 41–49. http://www.jstor.org/stable/24349808.

Levtzion, Nehemia, and J. F. P. Hopkins. *Corpus of Early Arabic Sources for West African History*. Princeton, NJ: Markus Wiener Publishers, 2011: 269–73.

Lopes, H. T., and I. Almeida. "The Mediterranean: The Asian and African Roots of the Cradle of Civilization." IntechOpen, 2017. https://www.intechopen.com/chapters/55745.

Mahmoud, Ahmed M. A. "Sudan's 'Forgotten' Pyramids Risk Being Buried by Shifting Sand Dunes." Fanack.com, 28 July 2021. https://fanack.com/environment-en/sudans-forgotten-pyramids-risk-being-buried-by-shifting-sand-dunes%7E213367/.

Mariscal, George. "The Role of Spain in Contemporary Race Theory." *Arizona Journal of Hispanic Cultural Studies*, 2, 1998: 7–22. http://www.jstor.org/stable/20641414.

Mark, J. J. "The Candaces of Meroe." World History Encyclopedia, 19 March 2018. https://www.worldhistory.org/The_Candaces_of_Meroe/.

Mark, J. J. "The Kingdom of Kush." World History Encyclopedia, 7 January 2022. https://www.worldhistory.org/Kush/.

Martin, J. P. *African Empires: Volume 1: Your Guide to the Historical Record of Africa*. Bloomington, IN: Trafford Publishing, 2016.

McKissack, Patricia, and F. McKissack. *The Royal Kingdoms of Ghana, Mali, and Songhay: Life in Medieval Africa*. Illustrated ed. New York: Square Fish Books, 1995.

Ndoro, Webber. "Great Zimbabwe." *Scientific American*, 1 January 2005. https://www.scientificamerican.com/article/great-zimbabwe-2005-01/?error=cookies_not_supported&code=2758ded2-1d1f-4050-b09f-4c20879bcdbf.

New King James Version. Psalm 68:31. https://biblehub.com.

Niane, D. T., and G. D. Pickett. *Sundiata: An Epic of Old Mali*. Revised ed. Longman African Writers. New York: Pearson College Division, 2006.

Oliver, J. P. *Mansa Musa and the Empire of Mali*. CreateSpace Independent Publishing Platform, 2013.

Painter, Nell Irvin. "White Identity in America Is Ideology, Not Biology. The History of 'Whiteness' Proves It." NBC News, 27 June 2020. https://www.nbcnews.com/think/opinion/white-identity-america-ideology-not-biology-history-whiteness-proves-it-ncna1232200.

Patterson, O. *Slavery and Social Death: A Comparative Study*. 2nd ed. Boston: Harvard University Press, 2018.

Perry, Philip. "Did This Medieval African Empire Invent Human Rights?" Big Think, 22 January 2017. https://bigthink.com/politics-current-affairs/did-this-medieval-african-empire-invent-human-rights/.

Ptah-Hotep. *The Instruction of Ptah-hotep: and the Instruction of Ke'gemni*. Berkeley: University of California Libraries, 1912.

Roberts, S. "Patricia McKissack, Prolific Author Who Championed Black Heroes, Dies at 72." *New York Times,* 12 April 2017. https://www.nytimes.com/2017/04/12/books/obituary -patricia-mckissack-dead-childrens-book-author.html.

Rodney, Walter, and Angela Davis. *How Europe Underdeveloped Africa*. New York: Verso Books, 2018: 69.

Sandberg, C. "Jazz Have a Healing Role in a World Divided by Conflicting Ideologies?" Meridian International Center. http://www.meridian.org/jazzambassadors/.

Sandomir, R. "John Mbiti, 87, Dies; Punctured Myths About African Religions." *New York Times,* 24 October 2019. https://www.nytimes.com/2019/10/24/world/africa/john-mbiti -dead.html.

Sato, S. "'Operation Legacy': Britain's Destruction and Concealment of Colonial Records Worldwide." *Journal of Imperial and Commonwealth History* 45, no. 4, 2017: 697–719. https://doi.org/10.1080/03086534.2017.1294256.

Simpson, W. K., R. K. Ritner, V. A. Tobin, and E. Wente Jr. *The Literature of Ancient Egypt: An Anthology of Stories, Instructions, Stelae, Autobiographies, and Poetry*. 3rd revised and enlarged ed. New Haven, CT: Yale University Press, 2003: 131.

Universität Mainz. "Ant Colonies: Behavioral Variability Wins." *ScienceDaily*, 11 July 2011. http://www.sciencedaily.com/releases/2011/07/110710204242.htm.

van Sertima, Ivan. *They Came Before Columbus: The African Presence in Ancient America*. New York: Random House Trade Paperbacks, 2003.

Chapter Six: Scattered Lives

Adi, H. "Women and Pan-Africanism." Oxford Research Encyclopedia of African History, 2019. https://doi.org/10.1093/acrefore/9780190277734.013.559.

Alice Kinloch Jackson, J. V., and Cothran, M. E. Black Versus Black: The Relationships Among African, African American, and African Caribbean Persons. *Journal of Black Studies* 33, no. 5, 2003: 576–604. http://www.jstor.org/stable/3180977.

BBC TWO. "This Painting Is a Snapshot of a World We've Forgotten [video]." Facebook, 2018. https://www.facebook.com/watch/?v=2192241050791082.

BBC World Service. "The Story of Africa: Slavery." https://www.bbc.co.uk/worldservice/africa /features/storyofafrica/9chapter2.shtml.

Blackburn, R. "The Old-World Background to European Colonial Slavery." *William and Mary Quarterly* 54, no. 1, 1997: 65–102. https://doi.org/10.2307/2953313.

Butler, Alban. *The Lives of the Fathers, Martyrs, and Principal Saints: Compiled from Original Monuments, and Other Authentic Records*. Illustrated with remarks. Vol. 9 of 12 vols. Detroit: Gale ECCO, 2018: 265.

Canadian Museum for Human Rights. "The Story of Africville." https://humanrights.ca /story/the-story-of-africville.

CBS News. "Barbados Declares Itself a Republic, Cutting Colonial-Era Ties with Britain and Queen Elizabeth II." CBS News, 30 November 2021. https://www.cbsnews.com/news /barbados-independence-republic-colonial-britain.

Césaire, Aimé. *The Complete Poetry of Aimé Césaire*. Wesleyan Poetry Series. Translated by Clayton Eshleman and A. James Arnold. Middletown, CT: Wesleyan University Press, 2017: 27.

Césaire, Aimé, and J. Pinkham. *Discourse on Colonialism*. New York: Monthly Review Press, 2022.

Cohn, Samuel K. "The Black Death and the Burning of Jews." *Past & Present*, no. 196, 2007: 3–36. http://www.jstor.org/stable/25096679.

Coles, Robert. "Pushkin's Black Consciousness." *CLA Journal* 43, no. 1, 1999: 54–72. http://www.jstor.org/stable/44324993.

Encyclopedia Britannica, eds. "Western Colonialism: The New Imperialism (c. 1875–1914)." https://www.britannica.com/topic/Western-colonialism/The-new-imperialism-c-1875-1914.

Freedman, Dan. "Why Were Jews Blamed for the Black Death?" *Moment*, 28 December 2021. https://momentmag.com/why-were-jews-blamed-for-the-black-death/.

Gabbatiss, Josh. "Oldest Drawing Ever Found Discovered in South African Cave, Archaeologists Say." *Independent*, 12 September 2018. https://www.independent.co.uk /news/science/archaeology/oldest-drawing-ever-south-africa-blombos-cave-art-hashtag-rock -ochre-a8534696.html.

Gipson, Ferren. "The Story of the Black Madonnas." Art UK, 11 October 2018). https://artuk .org/discover/stories/the-story-of-the-black-madonnas.

Gobineau, J. D., A. Collins, and O. Levy. "Essay on the Inequality of Human Races." Independently published, 1855: 313.

Gomez, M. A. *Reversing Sail: A History of the African Diaspora*. New Approaches to African History. Cambridge, UK: Cambridge University Press, 2005: 13.

Hawks, John, K. Hunley, S. H. Lee, and M. Wolpoff. "Population Bottlenecks and Pleistocene Human Evolution." *Molecular Biology and Evolution*, 17, no. 1, 2000: 2–22. https://doi.org /10.1093/oxfordjournals.molbev.a026233.

Jayasuriya, D. S. S., and J. Angenot. *Uncovering the History of Africans in Asia*. Leiden, Netherlands: Brill Publishers, 2008: 155–65.

Jordan, W. D., C. L. Brown, and P. H. Wood. *White Over Black: American Attitudes Toward the Negro, 1550–1812*. 2nd ed. Chapel Hill: Omohundro Institute and University of North Carolina Press, 2012.

Kaufmann, Miranda. *Black Tudors: The Untold Story*. Reprint ed. London: Oneworld Publications, 2018: 8–9.

Marean, Curtis W. "The Most Invasive Species of All." *Scientific American*, 313, no. 2, 215: 32–39. https://www.jstor.org/stable/26046104.

Mohamud, B. N. "Yasuke: The Mysterious African Samurai." BBC News, 14 October 2019. https://www.bbc.com/news/world-africa-48542673.

Natural History Museum. "Cheddar Man FAQ." Natural History Museum. https://www .nhm.ac.uk/our-science/our-work/origins-evolution-and-futures/human-adaptation-diet -disease/cheddar-man-faq.html.

Ohio State University. "White Slavery Was Much More Common Than Believed." Newswise, 8 March 2004. https://www.newswise.com/articles/white-slavery-was-much-more-common -than-believed.

Prince, C. "The Historical Context of Arabic Translation, Learning, and the Libraries of Medieval Andalusia." Library History, 18, no. 2, 2002: 73–87. https://doi.org/10.1179/lib .2002.18.2.73.

Riddell, William R. "Le Code Noir." *Journal of Negro History*, 10, no. 3, July 1925: 321–29. Chicago: University of Chicago Press, 1925. https://doi.org/10.2307/2714119.

Roark, J. L. (1971). "American Black Leaders: The Response to Colonialism and the Cold War, 1943–1953." *African Historical Studies* 4, no. 2, 1971: 253–70. https://doi.org/10.2307 /216417.

Rodriguez, J. P. *Encyclopedia of Slave Resistance and Rebellion*. Netherlands: Amsterdam University Press, 2007.

Roychowdhury, Adrija. "African Rulers of India: That Part of Our History We Choose to Forget." *Indian Express*, 5 June 2016. https://indianexpress.com/article/research/african -rulers-of-india-that-part-of-our-history-we-choose-to-forget.

Sieff, Kevin. "An African Country Reckons with Its History of Selling Slaves." *Washington Post*, 29 January 2018. https://www.washingtonpost.com/world/africa/an-african-country -reckons-with-its-history-of-selling-slaves/2018/01/29/5234f5aa-ff9a-11e7-86b9 -8908743c79dd_story.html.

Sky HISTORY. "The History of Black Britain: Roman Africans." https://www.history.co.uk /article/the-history-of-black-britain-roman-africans.

SlaveVoyages. "Explore the Origins and Forced Relocations of Enslaved Africans Across the Atlantic World." https://www.slavevoyages.org.

Sutter, John. "Slavery's Last Stronghold." CNN.com, March 2012. https://edition.cnn.com /interactive/2012/03/world/mauritania.slaverys.last.stronghold/index.html.

Tattersall, Ian. "Human Origins: Out of Africa." PNAS, 22 September 2009. https://www .pnas.org/content/106/38/16018.

Twinam, A. *Purchasing Whiteness: Pardos, Mulattos, and the Quest for Social Mobility in the Spanish Indies*. Redwood City, CA: Stanford University Press, 2015: 159.

United Nations. United Nations General Assembly Official Records, 20th Plenary Meeting, Thursday, 4 October 1984, at 10.40 a.m., New York, (A/39/PV.20), pp. 405–10.

van Sertima, I. *The African Presence in Early Europe*. New York: Macmillan Publishers, 1985: 108–16.

World Monuments Fund. "Rock-Hewn Churches." https://www.wmf.org/project/rock-hewn churches.

Yale University. "Anna Pauline (Pauli) Murray, Yale 1965 J.S.D., 1979 Hon. D.Div." Office of Public Affairs & Communications, 9 May 2019. https://communications.yale.edu /media/media-kits/anna-pauline-pauli-murray-yale-1965-jsd-1979-hon-ddiv.

Yeginsu, C., and C. Zimmer. "'Cheddar Man,' Britain's Oldest Skeleton, Had Dark Skin, DNA Shows." *New York Times,* 7 February 2018. https://www.nytimes.com/2018/02/07/world /europe/uk-cheddar-man-skeleton-skin.htm.

Chapter Seven: Appropriate(d) Culture

Antonio's Manufacturing Inc. Beauty Supplier, Barber Supplier, Styling Combs, Styling Piks. Antonio's Manufacturing. Retrieved October 14, 2021, from http://www.antoniosmfg .com/am_about.html

Bate, W. J. *John Keats*. Boston: Harvard University Press, 2009: 443.

Bhutta, N. "Black Families' Median and Mean Wealth Is Less Than 15 Percent." In *Disparities in Wealth by Race and Ethnicity in the 2019 Survey of Consumer Finances,* 28 September 2020. Federal Reserve. https://www.federalreserve.gov/econres/notes/feds -notes/disparities-in-wealth-by-race-and-ethnicity-in-the-2019-survey-of-consumer -finances-20200928.htm.

Butler, N. "Ten Things Everyone Should Know About Lowcountry Rice." Charleston County Public Library. March 2, 2017. https://www.ccpl.org/charleston-time-machine/ten-things -everyone-should-know-about-lowcountry-rice.

Byrd, A. X. *Captives and Voyagers: Black Migrants Across the Eighteenth-Century British Atlantic World*. Baton Rouge, LA: LSU Press, 2008.

Cowell, S. R., C. Seeger, and J. Handcox. "There Is Mean Things Happening in This Land." Audio recording, 1937. Washington, DC. https://www.loc.gov/item/afc9999005 .6543?loclr=blogtea.

Dews, Fred. "Charts of the Week: Black Men's Life Expectancy; Student Debt and Black Households; Struggling Families." Brookings, 26 February 2021. https://www.brookings .edu/blog/brookings-now/2021/02/26/charts-of-the-week-black-mens-life-expectancy -student-debt-and-black-households-struggling-families.

Dobson, J. M. *Bulls, Bears, Boom, and Bust: A Historical Encyclopedia of American Business Concepts*. Santa Barbara, CA: ABC-CLIO, 2006: 146.

F. Fiona Moolla. "When Orature Becomes Literature," *Comparative Literature Studies* 49, no. 3, 2012: 434. https://doi.org/10.5325/complitstudies.49.3.0434.

Farmer, F. M. *The Boston Cooking-School Cook Book*. 8th ed. New York: Little, Brown and Company, 2022.

Floyd, S. A., Jr. *The Power of Black Music: Interpreting Its History from Africa to the United States*. London: Oxford University Press, 1996.

Foner, P. S., and R. L. Lewis, eds. "The Southern Tenant Farmers Union." In *Black Worker*, Volume 7: The Black Worker from the Founding of the CIO to the AFL-CIO Merger, 1936–1955. Philadelphia: Temple University Press, 1983. https://doi.org/10.2307/j .ctvn1tch8.6.

Gates Jr., Henry Louis. *Stony the Road: Reconstruction, White Supremacy, and the Rise of Jim Crow*. Reprint ed. New York: Penguin Books, 2020: 216.

Gates Jr., Henry Louis, and M. Tatar. *The Annotated African American Folktales*. Annotated ed. New York: Liveright Publishing Corporation, 2017: 73–77.

Gillette, F. L., and Hugo Ziemann. *White House Cook Book: A Comprehensive Cyclopedia of Information for the Home*. 1887 ed. Media Solution Services, 2021.

Gordon, L. *The Second Coming of the KKK: The Ku Klux Klan of the 1920s and the American Political Tradition*. New York: Liveright Publishing Corporation, 2018.

Greenwood, Veronica. "Where Your Watermelon Came From," *New York Times*, 28 May 2021. https://www.nytimes.com/2021/05/28/science/watermelons-genome-origins.html.

Handcox, J. L. "Roll the Union On." Smithsonian Folkways Recordings, 1947. https:// folkways.si.edu/john-handcox/roll-the-union-on/american-folk-struggle-protest/music /track/smithsonian.

Honey, M. K. *Sharecropper's Troubadour: John L. Hancox, the Southern Tenant Farmers' Union, and the African American Song Tradition*. New York: Palgrave Macmillan, 2013.

Hopkins, P., and D. McDowell. *Of One Blood: Or, the Hidden Self: The Givens Collection*. New York: Washington Square Press, 2004.

Kai, N. *Kuma Malinke Historiography: Sundiata Keita to Almamy Samori Toure*. Illustrated ed. New York: Lexington Books, 2014.

Larson, J. B. "Tina Bell's Hidden Legacy: The Black Woman Who Created the Sound of Grunge." PleaseKillMe. September 3, 2020. https://pleasekillme.com/bam-bam-tina-bell.

Library of Congress. "Railroads in the Late 19th Century." https://www.loc.gov/classroom
-materials/united-states-history-primary-source-timeline/rise-of-industrial-america-1876
-1900/railroads-in-late-19th-century.

Lott, E. *Black Mirror: The Cultural Contradictions of American Racism*. Boston: The Belknap
Press, 2013: 33–34.

Lott, E., and G. Marcus. *Love & Theft: Blackface Minstrelsy and the American Working Class*.
20th ed. London: Oxford University Press, 2013: 122.

Marovich, Pete. "Can These Descendants of Enslaved Africans Save Their Unique Culture?"
Washington Post, 18 October 2018. https://www.washingtonpost.com/graphics/2018
/lifestyle/magazine/amp-stories/gullah-geechee-culture-south-carolina/.

Mathers, M. Eminem. "Without Me" (lyrics). *The Eminem Show*, 2002. https://genius.com
/Eminem-without-me-lyrics.

McClay, B. C. "Why Black TikTok Creators Have Gone on Strike." BBC News, 15 July 2021.
https://www.bbc.com/news/world-us-canada-57841055.

National Park Service. "John Henry and the Coming of the Railroad." New River Gorge
National Park and Preserve, 26 January 2021. https://www.nps.gov/neri/learn
/historyculture/john-henry-and-the coming-of-the-railroad.htm.

National Resource Council. *Lost Crops of Africa: Volume II: Vegetables by Security, and
Cooperation Development*, 27 November 2006. Washington, DC: National Academies
Press. https://infonet-biovision.org/sites/default/files/lost_crops_of_africa_vol_2
_vegetables.pdf.

Niane, D. T., and G. D. Pickett. *Sundiata: An Epic of Old Mali*. Revised ed. Victoria, BC:
Pearson College, 2006: vii.

Olsen, A., and C. McHose. *The Place of Dance: A Somatic Guide to Dancing and Dance Making*.
Illustrated ed. Middletown, CT: Wesleyan University Press, 2014: 50.

Omer, R. "The Modern and the Traditional African Women and Colonial Morality."
International Journal of Culture and History 5, no. 1, 2018: 30. https://doi.org/10.5296
/ijch.v5i1.13311.

Pennink, H. "Pete Seeger's Uneasy Coexistence with Wealth." *Star Tribune*, 28 January 2014.
https://www.startribune.com/pete-seeger-s-uneasy-coexistence-with-wealth/242445471
/?refresh=true.

Pérez, P., et al. "Conscious Processing of Narrative Stimuli Synchronizes Heart Rate Between
Individuals." *Cell Reports* 36, no. 11, 2021: 109692. https://doi.org/10.1016/j.celrep.2021
.109692.

Rice, Kym S., and Martha B. Katz-Hyman. *World of a Slave: Encyclopedia of the Material Life of
Slaves in the United States*. Westport, CT: Greenwood Publishing Group, 2010.

Risen, C. "When Jack Daniel's Failed to Honor a Slave, an Author Rewrote History." *New York
Times*, 15 August, 2017. https://www.nytimes.com/2017/08/15/dining/jack-daniels
-whiskey-slave-nearest-green.html.

Roberts, Amy Lotson, et al. *Gullah Geechee Heritage in the Golden Isles*. American Heritage.
Cheltenham, UK: The History Press, 2019.

Rubin, R. "'Black Panther' Surpasses 'The Avengers' as Highest-Grossing Superhero Movie of
All Time in U.S." Variety.com, 25 March 2018. https://variety.com/2018/film/box-office
/black-panther-surpasses-avengers-highest-grossing-superhero-movie-1202735863/.

Smith, C. Y. N. "Oral Tradition and the Kennewick Man." *Yale Law Journal,* 3 November 2016. https://www.yalelawjournal.org/forum/oral-tradition-and-the-kennewick-man.

Sprague, Kevin. "The Kola Nut: West African Commodity in the Atlantic World." UCLA Global, 15 December 2017. https://www.international.ucla.edu/institute/academics /article/186740.

Thurman, W. *Infants of the Spring.* Reprint ed. Mineola, NY: Dover Publications, 2013: 142.

Twain, M., B. Griffin, and H. E. Smith. *Autobiography of Mark Twain. Vol. 2: The Complete and Authoritative Edition.* Mark Twain Papers. Berkeley: University of California Press, 2013.

Wallach, J. J. *Every Nation Has Its Dish: Black Bodies and Black Food in Twentieth-Century America.* Illustrated ed. Chapel Hill: University of North Carolina Press, 2019: 145.

Weber, B. "Jeni LeGon, Singer and Solo Tap-Dancer, Dies at 96." *New York Times,* 17 December 2012. Retrieved October 18, 2021, from https://www.nytimes.com/2012 /12/17/arts/dance/jeni-legon-singer-and-solo-tap-dancer-dies-at-96.html.

Chapter Eight: The Fabric of America

Allen, D. "Prince Hall, American Revolutionary." *The Atlantic,* 10 February 2021. https:// www.theatlantic.com/magazine/archive/2021/03/prince-hall-forgotten-founder/617791.

Architect of the Capitol. "Apotheosis of Washington." https://www.aoc.gov/explore-capitol -campus/art/apotheosis-washington.

Armistead, G. "Official Account of the Bombardment of Fort McHenry," 24 September 1814. https://amhistory.si.edu/starspangledbanner/pdf/TRANSCRIPT%20Official%20 Account%20of%20the%20Bombardment%20of%20Fort%20McHenry.pdf.

Bill of Rights Institute. "Fort McHenry and the War of 1812." https://billofrightsinstitute.org /essays/fort-mchenry-and-the-war-of-1812.

Bolster, J. W. "Letters by African American Sailors, 1799–1814." *William and Mary Quarterly* 64, no. 1, 2007: 167–82.

Brockell, G. "Before 1619, There Was 1526: The Mystery of the First Enslaved Africans in What Became the United States." *Washington Post,* 7 September 2019, https://www .washingtonpost.com/history/2019/09/07/before-there-was-mystery-first-enslaved-africans -what-became-us.

Bryant, C. "Without Representation, No Taxation: Free Blacks, Taxes, and Tax Exemptions Between the Revolutionary and Civil Wars." *Michigan Journal of Race & Law* 21.1, 2015: 91. https://doi.org/10.36643/mjrl.21.1.without.

Casas, B., B. de las Casas, H. Briffault, and B. Donovan. *The Devastation of the Indies.* Amsterdam University Press, 1992: 33.

Colburn, D., and Landers, J. *The African American Heritage of Florida.* Reissue ed. Gainesville: LibraryPress@UF, 2018: 23.

Columbus, Christopher. *The Diario of Christopher Columbus's First Voyage to America, 1492– 1493.* Vol. 70. Translated by Oliver Dunn and James E. Kelley. American Exploration and Travel Series. Reprint ed. Norman: University of Oklahoma Press, 1991.

Dennis, Y. W., A. Hirschfelder, and S. R. Flynn. *Native American Almanac: More Than 50,000 Years of the Cultures and Histories of Indigenous Peoples.* Illustrated ed. Canton, MI: Visible Ink Press, 2016.

Douglass, F. "The Hypocrisy of American Slavery." 1852. Frederick Douglass Heritage. Retrieved December, 15 2022, from http://www.frederick-douglass-heritage.org/speech-the -hypocrisy-of-american-slavery/.

Estevez, J. B. "On Indigenous Peoples' Day, Meet the Survivors of a 'Paper Genocide.'" *National Geographic*, October 14, 2019. https://www.nationalgeographic.com/history/article/meet -survivors-taino-tribe-paper-genocide.

Fling, S. "Enslaved Labor and the Construction of the U.S. Capitol." WHHA. https://www .whitehousehistory.org/enslaved-labor-and-the-construction-of-the-u-s-capitol.

Francis, M. J., G. Mormino, and R. Sanderson. "Slavery Took Hold in Florida Under the Spanish in the 'Forgotten Century' of 1492–1619." *Tampa Bay Times*, 29 August, 2019. https://www .tampabay.com/opinion/2019/08/29/before-1619-africans-and-the-early-history-of-spanish -colonial-florida-and-america-column/.

Ganz, C. R. *The 1933 Chicago World's Fair: A Century of Progress*. Urbana: University of Illinois Press, 2008.

Gilley, B. (2018). "The Case for Colonialism." *Academic Questions*, 31(2), 167–85. https://doi .org/10.1007/s12129-018-9696-2.

Gordon, R. A. "Following Estevanico: The Influential Presence of an African Slave in Sixteenth-Century New World Historiography." *Colonial Latin American Review* 15, no. 2, 2006: 183–206. https://doi.org/10.1080/10609160600958645.

Gugliotta, Guy. "The Other Jefferson Davis." *Humanities* 33, no. 5, September/October 2012. https://www.neh.gov/humanities/2012/septemberoctober/feature/the-other-jefferson-davis.

Hannah-Jones, N. and *New York Times*. "The 1619 Project." *New York Times*, 14 August, 2019. Retrieved December 5, 2022, from https://www.nytimes.com/interactive/2019/08/14 /magazine/1619-america-slavery.html.

Helps, A. S. (1855). *The Spanish Conquest in America and Its Relation to the History of Slavery and to the Government of Colonies*. Volume 1 of 4. London: J.W. Parker and Son, 214.

Holland, J. *Black Men Built the Capitol: Discovering African-American History in and Around Washington, DC*. Lanham, MD: Lyons Press, 2017: 5–7.

Key, Francis Scott. Lyrics ("Star Spangled Banner"). 1814. Historic American Sheet Music, Rare Book, Manuscript, and Special Collections Library, Duke University. https://library .duke.edu/rubenstein/scriptorium/sheetmusic/lyrics/Smith__Star_spangled_banner.html.

Kiley, Gillian. "Colonial Enslavement of Native Americans Included Those Who Surrendered, Too." Brown University, 15 February 2017. https://www.brown.edu/news/2017-02-15 /enslavement.

King Jr., Martin Luther. "The American Dream." 1965. The Martin Luther King, Jr., Research and Education Institute. Retrieved December 3, 2022, from https://kinginstitute.stanford .edu/king-papers/publications/knock-midnight-inspiration-great-sermons-reverend-martin -luther-king-jr-4.

Leon-Portilla, Miguel. *The Broken Spears: The Aztec Account of the Conquest of Mexico*. Boston: Beacon Press, 1992.

Meehan, Thomas A. "Jean Baptiste Point du Sable, the First Chicagoan." *Journal of the Illinois State Historical Society* (1908–1984) 56, no. 3, 1963: 439–53. http://www.jstor.org/stable /40190620.

Miller, G. "Maps Show How Tearing Down City Slums Displaced Thousands." *National Geographic*, 15 December 2017. https://www.nationalgeographic.com/history/article/urban -renewal-projects-maps-united-states.

Nobile, P. "The David McCullough Nobody Knows." History News Network. Retrieved December 5, 2022, from https://hnn.us/articles/157.html.

PBS. "British Navy Impressment." *History Detectives*. https://www.pbs.org/opb/history detectives/feature/british-navy-impressment/.

Pearson, E. "Death of Seneca Village." *Gotham Gazette,* July 21, 2003. https://www.gotham gazette.com/environment/1902-death-of-seneca-village.

Peck, D. T. Lucas Vásquez de Ayllón's Doomed Colony of San Miguel de Gualdape. *Georgia Historical Quarterly* 85(2), 2001: 183–98. http://www.jstor.org/stable/40584407.

Rushforth, B. *Bonds of Alliance: Indigenous and Atlantic Slaveries in New France*. Reprint ed. Chapel Hill: University of North Carolina Press and Omohundro Institute of Early American History and Culture, 2014.

Schmidt-Nowara, Christopher. *Slavery, Freedom, and Abolition in Latin America and the Atlantic World*. Diálogos Series. Albuquerque: University of New Mexico Press, 2011.

Smith, J. C., and N. Giovanni. *Complete Encyclopedia of African American History*: Canton, MI: Visible Ink Press/African American Publications, 2018.

Staples, B. "The Death of the Black Utopia." *New York Times,* 28 November 2019. https:// www.nytimes.com/2019/11/28/opinion/seneca-central-park-nyc.html.

Stephens, Ronald J., La Wanna M. Larson, and Black American West Museum. *African Americans of Denver*. Illustrated ed. Mt. Pleasant, SC: Arcadia Publishing, 2008.

The Geography of Slavery in Virginia. "Official Records—Virginia Laws 1751–1800." University of Virginia. http://www2.vcdh.virginia.edu/gos/laws1751-1800.html.

Trinidad and Tobago National Library. "The Merikins: Free Black Settlers 1815–1816." National Library and Information System Authority. Retrieved December 11, 2022, from https://www.nalis.gov.tt/Resources/Subject-Guide/Merikins.

US National Park Service. "Grace Wisher." Fort McHenry National Monument and Historic Shrine. https://www.nps.gov/fomc/learn/historyculture/grace-wisher.htm.

US National Park Service. "William Williams." Fort McHenry National Monument and Historic Shrine. https://www.nps.gov/fomc/learn/historyculture/william-williams.htm.

Wesley, C. H. "Prince Hall: Life and Legacy." United Supreme Council, Southern Jurisdiction, Prince Hall Affiliation, 1977: 89.

Wilson, C. "Where's the Debate on Francis Scott Key's Slave-Holding Legacy?" *Smithsonian Magazine,* 1 July 2016. https://www.smithsonianmag.com/smithsonian-institution/wheres -debate-francis-scott-keys-slave-holding-legacy-180959550.

York, Neil L. *The Boston Massacre: A History with Documents*. Oxfordshire, UK: Routledge Company, 2010.

Chapter Nine: Resistance! Resistance! Resistance!

Alexander, Leslie M., and Walter C. Rucker. *Encyclopedia of African American History* [3 volumes]. Santa Barbara, CA: ABC-CLIO, 2010: 477.

Alexander, Michelle. *The New Jim Crow: Mass Incarceration in the Age of Colorblindness*. 10th anniversary ed. New York: The New Press, 2020: 2.

Ball, E. "Retracing Slavery's Trail of Tears." *Smithsonian Magazine.* November 2015. https://
www.smithsonianmag.com/history/slavery-trail-of-tears-180956968.

Berry, J. *City of a Million Dreams: A History of New Orleans at Year 300.* Chapel Hill:
University of North Carolina Press, 2021: 95.

Blakemore, E. "The Louisiana Purchase Was a Bargain. But It Came at a Great Human Cost."
History, 2021. https://www.nationalgeographic.com/history/article/louisiana-purchase
-bargain-came-great-human-cost?loggedin=true.

Coffin, L. (2014b). *Reminiscences of Levi Coffin: The Reputed President of the Underground
Railroad; Being a Brief History of the Labors of a Lifetime in Behalf of the . . . Instrumentality,
and Many Other Incidents.* Calumet, MI: CreateSpace Independent Publishing Platform,
2014: 298.

Dubois, Leslie. *Avengers of the New World: The Story of the Haitian Revolution.* Boston: The
Belknap Press, 2005: 110.

Dun, J. A. *Dangerous Neighbors: Making the Haitian Revolution in Early America.*
Philadelphia: University of Pennsylvania Press, 2016: 144.

Eakin, Emily. "Bigotry as Mental Illness or Just Another Norm." *New York Times,* 15 January
2000. https://www.nytimes.com/2000/01/15/arts/bigotry-as-mental-illness-or-just
-another-norm.html.

Eberhart, George. "Newsmaker: Eric Foner—Historian Discusses Slavery's Hidden History."
American Libraries Magazine, 27 October 2015. https://americanlibrariesmagazine.org
/2015/10/27/slaverys-hidden-history-eric-foner/.

Egerton, Douglas R. *He Shall Go Out Free: The Lives of Denmark Vesey.* Lanham, MD:
Rowman & Littlefield, 2004.

Encyclopedia.com. "American Reaction to the Haitian Revolution." Retrieved December 27,
2021, from https://www.encyclopedia.com/history/encyclopedias-almanacs-transcripts
-and-maps/american-reaction-haitian-revolution.

Foner, Eric. *Gateway to Freedom: The Hidden History of the Underground Railroad.* Reprint ed.
New York: W. W. Norton & Company, 2016.

Funk, William H. "The Dismal Swamp: One Road Out of Slavery Took You Straight into the
Boggiest Place You've Ever Been." *Humanities* 38, no. 2, Spring 2017. https://www.neh
.gov/humanities/2017/spring/feature/the-dismal-swamp-one-road-out-slavery-took-you
-straight-the-boggiest-place-you%E2%80%99ve-ever-been.

Gay, Sydney H. "Sydney Howard Gay's 'Record of Fugitives.'" Columbia University Libraries
Online Exhibitions, 1855–1856. https://exhibitions.library.columbia.edu/exhibits
/show/fugitives/record_fugitives.

Griffith, Janelle. "Teacher's Alleged Mock Slave Auction in 5th Grade Class Prompts AG
Response." NBC News, 11 March 2019. https://www.nbcnews.com/news/us-news/teacher
-s-alleged-mock-slave-auction-5th-grade-class-prompts-n981886.

Hart, Scott. "The Underground Railroad to Mexico." West Des Moines Historical Society,
2021. https://www.wdmhs.org/the-underground-railroad-to-mexico/.

Herskovits, M. *The Myth of The Negro Past.* Amsterdam, the Netherlands: Amsterdam
University Press, 1990: 102.

Heywood, L. M. *Njinga of Angola: Africa's Warrior Queen.* Reprint ed. Boston: Harvard
University Press, 2019.

Hodal, Kate. "One in 200 people Is a Slave. Why?" *Guardian*, 25 February 2020. https://
    www.theguardian.com/news/2019/feb/25/modern-slavery-trafficking-persons-one-in
    -200.
Jackson, M., and Bacon, J. *African Americans and the Haitian Revolution*. New York: Taylor &
    Francis, 2010: 209.
Lee, Anna. "South Carolina Fifth-Graders Told to Pick Cotton, Sing Slave Song on Field Trip."
    USA Today, 24 February 2019. https://eu.usatoday.com/story/news/nation/2019/02/24
    /students-pick-cotton-sing-slave-songs-field-trip/2971819002m.
MacKaye, James Morris, J. B. "Life in the Swamp." *New York Times*, 19 October 2013. https://
    opinionator.blogs.nytimes.com/2013/10/19/life-in-the-swamp/.
Morrison. "The Mastership and Its Fruits: The Emancipated Slave Face to Face with His Old
    Master." Library of Congress, 1864.
Mustakeem, S. M. *Slavery at Sea: Terror, Sex, and Sickness in the Middle Passage*. New Black
    Studies Series. Illustrated ed. Urbana: University of Illinois Press, 2016.
National Endowment for the Humanities. "The Slave Who Mailed Himself to Freedom."
    12 February 2019. https://www.neh.gov/news/slave-who-mailed-himself-freedom.
Nzinga Mbemba. "Letters (1526 CE) from the King of Kongo (Nzinga Mbemba) to the King of
    Portugal (Manuel I)." Rowan University. Digital History. https://users.rowan.edu/%7
    Emcinneshin/5394/wk07/LettersToPortugal.htm.
Ohio History Central. Margaret Garner—Ohio History Central. Retrieved December 31,
    2021, from https://ohiohistorycentral.org/w/Margaret_Garner.
Ohio History Central. Tice Davids—Ohio History Central. https://ohiohistorycentral
    .org/w/Tice_Davids.
Paquette, R. L. "'A Horde of Brigands?' The Great Louisiana Slave Revolt of 1811
    Reconsidered." *Historical Reflections/Réflexions Historiques* 35, no.1, Spring 2009: 72.
    https://link.gale.com/apps/doc/A196534983/AONE?u=anon~38e04c58&sid=google
    Scholar&xid=91ead91e.
Pinheiro, H. A., Jr. "Northern Black People's Freedom Struggle in the Nineteenth Century."
    AAIHS. 21 March 2022. https://www.aaihs.org/northern-black-peoples-freedom-struggle
    -in-the-nineteenth-century/.
Powell, Timothy B. "Ebos Landing." New Georgia Encyclopedia, 17 July 2020. https://www
    .georgiaencyclopedia.org/articles/history-archaeology/ebos-landing/.
Rediker, M. *The Slave Ship: A Human History*. Reprint ed. New York: Penguin Books, 2008:
    14–16.
Robinson, Halee. "Black Women's Voices and the Archive." Black Perspectives, 15 November
    2017. https://www.aaihs.org/black-womens-voices-and-the-archive/.
Rutgers University. "African-Americans More Likely to Be Misdiagnosed with Schizophrenia
    Study Finds: The Study Suggests a Bias in Misdiagnosing Blacks with Major Depression and
    Schizophrenia." *ScienceDaily*, March 2019. http://www.sciencedaily.com/releases/2019/03
    /190321130300.htm.
Shuler, Jack. *Calling Out Liberty: The Stono Slave Rebellion and the Universal Struggle for
    Human Rights*. Jackson: University Press of Mississippi, 2009: 70–73.
Sowell, Thomas. *Conquests and Cultures: An International History*. Adfo Books, 2021.
Stone, Lester B. *War and the Market Economy*. New York: Alpha Edition, 2017.

Taylor, Y., and C. Johnson. *I Was Born a Slave: 1772–1849*. New York: McGraw-Hill Education, 1999: 657.

Teixeira, Fabio. "Picked by Slaves: Coffee Crisis Brews in Brazil." Reuters, 12 December 2019. https://www.reuters.com/article/us-brazil-coffee-slavery/picked-by-slaves-coffee-crisis-brews-in-brazil-idUSKBN1YG13E.

The Cultural Resources Office. St. Louis Historic Preservation. City of St. Louis. "Mound City on the Mississippi: A St. Louis History." https://dynamic.stlouis-mo.gov/history/peopledetail.cfm?Master_ID=1126.

Thiong'O, N. W. *Wizard of the Crow*. Reprint ed. New York: Anchor, 2007.

Thompson, T. M. "National Newspaper and Legislative Reactions to Louisiana's Deslondes Slave Revolt of 1811." *Journal of the Louisiana Historical Association* 33, no. 1, 1992: 5–29. https://www.jstor.org/stable/4232918.

University of Houston. "What Was Life Like Under Slavery," Digital History, 2021. https://www.digitalhistory.uh.edu/disp_textbook.cfm?smtid=2&psid=3040.

Weil, J. A. B. "Who Owned Slaves in Congress? A List of 1,800 Enslavers in Senate, House History." *Washington Post*, 10 January 2022. https://www.washingtonpost.com/history/interactive/2022/congress-slaveowners-names-list/.

Williams, E. *Capitalism and Slavery*. Chapel Hill: University of North Carolina Press, 1994.

Williams, H. A. *American Slavery: A Very Short Introduction*. Very Short Introductions. Illustrated ed. London: Oxford University Press, 2014: 1–2.

Chapter Ten: Civil War

American Battlefield Trust. "Fort Wagner." https://www.battlefields.org/learn/articles/fort-wagner.

Anastaplo, G. *Reflections on Slavery and the Constitution*. Reprint ed. New York: Lexington Books, 2013: 175.

Ayton, M. *Plotting to Kill the President: Assassination Attempts from Washington to Hoover*. Illustrated ed. Stirling, VA: Potomac Books, 2017.

Carrillo, K. J. *African American History Day by Day: A Reference Guide to Events*. Westport, CT: Greenwood Publishing Group, 2012: 188.

Cavanaugh, Ray. "Our American Cousin: Lincoln's Fateful Night at the Theatre." *The Guardian*, 22 September 2020. https://www.theguardian.com/stage/2015/apr/06/our-american--cousin-lincoln-theatre-john-wilkes-booth.

Chan, Sewell. "The Unofficial History of Memorial Day." *New York Times,* 26 May 2018. https://www.nytimes.com/2018/05/26/us/the-unofficial-history-of-memorial-day.html.

Commonwealth of Virginia. *Annual Reports of Officers, Boards and Institutions of the Commonwealth of Virginia*. William F. Ritchie, Public Printer, 1859: 116.

Conrad, Earl. "General Tubman." Harriet Tubman, Campaign on the Combahee, 1863. http://www.harriettubman.com/tubman2.html.

Cotham Jr., E. T. *Juneteenth: The Story Behind the Celebration*. Kerrville, TX: State House Press, 2021: 241.

Davis, J., V. H. Borcke, R. E. Lee, F. H. Alfriend, and J. E. Cooke. *REBEL YELL: History of the Confederacy, Memoirs and Biographies of the Confederate Leaders & Official Documents: History of the Confederate States, The . . . of the Confederate States and More*. Czech Republic: Madison & Adams Press, 2017.

Dease, Jared, and Alyssa Putt. "Buffaloes." NCpedia, 1 January 2006. Encyclopedia of North Carolina, Chapel Hill: University of North Carolina Press, 2006. https://www .ncpedia.org/buffaloes.

Douglass, Frederick. *Frederick Douglass: Selected Speeches and Writings.* The Library of Black America series. Edited by Philip S. Foner and Yuval Taylor. Chicago: Chicago Review Press, 2000: 447.

Editor. "A Legacy of Lies: 'Lost Cause' Myth Distorted Civil War History to Infect America's Soul with White Supremacy." *Milwaukee Independent*, 12 June 2020. http://www .milwaukeeindependent.com/articles/a-legacy-of-lies-lost-cause-myth-distorted-civil-war -history-to-infect-americas-soul-with-white-supremacy/.

Edwards, W. C., and E. Steers. *The Lincoln Assassination: The Evidence.* Annotated ed. Urbana: University of Illinois Press, 2009: 1153–54.

Egerton, Douglas R. *Thunder at the Gates: The Black Civil War Regiments That Redeemed America.* New York: Basic Books, 2016.

Fletcher, F. "Sergeant Francis Fletcher of the 54th Massachusetts on Equal Pay for Black Soldiers, 1864, Gilder Lehrman Institute of American History. https://www .gilderlehrman.org/history-resources/spotlight-primary-source/sergeant-francis -fletcher-54th-massachusetts-equal-pay.

Fuchs, R. *An Unerring Fire: The Massacre at Fort Pillow.* Stackpole Classics. Reprint ed. Mechanicsburg, PA: Stackpole Books, 2017.

Fuller, A. James. "The Draft and the Draft Riots of 1863." Bill of Rights Institute. https:// billofrightsinstitute.org/essays/the-draft-and-the-draft-riots-of-1863.

Gardner, Eric. "African American Civil War Poetry." Black Print Culture, 29 August 2015. https://www.blackprintculture.com/bpu-blog/african-american-civil-war-poetry.

Gilpin, B. R. *John Brown Still Lives!: America's Long Reckoning with Violence, Equality, and Change.* Reprint ed. Chapel Hill: University of North Carolina Press, 2014: 18.

Headley, J. T. *The Great Riots of New York 1712 to 1873.* Project Gutenburg, November 2004. https://www.gutenberg.org/files/6856/6856-h/6856-h.htm.

Howe, L., and P. Kirwan. *Famine Pots: The Choctaw-Irish Gift Exchange, 1847–Present.* American Indian Studies. Illustrated ed. East Lansing: Michigan State University Press, 2020.

Jenkins, S. "In Civil War's Early Days, Battlefield Deaths an Abstract Notion in North and South." *Washington Post*, 11 April 2011. https://www.washingtonpost.com/lifestyle/style /in-civil-wars-early-days-battlefield-deaths-an-abstract-notion-in-north-and-south/2011 /03/28/AF3CD8LD_story.html.

Jensen, G. *The Routledge Handbook of the History of Race and the American Military.* Routledge History Handbooks. Oxfordshire, UK: Routledge, 2018: 75–80.

Kurin, R. *The Smithsonian's History of America in 101 Objects.* Reprint ed. New York: Penguin Books, 2016: 226.

McPherson, James M. *Defining Documents in American History: Civil War (1860–1865).* Pasadena, CA: Salem Press, 2014: 258–62.

McPherson, James M. "Southern Comfort." *New York Review of Books*, 12 April 2001. https:// www.nybooks.com/articles/2001/04/12/southern-comfort/.

McPherson, James M., and George Henry Davis. *Battle Cry of Freedom: The Civil War Era.* Oxford History of the United States, book 6. New York: Oxford University Press, 1988.

Mintz, Steven. "Historical Context: Black Soldiers in the Civil War." Gilder Lehrman Institute of American History, History Resources. https://www.gilderlehrman.org/history-resources /teaching-resource/historical-context-black-soldiers-civil-war.

Moss, J. P. *Forgotten Black Soldiers Who Served in White Regiments During the Civil War.* Vol. II. Berwyn Heights, MD: Heritage Books, Inc., 2019.

Norris, Wesley. "Robert E. Lee: His Brutality to His Slaves." Fair Use Repository, 1866.

Ottenheimer, David. "Devil's Punch Bowl in Natchez: Confederate Disaster and Propaganda Campaign." Flying Penguin, 2021. https://www.flyingpenguin.com/?p=33699.

Reekie, J. "African Americans Collecting Bones of Soldiers Killed in Cold Harbor, Virginia, April 1865." Iowa Department Cultural Affairs, 2019. https://iowaculture.gov/history /education/educator-resources/primary-source-sets/african-americans-and-civil-war/african.

Reynolds, D. S. *John Brown, Abolitionist: The Man Who Killed Slavery, Sparked the Civil War, and Seeded Civil Rights.* Reprint ed. New York: Vintage, 2006: 169.

Santayana, G. (2022). *Soliloquies in England and Later Soliloquies.* Independently published.

Schwartz, A. "'Is God Dead?': Frederick Douglass's Recollection of a Contentious Moment in Antislavery History." *New North Star* 3, 2021. https://doi.org/10.18060/25879.

Stephens, Alexander H. "Cornerstone Speech: Savannah, Georgia, 21 March 1861." American Battlefield Trust. https://www.battlefields.org/learn/primary-sources/cornerstone-speech.

Taylor, Susie King. "Reminiscences of My Life in Camp with the 33d United States Colored Troops Late 1st S. C. Volunteers." Documenting the American South, 1902. https:// docsouth.unc.edu/neh/taylorsu/summary.html.

Varon, Elizabeth R. "Freedom Days: Juneteenth and the Process of Emancipation." Nau Center for Civil War History, 2020. University of Virginia. https://naucenter.as.virginia.edu/blog -page/1221.

White, S. *Prince of Darkness: The Untold Story of Jeremiah G. Hamilton, Wall Street's First Black Millionaire.* New York: St. Martin's Press, 2015.

Wilder, Burt G. *Practicing Medicine in a Black Regiment: The Civil War Diary of Burt G. Wilder, 55th Massachusetts.* Edited by Richard M. Reid. Amherst: University of Massachusetts Press, 2010.

Chapter Eleven: Dawn to Dusk

Asante, M. *African Intellectual Heritage* (African American Studies). Temple University Press, 1996: 648.

Avalon Project. "Madison Debates: June 26." Yale Law School, 1787. https://avalon.law.yale .edu/18th_century/debates_626.asp.

Bachan, Kyle. "Still Searching Out Zora Neale Hurston." *Ms.*, 25 June 2020. https:// msmagazine.com/2011/02/02/still-searching-out-zora-neale-hurston.

Boney, F. N., R. L. Hume, and R. Zafar. *God Made Man, Man Made the Slave: The Autobiography of George Teamoh.* Macon, GA: Mercer University Press, 1992.

Britannica, The Editors of Encyclopedia. "Andrew Johnson." *Encyclopedia Britannica.* https:// www.britannica.com/biography/Andrew-Johnson.

Du Bois, W. E. B., and D. L. Lewis. *Black Reconstruction in America, 1860–1880.* 12.2.1997 ed. New York: Free Press, 1998.

Equal Justice Initiative. "On This Day—Nov. 22, 1865: Mississippi Authorizes 'Sale' of Black Orphans to White 'Masters or Mistresses.'" A History of Racial Injustice. https://calendar .eji.org/racial-injustice/nov/22.

Feuerherd, Peter. "Why Ulysses S. Grant Was More Important Than You Think." JSTOR, 2 April 2020. https://daily.jstor.org/why-ulysses-s-grant-was-more-important-than-you-think/.

Fleming, W. L. *Documentary History of Reconstruction, Vol. 1: Political, Military, Social, Religious, Educational Industrial, 1865 to the Present Time.* London: Forgotten Books, 2018.

Foner, Eric. *Reconstruction: America's Unfinished Revolution 1863–1877.* Updated ed. New York: HarperPerennial Modern Classics, 2014.

Formwalt, L. W. "The Camilla Massacre of 1868: Racial Violence as Political Propaganda." *Georgia Historical Quarterly* 71, no. 3, 1987: 399–426. https://www-jstor-org.libproxy .bellarmine.edu/stable/40581696?seq=19#metadata_info_tab_contents.

Frankel, Noralee. "From Slave Women to Free Women." National Archives, 1997. https:// www.archives.gov/publications/prologue/1997/summer/slave-women.

Freedmen and Southern Society Project. "Meeting Between Black Religious Leaders and Union Military Authorities, January 12, 1865." University of Maryland. http://www.freedmen .umd.edu/savmtg.htm.

Freeman, J. B. *The Field of Blood: Violence in Congress and the Road to Civil War.* Reprint ed. London: Picador, 2019.

History, Art & Archives. "Walls, Josiah Thomas. United States House of Representatives." https://history.house.gov/People/Detail/23324.

Johnson, H. T. *The Negro Tried and Triumphant, or, Thoughts Stirred by Race Conflict.* Philadelphia: A.M.E. Publishing House, 1895. https://www.loc.gov/item/91898150/.

Jones, LaDawn LBJ. "The 'Original 33' from the Georgia General Assembly." GeorgiaPol, 1 February 2018. https://www.georgiapol.com/2018/02/01/original-33-georgia-general -assembly.

Kleinfeld, R. *A Savage Order: How the World's Deadliest Countries Can Forge a Path to Security.* Reprint ed. New York: Vintage, 2019: 49.

Latson, Jennifer. "How the First Black U.S. Senator Was Nearly Kept from His Seat. *Time,* 25 February 2015. https://time.com/3714088/hiram-revels.

Lee, Karis. *The 1868 Mayoral Election, African-American Vote, and Riots That Followed.* Boundary Stones, 12 March 2020. WETA's Washington, D.C., History Blog. https:// boundarystones.weta.org/2020/03/12/1868-mayoral-election-african-american-vote-and -riots-followed.

Marable, M. "The Politics of Black Land Tenure: 1877–1915." *Agricultural History* 53, no. 1, 1979: 142–52. http://www.jstor.org/stable/3742866.

McAfee, W. M. *Religion, Race, and Reconstruction: The Public School in the Politics of the 1870s.* SUNY Series, Religion and American Public Life. Albany: State University of New York Press, 1998.

McMillen, Neil R. "Isaiah T. Montgomery, 1847–1924 (Part II)." Mississippi Department of Archives and History, February 2007. https://www.mshistorynow.mdah.ms.gov/issue /isaiah-t-montgomery-1847-1924-part-ii.

Mitchell, E. *Liberty's Torch: The Great Adventure to Build the Statue of Liberty.* Reprint ed. New York: Grove Press, 2015: 258.

Morey, Michael. *Fagen: An African American Renegade in the Philippine-American War.*
Illustrated ed. Madison: University of Wisconsin Press, 2019.

Morrow, Emerald. "Grave of Florida Sen. Robert Meacham, a Former Slave, Could Be Under
Tampa Lot. Lawmakers React." *Tampa Bay News,* 22 June 2021. https://www.wtsp.com
/article/news/special-reports/erased/former-slave-state-senator-robert-meacham-grave
-tampa/67-58e4e8bc-4cba-47b2-a6d2-310a9cef25b1.

Myers, B. "Sherman's Field Order No. 15." New Georgia Encyclopedia, 2021. https://www
.georgiaencyclopedia.org/articles/history-archaeology/shermans-field-order-no-15/.

National Constitution Center. "Andrew Johnson: The Most-Criticized President Ever?" NCC,
31 July 2019. https://constitutioncenter.org/blog/marking-the-passing-of-maybe-the-most
-criticized-president-ever.

National Constitution Center. "The 15th Amendment: Right to Vote Not Denied by Race."
National Constitution Center. https://constitutioncenter.org/interactive-constitution
/amendment/amendment-xv.

National Park Service. "Abolition." Statue of Liberty National Monument. https://www.nps
.gov/stli/learn/historyculture/abolition.htm.

Rich, Grant J., and Neeta A. Ramkumar. *Psychology in Oceania and the Caribbean.*
International and Cultural Psychology. Singapore: Springer, 2021: 90.

Schuessler, Jennifer. "Liberation as Death Sentence." *New York Times,* 10 June 2012. https://
www.nytimes.com/2012/06/11/books/sick-from-freedom-by-jim-downs-about-freed
-slaves.html.

Smith, John David. *We Ask Only for Even-Handed Justice: Black Voices from Reconstruction, 1865–
1877.* Revised and expanded ed. Amherst: University of Massachusetts Press, 2014.

The Cline Center. "It Was an Attempted Coup: The Cline Center's Coup D'état Project
Categorizes the January 6, 2021 Assault on the US Capitol." University of Illinois. Cline
Center for Advanced Social Research, 2021. https://clinecenter.illinois.edu/coup-detat
-project-cdp/statement_jan.27.2021.

Tillman, B. "'Their Own Hotheadedness': Senator Benjamin R. 'Pitchfork Ben' Tillman
Justifies Violence Against Southern Blacks." George Mason University. History Matters,
1900. http://historymatters.gmu.edu/d/55.

TreasuryDirect KIDS. "The History of U.S. Public Debt: The Civil War (1861–1865)." https://
www.treasurydirect.gov/kids/history/history_civilwar.htm.

Trefousse, H. L. *Thaddeus Stevens: Nineteenth-Century Egalitarian.* Chapel Hill: University of
North Carolina Press, 2005.

Tunnell, T. "Creating 'The Propaganda of History': Southern Editors and the Origins of
'Carpetbagger and Scalawag.'" *Journal of Southern History* 72, no. 4, , 2006: 789–822.
https://doi.org/10.2307/27649233.

United States. Congress. Senate. *Reports of Committees: 30th Congress, 1st Session–48th
Congress, 2nd Session Volume 2, Part 2.* Saskatoon, Canada: HardPress, 2019.

Walls, Josiah. Digital Harrisburg, 2020. https://digitalharrisburg.com/josiah-walls/.

Warren, Joyce Pualani. "Reading Bodies, Writing Blackness: Anti-/Blackness and
Nineteenth-Century Kanaka Maoli Literary Nationalism." *American Indian Culture and
Research Journal* 43, no. 2, 2019: 49–72. https://doi.org/10.17953/aicrj.43.2.warren.

Washington, Booker T., L. R. Harlan, and R. Smock. *Booker T. Washington Papers.* Vol. 9.
Amsterdam, the Netherlands: Amsterdam University Press, 1980: 309.

Woodward, C. Vann. *Reunion and Reaction: The Compromise of 1877 and the End of Reconstruction*. New York: Oxford University Press, 1991.

Zuczek, R. *Encyclopedia of the Reconstruction Era*. Greenwood Milestones in African American History, Vol. 1: A–L. Westport, CT: Greenwood Publishing Group, 2006.

Chapter Twelve: A Portrait of Suffering

"100 Years Later, What's the Legacy of 'Birth of a Nation'?" NPR, 8 February 2015. https://www.npr.org/sections/codeswitch/2015/02/08/383279630/100-years-later-whats-the-legacy-of-birth-of-a-nation.

Addams, Jane. "Jane Addams: The Subjective Necessity for Settlements." Hanover College, 1892. https://history.hanover.edu/courses/excerpts/336addams.html.

Alexander, Shawn Leigh. *T. Thomas Fortune, the Afro-American Agitator: A Collection of Writings, 1880–1928*. Gainesville: University Press of Florida, 2010.

Anand, K. J. S. "Discovering Pain in Newborn Infants." *Anesthesiology* 131, no. 2, 2019: 392–95. https://doi.org/10.1097/aln.0000000000002810.

BBC News. "Joe Biden Signs Anti-lynching Bill in Historic First." BBC, 29 March 2022. https://www.bbc.com/news/world-us-canada-60679930.

Birnbaum, Jonathan, and Clarence Taylor. *Civil Rights Since 1787*. New York: New York University Press, 2000: 177.

Black in Appalachia. "The Corbin Expulsion of 1919." https://www.blackinappalachia.org/corbin-expulsion.

Block, Melissa. "Yes, Women Could Vote After the 19th Amendment—But Not All Women. or Men." NPR, 26 August 2020. https://www.npr.org/2020/08/26/904730251/yes-women-could-vote-after-the-19th-amendment-but-not-all-women-or-men.

Bogel-Burroughs, Nicholas. "Prosecutors Say Derek Chauvin Knelt on George Floyd for 9 Minutes 29 Seconds, Longer Than Initially Reported." *New York Times,* 30 March 2021. https://www.nytimes.com/2021/03/30/us/derek-chauvin-george-floyd-kneel-9-minutes-29-seconds.html.

Bordewich, F. M. *Bound for Canaan: The Epic Story of the Underground Railroad, America's First Civil Rights Movement*. New York: Amistad Press, 2021: 373.

Cahill, C. D. *Recasting the Vote: How Women of Color Transformed the Suffrage Movement*. Chapel Hill: University of North Carolina Press, 2020: 106.

Central Iowa Community Museum. "Toward a Universal Suffrage: From Slavery to Suffrage." https://centraliowamuseum.com/towarduniversalsuffrage/slaverytosuffrage.

Chestnut, Trichita M. "Lynching: Ida B. Wells-Barnett and the Outrage over the Frazier Baker Murder." National Archives, 2008. https://www.archives.gov/files/publications/prologue/2008/fall/lynching.pdf.

Clark, Kenneth B., and Mamie P. Clark. "Emotional Factors in Racial Identification and Preference in Negro Children." *Journal of Negro Education* 19, no. 3, 1950: 341. https://doi.org/10.2307/2966491.

@common. "Black Massacres—Pick a Massacre and Research It!" Twitter, 31 May 2021. https://twitter.com/common/status/1399425644375822342?.

Early Chicago: "The 1893 World's Fair." WTTW Chicago, 2018. https://interactive.wttw.com/dusable-to-obama/1893-worlds-fair.

Equal Justice Initiative. "Alabama Congressman Shoots Black Man for Swearing in Presence of White Woman; Receives Outpouring of Support." EJI, 27 March 1908. https://calendar.eji .org/racial-injustice/mar/27.

Equal Justice Initiative. "Reconstruction in America: Racial Violence after the Civil War." Report Overview, 15 November 2021. https://eji.org/reports/reconstruction-in-america -overview.

Field Museum. "Fun Facts About the World's Columbian Exposition." 2018. https://www .fieldmuseum.org/fun-facts-about-worlds-columbian-exposition.

Greenidge, Kerri. *Black Radical: The Life and Times of William Monroe Trotter*. New York: Liveright Publishing Corporation, 2021.

Greenidge, Kerri. "The Radical Black Newspaper That Declared 'None Are Free Unless All Are Free.'" *The Guardian*, 3 January 2020. https://www.theguardian.com/us-news/2020/jan /03/boston-guardian-william-monroe-trotter-newspaper.

Hunn, David, and Kim Bell. "Why Was Michael Brown's Body Left There for Hours?" *St. Louis Post-Dispatch*, 14 September 2014. https://www.stltoday.com/news/local/crime -and-courts/why-was-michael-browns-body-left-there-for-hours/article_0b73ec58 -c6a1-516e-882f-74d18a4246e0.html.

Jones, Seth G., Catrina Doxsee, Nicholas Harrington, Grace Hwang, and James Suber. "The War Comes Home: The Evolution of Domestic Terrorism in the United States." Center for Strategic and International Studies, October 2020. https://csis-website-prod.s3.amazonaws .com/s3fs-public/publication/201021_Jones_War_Comes_Home_v2.pdf.

Kinni, F. K. *Pan-Africanism: Political Philosophy and Socio-Economic Anthropology for African Liberation and Governance*. Vol. 1. Bamenda, Cameroon: Langaa RPCIG, 2015: 565.

Laqueur, W. *A History of Terrorism*. Oxfordshire, UK: Routledge, 2001.

Logan, R. W. *The Betrayal of the Negro: From Rutherford B. Hayes to Woodrow Wilson*. Originally published as: *The Negro in American Life and Thought: The Nadir: 1877–1901*. New, enlarged ed., 5th printing. New York: Collier Books, 1970.

Matz, L., and R. Jackson. "A Radical Black Voice: William Monroe Trotter and His Effort to Hold a Mirror up to Nature." *Milwaukee Independent*, 2020. http://www .milwaukeeindependent.com/featured/a-radical-black-voice-william-monroe-trotter-and -his-effort-to-hold-a-mirror-up-to-nature.

McDaniels III, P. "African American Soldiers (USA)." International Encyclopedia of the First World War, 2014. https://encyclopedia.1914-1918-online.net/article/african_american _soldiers_usa.

McGerr, Michael. *A Fierce Discontent: The Rise and Fall of the Progressive Movement in America, 1870–1920*. New York: Oxford University Press, 2005.

Mjagkij, N. (2011). *Loyalty in Time of Trial: The African American Experience During World War I*. The African American Experience Series, 2011. Lanham, MD: Rowman & Littlefield Publishers, 162.

Reicher, S. D. "The St. Pauls' Riot: An Explanation of the Limits of Crowd Action in Terms of a Social Identity Model." *European Journal of Social Psychology* 14, no. 1, 1984: 1–21. https://doi.org/10.1002/ejsp.2420140102.

"Research Guides: American Women: Topical Essays: Marching for the Vote: Remembering the Woman Suffrage Parade of 1913." Library of Congress. https://guides.loc.gov/american -women-essays/marching-for-the-vote.

Schechter, P. A. *Ida B. Wells-Barnett and American Reform, 1880–1930*. Chapel Hill: University of North Carolina Press, 2001: 41.

Scott, Emmett J. "Scott's Official History of the American Negro in the World." Archive, 1919. https://archive.org/details/scottsofficialhi00scot/page/8/mode/2up.

Segrave, Kerry. *Lynchings of Women in the United States: The Recorded Cases, 1851–1946*. Twenty-First Century Works. Jefferson, NC: McFarland & Company, 2010: 292.

Stockley, Grif. "Elaine Massacre of 1919." Butler Center for Arkansas Studies. Encyclopedia of Arkansas, 18 November 2020. https://encyclopediaofarkansas.net/entries/elaine-massacre -of-1919-1102/.

Taper, Bernard. *Gomillion Versus Lightfoot: The Tuskegee Gerrymander Case*. New York: McGraw-Hill, 1962.

Terrell, Mary Church, and D. N. Ham. *A Colored Woman in a White World*. Adfo Books, 2005: 169–70.

Tolnay, S. E., and E. M. Beck. *A Festival of Violence: An Analysis of Southern Lynchings, 1882–1930*. Urbana: University of Illinois Press, 1995: 23.

Wells, Ida B. *Crusade for Justice: The Autobiography of Ida B. Wells*. 2nd ed. Edited by Alfreda M. Duster. Negro American Biographies and Autobiographies. Chicago: University of Chicago Press, 2020: 39, 48, 370.

Wells, Ida. B. *The Light of Truth: Writings of an Anti-lynching Crusader*. Edited by Mia Bay and Henry Louis Gates Jr. New York: Penguin Random House, 2014: 501.

Wells-Barnett, Ida B. "'Lynching Is Color-Line Murder': The Blistering Speech Denouncing America's Shame." *The Guardian*, 27 April 2018. https://www.theguardian.com/world /2018/apr/27/ida-b-wells-barnett-national-negro-conference-chicago-speech.

Wells-Barnett, I. B. "Southern Horrors: Lynch Law in All Its Phases." Archives of Women's Political Communication, 5 October 1892. https://awpc.cattcenter.iastate.edu/2020/09 /21/southern-horrors-lynch-law-in-all-its-phases-oct-5-1892/.

White House Historical Association. "William Monroe Trotter Challenges President Wilson. White House History." https://www.whitehousehistory.org/william-monroe-trotter -challenges-president-wilson.

"White Man's War?" *TIME*, 2 March 1942. http://content.time.com/time/subscriber/article /0,33009,773068-1,00.html.

Williams, C. L. *Torchbearers of Democracy: African American Soldiers in the World War I Era*. The John Hope Franklin African American History and Culture. Illustrated ed. Chapel Hill: University of North Carolina Press, 2013: 223–224

Wrobel, D. M. *America's West: A History, 1890–1950*. Cambridge Essential Histories. Cambridge, UK: Cambridge University Press, 2017: 123.

Zahniser, Jill Diane, and Amelia R. Fry. *Alice Paul: Claiming Power*. New York: Oxford University Press, 2014: 138.

Chapter Thirteen: Jim Crow Took a Road Trip

Abel, E. *Signs of the Times: The Visual Politics of Jim Crow*. Berkeley: University of California Press, 2010.

Abt, T. *Bleeding Out: The Devastating Consequences of Urban Violence—and a Bold New Plan for Peace in the Streets*. New York: Basic Books, 2019.

Ahmed, Amal. "Robert Bullard Isn't Done Yet." *Texas Observer*, 3 May 2021. https://www .texasobserver.org/robert-bullard-isnt-done-yet.

American Public Media. "Surviving Jim Crow." Remembering Jim Crow, 2018. http:// americanradioworks.publicradio.org/features/remembering/surviving.html.

Ayres, I., F. E. Vars, and N. Zakariya. "To Insure Prejudice: Racial Disparities in Taxicab Tipping." *SSRN Electronic Journal*, 2003. https://doi.org/10.2139/ssrn.401201.

Bay City News. "Oakland Homicides Reach 100 in 2020, a 47% Jump from Last Year." NBC Bay Area, 8 December 2020. https://www.nbcbayarea.com/news/local/east-bay/oakland -homicides-reach-100-in-2020-a-47-jump-from-last-year/2418372/.

BBC News. "US Senator Tom Cotton Defends Slavery Remarks." BBC, 27 July 2020. https:// www.bbc.com/news/world-us-canada-53550882.

Blackmon, D. A. *Slavery by Another Name: The Re-Enslavement of Black Americans from the Civil War to World War II*. Reprint ed. New York: Anchor, 2009: 4.

Blake, H. "When We Worked on Shares, We Couldn't Make Nothing." George Mason University. http://historymatters.gmu.edu/d/6377/.

Bracken, Hailey. "Was Jesse Owens Snubbed by Adolf Hitler at the Berlin Olympics?" Encyclopedia Britannica. https://www.britannica.com/story/was-jesse-owens-snubbed by -adolf-hitler-at-the-berlin-olympics.

Bullard, Sara, and Julian Bond. *Free at Last: A History of the Civil Rights Movement and Those Who Died in the Struggle*. Reprint ed. New York: Oxford University Press, 1994.

Caro, R. A. *Master of the Senate: The Years of Lyndon Johnson*. New York: Vintage, 2003: 954.

Carper, N. G. "Martin Tabert, Martyr of an Era." *Florida Historical Quarterly*, 52, no. 2, 1973: 115–31. http://www.jstor.org/stable/30149028.

Chavez, N. C. "Tulsa Massacre Survivor at 107 Years Old Testifies That the Horror of That Day Never Goes Away." CNN, 20 May 2021. https://edition.cnn.com/2021/05/19/us/tulsa -massacre-survivors-congress/index.html.

CSU Channel Islands. "Japanese Internment." https://library.csuci.edu/collections/internment -camp.

Daniels, R., S. C. Taylor, and H. H. Kitano. L. *Japanese Americans: From Relocation to Redress*. Revised ed. Seattle: University of Washington Press, 1991: 5.

DeWitt, L. "The Decision to Exclude Agricultural and Domestic Workers from the 1935 Social Security Act." Social Security Administration Research, Statistics, and Policy Analysis, 1 November 2010. https://www.ssa.gov/policy/docs/ssb/v70n4/v70n4p49.html.

Fain, K. "The Devastation of Black Wall Street." JSTOR Daily, 2020. https://daily.jstor.org/the -devastation-of-black-wall-street.

Falk, R., M. Wallinius, S. Lundström, T. Frisell, H. Anckarsäter, and N. Kerekes. "The 1% of the Population Accountable for 63% of All Violent Crime Convictions." *Social Psychiatry and Psychiatric Epidemiology* 49, no. 4, 2013: 559–71. https://doi.org/10.1007/s00127-013 -0783-y.

Ferris State University. "Pullman Porters." Jim Crow Museum, 2021. https://www.ferris.edu /HTMLS/news/jimcrow/question/2021/august.htm.

Fomerand, J. *Historical Dictionary of Human Rights*. (Historical Dictionaries of Religions, Philosophies, and Movements Series). 2nd ed. Lanham, MD: Rowman & Littlefield Publishers, 2021.

Funk & Wagnalls Company. *The Slaves of Turpentine*. New York: Literary Digest, 1914: 1490–91.

Gilder Lehrman Center for the Study of Slavery, Resistance, and Abolition. "Frederick Douglass and Richard T. Greener on the Negro Exodus, 1879." Yale University, 7 April 2015. https://glc.yale.edu/frederick-douglass-and-richard-t-greener-negro-exodus-1879.

Gilder Lehrman Institute of American History. "FDR on Racial Discrimination, 1942." Retrieved November 25, 2021, from https://www.gilderlehrman.org/history-resources /spotlight-primary-source/fdr-racial-discrimination-1942.

Green, Victor H. *The Negro Motorist Green Book*. Smithsonian, 1958. https://transcription.si .edu/project/7955.

Harrington, O. *Soul Shots: Political Cartoons*. A Daily World Book. Chicago: Long View Publishing, 1972.

Hautzinger, D. "How Pullman Porters Laid Groundwork for the Civil Rights Movement." WTTW Chicago, 22 February 2019. https://interactive.wttw.com/playlist/2019/02/22 /pullman-porters.

Holbrook, S. H. "Life of a Pullman Porter." *Esquire*, November 1939. https://classic.esquire .com/article/1939/11/1/life-of-a-pullman-porter.

Hudson, L. M. *West of Jim Crow: The Fight Against California's Color Line*. Urbana: University of Illinois Press, 2020.

James, Rawn, Jr. *The Double V: How Wars, Protest, and Harry Truman Desegregated America's Military*. Reprint ed. London: Bloomsbury Publishing, 2014: 222.

Johll, M. *Investigating Chemistry: A Forensic Science Perspective*. New York: W. H. Freeman and Company, 2008: 184.

Kersten, Andrew E. *A. Philip Randolph: A Life in the Vanguard*. The African American Experience Series. Lanham, MD: Rowman & Littlefield Publishers, 2006: 37.

Keyes, A. "A Long-Lost Manuscript Contains a Searing Eyewitness Account of the Tulsa Race Massacre of 1921." *Smithsonian Magazine*, 27 May 2016. https://www.smithsonianmag .com/smithsonian-institution/long-lost-manuscript-contains-searing-eyewitness-account -tulsa-race-massacre-1921-180959251.

Lee, J. "Samuel Bowers, 82, Klan Leader Convicted in Fatal Bombing, Dies." *New York Times*, 6 November 2006. https://www.nytimes.com/2006/11/06/us/06bowers.html.

Lee, T. "New Deal, Old South: How FDR Propped Up Jim Crow [Review of Fear Itself: The New Deal and the Origins of Our Time, by I. KATZNELSON]." *Foreign Affairs* 92, no. 5, 2013: 146–51. http://www.jstor.org/stable/23527524.

Lemann, Nicholas. *The Promised Land: The Great Black Migration and How It Changed America*. New York: Vintage, 1992: 6, 47.

Lescaze, L. "Reagan Blames Crime on 'Human Predator.'" *Washington Post*, 29 September 1981. https://www.washingtonpost.com/archive/politics/1981/09/29/reagan-blames -crime-on-human-predator/2892636f-d176-48fb-b06b-39012eace1f4.

Library of Congress. "Race Massacre: Topics in Chronicling America: Search Strategies & Selected Articles." https://guides.loc.gov/chronicling-america-tulsa-race-riots/selected -articles.

Loewen, J. W. *Sundown Towns: A Hidden Dimension of American Racism*. Illustrated ed. New York: The New Press, 2018: 23–28.

Long, M. "Was Mister Rogers Racist? Twelve Facts About Our Favorite Neighbor." HuffPost, 7 August 2016. https://www.huffpost.com/entry/was-mister-rogers-racist-_b_7939498.

Martin Tabert: Boyle, K. "Closing the Racial Inequality Gaps." CitiGPS, September 2020. https://www.citivelocity.com/citigps/closing-the-racial-inequality-gaps/.

Maxedon, Tom. "A Lesser Known Piece of 'The Great Migration': Phoenix And McNary, Arizona." KJZZ, 26 February 2021. https://kjzz.org/content/1661220/lesser-known-piece-great-migration-phoenix-and-mcnary-arizona.

McAboy, K. "California Cities Grapple with Racist History of Sundown Towns." FOX 11 Los Angeles, 2022. https://www.foxla.com/news/california-cities-grapple-with-racist-history-of-sundown-towns.

Merrefield, C. "The 1921 Tulsa Race Massacre and Its Enduring Financial Fallout." *Harvard Gazette*, 19 June 2020. https://news.harvard.edu/gazette/story/2020/06/the-1921-tulsa-race-massacre-and-its-enduring-financial-fallout/.

Murray, P., and D. Douglas. *States' Laws on Race and Color.* Studies in the Legal History of the South. Reprint ed. Athens: University of Georgia Press, 2016: 290.

Musick, D., and K. Gunsaulus-Musick. *American Prisons: Their Past, Present and Future.* Oxfordshire, UK: Routledge, 2017: 12.

Nittle, N. "Why Aunt Jemima, Uncle Ben, and Other Racist Food Mascots Were Rebranded in 2020." Eater, 25 May 2021. https://www.eater.com/22450623/racist-brand-mascot-logo-changes-aunt-jemima-uncle-bens-land-o-lakes.

Parrish, J. M. E. *Events of the Tulsa Disaster.* Independently published, 1923.

Parshina-Kottas, Y., A. Singhvi, A. D. S. Burch, T. Griggs, M. Gröndahl, L. Huang, T. Wallace, J. White, and J. Williams. "What the 1921 Tulsa Race Massacre Destroyed." *New York Times* 15 November 2021. https://www.nytimes.com/interactive/2021/05/24/us/tulsa-race-massacre.html.

Pattillo, Alicia. "The Great Migration of African Americans." KTNV Las Vegas, 27 February 2020. https://www.ktnv.com/news/the-great-migration-of-african-americans.

Pepin, Elizabeth, and Lewis Watts. *Harlem of the West: The San Francisco Fillmore Jazz Era.* Illustrated ed. San Francisco: Chronicle Books, 2005.

Phillips Collection. "Troy, Alabama." Jacob Lawrence: The Migration Series, 17 October 1916. https://lawrencemigration.phillipscollection.org/culture/migrant-life/troy-alabama-october-17-1916.

Pollard, S. "Sammy Davis, Jr. Endured Horrific Racist Abuse in the Army." *American Masters.* https://www.pbs.org/wnet/americanmasters/sammy-davis-jr-endured-horrific-racist-abuse-in-the-army/14981/.

Post, A. "Amazon Did Everything It Could to Bust the Staten Island Union. They Overcame It All." The Intercept, 2 April 2022. https://theintercept.com/2022/04/02/amazon-union-staten-island/.

Randolph, A. Philip. "World War II and the Post War Years—NAACP." A Century in the Fight for Freedom. Library of Congress. https://www.loc.gov/exhibits/naacp/world-war-ii-and-the-post-war-years.html#obj1.

Rothstein, Richard. *The Color of Law: A Forgotten History of How Our Government Segregated America.* Reprint ed. New York: Liveright Publishing Corporation, 2018.

Rutkowski, S. *Literary Legacies of the Federal Writers' Project: Voices of the Depression in the American Postwar Era*. American Literature Readings in the 21st Century. New York: Palgrave Macmillan, 2017: 37.

Rutkowski, Sara. *Literary Legacies of the Federal Writers' Project: Voices of the Depression in the American Postwar Era*. American Literature Readings in the 21st Century. New York: Palgrave Macmillan, 2018: 37.

State of Oklahoma. *The Tulsa Race Riot: A Report by the Oklahoma Commission to Study the Tulsa Race Riot of 1921*. Oklahoma Commission to Study the Tulsa Race Riot of 1921, March 2001. https://www.okhistory.org/research/forms/freport.pdf.

Strauss, Valerie. "School Apologizes for Black History Month Lunch of Watermelon, Fried Chicken." *Washington Post*, 6 February 2014. https://www.washingtonpost.com/news/answer-sheet/wp/2014/02/06/school-apologizes-for-black-history-month-lunch-of-watermelon-fried-chicken/.

Taylor, Quintard. "The Great Migration: The Afro-American Communities of Seattle and Portland During the 1940s." *Arizona and the West* 23, no. 2, 1981: 109–26. http://www.jstor.org/stable/40169136.

Tribune, T. T. "Nab Negro for Attacking Girl in an Elevator." *Tulsa World*, 1921. https://tulsaworld.com/archive/nab-negro-for-attacking-girl-in-an-elevator/article_758e0217-1077-5282-bdb9-4eef81f8e12d.htm.

Waite, Kevin. "Black California: A Review of West of Jim Crow." Boom California, 12 February 2021. https://boomcalifornia.org/2021/02/12/black-california-a-review-of-west-of-jim-crow/.

Walker, Finch. "White Brevard County Firefighter Fired After Halloween Party Blackface Incident." *Florida Today*, 26 February 2022. https://eu.floridatoday.com/story/news/2022/02/26/brevard-firefighter-fired-after-blackface-incident-halloween-party/6937714001/.

Wang, Tabitha. "Detroit Race Riot (1943)." Black Past, 3 July 2003. https://www.blackpast.org/african-american-history/detroit-race-riot-1943.

Weber, G. M. H. H. *Politics as a Vocation*. London: Oxford University Press, 1946: 122–23.

Whitman, J. Q. *Hitler's American Model: The United States and the Making of Nazi Race Law*. Princeton, NJ: Princeton University Press, 2018.

Wilkerson, I. *The Warmth of Other Suns*. Penguin Random House, 2010: 162, 225, 371.

Wills, S. "Origins of Black Wall Street." Investopedia, 3 March 2022. https://www.investopedia.com/insights/origins-black-wall-street.

Zelizer, J. "The Power of Lyndon Johnson Is a Myth." *Washington Post*, 11 January 2015. https://www.washingtonpost.com/news/monkey-cage/wp/2015/01/11/the-power-of-lyndon-johnson-is-a-myth/.

Zraick, K. "Alice Dunnigan, First Black Woman to Cover White House, Will Get Statue at Newseum." *New York Times*, 27 August 2018. https://www.nytimes.com/2018/08/23/us/alice-allison-dunnigan-newseum-statue.html.

Zraick, Karen. "Alice Dunnigan, First Black Woman to Cover White House, Will Get Statue at Newseum." *New York Times*, 23 August 2018. https://www.nytimes.com/2018/08/23/us/alice-allison-dunnigan-newseum-statue.html.

Chapter Fourteen: Excellence or Equality

African American Registry. "Thu, 05.01.1924 Evelyn Granville, Math Educator Born." https://aaregistry.org/story/math-educator-extraordinaire-evelyn-granville.

Ali, Muhammad, and Hana Yasmeen Ali. *The Soul of a Butterfly: Reflections on Life's Journey.* New York: Simon & Schuster, 2013: 119.

Anderson, D. "All Regains Title, Flooring Foreman." *New York Times,* 30 October 1974. https://www.nytimes.com/1974/10/30/archives/ali-regains-title-flooring-foreman-ali-knocks-out-foreman-in-8th.html.

Bishir, Catherine W. *Crafting Lives: African American Artisans in New Bern, North Carolina, 1770–1900.* Illustrated ed. Chapel Hill: University of North Carolina Press, 2015.

Chambers, Veronica. "Mary Ellen Pleasant." *New York Times,* 13 February 2019. https://www.nytimes.com/interactive/2019/obituaries/mary-ellen-pleasant-overlooked.html.

Chisholm, Shirley, Scott Simpson, Shola Lynch, and Donna Brazile. *Unbought and Unbossed.* Expanded 40th Anniversary Edition. Charlotte, NC: Take Root Media, 2010.

Decker, E., & Mabunda, L. M. *Contemporary Black Biography.* 9th ed. Cengage Gale, 1995.

Dunigan, R., and Daniel Murray Collection. *How to Succeed.* Memphis, TN: Neilson Print. Co., 1919. Retrieved from the Library of Congress, https://www.loc.gov/item/96100239/.

Estrada, W. D. "The Life and Times of Pío Pico, Last Governor of Mexican California." KCET, 10 October, 2017. https://www.kcet.org/shows/lost-la/the-life-and-times-of-pio-pico-last-governor-of-mexican-california.

Farkus, Mackenzie. "As Part of Watergate, FBI Investigated a Fake Press Release on Hubert Humphrey Campaign Stationery Targeting Shirley Chisholm." MuckRock, 29 March 2019. https://www.muckrock.com/news/archives/2019/mar/29/fbi-watergate-chisholm/.

"First Constitution of California, 1849." US Capitol Visitor Center. https://www.visitthecapitol.gov/exhibitions/artifact/first-constitution-california-1849.

Fisher, Julia Freeland. "How to Get a Job Often Comes Down to One Elite Personal Asset, and Many People Still Don't Realize It." CNBC, 27 December 2019. https://www.cnbc.com/2019/12/27/how-to-get-a-job-often-comes-down-to-one-elite-personal-asset.html.

Franklin, Ben A. "Humphrey Names Donors; 121 Gave $1,000 or More." *New York Times,* 15 March 1972. https://www.nytimes.com/1972/03/15/archives/humphrey-names-donors-121-gave-1000-or-more.html.

Frazier, F. E. *Black Bourgeoisie: The Book That Brought the Shock of Self-Revelation to Middle-Class Blacks in America.* New York: Free Press, 1997: 127.

Gatewood, Willard B. "Aristocrats of Color: South and North The Black Elite, 1880–1920." *Journal of Southern History* 54, no. 1, February 1988: 3–20. https://doi.org/10.2307/220851.

Hauser, T. *Muhammad Ali: His Life and Times.* Reprint ed. New York: Simon & Schuster, 1992.

House of Representatives. "'Catalyst for Change': 1972 Presidential Campaign of Representative Shirley Chisholm." *Art & Archives,* 14 September 2020. https://history.house.gov/Blog/2020/September/9-14-Chisholm-1972/.

Jackson, Shareef. "Ed Dwight Was Going to Be the First African American in Space. Until He Wasn't." *Smithsonian Magazine,* 18 February 2020. https://www.smithsonianmag.com/history/ed-dwight-first-african-american-space-until-wasnt-180974215/.

Jefferson, Thomas, and M. D. Peterson. *Thomas Jefferson Writings.* Library of America #17 Founders Collection Book 1, 1984.

Jones, Martha. "Improvement in Corn-Husker, Sheller." Google Patents, 5 May 1868. https://
       patents.google.com/patent/US77494A/en.
Joseph, P. E. "The Black Power Movement: A State of the Field." *Journal of American History*
       96, no. 3, 2009: 751–76. http://www.jstor.org/stable/25622477.
Kilpatrick, C. "Nixon Tells Editors, 'I'm Not a Crook.'" *Washington Post*, 18 November 1973.
       https://www.washingtonpost.com/politics/nixon-tells-editors-im-not-a-crook/2012/06/04
       /gJQA1RK6IV_story.html.
Kurzius, R. "This GIF Shows How the D.C. Area's Demographics Have Changed Since 1970."
       DCist, 14 January 2020. https://dcist.com/story/20/01/14/this-gif-shows-how-the-d-c
       -areas-demographics-have-changed-since-1970/.
Lemert, C., and E. Bhan. *The Voice of Anna Julia Cooper: Including a Voice from the South and
       Other Important Essays, Papers, and Letters.* Legacies of Social Thought Series. Lanham,
       MD: Rowman & Littlefield Publishers, 1998: 86.
Luckerson, V. "Black Wall Street: The African American Haven That Burned and Then Rose
       from the Ashes." The Ringer, 28 June 2018. https://www.theringer.com/2018/6/28
       /17511818/black-wall-street-oklahoma-greenwood-destruct.
Maple, Taylor. "Katherine Johnson, Real-Life Subject of 'Hidden Figures' Receives Standing
       Ovation." ABC News, 26 February 2017. https://abcnews.go.com/Entertainment
       /real-life-subject-hidden-figures-receives-standing-ovation/story?id=45755913.
McQuaid, Kim. "Race, Gender, and Space Exploration: A Chapter in the Social History of the
       Space Age." *Journal of American Studies* 41, no. 2, 2007: 405–34. http://www.jstor.org
       /stable/27558000.
Meares, H. "Biddy Mason, One of LA's First Black Real Estate Moguls." Curbed LA, 1 March
       2017. https://la.curbed.com/2017/3/1/14756308/biddy-mason-california-black-history.
Meares, Hadley. "Free Forever: The Contentious Hearing That Made Biddy Mason a Legend."
       LAist, 18 November 2021. https://laist.com/news/la-history/biddy-mason-free-forever
       -the-contentious-hearing-that-made-her-a-legend-los-angeles-black-history.
Messer, Chris M., Thomas E. Shriver, and Alison E. Adams. "The Destruction of Black Wall
       Street: Tulsa's 1921 Riot and the Eradication of Accumulated Wealth." *American Journal of
       Economics and Sociology* 77, nos. 3–4, 2018: 789–819. https://doi.org/10.1111/ajes.12225.
Miller, B. *George Washington Carver: God's Ebony Scientist.* New York: Penguin Random
       House, 1943: 128.
Mills, Michelle. "Exhibit Explores the African Ancestry of the Founders of Los Angeles. San
       Gabriel Valley Tribune." *San Gabriel Valley Tribune*, 4 February 2016. https://www
       .sgvtribune.com/2016/02/04/exhibit-explores-the-african-ancestry-of-the-founders-of
       -los-angeles.
Missouri Department of Agriculture. "George Washington Carver." https://agriculture
       .mo.gov/gwc.php#:~:text=Alabama%20residents%20saw%20cotton%20oil,southern%20
       part%20of%20the%20U.S.
Moore, S. A. W. *Sweet Freedom's Plains: African Americans on the Overland Trails, 1841–1869.*
       Norman: University of Oklahoma Press, 2016: 197.
Mueller, M. P. *Race and the Making of the Mormon People.* Amsterdam, the Netherlands:
       Amsterdam University Press, 2017: 131.

Munthali, Towela M. "Pushing the Glass Ceiling: Shirley Chisholm & the Democratic Party." *Women Leading Change: Case Studies on Women, Gender, and Feminism* 3, no. 2, 2018. https://journals.tulane.edu/ncs/article/view/1334.

Musgrove, G. D. "Black Power in Washington, D.C. 1961–1998." ArcGIS, 2017. https://experience.arcgis.com/experience/5e17e7d1c4a8406b9eaf26a4eae77103/.

National Inventors Hall of Fame. "How Elijah McCoy Invented 'The Real McCoy.'" 28 January 2022. https://www.invent.org/blog/inventors/elijah-mccoy-automatic-lubricator.

National Park Service. "Bridget 'Biddy' Mason." https://www.nps.gov/people/biddymason.htm.

New York Times. "More Spilled Milk." 28 March 1974. https://www.nytimes.com/1974/03/28/archives/more-spilled-milk.html.

Noel, N., D. Pinder, S. Stewart, and J. Wright. "The Economic Impact of Closing the Racial Wealth Gap." McKinsey & Company, 2021. https://www.mckinsey.com/industries/public-and-social-sector/our-insights/the-economic-impact-of-closing-the-racial-wealth-gap.

Office of Legacy Management. "LM Highlights 3 Accomplished Scientists in Honor of Black History Month." Department of Energy, 10 February 2021. https://www.energy.gov/lm/articles/lm-highlights-3-accomplished-scientists-honor-black-history-month.

Quillian, Lincoln, et al. "Meta-analysis of Field Experiments Shows No Change in Racial Discrimination in Hiring over Time." *Proceedings of the National Academy of Sciences* 114, no. 41, 2017: 10870–875. https://doi.org/10.1073/pnas.1706255114.

Rasmussen, C. "In Key Court Case, Slave Tested State's Commitment to Freedom." *Los Angeles Times*, 27 January 2002. https://www.latimes.com/archives/la-xpm-2002-jan-27-me-25048-story.html

Robinson, Henry. S. "The M Street High School, 1891–1916." *Records of the Columbia Historical Society*, Washington, DC, 51, 1984: 119–43. https://www.jstor.org/stable/4006784.

Rodriguiz, M. L. "Matilda A. Evans" University History. University of South Carolina. https://sc.edu/about/our_history/university_history/presidential_commission/commission_reports/final_report/appendices/appendix-3/evans-matilda-a/index.php.

Rothwell, Jonathan, Andre M. Perry, and Mike Andrews. "The Black Innovators Who Elevated the United States: Reassessing the Golden Age of Invention." Brookings, 23 November 2020. https://www.brookings.edu/research/the-black-innovators-who-elevated-the-united-states-reassessing-the-golden-age-of-invention.

Rustin, B. "Black Power and Coalition Politics." *Commentary Magazine*, 3 September 2015. https://www.commentary.org/articles/bayard-rustin-2/black-power-and-coalition-politics/.

Schneider, B. "The Incredible Story of William Leidesdorff, San Francisco's Black Founding Father." *San Francisco Examiner*, 9 December 2021. https://www.sfexaminer.com/news/the-incredible-story-of-william-leidesdorff-san-franciscos-black-founding-father/.

Science History Institute. "Marie Maynard Daly." 9 November 2018. https://www.sciencehistory.org/historical-profile/marie-maynard-daly.

Sowell, Thomas. "The Education of Minority Children." Thomas Sowell, 2001. https://www.tsowell.com/speducat.html.

Taylor, Herman A., Tulani Washington-Plaskett, and Arshed A. Quyyumi. "Perspective: Black Resilience—Broadening the Narrative and the Science on Cardiovascular Health and Disease Disparities." *Ethnicity & Disease* 30, no. 2, 2020: 365–68. https://doi.org/10.18865/ed.30.2.365.

The Historical Society of Washington, DC, and the DC Heritage Tourism Coalition (now Cultural Tourism DC). *City Within a City: Greater U Street Heritage Trail.* https://www.culturaltourismdc.org/portal/c/document_library/get_file?uuid=5ca6dfd0-fbc3-4881-95ff-e50da27bf64a&groupId=701982.

The Planetary Society. "How Much Did the Apollo Program Cost?" https://www.planetary.org/space-policy/cost-of-apollo.

Ture, K., and C. V. Hamilton. *Black Power: The Politics of Liberation.* New York: Vintage, 1992.

Van Horne, W. A. "The Concept of Black Power: Its Continued Relevance." *Journal of Black Studies* 37, no. 3, 2007: 365–89.

Wolff, C. "Travers J. Bell Jr., 46, Founder of Only Black Firm on Exchange." *New York Times,* 27 January 1988. https://www.nytimes.com/1988/01/27/obituaries/travers-j-bell-jr-46-founder-of-only-black-firm-on-exchange.html.

Chapter Fifteen: Are We a Democracy Yet?

Albanese, Catherine L. *America: Religions and Religion.* 5th ed. Belmont, CA: Thomson Wadsworth, 2012: 146.

Associated Press. "The Remnants of One of the Nation's Oldest Black Churches Have Just Been Found." NPR, 7 October 2021. https://www.npr.org/2021/10/07/1043964120/colonial-williamsburg-remnants-of-one-of-the-nations-oldest-black-churches.

Barga, Michael. "Free African Society (1787–1794)." Social Welfare History Project. https://socialwelfare.library.vcu.edu/eras/colonial-postrev/free-african-society.

Bill of Rights Institute. "Charles Pinckney." https://billofrightsinstitute.org/founders/charles-pinckney.

Blain, K. N. *Until I Am Free: Fannie Lou Hamer's Enduring Message to America.* Boston: Beacon Press, 2021.

Cantarow, Ellen, and Susan G. O'Malley. *NAACP, SCLC, SNCC, Ella Baker Got Them Moving.* New York: Matilda Publications, 1980.

Cobb, Charles E. *This Nonviolent Stuff'll Get You Killed: How Guns Made the Civil Rights Movement Possible.* Reprint ed. Durham, NC: Duke University Press Books, 2015.

Cogliano, F. D., and K. E. Phimister. *Revolutionary America, 1763–1815: A Sourcebook* Oxfordshire, UK: Routledge Company, 2010: 130.

Colbert, S. D. *Radical Vision: A Biography of Lorraine Hansberry.* New Haven, CT: Yale University Press, 2021: 49.

Cose, Ellis. "The Saga of the Scottsboro Boys." In *Democracy, If We Can Keep It.* New York: The New Press, 2020. https://www.aclu.org/issues/racial-justice/saga-scottsboro-boys.

Douglass, F. "Frederick Douglass's, 'What to the Slave Is the Fourth of July?'" NEH-Edsitement, 1852. https://edsitement.neh.gov/student-activities/frederick-douglasss-what-slave-fourth-july.

Einboden, J. *Jefferson's Muslim Fugitives: The Lost Story of Enslaved Africans, Their Arabic Letters, and an American President.* New York: Oxford University Press, 2020.

Eschner, K. "For a Few Decades in the 18th Century, Women and African Americans Could Vote in New Jersey." *Smithsonian Magazine,* 16 November 2017. https://www.smithsonianmag.com/smart-news/why-black-people-and-women-lost-vote-new-jersey-180967186/.

Fraser, G. "Ella Baker, Organizer for Groups in Civil-Rights Movement in South." *New York Times,* 17 December 1986. https://www.nytimes.com/1986/12/17/obituaries/ella-baker -organizer-for-groups-in-civil-rights-movement-in-south.html.

Fumurescu, A., and A. M. Schön. *Foundations of American Political Thought: Readings and Commentary.* Cambridge, UK: Cambridge University Press, 2021: 325.

Havis, Devonya N. "The Parrhesiastic Enterprise of Black Philosophy." *Black Scholar* 43, no. 4, 2013: 52–58. https://www.jstor.org/stable/10.5816/blackscholar.43.4.0052.

Hemenway, R. E., and A. Walker. *Zora Neale Hurston: A Literary Biography.* Urbana: University of Illinois Press, 1980: 281.

Hoover, J. Edgar. "The FBI Sets Goals for COINTELPRO." The City University of New York. Resources for Teachers. https://shec.ashp.cuny.edu/items/show/814.

Hudson Jr., D. L. "Black History Month: Remembering Angelo Herndon." Freedom Forum Institute, 2011. https://www.freedomforuminstitute.org/2011/02/23/black-history-month -remembering-angelo-herndon.

Hutson, J. "The Founding Fathers and Islam." Library of Congress, 2002. https://www.loc.gov /loc/lcib/0205/tolerance.html.

Judge, Mark G. "Justice to George S. Schuyler." Hoover Institution, 1 August 2000. https:// www.hoover.org/research/justice-george-s-schuyler.

Kenton, Luke. "Gun Ownership Among Black Americans Surged 58% in First Half of 2020." *Daily Mail,* 5 November 2020. https://www.dailymail.co.uk/news/article-8917563/Gun -ownership-black-Americans-surged-58-half-2020-report-finds.html.

King Jr., Martin Luther. *Montgomery Bus Boycott.* Houston: University of Houston, 1955. https://www.digitalhistory.uh.edu/disp_textbook.cfm?smtid=3&psid=3625.

Knight, A. *Pauline Hopkins and the American Dream: An African American Writer's (Re) Visionary Gospel of Success.* Knoxville: University of Tennessee Press, 2012: 80.

Levy, A. "The Anti-Jefferson: Why Robert Carter III Freed His Slaves (And Why We Couldn't Care Less)." *American Scholar* 70, no. 2, 2001: 15–35. http://www.jstor.org/stable /41213139.

Lincoln, Abraham. "First Inaugural Address of Abraham Lincoln." The Avalon Project, 1861. https://avalon.law.yale.edu/19th_century/lincoln1.asp.

Mays, Benjamin E., and G. Joseph W. Nicholson. *The Negro's Church.* Eugene, OR: Wipf and Stock Publishers, 2015.

National Lawyers Guild. *Counterintelligence: A Documentary Look at America's Secret Police.* National Lawyers Guild, 1980. https://archive.org/details/Counterintelligence -Documentary-Look-1980.

Nelson, A. F. "The Message of the Hush Harbor: History and Theology of African Descent Traditions." *South Carolina United Methodist Advocate,* 1 March 2019. https://advocatesc.org /2019/03/the-message-of-the-hush-harbor-history-and-theology-of-african-descent-traditions.

New York Historical Society. "Jarena Lee 1783–1849." Women and the American Story, 2017. https://blog.nyhsdev2.org/sites/default/files/newfiles/cwh-curriculum/Module%202/Life %20Stories/Jarena%20Lee%20Life%20Story.pdf.

Robinson, Jontyle, and Charles Austin Page Jr.. "Titus Kaphar: Knockout." Tuskegee Institute, 2019. https://www.tuskegee.edu/Content/Uploads/Tuskegee/files/Events/2019.09%20 Knockout%20brochure.pdf.

Rosa, M. "1503: America's First Muslim Ban." Yaqeen Institute for Islamic Research, 2018. https://yaqeeninstitute.org/read/paper/1503-americas-first-muslim-ban.

Schuyler, George. "The Harlem Renaissance: George Schuyler Argues Against 'Black Art.'" George Mason University. http://historymatters.gmu.edu/d/5129/.

Schuyler, George. S., and J. B. Leak. *Rac(e)Ing to the Right: Selected Essays George S. Schuyler.* Knoxville: University of Tennessee Press, 2011.

Sowell, Thomas. *The Thomas Sowell Reader.* New York: Basic Books, 2011.

Stobaugh, J. P. *American Literature: Cultural Influences of Early to Contemporary Voices.* Green Forest, AZ: New Leaf Publishing Group, 2012: 390.

Taylor, C. H. J. "Whites and Blacks; or, the Question Settled." Internet Archive, 1889. https://archive.org/details/whitesblacksorqu00tayl/mode/2up.

The Combahee River Collective. *The Combahee River Collective Statement.* Amsterdam, the Netherlands: Amsterdam University Press: 1986.

The David Walker Memorial Project. "The Death of David Walker." Retrieved June 28, 2022, from https://www.sites.google.com/site/davidwalkermemorial/david-walker/death-of-david-walker.

Virginia General Assembly. "'An Act Declaring That Baptisme of Slaves Doth Not Exempt Them from Bondage' (1667)." *Encyclopedia Virginia.* https://encyclopediavirginia.org/entries/an-act-declaring-that-baptisme-of-slaves-doth-not-exempt-them-from-bondage-1667.

Walker, David. *Walker's Appeal, in Four Articles: Together with a Preamble, to the Coloured Citizens of the World, but in Particular, and Very Expressly, to Those of the United States of America.* 3rd ed. Carolina Population Center, 2011. University of North Carolina. https://docsouth.unc.edu/nc/walker/walker.html.

Williams, F. R., Martin Luther King Jr., and T. Nelson. *Negroes with Guns.* Eastford, CT: Martino Fine Books, 2020.

Williams, J. *From the Bullet to the Ballot: The Illinois Chapter of the Black Panther Party and Racial Coalition Politics in Chicago.* The John Hope Franklin Series in African American History and Culture. Illustrated ed. Chapel Hill: University of North Carolina Press, 2015: 4.

Worthington, L., R. C. Donaldson, and J. W. White. *Challenging History: Race, Equity, and the Practice of Public History.* The Carolina Lowcountry and the Atlantic World. Columbia: University of South Carolina Press, 2021: 22.

X, Malcolm. *Malcolm X Speaks: Selected Speeches and Statements.* Edited by George Breitman. Reprint ed. New York: Grove Press, 1994: 26.

Chapter Sixteen: The Crossroads of History

Allosso, Dan. "12. The New Right" US History II: Gilded Age to Present. Minnesota Libraries Publishing Project. https://mlpp.pressbooks.pub/ushistory2/chapter/the-new-right/.

Anderson, Monica. "3. The Hashtag #BlackLivesMatter Emerges: Social Activism on Twitter." Pew Research Center, 15 August 2016. https://www.pewresearch.org/internet/2016/08/15/the-hashtag-blacklivesmatter-emerges-social-activism-on-twitter/.

Associated Press. "Boston U. Panel Finds Plagiarism by Dr. King." *New York Times*, 11 October 1991. https://www.nytimes.com/1991/10/11/us/boston-u-panel-finds-plagiarism-by-dr-king.html.

Baldwin, James. *The Price of the Ticket: Collected Nonfiction: 1948–1985.* Reprint ed. Boston: Beacon Press, 2021: 375.

Balliett, W. *American Musicians II: Seventy-one Portraits in Jazz*. Jackson: University Press of Mississippi, 2006: 93.

Campbell, S. "Black Lives Matter Secretly Bought a $6 Million House." *New York Magazine*, 4 April 2022. https://nymag.com/intelligencer/2022/04/black-lives-matter-6-million -dollar-house.html.

Compton, M. T. *The American Opioid Epidemic: From Patient Care to Public Health*. Washington, DC: American Psychiatric Association Publishing, 2019: 110.

Dorrien, G. *American Democratic Socialism: History, Politics, Religion, and Theory*. New Haven, CT: Yale University Press, 2021: 548.

Eggers, Andrew C., Haritz Garro, and Justin Grimmer. "No Evidence for Systematic Voter Fraud: A Guide to Statistical Claims About the 2020 Election." CrimRxiv, 2 November 2021. https://doi.org/10.21428/cb6ab371.98f5d828.

Elam, Michele. *The Cambridge Companion to James Baldwin*. Cambridge, UK: Cambridge University Press, 2015.

Gade, Christian B. N. "What Is Ubuntu? Different Interpretations Among South Africans of African Descent." *South African Journal of Philosophy* 31, no. 3, 2012: 484–503. https://doi .org/10.1080/02580136.2012.10751789.

Greenlee, Cynthia. "A Priceless Archive of Ordinary Life." *Atlantic*, 8 February 2021. https:// www.theatlantic.com/culture/archive/2021/02/race-save-black-history-archives/617932/.

Honey, Maureen. *Aphrodite's Daughters: Three Modernist Poets of the Harlem Renaissance*. New Brunswick, NJ: Rutgers University Press, 2016.

Johnson, D. B. *National Party Platforms of 1980*. Amsterdam, the Netherlands: Amsterdam University Press, 1982.

Kilander, G. "Breonna Taylor's Mother Blasts Black Lives Matter Movement." *The Independent*, 17 April 2021. https://www.independent.co.uk/news/world/americas/breonna-taylor -tamika-palmer-blm-b1833123.html.

Kilgannon, C. "9/11 Victims Are Still Being Identified, 20 Years Later." *New York Times*, September 6, 2021. https://www.nytimes.com/2021/09/06/nyregion/9-11-ground-zero -victims-remains.html.

King, A. *Urban Warfare in the Twenty-First Century*. Cambridge, UK: Polity Publisher, 2021.

Lewis, William Dodge. *Democracy's High School*. Sydney, Australia: Wentworth Press, 2019: 221.

Maccash, Doug. "Mysterious Enslaved Teen Appeared in a 1837 Painting, Was Blotted Out, Then Rediscovered." NOLA.com, 11 November 2021. https://www.nola.com /entertainment_life/arts/article_286827ae-3b43-11ec-bdab-0355a7888fe5.html.

Mattingly, David. "Gregory Bush: Kroger Killer Sentenced to Life in Prison +10 Years." WBKO News, 24 June 2021. https://www.Wave3.Com. https://www.wave3.com /2021/06/24/gregory-bush-kroger-killer-sentenced-life-prison-10-years/.

Morice, Jane. "Thousands of 'Freedom Fighters' in Cleveland for First National Black Lives Matter Conference." Cleveland.com, 26 July 2015. https://www.cleveland.com/metro/2015 /07/thousands_of_freedom_fighters.html.

Nagourney, Adam, Jim Rutenberg, and Brian Knowlton. "Obama's Team Tries to Temper Expectations." *New York Times,* 6 November 2008. https://www.nytimes.com/2008/11/06 /world/americas/06iht-dems.4.17602593.html.

Nash, C. "Ronnie Lee Henderson a Man of Action, a Man of Faith." Bravest Memorial. http:// bravestmemorial.net/html/members_individual/henderson_ronnie/newsday_com.html.

National Museum of American History. "Reckoning with Remembrance: History, Injustice, and the Murder of Emmet Till." Closed as of November 2, 2021. https://americanhistory .si.edu/exhibitions/reckoning-remembrance-emmett-till.

National Urban League. "'BreonnaCon' Convention in Louisville, August 22–25." National Urban League, 8 June 2022. https://nul.org/news/breonnacon-convention-louisville -august-22-25.

Ndgo, Y. "Tell No Lies. Statement from the Frontlines of BLM." Black Lives Matter, 10 June 2021. https://www.blmchapterstatement.com.

Obama, Barack. "Barack Obama's Feb. 5 Speech." *New York Times*, 2008. https://www .nytimes.com/2008/02/05/us/politics/05text-obama.html.

Obama, Barack. *Dreams from My Father: A Story of Race and Inheritance*. New York: Times Books, 1995.

Penn State University Library. "William H. Dorsey Scrapbook Collection." Penn State University Library. https://digital.libraries.psu.edu/digital/collection/contest/id/2419/.

Perry, I. "Stop Hustling Black Death." *New York Magazine*, The Cut, 24 May 2021. https:// www.thecut.com/article/samaria-rice-profile.html.

Reagan, Ronald. *An American Life: The Autobiography*. Reprint ed. New York: Simon & Schuster, 2011.

Samuels, Robert, and Toluse Olorunnipa. *His Name Is George Floyd: One Man's Life and the Struggle for Racial Justice*. New York: Viking, 2022.

Sarkar, Pia, and Noreen Nasir. "Buffalo Shooting Leaves Neighborhood Without a Grocery Store. AP, 18 May 2022. https://apnews.com/article/buffalo-supermarket-shooting -health-shootings-69162d957dbeb6e6a67f242a32c10f52.

Shetterly, Robert. "How to Think About Frederick Douglass's Feet of Clay." Americans Who Tell the Truth, 1 May 2019. https://www.americanswhotellthetruth.org/blog/how-to -think-about-frederick-douglasss-feet-of-clay.

Stohr, M. K., and A. Walsh. *Corrections: From Research, to Policy, to Practice*. 2nd ed. Thousand Oaks, CA: SAGE Publications, Inc, 2020.

The Associated Press. "Obama Draws About 150,000 to Colo. Rallies." *Denver Post*, 26 October 2008. https://www.denverpost.com/2008/10/26/obama-draws-about-150000-to-colo-rallies/.

Thursby, Jacqueline S. *Critical Companion to Maya Angelou: A Literary Reference to Her Life and Work*. Illustrated ed. New York: Facts on File, 2011: 89.

INDEX

ABOUT THE AUTHOR

Born in Louisville, Kentucky, **Jermaine Fowler** is a storyteller and self-proclaimed intellectual adventurer who spent his youth seeking knowledge on the shelves of his local free public library. Between research and lecturing, he is the host of the top-rated history podcast *The Humanity Archive*, which has been praised as a must-listen by *Vanity Fair*. Challenging dominant perspectives, Fowler goes outside the textbooks to find stories that are recognizably human. Connecting current issues with the heroic struggles of those who've come before us, he brings hidden history to light and makes it powerfully relevant.